Money and political economy in the Enlightenment

Money and political economy in the Enlightenment

Edited by

DANIEL CAREY

VOLTAIRE FOUNDATION
OXFORD

www.voltaire.ox.ac.uk

© 2014 Voltaire Foundation, University of Oxford
ISBN 978 0 7294 1138 7
Oxford University Studies in the Enlightenment 2014:05
ISSN 0435-2866

Voltaire Foundation
99 Banbury Road
Oxford OX2 6JX, UK
www.voltaire.ox.ac.uk

A catalogue record for this book is available from the British Library

The correct style for citing this book is
D. Carey (ed.), *Money and political economy in the Enlightenment*,
Oxford University Studies in the Enlightenment
(Oxford, Voltaire Foundation, 2014)

Cover illustration: Recoinage era silver crown. Obverse: William III crown,
1696 (Christ Church College collection, Ashmolean Museum). Reverse:
William III crown, 1696 (R. Finch, Ashmolean Museum). Photography by
Daniel Carey. Reproduced by permission of the Ashmolean Museum.

This publication was grant-aided by the Publications Fund of
National University of Ireland, Galway.

FSC® (the Forest Stewardship Council) is an independent organization established to
promote responsible management of the world's forests.

This book is printed on acid-free paper

Printed in the UK by TJ International Ltd, Padstow, Cornwall

OXFORD UNIVERSITY STUDIES IN THE ENLIGHTENMENT

MONEY AND POLITICAL ECONOMY IN THE ENLIGHTENMENT

Key events, from the Recoinage crisis in the 1690s to the South Sea Bubble in the 1720s and the consequences of the French Revolution, sharpened the need for a more dynamic conception of economic forces in the midst of the Financial Revolution. Political economy emerged as a disruptive force, challenging philosophers to debate and define unstable phenomena in a new climate of expanding credit, innovation in money form, political change and international competition. In *Money and political economy in the Enlightenment* contributors investigate received critical assumptions about what was progressive and what was backward-looking, and reconsider traditional attempts to periodise the Enlightenment.

History of ideas / economic history

Histoire des idées / histoire économique

Contents

Acknowledgements

In preparing this volume I have received support from the National University of Ireland, Galway, which awarded me a Grant-in-aid of publication. I am grateful to Gary Lupton of the Research Office for his help. Research was carried out with assistance from the Irish Research Council and a grant from the Higher Education Authority in Ireland under the Programme for Research in Third Level Institutions.

Many individuals have made this volume possible. I am especially indebted to Jonathan Mallinson, General editor of Oxford University Studies in the Enlightenment, and to Lyn Roberts, Senior publishing manager, who have provided enormous assistance with unfailing generosity. I also wish to thank Nicholas Cronk, Director of the Voltaire Foundation, who supported this project from an early stage.

While completing the editing process I benefited from the intellectual resources of the Winton Institute for Monetary History in the Ashmolean Museum in Oxford, led by Nicholas Mayhew. I appreciate being appointed to an associate fellowship of the Institute during research leave in Oxford. On questions of economic, financial and intellectual history, I have learned a great deal from conversations and exchanges with many friends and colleagues, among whom Perry Gauci, Aaron Graham, Anthony Hotson, Patrick Kelly, John Marshall, Nick Mayhew, Anne Murphy, Guy Rowlands and Carl Wennerlind have been especially helpful. Above all I appreciate the scholarship and insight of the contributors to this collection.

For assistance with the production of the volume I want to thank Gábor Gelléri, Emer McHugh and Peter Shine at NUI Galway, Susan Jones, and Megan Hiatt, who expertly prepared the index. The Recoinage-era coins featured in the cover illustration come from the collection of the Ashmolean Museum. Nick Mayhew made this possible and kindly offered his expertise.

This book is dedicated to two people who nurtured my interests in economic and intellectual history – Julian Simon, and my father, James W. Carey.

List of illustrations

Introduction: money and political economy in the era of Enlightenment

DANIEL CAREY

When the Edinburgh philosopher and educationalist Dugald Stewart gave his course of lectures on political economy in 1800-1801, he addressed a core of familiar topics by drawing on an established literature to which he made frequent reference. The canon of authors included John Locke, 'that profound writer',[1] George Berkeley and three of his countrymen – David Hume, Sir James Steuart and Adam Smith – all of whom he quoted, commented on and modified. The emergence of political economy as an intellectual priority, exemplified by Stewart's lectures, constitutes one of the defining features of the era of Enlightenment. Over the course of the seventeenth and eighteenth centuries, the orientation of economic discussions around largely mercantilist concerns with international trade, competition and the accumulation of precious metals gave way to a more dynamic conception of economic forces, spurred on by rapid innovations in financial instruments, credit and money form. These developments, occurring as part of what has been termed the Financial Revolution, resulted from and in turn influenced the need for war finance, the shifting balance of power within Europe and ongoing rivalries in trade and colonial territory across the globe. The results were at times cataclysmic, as the South Sea Bubble and collapse of the Mississippi Scheme testify, but they placed discussion of economic issues, which had once been peripheral, in the foreground of philosophy.[2]

Although they wrote in very different forms, the major thinkers whom

1. Dugald Stewart, *Lectures on political economy*, in *The Collected works of Dugald Stewart*, ed. Sir William Hamilton, 11 vols (Edinburgh, 1854-1858), vol.8, p.389.
2. The contrast is apparent in comparing *The Cambridge history of political thought 1450-1700*, ed. J. H. Burns, with the assistance of Mark Goldie (Cambridge, 1991), with *The Cambridge history of eighteenth-century political thought*, ed. Mark Goldie and Robert Wokler (Cambridge, 2006). The 1450-1700 volume has no index entry on 'economy' or 'economics'; the signal exception is the discussion by James Tully of the introduction of money in his chapter on John Locke, focusing on Locke's 'Second treatise' of government (p.633-43). The eighteenth-century volume, on the contrary, has major chapters on political economy by Istvan Hont, T. J. Hochstrasser, Donald Winch, Michael Sonenscher and Keith Tribe, as well as various subsections devoted to the topic in other chapters.

Stewart considered, from Locke to Hume and Smith, devoted substantial attention to questions of money, trade, interest rates and economic competition in ways that would not have engaged their counterparts in philosophy a century earlier. It is instructive in this regard that the great philosophical irritant of the eighteenth century was Bernard Mandeville, author of *The Fable of the bees*,[3] while Machiavelli and Hobbes, in previous periods, occupied similarly demonised positions without achieving this status on the basis of their pronouncements on economic matters.

Yet there was no 'Enlightenment' position on political economy, in contrast with recognisable attitudes (if not consensus) in relation to subjects such as reason, superstition, toleration or science. Financial innovation met with as many critics as exponents among figures with an accepted 'enlightened' pedigree. Adam Smith's reservations about paper money were not shared by others in Scotland, like John Law and Sir James Steuart, for example, while bank projects attracted enthusiastic support and equally vociferous objection. Nor did philosophers always take positions in the context of political economy that we might expect, given some of their other commitments. Berkeley, as hostile as anyone to 'freethinkers' with enlightened agendas, was an advocate of banking and monetary innovation; he and John Toland arrived on this occasion at similar conclusions. Crises created divisions as well as unusual alliances – as when Jonathan Swift dedicated the fifth of his *Drapier's letters* (1724), during the controversy in Ireland over Wood's halfpence, to Robert Molesworth, with whom he otherwise had considerable political and philosophical differences.[4] What we can conclude is that political economy established itself as a shared intellectual concern in a striking fashion that continues to merit investigation into the pathways and paradoxes of this historical era.

This volume looks at the interweaving of money, banking, credit and political thought in the long eighteenth century. The interventions of a range of leading authorities in these debates occurred against the backdrop of earlier contributions dominated by mercantilist priorities. By the end of the period, a series of alternative perspectives had come into play, re-evaluating received assumptions without disengaging entirely from inherited views. The focus on English, Irish and Scottish sources here is complemented by looking finally at the interplay with French

3. Mandeville initially published the poem under the title *The Grumbling hive: or, Knaves turn'd honest* in 1705. In 1714 he reprinted the work together with a commentary as *The Fable of the bees: or, private vices publick benefits*; he added further sections in editions of 1723 and 1724. See M. M. Goldsmith, *Private vices, public benefits: Bernard Mandeville's social and political thought* (Cambridge, 1985).

4. For some discussion of the fifth letter, see Seán D. Moore, *Swift, the book, and the Irish financial revolution: satire and sovereignty in colonial Ireland* (Baltimore, MD 2010), p.146-48.

analyses and the response to the work of Adam Smith. Several leading themes emerge from this discussion. First of all, determining what was progressive and what was backward-looking proves more difficult than we might expect on closer consideration. We find this in the opening chapter in Johann Sommerville's discussion of Sir Robert Filmer's views on the taking of interest, and also in the case of John Locke, who was indebted to much earlier assumptions about money even as he articulated a forceful position with considerable influence in the eighteenth century. Conversely, Justin Champion's shows that republican thought – regarded by some scholars as ill-equipped to deal with the new financial innovations – in fact demonstrated a more responsive approach than we have commonly assumed. The challenges of periodisation posed by this material disrupt existing narratives of Enlightenment, and complicate the process of absorbing political economy into received accounts of intellectual history. Telling the story through political affiliation again produces a complex picture, with the Whig Locke appearing less progressive than the Tory Charles Davenant, who endorsed credit, while Locke actually coincided with Filmer on the subject of interest, to whom he was otherwise politically opposed. The later republican moment studied by Thomas Hopkins, in revolutionary France, confronted its own challenges in accommodating the priorities of commercial culture.

The topic of money represents a running theme throughout this volume. Already a well-established issue in earlier discussion, it remained a central subject of debate in the eighteenth century, with a series of competing definitions surfacing in connection with credit, banking and trade. These arguments occurred in the context of a bimetallic currency system in which silver and gold constituted the circulating medium, supplemented by new credit instruments and experimentation in some quarters with paper money. The bimetallic arrangement was beset by a series of endemic problems. Price ratios between the two metals created arbitrage opportunities between different countries.[5] Individual nations set a Mint price which served as the unit of account, but silver and gold also constituted commodities, possessing their own market price in the form of bullion, with attendant fluctuations that often destabilised national economies. Internationally, trade was conducted to a large

---

5. This problem was noted in early discussion, for example by Edward Misselden, *Free trade. Or, the meanes to make trade florish* (London, Iohn Leggatt for Simon Waterson, 1622), p.11; nor did it escape the notice of Gerard Malynes in the context of his discussion of royal intervention in the value of coin. See *Consuetudo, vel lex mercatoria, or The Ancient law-merchant* (London, Adam Islip, 1622), p.310. For discussion of the eighteenth century, see Pilar Nogués-Marco, 'Competing bimetallic ratios: Amsterdam, London, and bullion arbitrage in mid-eighteenth century', *Journal of economic history* 73:2 (2013), p.445-76.

extent through bills of exchange, but the demands of final settlement in specie meant that the need for precious metals and a favourable trade balance did not disappear. In a domestic context, conditions of scarcity in the supply of coin exerted ongoing economic pressure, particularly in marginal or colonial economies, as Berkeley among others recognised.[6]

The studies published here investigate the challenge these commentators faced in understanding economic forces and reconciling them with their political priorities. Collectively, they illustrate a set of tensions and inconsistencies as much as the rigour of the solutions when leading figures intervened in such disputes. Before reviewing the different arguments covered here, this introduction contextualises the discussion by considering different assessments of the origins of political economy as well as the protracted deliberation over the question of money form in the era of Enlightenment.

Political economy: origins and traditions

Various genealogies for political economy have been suggested, but we can begin by observing the limited purchase of economic thinking in the political thought of some leading early modern predecessors. Although the notion that money represented the sinews of war had become commonplace in the early modern period (drawing on remarks in Plutarch and Cicero),[7] Machiavelli was content to dispute this view in his *Discorsi*.[8] Machiavelli remained preoccupied by different questions, with wealth as an important but still ancillary consideration to his analysis of power and authority.[9] As for Hobbes, Istvan Hont has pointed

---

6. On this subject see Daniel Carey and Christopher J. Finlay (eds), *The Empire of credit: the financial revolution in the British Atlantic world, 1688-1815* (Dublin, 2011).
7. Plutarch, *Parallel lives*, trans. Bernadette Perrin, 11 vols (London, 1914-26), Agis and Cleomenes, xxvii.1-2; Cicero, *Philippics*, 5.5, speaking against the proposition that Marc Anthony would be assigned Outer Gaul, comments that this would present him with the weapons for civil war: 'first, the sinews of war, a limitless supply of money' (Quid est [...] primum nervos belli, pecuniam infinitam'. Cicero, *Philippics 1-6*, ed. and trans. D. R. Shackleton Bailey, rev. John T. Ramsey and Gesine Manuwald (Cambridge, MA, 2009). For early modern references, see for example Richard Hakluyt, 'A discourse of western planting', in *The Original writings & correspondence of the two Richard Hakluyts*, ed. E. G. R. Taylor, 2 vols (London, 1935), vol.2, p.249, as part of an argument for acting against Spanish interests in the New World; and Misselden, *Free trade*, p.7, who remarked that 'Money [...] hath obtained the title of *sinewes* of *warre* and of *State*'.
8. Machiavelli, *Discourses on Livy*, trans. Harvey C. Mansfield and Nathan Tarcov (Chicago, IL, 1996), II.10 (p.147-50). At II.10.1, Machiavelli states 'Nor can the common opinion be more false that says that money is the sinew of war'. In his estimation, 'Money is quite necessary in second place, but it is a necessity that good soldiers win it by themselves; for it is impossible for money to be lacking to good soldiers as for money by itself to find good soldiers' (II.10.2).
9. On this point see the comment on Livy and Machiavelli in Nicholas Barbon, *A Discourse of*

out that 'there is no place for an economy in his politics in any important sense. It is practically pure politics'.[10] Yet Hont has argued that the perspectives of Machiavelli and Hobbes nonetheless shaped the appearance of political economy, or at least one strand of it, in the form of the 'jealousy of trade' emerging out of the competition between states for pre-eminence. On this analysis, distinct traditions of republicanism, reason of state and natural law can be understood as synthesising in the later seventeenth and eighteenth centuries, in a recognition of the economic conditions necessary for national survival.

An alternative genealogy of political economy has been suggested, based more closely on the views associated with a group of seventeenth-century commentators on economic questions, especially Thomas Mun, Gerard Malynes and Edward Misselden, whose work in the 1620s was reprinted throughout the century.[11] Their positions, which have conveniently been labelled 'mercantilist', focused on the interests of international trade and the imperative of accumulating precious metals. Such a priority was not detached from politics, on the assumption that success in this endeavour came at the expense of a country's competitors, in an equation of wealth and power, with government assigned a role in controlling consumption and production.

Scholars have disputed the adequacy of mercantilism as a label for the different positions taken in the period, and caution is appropriate in order to avoid totalising the account we give of it.[12] Still, there is value in indicating a number of leading assumptions, some of which survive and some of which later come under dispute in the eighteenth century. Five relevant positions or attitudes can be identified.[13] The first is that economic policy should privilege national interests alone; second, the

---

trade (London, Tho. Milbourn for the author, 1691), sig.A3r-v, echoed by David Hume (as noticed by Istvan Hont, *Jealousy of trade: international competition and the nation-state in historical perspective* (Cambridge, MA, 2005), p.8n).

10. Hont, *Jealousy of trade*, p.2.

11. On these figures, see Andrea Finkelstein, *Harmony and the balance: an intellectual history of seventeenth-century English economic thought* (Ann Arbor, MI, 2000).

12. See Philip J. Stern and Carl Wennerlind (eds), *Mercantilism reimagined: political economy in early modern Britain and its empire* (Oxford, 2013); Steve Pincus, 'Rethinking mercantilism: political economy, the British Empire, and the Atlantic World in the seventeenth and eighteenth centuries', *William and Mary quarterly* 69:1 (2012), p.3-34. The classic account, regarding mercantilism as what he calls an *'agent of unification'*, is Eli F. Heckscher, *Mercantilism* [1935], trans. Mendel Shapiro, revd edn, ed. E. F. Söderlund, 2 vols (London, 1955), p.22; see also Heckscher, 'Revisions in economic history: V. Mercantilism', *Economic history review* 7:1 (1936), p.44-54, responding to critics and seeing mercantilism as a 'convenient term' which is nonetheless 'governed by an inner harmony' as a doctrine (p.54).

13. I have drawn on and adapted the discussion in Jacob Viner, 'Mercantilist thought', in Viner, *Essays on the intellectual history of economics*, ed. Douglas A. Irwin (Princeton, NJ, 1991), p.262-76.

stock of precious metals must be the focus of trade and economic policy; third, exports must outweigh imports as the method of augmenting that stock; fourth, attaining favourable trade balances requires legal and political action to restrict imports and promote exports; and fifth, that security of the state depends on economic strength, requiring a coordination between economic and foreign policy.

In his recent account of the thought of Mun, Misselden and Malynes, Carl Wennerlind has emphasised these figures' fundamental concern with the problem of the scarcity of money in the 1620s.[14] Although from a 'modern' economic perspective there can be no shortage of money as such, the organisation of the seventeenth-century (and earlier) currency system around coins fashioned with precious metals meant that trade was vulnerable to movements in the supply of money.[15] To address this predicament, high priority was placed on creating inflows of coin (as behoved a country like England without its own gold or silver mines).[16] As a result, the balance of trade remained an abiding consideration in regulating economic activity. Thomas Mun put it succinctly: the goal was to 'observe this rule; to sell more to strangers yearly than we consume of theirs in value'.[17] In short, the basic solution was to increase exports and decrease consumption. The loss of specie due to trade in exotic commodities in the Levant, Persia and East Indies was subject to criticism for this reason. Misselden, for example, complained of the drain on 'ready money' that this caused.[18] Mun, an East India Company merchant, unsurprisingly contested this view, arguing instead that the exportation of money was ultimately beneficial by facilitating trade with goods purchased abroad that could then be re-exported, though he recognised

14. Carl Wennerlind, *Casualties of credit: the English Financial Revolution, 1620-1720* (Cambridge, MA, 2011), ch.1, 'The scarcity of money problem and the birth of English political economy'. It is worth noting, as Wennerlind points out, that there were hot disputes between these three figures and that they had different specific remedies to propose.

15. Malynes mentions the use of tokens and base money coins of various kinds in *Consuetudo*, p.278. These small-value coins offered some relief for local trade (and charity) and he hoped would prevent export of coinage, but for international transactions coinage in precious metal was required. In 1613 Malynes was granted a patent to coin copper and brass farthings. Perry Gauci, 'Malynes, Gerard (fl. 1585–1641)', in *Oxford dictionary of national biography* (Oxford, 2004). For a study of the widespread operation of private systems of credit, see Craig Muldrew, *The Economy of obligation: the culture of credit and social relations in early modern England* (Houndmills, 1998).

16. Again, bills of exchange provided the basis for international transactions, but the final means of settlement was hard currency. Philipp Robinson Rössner argues that bills of exchange did not contribute to the monetary base properly but rather to the velocity by raising the number of transactions that coin could cover. *Deflation – devaluation – rebellion: Geld im Zeitalter der Reformation* (Stuttgart, 2012), p.75-85, 190-204.

17. Thomas Mun, *England's treasure by forraign trade* (London, J. G. for Thomas Clark, 1664), p.11. See also Misselden, *Free trade*, p.13.

18. Misselden, *Free trade*, p.19.

he was contradicting 'common opinion'.[19] Although colonial possessions were fitful in becoming established, the commercial exploitation they afforded offered one avenue for improving the situation, while sumptuary laws remained a popular answer to the consumption of expensive foreign goods.

The contribution of seventeenth-century commentators to the formation of political economy is clearly much wider than the mercantilist strain alone. Innovative proposals on money, banking and credit developed in the Civil War period in connection with the Hartlib Circle, as Wennerlind has shown in detail.[20] Troubled by the scarcity of money, in common with 'mercantilists', William Potter proposed not to concentrate on the balance of trade but to think instead about alternative money forms from gold and silver. Credit based on land was Potter's recommendation, made feasible by establishing a land bank issuing notes to expand the money stock. Other banking schemes were endorsed, some on Continental models, with the same purpose of introducing a wider circulation of money on the basis of credit.

Among the participants in the Hartlib Circle was William Petty, who introduced the notion of political arithmetic.[21] His approach, shared by John Graunt, and later by Gregory King and others in the seventeenth century, had lasting impact in a variety of contexts. At one level we can define political arithmetic as the accumulation of numerical data and demographic information, together with the application of statistics in order to address questions of public health, colonial administration and a host of areas of government policy, including economic matters. Thus it is partly a methodological innovation or orientation on politics and social planning with a wide scope of attention and influence. We can situate this in conjunction with Hartlib and the impulse of reform, but the progress of political events in the century and the wide applicability of this method makes it difficult to tie political arithmetic to specific party or ideological allegiances. John Locke came under Petty's influence but the Tory economic thinker Charles Davenant also inherited his approach.[22]

19. Mun, *England's treasure*, p.34.
20. Wennerlind, *Casualties of credit*, ch.2.
21. See especially William Petty, *Political arithmetick* (London, Robert Clavel and Hen. Mortlock, 1690), but he used the phrase in the title of several earlier works; on Petty see Ted McCormick, *William Petty and the ambitions of political arithmetic* (Oxford, 2009).
22. On Locke and Petty, see Patrick Hyde Kelly, 'General introduction: Locke on money', in *Locke on money*, ed. Patrick Hyde Kelly, 2 vols (Oxford, 1991), vol.1, p.34, 97-98. On Davenant and developments in the eighteenth century, see William Peter Deringer, 'Calculated values: the politics and epistemology of economic numbers in Britain, 1688-1738' (Doctoral dissertation, Princeton University, 2012). See also Terence Hutchison, *Before Adam Smith: the emergence of political economy, 1662-1776* (Oxford, 1988), ch.3 and 4.

Petty's specifically economic writings introduce a number of important observations and statements on taxation, income, labour, money and other issues. Antoin Murphy has stressed Petty's breakthrough in conceptualising and measuring national income and expenditure, and therefore his advances in macroeconomic analysis (based on Petty's *Verbum sapienti* [1665; published 1691].[23] He shared Potter's innovative ideas on banking and he developed, if only by way of suggestion rather than in a systematic fashion, the notion of the velocity of money in circulation.[24]

The vicissitudes of English political experience took another sharp turn with the Glorious Revolution of 1688-1689 and the arrival of William and Mary on the throne (with William ruling alone after Mary's death in 1694). The advent of a Dutch monarch resulted in plunging the country into the Nine Years' War with France (1688-1697) and the start of a protracted economic crisis centring on English coinage. The need to send remittances to William's armies and allies on the Continent incentivised illegal clipping of coins to such an extent that, by the mid-1690s, 50 per cent of the silver, on average, had been removed.[25] The fiscal burden created by the war led to a series of important developments (traditionally identified as inaugurating the Financial Revolution).[26] The most notable, institutionally, was the founding of the Bank of England in 1694, chartered by Parliament in order to lend money to government, thereby establishing for the first time a national (rather than royal) debt. This period also saw the appearance of a range of different financial instruments, from exchequer bills (secured against future tax takings) to interest-bearing sealed bills in large denominations (issued by the Bank of England), running cash notes and other forms of transferable credit.[27] Further initiatives in the period included the

23. Antoin E. Murphy, *The Genesis of macroeconomics: new ideas from Sir William Petty to Henry Thornton* (Oxford, 2009), p.21-41; see also Paul Slack, 'Measuring the national wealth in seventeenth-century England', *Economic history review* 57:4 (2004), p.607-35.
24. On Petty and banking, see Murphy, *Genesis of macroeconomics*, p.38-39, although he does not see the connection with Potter. On the question of whether Petty or Locke is the direct inspiration for Richard Cantillon's elaboration of the idea of velocity (or *vitesse*) in his *Essai sur la nature du commerce en général* (London, Fletcher Gyles, 1755), see Tony Aspromourgos, *On the origins of classical economics: distribution and value from William Petty to Adam Smith* (London, 1996), p.114-15.
25. See especially D. W. Jones, *War and economy in the Age of William III and Marlborough* (Oxford, 1988).
26. See the founding work of P. G. M. Dickson, *The Financial Revolution in England: a study in the development of public credit 1688-1756* (London, 1967); and the briefer but valuable account by Henry Roseveare, *The Financial Revolution 1660-1760* (London, 1991).
27. See R. D. Richards, 'The Exchequer bill in the history of English governmental finance', *Economic history* 3:11 (1936), p.193-211. For a summary of the Bank of England's notes, see R. D. Richards, 'The first fifty years of the Bank of England', in *History of the principal public banks*, ed. J. G. van Dillen (The Hague, 1934), p.219-30.

complex tontine loan in 1692, the sale of other annuities and lotteries of various sorts, and rival banking proposals, with a mixed record of success and failure.[28] Integral to these schemes was a redevelopment of the tax system, not least because the attraction of investment often depended on nominating specific taxes to ensure repayment of government debt.[29]

There were several key dilemmas associated with these instruments, in particular regarding the terms on which they could be made convertible.[30] As for the Bank of England, it faced the challenge of sustaining a necessary fractional reserve of specie and the question of whether it could maintain confidence in its notes by guaranteeing payment on demand in cash. Writing to endorse the bank in 1694, Sir Humphry (or Humphrey) Mackworth asserted that a 'Bill of Credit from this Bank-Office is transferable from one Man to another *toties quoties*, and cannot fail, and is as good as Money in one's possession, and better'.[31] The reference to *toties quoties* – as often as desired – picked up on the public announcement of the act itself,[32] while he reassured readers that the bills would 'always be answered by Money on Demand'.[33] In fact the bank was forced into a suspension of cash payments on 6 May 1696 following a run on it during the recoinage. Two days earlier, clipped coins had ceased to

---

28. Dickson, *Financial Revolution*, p.52-54; Anne L. Murphy, *The Origins of English financial markets: investment and speculation before the South Sea Bubble* (Cambridge, 2009), p.40-41; R. D. Richards, 'The lottery in the history of English government finance', *Economic history* 3:9 (1934), p.57-76. For a clear summary, see Nicholas Mayhew, *Sterling: the rise and fall of a currency* (London, 1999), ch.3.

29. See John Brewer, *The Sinews of power: war, money and the English state, 1688-1783* (London, 1989); Patrick K. O'Brien, 'The political economy of British taxation, 1660-1815', *Economic history review* (2nd ser.) 41:1 (1988), p.1-32.

30. On the active secondary market trading in lottery tickets, bank shares, annuities, and other stocks and bonds, providing much needed liquidity and consequent support for public funds, see Murphy, *Origins of English financial markets*, p.58-61.

31. H. M. [Sir Humphry Mackworth], *England's glory, or, the great improvement of trade in general, by a royal bank, or office of credit* (London, T[homas]. W[arren]. for Tho. Bever, 1694), p.4. He remarked enthusiastically that he had 'heard of a Gentleman that had seen the same Money transmitted Nine times in one Morning, by writing off the Credit from one to another, and the Money *in specie* left untouched at last' (p.6-7).

32. As described in *An abstract of their majesties commission under the great seal, dated the 15th day of June 1694: for taking subscriptions for the bank, pursuant to the late act of parliament* (London, s. n., 1694), p.4. The same reassurance was given by one of the promoters of a land bank, John Briscoe, in *A Discourse of the late funds of the Million-Act, Lottery-Act, and Bank of England* (London, J. D. for Andrew Bell, 1696), p.25. Quoted in Ludovic Desmedt, 'Money in the "body politick": the analysis of trade and circulation in the writings of seventeenth-century political arithmeticians', *History of political economy* 37:1 (2005), p.92n.

33. Mackworth, *England's glory*, p.5-6. An anonymous author offered a tart reply on this point: *Some observations by way of answer, to a pamphlet, called England's glory; or, the royal bank* (London, John Whitlock, 1694), p.5. Mackworth remained confident that the scheme as a whole could not fail 'unless the Nation be destroyed' (p.7). Later in his career Mackworth himself issued unbacked bills as part of his mining schemes. William P. Griffith, 'Mackworth, Sir Humphry (1657-1727)', in *Oxford dictionary of national biography* (Oxford, 2004).

be accepted at face value but the bank had insufficient stores of reminted money to answer demand.[34] This episode was recalled long afterwards by Adam Smith in his critique of paper money in *Wealth of nations*.[35]

These innovations, together with the dilemma caused by the recoinage crisis, produced a flurry of arguments, proposals and counter-proposals, in a way that transformed thinking about economic questions and incorporated them centrally into public and philosophical debate. Many suggestions have been offered for how to account for the exceptional developments that mark this era. Regime change and the prospect of disastrous defeat to France clearly form a crucial part of the story and explain the motivation for financial experiment, but the specific solutions, as the work of Carl Wennerlind and Patrick O'Brien indicates, have to be set against a longer history of proposals and reforms.[36]

A provocative political and ideological analysis of this episode has been offered by Steve Pincus in a long chapter in *1688: the first modern revolution* (2009). He argues that a revolution in political economy was part of the intentions of the Whig actors who supported the defeat of James II and the installation of William III (together with more familiar concerns with religion and the constitution), rather than being an unforeseen consequence of these events.[37] His contrasting account sets up a strong division between a Tory conception of political economy (associated above all with Sir Josiah Child) in which property is finite and bound up with land, as opposed to a Whig vision in which manufactures and labour, which do not operate under the same limits, are the key to increasing wealth (a position endorsed by Locke among others). The larger context of Pincus's argument is his reconsideration of the place of commerce in political thought of the period. He disputes the assessment of J. G. A. Pocock that the Financial Revolution was a foreign imposition resisted by English commentators who shared, regardless of party affiliation, a basic view about the relationship between land, credit and trade – an essentially mercantilist understanding of property as defined by land, and trade as the exchange of goods produced from the land. Pincus also questions the alternative analysis (from Douglass North and Barry Weingast) that argues in favour of a post-revolutionary consensus in

---

34. See Sir John Clapham, *The Bank of England: a history*, 2 vols (Cambridge, 1944), vol.1, p.32, 35-36; Craig Rose, *England in the 1690s: revolution, religion and war* (Oxford, 1999), p.141.

35. Adam Smith, *An Inquiry into the nature and causes of the wealth of nations* [1776], gen. eds R. H Campbell and A. S. Skinner, textual ed. W. B. Todd, 2 vols (1976; Indianapolis, IN, 1982), II.ii.80 (p.318).

36. Wennerlind, *Casualties of credit*; Patrick K. O'Brien, 'Fiscal exceptionalism: Great Britain and its European rivals from Civil War to triumph at Trafalgar and Waterloo', in *The Political economy of British historical experience, 1688-1914*, ed. Donald Winch and Patrick K. O'Brien (Oxford, 2002), p.245-65.

37. Steve Pincus, *1688: the first modern revolution* (New Haven, CT, 2009), p.381, 393, 397.

support of capitalist institutions. Pincus stresses, on the one hand, the theoretical richness of debates and, on the other, the persistence of deep ideological divisions (along party lines). What the participants agreed on was the need for government intervention in economic matters, however different their ideas remained on the correct programme to back; thus neither party can be described as promoting 'possessive individualism' (contra C. B. Macpherson).[38]

The emphasis on richness and division is undoubtedly welcome but some of the contrasts are drawn too boldly to accommodate the complexity of positions taken on economic and political issues in the period. Before pursuing this point, more definition is required of the fault lines identified by Pincus. He focuses on a series of topics that defined Tory political economy, including support for the monopoly privileges granted to the East India Company and the Royal African Company, a tax policy which shifted the burden to excise rather than land, and an overall zero-sum view of economic competition articulated by Child. By contrast, the defeat of James II and enlistment of William III in a Whig political economy led to the removal of the Hearth Tax that had damaged manufacturing interests and to the passing of a new land tax; moves against the monopoly privileges of the Royal African Company and the 'larger target', the East India Company; and full support for the war effort against France. Most importantly, the Whigs backed the scheme for creating the Bank of England, which the Tories opposed as promoting the cause of manufactures and leading prospectively to a republic. The Tories had their own scheme in the form of a land bank, but the project approved by Parliament ultimately failed.[39]

Keeping the ideological lines straight in an era of disputed and uncertain orientations on economic questions proves decidedly difficult. One could argue that Pincus's account remaps some of the divisions between mercantilists and the Civil War era exponents of expanding credit onto later configurations, with Tories occupying the mercantilist

---

38. Pincus, *1688: the first modern revolution*, p.366-69, 372. This argument is developed more fully in Pincus, 'Neither Machiavellian moment nor possessive individualism: commercial society and the defenders of the English commonwealth', *American historical review* 103:3 (1998), p.705-36. For the positions he disputes, see J. G. A. Pocock, *The Machiavellian moment: Florentine political thought and the Atlantic republican tradition* (Princeton, NJ, 1975), p.423-505; Douglass C. North and Barry R. Weingast, 'Constitutions and commitment: the evolution of institutions governing public choice in seventeenth-century England', *Journal of economic history* 49:4 (1989), p.803-32; C. B. Macpherson, *The Political theory of possessive individualism: Hobbes to Locke* (Oxford, 1962).

39. Pincus, *1688: the first modern revolution*, esp. p.369-96. See also Steve Pincus and Alice Wolfram, 'A proactive state? The land bank, investment and party politics in the 1690s', in *Regulating the British economy, 1660-1850*, ed. Perry Gauci (Farnham, 2011), p.41-62; Dennis Rubini, 'Politics and the battle for the banks, 1688-1697', *English historical review* 85 (1970), p.693-714.

position and Whigs the more progressive one aligned with new credit instruments. But it is worth remembering that the bank proposals put forward in the Civil War period by Hartlibians were actually land banks (of the kind later embraced by Tories in the mid-1690s),[40] nor is it clear that all Whig thinkers were opposed to a zero-sum conception of economic competition, to the extent that they concentrated on international trade and the balance of payments in order to ensure an inflow of specie. This was certainly a priority for Locke. Pincus cites Locke as 'one of the earliest supporters of and investors in the Bank of England',[41] and it is true that he did invest in the bank, but he also invested in the monopolistic East India Company.[42] Furthermore, in an unpublished manuscript Locke questioned the arguments for establishing the Bank of England, and he was not alone in raising doubts about its merits.[43] The degree of Whig unanimity over the project can be considerably overstated.[44]

Certain evidence used to support ideological division looks different on closer inspection. The author of the *England's glory* (1694), H. M., is described by Pincus as 'The most eloquent proponent of the Bank of England'.[45] This in fact was Sir Humphry Mackworth, whom I quoted above. Mackworth was a significant figure. He married into a Welsh landowning family and developed extensive mining interests starting in 1695 in the property in Neath in west Glamorgan, and the surrounding area, becoming deputy-governor of the Company of Mine Adventurers of England in 1698. Far from adhering to a Whig outlook, Mackworth was a committed Tory who had been loyal to James II, and entered Parliament as an MP for Cardiganshire in 1701 with the backing of the Mine Adventurers with whom he shared high-church toryism. According to William Griffith, 'Mackworth proved an assertive upholder of their [Tory] principles and protestantism in parliament and through pamphlets', and 'His anti-whig and anti-court views led to his attacks on the king's ministers in 1701 and on Robert Harley as speaker in 1704-1705'.[46]

40. Wennerlind, *Casualties of credit*, p.73-75.
41. Pincus, *1688: the first modern revolution*, p.371.
42. Bodleian Library, Oxford, MS Locke f.10, fols 380, 406, 410, 461, 462-3, 487, 492, 493, 495, 495, 497, 533, 560, 588 and 599.
43. Bodleian Library MS Locke b.3, p.35-37. Rose, *England in the 1690s*, p.134-35, notes Locke's reservations, quoting a letter from Locke to John Freke and Edward Clarke of 18 February 1695. Richard A. Kleer, ' "Fictitious cash": English public finance and paper money, 1689-1697', in *Money, power, and print: interdisciplinary studies on the Financial Revolution in the British Isles*, ed. Charles Ivar McGrath and Chris Fauske (Newark, DE, 2008), p.70-103, indicates a considerable division within proponents of the bank about its merits.
44. There were also plenty of critics of creating a national debt with which the Bank was associated; see Dickson, *Financial Revolution*, ch.2.
45. Pincus, *1688: the first modern revolution*, p.391.
46. Griffith, 'Mackworth, Sir Humphry (1657-1727)'.

We might say that Mackworth is representative of nothing but himself,[47] but then the same could be suggested on careful examination of a number of others individuals who produced quite hybrid and paradoxical positions on matters of money and political economy in the period which do not always lend themselves to easy characterisation.

The story of political economy in the period looks rather different if we place the recoinage controversy in a more central position. Pincus does not discuss the recoinage but certainly in terms of the sheer volume of contributions to economic debate the question of how to address the deterioration of English currency occupied a dominant position in the 1690s, even if the role that might be played by various kinds of banks in resolving it was not unrelated.[48] There were two main options that received backing, both of which by 1695 required coins in circulation to be recalled and reminted. The first option was to remint them at the existing standard of silver weight at the Mint of 5s. 2d. per ounce, in effect a 'restoration' of the missing silver depleted at this point by 50 per cent on average by clipping. The second option was to engage in a devaluation and not to remint at the old rate but at a new, higher Mint price (a strategy referred to in the period as 'raising' the coin). Both schemes had backers in Parliament. The Treasury commissioned a famous *Report* from its secretary, William Lowndes, advocating a devaluation of the coin by 20 per cent by raising the price at the Mint to 6s. 5d. per ounce.[49] The main figures opposing this were John Locke and his political associates who argued in favour of retaining the existing standard. Locke's side prevailed in Parliament and the recoinage began in 1696 on the principle of a restoration, though not all of Locke's provisions for implementation were followed. These rival proposals had many important implications, not all of them foreseen by the participants. In particular the deflationary consequences of Locke's solution were dramatic; the money supply would also have shrunk under Lowndes's proposals but not to the same extent.[50]

---

47. The *History of Parliament* entry on Mackworth by D. W. Hayton opens with the statement that 'Mackworth was a collection of apparent paradoxes: a Country Tory industrialist and financial "projector"; a godly-minded High Churchman; and a publicly pious and philanthropic swindler for whom not one among his contemporaries could find a kind word'. *The History of Parliament: the House of Commons 1690-1715*, ed. Eveline Cruickshanks, Stuart Handley and D. W. Hayton, 5 vols (Cambridge, 2002), vol.4, p.724.

48. For a bibliography, see J. Keith Horsefield, *British monetary experiments 1650-1710* (Cambridge, MA, 1960). For discussion see also Kwasi Kwarteng, 'The political thought of the recoinage crisis of 1695-1697' (Doctoral dissertation, University of Cambridge, 2000).

49. William Lowndes, *A Report containing an essay for the amendment of the silver coins* (London, Charles Bill and the executrix of Thomas Newcomb, 1695).

50. For the clearest discussion, see Horsefield, *British monetary experiments*; see also Ming-Hsun Li, *The Great Recoinage of 1696 to 1699* (London, 1963). Apparently Lowndes did not grasp

The focus of contemporary discussion was not on deflation, but on a series of other critical issues such as the correct understanding of the nature of money. For Locke, silver was not just a means of measurement (as in a unit of account); it also constituted the thing bargained for.[51] In other words, he claimed that people made agreements according to the amount of silver by weight, not in terms of the 'nominal' or face value of coinage in tale. Locke emphasised a view that had been long held and was widely shared that the value of silver was in that sense 'intrinsic' to it by weight, not conferred by something extrinsic like its stamp. This notion, which he regarded as axiomatic, enabled him to draw a series of conclusions, but a form of proof was available in noting that international trade was conducted according to silver by weight. An isolated economy might be able to organise its affairs differently; England had no choice, as a trading nation, other than to respect the role of silver and to revalue its coinage accordingly.[52] Ultimately Locke saw himself as protecting money as a form of property, on the assumption that contracts had been made in silver by weight, and that any tampering with the standard violated such contracts. Money was therefore emphatically political.

Not everyone subscribed to Locke's position. Various motives existed for dissenting from it. Some respondents flatly contradicted him and asserted that the value of money did not reside solely in silver content.[53] On the contrary, the stamp on coin did confer value. There was a sound basis for this argument since lightweight money had in fact circulated by tale (that is, at face value) for long periods in domestic transactions.[54] The loss of silver represented, paradoxically, an economic boost by expanding the money supply.[55] Locke countered with its adverse effect

---

the deflationary impact either, since he commented that his plan had the advantage of allowing for a revaluation of coin at the old standard once economic affairs had settled, presumably after the war. *Report*, p.87-88.

51. *Further considerations concerning raising the value of money* (1695), in *Locke on money*, ed. Patrick Hyde Kelly, 2 vols (Oxford, 1991), vol.2, p.412.

52. *Some considerations of the consequences of the lowering of interest, and raising the value of money* (1692), in *Locke on money*, vol.1, p.264.

53. See for example Nicholas Barbon, *A Discourse concerning coining the new money lighter* (London, Richard Chiswell, 1696); James Hodges, *The Present state of England, as to coin and publick charges* (London, Andr. Bell, 1697).

54. In any case, coins were hardly of a standard weight in circulation, partly due to wear and tear, and partly because they were hand-tooled and difficult to make consistent. 'Hammered' coin of this kind was complemented, starting in 1662, by the introduction of 'milled' money which was more standardised but still varied in weight (and it represented a small percentage of the circulating medium).

55. See Joyce Oldham Appleby, 'Locke, liberalism, and the natural law of money', *Past & present* 71 (May 1976), p.43-69. The historian D. W. Jones remarks, 'Far from being the villain of the piece, clipping was England's salvation' during the Nine Years' War. *War and economy in the age of William III and Marlborough*, p.247.

in raising prices and the arbitrage opportunities it created. The alternative to Locke's position privileged the needs of the national economy, which required an adequate medium of exchange to facilitate trade rather than the more restricted demands of international exchange conducted in terms of silver by weight alone. Locke's Whig outlook was thus not dissimilar to a mercantilist concern with the balance of trade as the way to secure a net surplus of precious metals.[56]

The place of credit in these discussions requires some comment. For Locke it played a very limited part in his system; he remained dubious about how effectively credit notes could be made convertible since third parties had no real incentive to accept them, although he acknowledged that such an arrangement would be preferable to doing without an adequate medium of exchange altogether.[57] His model seems to have been based on debts between individuals entering into wider circulation rather than more elaborate schemes for backing credit devised at the time. By contrast, Davenant was much more open to credit than Locke as a solution to the recoinage crisis, despite sharing his understanding of intrinsic value.[58]

These considerations leave us with a dilemma in determining what was progressive and what was backward looking in political economy at this moment in time. Locke's importance makes him a key figure to examine. His response to the recoinage crisis could be described as conservative – insisting on preserving the existing standard in order to ensure the interests of landlords and creditors with existing contracts who expected payment in full-weight coin. But devaluation of the currency would also have left those holding government debt with a loss. In his view, such a mistaken course of action threatened English credit at a time when borrowing to fund the war was absolutely essential. From another perspective, we could see Locke as articulating a position in which the monetary standard was not subject to manipulation either by the sovereign or by Parliament, aligning him with a much more 'liberal', even

---

56. Appleby situates Locke in a mercantilist paradigm in which 'the sterility of domestic trade, the inelasticity of demand, and the beggar-thy-neighbour approach to international commerce' prevailed. 'Locke, liberalism, and the natural law of money', p.67. We could, however, attribute Locke's position to his sense of how best to defend the country in time of war in which international financial obligations were paramount due to the need for remittances and indebtedness to the Dutch.

57. See Daniel Carey, 'John Locke, money, and credit', in *The Empire of credit: the financial revolution in the British Atlantic world, 1688-1815*, ed. Daniel Carey and Christopher J. Finlay (Dublin, 2011), p.25-51.

58. For Davenant's acknowledgement that international trade was conducted in terms of the intrinsic value of coin, see 'A memorial concerning the coyn of England: November, 1695', in *Two manuscripts by Charles Davenant*, ed. Abbott Payson Usher (Baltimore, MD, 1942), p.17.

radical agenda.[59] His attitude to credit suggests a more limited outlook on economic experiment, while his passionate defence of the state in a moment of crisis places him in the political vanguard endorsing a Protestant settlement. That all these things could be true at the same time gives some indication of why money and political economy should complicate our picture of Enlightenment.

Money form

Deliberations over money form in the eighteenth century represent some of the most striking and significant contributions to political economy in the long eighteenth century. As we have seen, Locke committed himself to a traditional definition of money as constituted by precious metal. Although he encountered difficulties in addressing the relationship between silver and gold – preferring a single unit of measure rather than two rival ones – he had no doubt that value was tied to the precious metal in coin, intrinsically. Perhaps the most famous challenge to this account in the early eighteenth century came from the Scottish economist and projector, John Law. In *Money and trade considered* (1705), Law made a theoretical separation between money and bullion, an insight of considerable importance. Law's openness to this notion no doubt owes a considerable amount to his Scottish experience, as Murray Pittock and others have argued.[60] The chronic lack of specie in Scotland led to significant innovations in banking, credit and note issue associated with the founding of the Bank of Scotland in 1695, to the point where, as S. G. Checkland observes, 'gold and silver virtually disappeared'.[61] Law argued in *Money and trade considered* and his unpublished 'Essay on a land bank' of 1704 that the shortage of reserves in specie limited the capacity of the Bank of Scotland to extend credit, which prompted Law to propose land as a more suitable backing and security. The precarious hard currency of Scotland – composed of a mixture of foreign and domestic coins of variable fineness – could be remedied by land with more certain value. Ironically, Law criticised the Bank of England for its limited reserve of 20-25 per cent in silver against its bank notes, on the grounds that this would expose it to the risk of a run.

59. His critic James Hodges certainly thought that Locke's insistence on keeping the current monetary standard was an abrogation of royal power. *The Present state of England, as to coin and publick charges*, p.x, 155, 263-78.
60. M. G. H. Pittock, 'John Law's theory of money and its roots in Scottish culture', *Proceedings of the antiquarian society of Scotland* 133 (2003), p.391-403. Pittock emphasises Law's familial tradition (as goldsmiths). See also Antoin E. Murphy, *John Law: economic theorist and policy-maker* (Oxford, 1997).
61. S. G. Checkland, *Scottish banking: a history* (Glasgow, 1975), p.xvii-xviii. The scale of the note issue was what set the Scottish experiment apart. See Richard Saville, *Bank of Scotland: a history 1695-1995* (Edinburgh, 1996), p.21-3.

In spite of Law's significance, this brief sketch already sufficiently suggests that the extent of his originality can be exaggerated.[62] Land-bank schemes had been proposed in the 1690s, notably by Hugh Chamberlen, John Briscoe, Nicholas Barbon and John Asgill, and earlier in the Civil War period as we have seen. Asgill was especially clear that the poor condition of English coinage in the mid-1690s meant that it was essential, as the title of his book indicated, to *Create another species of money than gold and silver* (1696), based on land. Asgill argued that 'whatever hath all the qualities of a thing, ceases to be a likeness, and is become that very thing'.[63] This did not mean that any entity with the qualities of money somehow became gold and silver, but it could become *money* (just as gold is money and silver is money, but gold is not silver, nor silver gold). Consistent with this, Asgill spoke of 'forming' land (or securities based on it) into the qualities of money.[64]

Law became notorious because of his involvement in the failure of the Mississippi System (after his elevation to the equivalent of French chief minister and finance minister). When he introduced his scheme in France it was elaborated in considerable detail in terms of the structure and resources of his bank, which weakened it fatally, in part due to the assumption of the national debt and the complex relationship to different trading companies it incorporated and obligations to shareholders.[65] Adam Smith's critical discussion of Law in his *Lectures on jurisprudence* accused him of the mistaken view that 'opulence consists in money' and that the value of gold and silver was arbitrary and dependent on agreement, a conviction that allowed Law to imagine that 'the idea of value might be brought to paper'. Smith traced this notion to the absence of precious metals in Scotland which might be substituted by paper and an Edinburgh land bank. In his account of the French career of Law, Smith seems to have regarded the scheme as viable up to a point – that is, if Law had quit when he was ahead. But Law ended up, unfortunately, 'the dupe of it himself'.[66]

---

62. In acknowledging this point, Antoin Murphy argues that Law's proposals 'outshone all of these contemporary writings by the sheer scale of the macroeconomic vision and modernity of its economic conceptualization' (*The Genesis of macroeconomics*, p.46).
63. John Asgill, *Several assertions proved, in order to create another species of money than gold and silver* (London, s. n., 1696), p.17.
64. Asgill, *Several assertions*, p.22, 25, 44.
65. See Murphy, *John Law*; Murphy, 'John Law: a new monetary system', in Murphy, *The Genesis of macroeconomics*, p.43-71. For a recent study of Law's activities, see Larry Neal, *'I am not master of events': the speculations of John Law and Lord Londonderry in the Mississippi and South Sea Bubbles* (New Haven, CT, 2012).
66. Adam Smith, *Lectures on jurisprudence*, ed. R. L. Meek, D. D. Raphael and P. G. Stein (Oxford, 1978), p.515, 517, 519. For some discussion of Smith's views on Law, see Antoin E. Murphy, 'John Law and the Scottish Enlightenment', in *A History of Scottish economic thought*, ed. Alexander Dow and Sheila Dow (London, 2006), p.9-26.

George Berkeley separated money conceptually from specie, but he was unsuccessful in his attempts to persuade his Irish contemporaries to adopt his monetary or banking recommendations. In *The Querist* (published in three parts, 1735-1737), he composed a set of questions designed to unseat received assumptions about a host of economic matters (the final edition in his lifetime, of 1752, contains nearly 600 questions). On the subject of money his ideas were complicated by a series of rival commitments; nonetheless he invited consideration of the thesis that 'the true idea of money' was that of a 'ticket or counter'. Gold and silver had no special virtue (aside from motivating people's industry to acquire them); they functioned, effectively, as the unit of account (for 'reckoning, recording and transferring' value) but also as signs facilitating exchange. On this basis he concluded that it was of no 'great consequence what materials the tickets are made of'.[67] Nonetheless we should not exaggerate the degree to which Berkeley had arrived at a classical conception of money as having an inert function since he still regarded it as a key factor in production; he also wanted the notes issued by his proposed bank to be backed by a promise to pay specie on demand, despite being guaranteed against the stock of the nation, as Patrick Kelly shows in his chapter.[68] Berkeley's analysis was closely connected to the predicament of the Irish economy, beset by a shortage of small coins,[69] and the burden of payments and remittances to land-lords in precious metals. He wondered, for example, 'Whether if there was no silver or gold in the kingdom, our trade might not, nevertheless, supply bills of exchange, sufficient to answer the demands of absentees in England or elsewhere?' Rather than privilege the interests of inter-national exchange, Berkeley defined coinage as 'an affair entirely dom-estic'.[70] Locke himself had acknowledged the possibilities for conducting trade differently from the point of view of money form if the country were isolated from the rest of the world.[71] Berkeley followed through on

67. George Berkeley, *The Querist*, in *The Works of George Berkeley Bishop of Cloyne*, ed. A. A. Luce and T. E. Jessop, 9 vols (London, 1948-1957), vol.6, nos 23, 25, 35.
68. Joseph Schumpeter concluded on this basis that Berkeley remained a metallist. *History of economic analysis*, ed. Elizabeth Boody Schumpeter (New York, 1954), p.288.
69. Berkeley, *The Querist*, nos 469-76, 482, 485-87, 571. The relationship between Berkeley's proposals and Wood's half-pence is worth consideration. The successful thwarting of Wood's patent to import copper coinage (with no legal tender status) in 1724, only for cards, tokens and tickets to circulate in their place, is discussed in Constantine George Caffentzis, *Exciting the industry of mankind: George Berkeley's philosophy of money* (Dordrecht, 2000), p.65-77. From this perspective, the emphasis on money as a ticket in *The Querist*, Caffentzis points out, 'was not a theoretical insight of a future monetary state but a foregrounding of a widespread contemporary practice' (p.76).
70. Berkeley, *The Querist*, nos 32, 572.
71. *Some considerations*, in *Locke on money*, vol.1, p.264.

this logic. Together with the provision for an Irish Mint, the remedy was ultimately 'a national bank, and plenty of small cash'.[72]

Both David Hume and Adam Smith remained more cautious. David Hume's evaluation of paper credit led him to the conclusion that it amounted to 'counterfeit money', which he rejected on the basis that it could not be made acceptable to foreigners in payment, but it also posed a risk to national well-being since, as he put it, 'any great disorder in the state will reduce [it] to nothing'.[73] As Carl Wennerlind and Christopher Finlay have argued, Hume was in some sense philosophically open to the concept of credit and paper replacing specie, but in practical terms the necessary relationships of trust and compulsion could not be brought to bear internationally for such a system to work.[74] Smith similarly understood the utility of paper money as confined to domestic transactions, with specie operative beyond national borders. He had a much more developed account of the role of banking which was central to the issue of paper. In principle, paper turned 'dead stock' of gold and silver into 'active and productive' capital,[75] subject to the retention of a suitable reserve of cash to support value and prevent bank runs. The endemic problem was over-issue. Competition among banks he reckoned to be positive in forestalling this possibility, but the example of the collapse of the Ayr Bank in 1772 demonstrated just how real the danger could be.[76] Yet Pennsylvania showed the potential for successful colonial experimentation with paper money, suggesting that, if properly managed, a system of paper money was viable.[77] After the deaths of Hume and Smith, these questions entered a new phase with the Restriction of Payments in 1797 when the Bank of England no longer honoured the promise to redeem notes with cash – a decision necessitated by economic conditions in the midst of the French Revolutionary Wars.[78] An era of

72. Berkeley, *The Querist*, no.588.
73. David Hume, 'Of money' (1752), in *Essays, moral, political and literary*, ed. Eugene F. Miller (Indianapolis, IN, 1985), p.284.
74. See Carl Wennerlind, 'The link between David Hume's *Treatise of human nature* and his fiduciary theory of money', *History of political economy* 33:1 (2001), p.139-60; Wennerlind, 'An artificial virtue and the oil of commerce: a synthetic view of Hume's theory of money', in *David Hume's political economy*, ed. Carl Wennerlind and Margaret Schabas (London, 2008), p.105-26; Christopher J. Finlay, 'Commerce and the law of nations in Hume's theory of money' in *The Empire of credit: the financial revolution in the British Atlantic world, 1688-1815*, ed. Daniel Carey and Christopher J. Finlay (Dublin, 2011), p.53-72.
75. Smith, *Wealth of nations*, II.ii.86 (p.320).
76. On this incident see Nicholas Phillipson, *Adam Smith: an enlightened life* (London, 2011), p.206-208 (noting Hume's comments to Smith on this subject).
77. Alberto Giacomin, 'Paper money: a reassessment of Adam Smith's view', in *Money and markets: a doctrinal approach*, ed. Alberto Giacomin and Maria Christina Marcuzzo (London, 2007), p.181-99.
78. The suspension lasted until 1821. The key issue was whether the Bank of England's notes,

intensified discussion of monetary matters occurred in the light of this, with hundreds of contributions, including the most famous of them, the report in 1810 of the Bullion Committee, chaired by Francis Horner.[79]

New directions in money and political economy

This collection of essays advances the discussion of money and political economy in the seventeenth and eighteenth centuries in a variety of directions. Johann P. Sommerville's opening chapter, 'Sir Robert Filmer, usury and the ideology of order', shows the difficulty of integrating political economy into accepted narratives of intellectual history. Filmer's fame rests on his defence of royal authority in *Patriarcha* (published 1680, composed in the 1630s) and his equation of the sovereign's absolute authority with the power of Adam over his family. Yet the assumption that Filmer defended existing social hierarchies on the basis of Scripture, backed up by a conception of the natural world as structured by an orderly creation, fails to account for his role as a trenchant defender of usury in his *Quaestio quodlibetica, or A Discourse, whether it may bee lawfull to take use for money* (published 1653).[80] Filmer made the argument, furthermore, on the basis of secular reasoning, not through an appeal to traditional hierarchies or the interests of landowners, showing a sensitivity to economic evidence and treating the rent of money as no different conceptually to the renting of land. In fact his position coincides with (and may indeed have influenced) the one adopted on interest by John Locke,[81] his staunch opponent in matters of politics (as the first of the *Two treatises of government* amply testifies). Several important conclusions result from this discussion, including a

---

which had become inconvertible into gold, should be recognised as legal tender. See J. K. Horsefield, 'The duties of a banker II: the effects of inconvertibility', in *Papers in English monetary history*, ed. T. S. Ashton and R. S. Sayers (Oxford, 1953), p.16-36.

79. The text of the Bullion Report is reprinted in Edwin Cannan (ed.), *The Paper pound of 1797-1821*, 2nd edn (London, 1925), p.1-72. On the political and economic background of the Bullion Committee and Horner's role see Frank Whitson Fetter, *Development of British monetary orthodoxy 1797-1875* (Cambridge, MA, 1965), p.26-63.

80. Filmer responded directly to critics of usury such as Lancelot Andrewes, *De usuris, theologica determinatio*, his 1585 Cambridge degree exercise for the bachelor of divinity, published in *Opuscula quaedam posthuma* (London, Felix Kyngston for R[ichard] B[adger] & Andræa Hebb, 1629), p.111-38; George Downam, *Lectures on the XV. Psalme* (London, Adam Islip for Cuthbert Burbie, 1604); and the cleric Roger Fenton's *A Treatise of usurie, divided into three bookes* (London, Felix Kyngston for William Aspley, 1611). For discussion see David Hawkes, *The Culture of usury in Renaissance England* (New York, 2010). For the range of English opinions, some of them more moderate, see Norman Jones, *God and the moneylenders: usury and law in early modern England* (Oxford, 1989), ch.6.

81. See John Locke, *Some considerations*; on Locke and Filmer, see Kelly, 'General introduction', in *Locke on money*, vol.1, p.98.

serious revision of existing interpretations of Filmer. Both Filmer and Locke turn out to be on the secular and modern side of the argument over usury, indicating that, unexpectedly, patriarchalist royal absolutism and commitments to government as limited by consent appear equally compatible with defences of charging interest on money.

The larger point is that our customary genealogies of the Enlightenment need to be suspended when encountering this subject more generally. Periodisation remains problematic because texts circulate widely across the period, from manuscript to print and republication. Filmer's *Quaestio*, for example, was composed somewhere between 1629 and 1638, printed in 1653 and then republished in 1678.[82] Among the major 'mercantilist' texts, Thomas Mun's important *England's treasure by forraign trade*, written sometime in the 1620s, did not appear in print until 1664, with subsequent editions in 1669, 1713, 1718 and 1755. Gerard Malynes's influential *Consuetudo, vel, lex mercatoria, or, The Ancient law-merchant* (1622), published during his lifetime (he died in 1641) was reprinted in 1629, 1636, 1656 and 1686. Works on money from earlier in the seventeenth century were re-circulated during the recoinage crisis when their renewed significance became apparent.[83]

Determining whose work is conservative, and whose progressive in tendency, whose is derivative, and whose innovative, encounters similar complications. Locke's pronouncement on the coinage carried great weight and provided a lasting point of reference in monetary controversies, but by adhering to the concept of intrinsic value he arguably sacrificed an 'empirical' take on economic relationships in favour of a more dogmatic approach organised around first principles and rigorous, if sometimes rather narrow, deductions. His critic James Hodges, for example, asserted that Locke's reasonings would fail when brought 'to the Touch-stone of Matter of Fact'.[84] In doing so, was Locke merely defending the class of landlords and investors to which he belonged or was he making a far-sighted and essentially liberal case against political interference in contracts and property, defending the state against itself, in effect, in a moment of national danger and crisis?

Resolving such matters is far from straightforward, and rather than propose reductive solutions this collection opens out the discussion to a

---

82. See Filmer, *A Discourse whether it may be lawful to take use for money* (London, Will. Crook, 1678). For dating the composition of *Quaestio quodlibetica* to the period 1629-1638, see Sommerville's discussion below, p.35-37.

83. See for example Rice Vaughan, *A Discourse of coin and coinage* (London, Th. Dawks, for Th. Basset, 1675), which was reprinted in 1696. See also *A Further essay for the amendment of the gold and silver coins: with the opinion of Mr. Gerrard de Malynes, who was an eminent merchant in the reign of Queen Elizabeth, concerning the standard of England* (London, T. Hodgkin, 1695).

84. Hodges, *The Present state of England, as to coin and publick charges*, p.267.

wider set of answers and considerations. In my chapter on 'Locke's philosophy of money' I investigate what made Locke so insistent on the sacrosanctity of the monetary standard despite knowing that it had changed historically over time. Locke's challenge to William Lowndes's significant 1695 *Report* for the Treasury argued that existing contracts had been made in full weight silver, according to the Mint standard, and that the recoinage must restore the missing silver (despite the hardship associated with doing so) lost to illegal clipping and exportation. Against the view that a devaluation would extend the money supply, Locke maintained that any efforts to manipulate the standard would be exposed by foreign traders who calculated their prices not according to 'extrinsic' names and inflated values but by the weight of silver in each coin. They would settle accounts in full-weight silver or simply raise their prices. This led Locke to privilege international exchange over the domestic economy, a shortcoming in the view of his critics. Nonetheless, Locke's orientation had the benefit of declaring that the monetary standard was not ultimately under the control of the state or the Crown but existed outside the reach of internal power. It is not therefore surprising to find that Locke was less than persuaded by the potential of credit to expand economic activity (on the basis that bills and debts could not be made properly transferable). In this respect his position was not forward looking in the era of the Financial Revolution. Yet his reticence is perhaps understandable if we consider that Davenant, a supporter of expanding credit, described it nonetheless as a form of 'fictitious wealth' in his 1695 submission to the Lords Justices – the regency council governing in William's absence during the war (which was also addressed by Locke).[85]

In order to make sense of Locke's position we have to embed it in his wider philosophical commitments. These relate not merely to his views on property and political consent but to the philosophy of language presented in the *Essay concerning human understanding* (1690). Money belongs in a special category of terms that Locke describes as 'mixed modes', the significance of which is that their definition remains the responsibility and entitlement of individuals since mixed modes are conceptual, and any physical referent does not in itself convey their meaning. However, Locke does not resign himself to this condition but searches for something that will give stability to the situation. This he locates in the agreed public standard of weight and fineness of the coin – an 'external' criterion of meaning based, paradoxically, on its 'intrinsic' quality in terms of physical properties (of weight and fineness of the alloy).

---

85. Davenant, 'A memorial concerning the coyn of England', in *Two manuscripts*, p.26.

While the preoccupation with money and political economy has been recognised as characteristic of the era of Enlightenment, insufficient attention has been given to the recoinage controversy in the 1690s as a crucible for developments in reflection on the nature of credit and the function of the circulating medium.[86] Charles Larkin's essay on 'The Great Recoinage of 1696: Charles Davenant and monetary theory' confirms the importance of the recoinage as a pivotal moment, leading to the articulation of principles with far-reaching consequences, ranging from credit on the one hand to the eventual adoption of the gold standard on the other. For Larkin, the size of the devaluation proposed by Lowndes (20 per cent) made it problematic, coupled with Lowndes's assumption that taking this measure would serve as a panacea in relation to the problem of the balance of payments (by making English exports cheaper and raising the cost of imports). Neither Lowndes nor Locke understood the price-specie-flow mechanism, which was only described properly in the eighteenth century by Richard Cantillon and David Hume.[87] Locke's deflationary solution was more acceptable politically but he had no real strategy to respond adequately to the dilemma of a bimetallic monetary system (a limitation he shared with Lowndes).

Larkin focuses on the contribution of Davenant, the Tory writer and former commissioner of excise (from 1678-1688), who became a prominent commentator on economic policy. Several features of Davenant's outlook distinguish him from his contemporaries, including Locke, whose assumptions were often framed by mercantilist concerns. Davenant's work constitutes a transition to a more 'classical' understanding of economic issues. His intellectual background was rooted in political arithmetic – he made frequent reference to William Petty in his writings, and he displayed a readiness to engage in probable reasoning, to take an experimental approach, and to accumulate data in assessing economic questions. He accepted a number of premises about international trade and intrinsic value that Locke embraced, but he also saw that a wider role for credit was possible in order to address the problem of liquidity and sustain the domestic economy particularly during the Nine Years' War. The shift of attitude, Larkin argues, came in his understanding of money as a means of exchange rather than as the definition of wealth (the accusation famously made by Adam Smith,

---

86. For exceptions, see Horsefield, *British monetary experiments*; Ming-Hsun Li, *The Great Recoinage*); Kwarteng, 'The political thought of the recoinage crisis of 1695-1697'; see also Ludovic Desmedt, 'Les fondements monétaires de la "révolution financière" anglaise: le tournant de 1696', in *La Monnaie dévoilée par ses crises*, ed. Bruno Theret, 2 vols (Paris, 2007), vol.1, p.311-38.

87. Antoin E. Murphy, *Richard Cantillon: entrepreneur and economist* (Oxford, 1986), p.270-74.

unfairly one could say, against the mercantilists).[88] Part of this was due to a greater awareness by Davenant of the pattern of monetary flows and knowledge of the different media of exchange. His work provides a more integrated analysis of economic factors, from credit and government borrowing to taxation, and something that begins to be identifiable as monetary policy.

The political legacy of the seventeenth century's ideological conflicts continued in the domain of republican thought, led by figures like Robert Molesworth and John Toland. In the context of contemporaneous arguments about expanding credit, state finance and commercial culture the question has arisen whether this tradition was capable of producing anything more than a resistant and backward-looking analysis of such important developments, in part through an abiding attachment to agrarian interests and their association of landed property with political power and virtue. Different conclusions have been offered by Pocock and Pincus but the debate is re-explored in a carefully considered discussion by Justin Champion in his chapter '"Mysterious politicks": land, credit and commonwealth political economy, 1656-1722', which runs a course from the publication of James Harrington's *Oceana* to the aftermath of the South Sea Bubble. Toland, an assiduous defender of republican principles and ally of Viscount Molesworth, began his contributions with a translation of Bernardo Davanzati's 1588 work on money as *A Discourse upon coins* (1696) in order to assist the Lockean position on the recoinage; he extolled the Bank of England in 1700; and later proposed a scheme for a national bank in Ireland (*c*.1720) designed on the model of the Bank of Amsterdam. Clearly, republican thought on credit, banking and debt has been underestimated. The plan for Toland's bank was a cautious one, in fact, intended to facilitate commercial transactions rather than to expand credit or fund the national debt. Toland's views were not prompted by hostility to new institutions but by an effort to shape them in support of public rather than private interests. Of course the South Sea Bubble elicited a huge response, with some of the leading contributions inflected by commonwealth vocabularies and the drawing of parallels between modern corruption and various ancient conspiracies (described by Cicero, Livy, Sallust, as well as Machiavelli). Here too the object of attack, for example in *Cato's letters* (1720-1723), was not credit as such but its abuse; credit continued to have the valuable potential to bond communities and governments in links of trust. It was a social relationship rather than simply financial, and essential for national

---

88. Smith, *Wealth of nations*, IV.i.: 'Of the principle of the commercial, or mercantile system', vol.1, p.429-51.

well-being, but it was also in perpetual danger of being undermined by deceit, manipulation and credulity. Champion's research shows that far from being an enemy of investment and speculation, Molesworth used Toland to purchase stock in the South Sea Company, and they both drew on his reputation in Parliament to make the deal. Toland himself was actively involved in such matters despite his limited means and was, as Champion puts it, fully 'embedded in a culture and network of credit and debt'.

Harrington's own antagonism towards commerce, money, and finance has arguably been overplayed. He certainly stressed the primacy of landed property (in an English context); however, he was not unaware of other forms of property or indifferent to trade and industry. *Imperium* may for him have been founded 'in dominio' but it was possible to follow him and yet to expand the definition of property to include not merely land but also wealth acquired through mercantile exchange. Thus there were resources available in his position to engage with a new political and economic set of circumstances. As Champion argues, the prescriptive solution in Harrington might have required modification (for example in relation to agrarian laws) without his philosophy losing its analytical force. Certainly Toland's dedication of his 1700 edition of Harrington's works 'To the Lord Mayor, Aldermen, Sherifs, and Common Council of London' tells a different story to the received view. In Toland's *The Art of governing by partys* (1701) he extended the argument in a passionate defence of public credit, which was underpinned not only by public confidence but ultimately by private resources of individuals.

The fact that Bishop Berkeley – a tireless foe of freethinkers like Toland – was nonetheless an exponent of an innovative banking scheme for Ireland is a measure of how open we should be to the possibilities of the period in the context of political economy. Best known in this context for his philosophy of money articulated in *The Querist* (1735-1737), Berkeley had a complex, insightful and practical view of economic issues, above all governed by an acute sense of the needs of a small and struggling economy. Patrick Kelly's chapter, 'Berkeley and the idea of a national bank', offers a nuanced reading of Berkeley's position, which has often eluded critics. Ireland was beset by a range of problems, including a shortage of specie due in part to remittances to absentee landlords; the need for small change to facilitate transactions; a precarious system of private banks (issuing their own notes), which had seen the collapse in 1733 of the country's largest private bank, Burton and Falkiner; and a starving population in need of work. In advance of the legislative session of the Irish parliament in 1737 Berkeley reprinted his queries related to banking in a (failed) attempt to encourage the foundation of a national bank. Earlier attempts in Ireland of this kind had also failed in 1721 in the wake of the South Sea Bubble,[89] but Berkeley was convinced that a suitably cautious model would succeed. Unlike the Bank of England, Berkeley's bank was properly national in ownership, rather than held in private hands and founded by joint stock. Its security was ultimately underwritten by the Irish parliament. Paper money issued by his proposed bank was subject to tight controls on note issue and accounting, and it was backed by a tax on wine to provide an initial fund of £100,000. With this sum, bills were to be issued to individuals who would deposit specie or securities in land or goods. Thus a specie reserve (and provision for payment on demand) remained an important feature of his scheme rather than committing him entirely to a token system, though judging the precise level of note issue to authorise remained a particular challenge. The bank would become a national asset by reinvesting profits in the country and ensuring a wide distribution of credit through the four provinces. Berkeley's sense of the viability of his proposal was partly conditioned by exploiting the advantage of the fact that Ireland existed in a relatively closed economy whose notes would not be acceptable outside, precisely in order to stimulate domestic consumption and production. At the same time, Berkeley favoured restoring the link between Irish currency and English sterling by re-rating the coin. Here too paper money would assist the process by preventing hardship associated with a contraction of the supply of specie. Berkeley charted a remarkable path. On the one hand he benefited from hindsight in criticising the plans of John Law which had led to the disaster of the Mississippi Company, while on the other he drew on a number of key provisions of Law's system as set out in *Money and trade considered* (1705). He was also indebted to mercantilist principles in seeing a vital role for the state in managing the economy, but he freed himself from the fixation with gold and silver as the markers of wealth.

With the appearance of Adam Smith's *Wealth of nations* (1776) an emphatic and self-conscious movement away from mercantilism takes place, as he devoted the whole of Book IV to assailing a key set of assumptions he maintained had misled theorists as well as the wider public. Ryan Patrick Hanley and Maria Pia Paganelli, in their contribution to this volume, discuss the formation of Smith's objections, his account of money and his privileging of a system of 'natural liberty'. The accuracy of Smith's characterisations of his predecessors may be open to question, but there is little doubt that he believed it was necessary to counteract the widespread confusion between money and wealth, the narrowness of interest that allowed advocates to shape economic policies

---

89. See Michael Ryder, 'The Bank of Ireland, 1721: land, credit and dependency', *Historical journal* 25:3 (1982), p.557-82.

to their own ends, and the failure to appreciate the existence of an encompassing system of economic activity which was cooperative and orderly, irrespective of the motivation of individual agents. Natural market forces exhibited a superior wisdom to the interventions of self-deluded exponents of 'rationalist' or artificial systems, including advocates like John Law. As far as money is concerned, Smith regarded it as an epiphenomenon of commerce, which enabled him to conclude that the fixation with accumulating precious metals was based on a confusion. His argument is embedded in a broader philosophy which insists, in a Stoic vein, on the order and beauty of the system as a whole. Smith regarded it as essential to direct our attention to this larger good in order to appreciate the mutual improvement possible through economic relationships. The legislator's role is to inculcate such an understanding – a kind of pedagogic function – which would deter misguided efforts to intrude on such a system. The enlargement of perspective endorsed here parallels the progression from self to community and from nation to humanity in general set out in Smith's *Theory of moral sentiments* (1759). Unhindered international trade is consonant with this vision. As Smith puts it in a very interesting line in *Wealth of nations* quoted by Hanley and Paganelli, 'Were all nations to follow the liberal system of free exportation and free importation, the different states into which a great continent was divided would so far resemble the different provinces of a great empire'.[90] The 'liberal' simile of empire introduces a rather striking note into the argument, realised in colonial visions of political economy advanced by John Stuart Mill and others in the nineteenth century.[91]

This volume concludes with a chapter on 'Pierre-Louis Rœderer, Adam Smith and the problem of inequality' by Thomas Hopkins that takes the story forward in a new direction, looking at the reception of Adam Smith in the post-Revolutionary period of ferment in France. The questions raised here re-engage with themes that predominate in the collection as a whole, including the impact of revolutionary crises on economic thinking, the transition from mercantilist to 'classical' assumptions about the market, and above all the difficult issue of how ancient republicanism might be revived on the foundations of a modern commercial system, particularly in light of seemingly unavoidable social inequalities associated with such a system. The Jacobin rejection of this argument

90. Smith, *Wealth of nations*, IV.v.b.39 (p.538).
91. See Uday Singh Mehta, *Liberalism and empire: a study in nineteenth-century British liberal thought* (Chicago, IL, 1999); Jennifer Pitts, *A Turn to empire: the rise of imperial liberalism in Britain and France* (Princeton, NJ, 2005); Pratap Bhanu Mehta, 'Liberalism, nation, and empire: the case of J. S. Mill', in *Empire and modern political thought*, ed. Sankar Muthu (Cambridge, 2012), p.232-60.

was met by an alternative position, articulated through a complex series of contributions (some of them under the banner of *Idéologie*), which proved more ready to welcome commercial society. Smith's 'system of natural liberty' constituted a potential alternative and attracted a number of adherents, but it was by no means a straightforward solution, not least because of Smith's willingness to build inequalities into his account of human nature. The challenge of addressing this dilemma and creating a more egalitarian political economy – without conceding too much ground to the political 'levellers' – was taken up by Pierre-Louis Rœderer, a close ally of the abbé Emmanuel-Joseph Sieyès.

The account of the 'distinction of ranks' given by Smith was rooted in a moral theory of sentiments which went some way toward explaining why people are led to pursue riches in order to avoid poverty, and to hold in esteem not merely virtue but also power and wealth. The resulting inequality could be offset by recognising a pattern of mutual benefits in which the elaboration of production would lead to economic growth with a positive impact throughout society.[92] Yet accepting this scenario without objection was problematic in a republican moment. Adjustments required to make it viable were available to Rœderer from different sources, including the critique of Smith in Sophie de Grouchy's *Lettres sur la sympathie* appended to her French translation of *The Theory of moral sentiments* (1798). She assigned a greater role than Smith to the capacity for reflection as the means for establishing the desire to work on behalf of the general good, and located these processes in human physiology as a way of creating a more suitable republican moral psychology. The expansion of sympathy was also tied to the division of labour and the reciprocity this created. A different kind of balancing act was required to maintain natural equality in the midst of progressive accumulation. The division between capitalists and labourers in fact enabled the fruits of the earth to be distributed, while the institution of property stimulated productive capacities. Rœderer's answer is full of the ironies performed by history. Just as Smith's 'liberal' simile of empire reads differently from the perspective of nineteenth-century colonial expansion, Rœderer's paean to labour invites an immediate thought of Marx. It was labour, for Rœderer, that 'in developing every talent, multiplying all wealth, expanding the common inheritance, can alone ennoble and strengthen the relations between men'. Through labour the rich and the poor would recognise 'their mutual dependence, acknowledge and respect one another'. It also supported property holding by

---

92. Smith produced a more optimistic analysis of the effects of society on the individual than Rousseau famously allowed, by seeing the division of labour that occurred in an era of progress as also leading to a wider compass of communication, expanding the moral imagination in the circle of commerce.

teaching that labour is the means to acquire. Finally, he claimed, 'It is this institution that is the most powerful guarantee of liberty, because it doubles the need the rich have of the poor, and it liberates the poor from the degradation of dependence'.[93]

By looking closely at a series of connected questions and theorists, this volume provides alternative perspectives on the emergence of money and political economy as central preoccupations in the Enlightenment period. Rather than accept existing narratives that suggest too easy a separation between mercantilist and classical, the forward-looking and the regressive, the radical or conservative, we have considered instead the tensions, inconsistencies and moments of transition that feature in a range of contexts and thinkers. As discussion developed of money, credit, banking and public debt, it is clear that the social and political consequences of these issues made them crucial topics of investigation without producing an Enlightenment consensus or consistency.

93. I quote from Hopkins's adapted translation of Rœderer in Evelyn L. Forget, *The Social economics of Jean-Baptiste Say: markets and virtue* (London, 1999), p.194. For the original, see Pierre-Louis Rœderer, 'Précis des observations sur la question proposée par l'Institut national pour le sujet du premier prix de la Classe des Sciences Morales et Politiques', *La Décade philosophique, politique et littéraire*, l'an VI, 1er trimestre (Paris, Au Bureau de la Décade, 1797), p.536.

Sir Robert Filmer, usury and the ideology of order

JOHANN P. SOMMERVILLE

Sir Robert Filmer (1588?-1653), the English political theorist best known for his tract *Patriarcha*, was also the author of a treatise on the question of usury, entitled *Quaestio quodlibetica, or a discourse, whether it may bee lawfull to take use for money* (published 1653). One purpose of what follows is to describe the *Quaestio* and its arguments in some detail, since there exists remarkably little scholarly work on it. Another and broader goal is to use the *Quaestio* and Filmer's other writings to challenge the commonplace modern notion that he was a quintessentially conservative thinker, who wrote to support the existing social hierarchy and the old belief that it is natural and divinely established. It is often said that Filmer endorsed an ideology of order, which affirmed that human societies are and ought to be hierarchical, and that the existing social hierarchy reflects similar God-given hierarchies among angels, animals and all created things. Filmer famously claimed that the political power which states now wield is in essence the same as the power that Adam once held over his family by the right of fatherhood. Underlying this idea, so the modern argument goes, is the claim – central to the ideology of order – that different parts of creation, such as the state and the family, are linked by analogy or correspondence, and that it is therefore reasonable to draw conclusions about one institution from premises concerning the other.[1] Filmer supplemented such arguments from analogy, the case proceeds, with a highly literal interpretation of Scripture, which he took to be directly relevant to modern social and political life. When John Locke assailed Filmer's views in the first of his *Two treatises of government*, the argument continues, he broke not only with the ideas of one particular thinker, but with a whole school of thought. Locke, we are told,

---

1. Filmerian patriarchalism is portrayed as a specimen of the ideology of order, which centred on analogies and correspondences between different parts of creation, for example in W. H. Greenleaf, *Order, empiricism and politics: two traditions of English political thought 1500-1700* (London, 1964), p.87; J. C. D. Clark, *English society 1688-1832: ideology, social structure and political practice during the Ancien Régime* (Cambridge, 1985), p.64-92 (79). James Daly, *Sir Robert Filmer and English political thought* (Toronto, 1979), p.67 and n31, rightly insists that in Filmer's theory fatherly and political power are identical and not merely analogous; Daly rejects Greenleaf's depiction of Filmer as an exponent of the ideology of order (p.33-34).

challenged 'the ancient argument' that 'the authority of the King and that of a father were directly linked by scriptural authority and the natural laws of hierarchy'.[2] He 'severed the connection between family and state', rejected traditional ideas of social hierarchy and grounded state power 'in a contractual agreement among men'.[3] While Filmer relied uncritically upon the Bible, Locke based his case on reason, not Scripture, and proposed that 'political society consists of an amalgamation of individuals rather than an organic corpus mysticum'.[4] Filmer, in short, was a traditionalistic, pre-modern thinker, whose ideas reflected the prejudices of his age.[5] Locke, by contrast, broke decisively with the past, adopting a thoroughly individualistic, contractualist and secular worldview which was soon to become characteristic of Enlightenment thought.

Many of Filmer's political writings were republished in 1679 as Tory propaganda, and it was for the same purpose that his *Patriarcha* was for the first time printed in 1680. Tories supported the established Anglican church and the interests of the country gentry. Filmer had himself been a prosperous country gentleman, and the son-in-law of a bishop. Long after Filmer's day, it has been suggested, Filmerian patriarchalist ideas survived vigorously, and 'the mercantile or professional "bourgeosie" ' continued to defer to 'the landed elite'.[6] Filmer's ideas lost their appeal only after 'the triumph of Whig principles and of Whig institutions, the growth of rationalism and the steady expansion of urban, commercial and bourgeois culture'.[7] During Filmer's lifetime, it was common for the Anglican clergy to argue in favour of a traditional agrarian economy and to denounce moneylending – on which commerce relied – as immoral. In the dramatic literature of Filmer's time, usury was frequently condemned as an immoral device by which Jews and atheists victimised improvident young gentlemen, and so subverted the social order.[8]

In his writings on money, Locke dismissed traditional arguments against usury, barely bothering to discuss them. Many seventeenth-

---

2. Lawrence Stone, *The Family, sex and marriage in England 1500-1800* (New York, 1977), p.265.
3. Mary Beth Norton, *Founding fathers and mothers: gendered power and the forming of American society* (New York, 1997), p.5.
4. Paul Kléber Monod, *The Power of kings: monarchy and religion in Europe, 1589-1715* (New Haven, CT, 1999), p.269.
5. Peter Laslett, in the 'Introduction' to his edition of Sir Robert Filmer, *Patriarcha and other political works* (Oxford, 1949), p.41, argues that Filmer was 'the codifier of conscious and unconscious prejudice'.
6. Clark, *English society 1688-1832*, p.70.
7. Laslett, 'Introduction', in Filmer, *Patriarcha*, p.41.
8. Robert Ashton, 'Usury and high finance in the age of Shakespeare and Jonson', *University of Nottingham Renaissance and modern studies* 4 (1960), p.14-43 (14, 26-31); James Shapiro, *Shakespeare and the Jews* (New York, 1996), p.48, 99, 110, 185, 217.

century churchmen held that contracts requiring the payment of interest on borrowed money were sinful, as the Bible prohibited usury. Locke argued that the payment of interest on loans was not only a necessary and inevitable fact of life, but also 'as equitable and lawful, as receiving Rent for Land', despite 'the Opinion of some over-scrupulous Men'.[9] If, as we are told, Locke and Filmer held opposed world views, then we might expect that they would have adopted different positions on the question of usury. Given Locke's interest in trade, and the alliance of his Whig allies with London financiers and merchants, it is perhaps not surprising to find him rejecting traditional religious condemnations of usury. We might equally expect to find Filmer upholding traditional dogmas. As we have seen, he is commonly portrayed as a very much less secular thinker than Locke. Such leading Anglicans as Filmer's contemporaries Bishops Lancelot Andrewes and George Downam strongly condemned usury. Moreover, usurers were commonly regarded as social climbers who disrupted the natural hierarchy that Filmer supposedly held so dear.[10] Yet Filmer in fact adopted exactly the same position as Locke on usury. Both thinkers argued that taking interest on loans was quite as justifiable as taking rent on land.[11] Both rejected the conventional strictures of clerics against usury. Indeed, it has been suggested that Filmer's book directly influenced Locke.[12]

Locke's writings on money and interest have attracted fairly substantial scholarly attention. The same is not true of Filmer's contribution on this subject. The first section below describes his book and its main arguments, setting them in historical context. It is sometimes said that the rise of Calvinism or Puritanism helped to relax attitudes towards usury, and to pave the way for thinking like Filmer's and Locke's. The second section discusses this thesis, and concludes that although a number of Calvinists took a more liberal line on usury than many members of other religious groups, there is no clear link between specifically Calvinist or Puritan ideas on the one hand and arguments in defence of usury on the other. In the debate on usury, both Filmer and Locke were on the secular and modern side. A notable feature of Filmer's discussion of usury is his lack of concern with questions of social hierarchy, or with the interests of landowners as opposed to merchants.

---

9. John Locke, *Some considerations of the lowering of interest, and raising the value of money*, in *Locke on money*, vol.1, p.203-342 (251).
10. Norman Jones, *God and the moneylenders*, p.44-45, 173.
11. Locke, *Some considerations*, in *Locke on money*, p.249-50; Sir Robert Filmer, *Quaestio quodlibetica, or a discourse, whether it may bee lawfull to take use for money* (London, Humphrey Moseley, 1653), p.125-27.
12. Patrick Hyde Kelly, 'General introduction: Locke on money', in *Locke on money*, vol.1, p.1-109 (98).

The third section argues that Filmer was equally unconcerned about such questions in his political works. The idea that Filmer wrote to defend the existing social order as natural and God-given is groundless. Nor is it correct to suppose that he placed any great weight on arguments from analogies or correspondences. In Filmer's political theory, political and fatherly power are not analogous but identical. His central contention is that by nature the father in every independent family possesses the power of life and death over family members, and that since this is the key political power, families and states are not distinct institutions. Locke strongly distinguished between the state and the family, and denied that fathers have any power to execute those who are subject to their paternal authority. The views of both authors on these questions had support from earlier thinking. Locke said relatively little new on the relationship between the state and the family. Arguably, Filmer was the more original of the two thinkers on this subject.

Filmer's *Quaestio quodlibetica*

In December 1652 the well-known London publisher Humphrey Moseley (who issued Milton's *Poems* of 1645 and much else) brought out *Quaestio quodlibetica, or a discourse, whether it may bee lawfull to take use for money*.[13] The volume begins with a preface subscribed by Sir Roger Twysden and dated 9 October 1652. Twysden stated that he was publishing the book without the author's consent, and invited readers to raise any criticisms they might have of the work speedily, 'before the gravel stone or some infirmity make the Writer unable to give thee and the world further satisfaction'. Twysden said that the book had been 'written almost thirty years since by a very learned gentleman, for satisfaction of a person of worth, and relation unto him'. Twysden's preface was followed by another, written by the author himself and subscribed 'R. F.'.[14] Sir Robert Filmer was a 'lifetime associate' of Twysden, and long suffered from 'the stone', dying of it on 30 May 1653.[15] There can be little doubt that 'R. F.' is Sir Robert Filmer, and when William Crook published a reprint of the book in 1678, he attributed it to Filmer on the title page.[16]

13. Although the title page is dated 1653, George Thomason in his copy (now in the British Library) recorded the date of purchase of the book as 11 December 1652. No critical edition of the work exists. There is a manuscript of it in the Huntington Library, San Marino, California (HM 43212). I am grateful to Cesare Cuttica for this information, and for many illuminating conversations about Filmer and his writings over the years.

14. Filmer, *Quaestio quodlibetica*, sig. a2v (Twysden's subscription; stone), sig. a2r (almost thirty years since), sig.a8v ('R. F.').

15. Laslett, 'Introduction', in Filmer, *Patriarcha*, p.4, 5, 9.

16. Filmer, *A Discourse whether it may be lawful to take use for money* (London, 1678), sig. A1r. William Crook or Crooke also published a number of writings by Thomas Hobbes, including the 1682 edition of *Behemoth*. Filmer's book was republished under its original

The style is very like that of Filmer's other writings. A difference of substance is that in his political works Filmer quoted very frequently from Aristotle and Bodin, but he did not draw much upon them in *Quaestio quodlibetica.* This is easily explained, for Aristotle and Bodin both opposed usury, while Filmer wrote to justify it and, above all, to refute the arguments of the cleric Roger Fenton against it.[17] Filmer informs us that he selected Fenton's treatise for special scrutiny 'because it is the latest, and I find little of any moment but is in him'.[18] While Twysden suggested that the book had been written for a specific person, Filmer himself stated more vaguely that he had composed it to satisfy 'the tenderness of the conscience of others'. He insisted that he himself had not lent (though he had borrowed) money at interest.[19] Thus the book was not written to justify his own usurious activities, and there is no evidence to suggest he was linked to professional moneylenders, whose cause he espoused. Filmer owned a country estate in Kent, but he spent much of his time in Westminster.[20] Arguably, the work reflects familiarity with the economic realities of London trade as well as of rural landownership, but it was not written in the interests of any particular group.

According to Peter Laslett, the *Quaestio quodlibetica* was Filmer's first work, and was written in 'about 1630, or perhaps earlier'.[21] Norman Jones similarly styles the *Quaestio* 'Filmer's first book' and asserts that internal 'evidence indicates that it was written between 1624 and 1630', and Keith Wrightson dates it to 'the later 1620s'.[22] There are problems with dating the book. Filmer refers to the statute of 1624 which allowed usury at eight per cent, so the book is clearly later than that date.[23] The

---

title in *The Harleian miscellany,* ed. William Oldys and Thomas Park, 10 vols (London, 1808-1813), vol.10 ('the second supplemental volume', ed. Thomas Park, London, 1813), p.103-38; a facsimile of this last printing is in *The Usury debate in the seventeenth century: three arguments* (New York, 1972).

17. Aristotle, *Politics,* bk 1, ch.10 (1258b); *Nicomachean ethics,* bk 4, ch.1 (1121b-1122a), both in *The Complete works of Aristotle: the revised Oxford translation,* 2 vols, ed. Jonathan Barnes (Princeton, NJ, 1984). Aristotle's influence on the scholastic view of usury is discussed in John T. Noonan, Jr., *The Scholastic analysis of usury* (Cambridge, MA, 1957), p.46-47, 65-66, 394-95; also in Jean Bodin, *The Six bookes of a commonweale,* trans. Richard Knolles (1606), facsimile ed. Kenneth Douglas McRae (Cambridge, MA, 1962), p.572-73 (bk 5, ch.2). Filmer, *Quaestio quodlibetica,* p.111-12, briefly dismisses Aristotle's arguments; he does not mention Bodin.

18. Filmer, *Quaestio quodlibetica,* sig.a4*v* (Author's preface).

19. Filmer, *Quaestio quodlibetica,* sig.a4*r* (Author's preface).

20. Laslett, 'Introduction', in Filmer, *Patriarcha and other political works,* p.2.

21. Laslett, 'Introduction', in Filmer, *Patriarcha and other political works,* p.3. Daly, *Sir Robert Filmer,* p.4, asserts that Filmer circulated the book in manuscript in 'the 1630's', citing Laslett.

22. Jones, *God and the moneylenders,* p.159. Keith Wrightson, *Earthly necessities: economic lives in early modern Britain* (New Haven, CT, 2000), p.208.

23. Filmer, *Quaestio quodlibetica,* p.114.

author's preface mentions 'Dr Downam now Bishop of London-derry in Ireland' and 'learned Dr Andrewes late Bishop of Winchester'.[24] Lancelot Andrewes died in 1626 while George Downam lived until 1634, which would appear to place the book's composition in the years between 1626 and 1634. Filmer quotes from Andrewes's *De usuris, theologica determinatio*, which was first published in the bishop's *Opuscula quaedam posthuma* of 1629.[25] It is conceivable that Filmer quoted from a manuscript of Andrewes's work but he says nothing to suggest this, which implies that Filmer's book dates to 1629 or later. In his preface, Filmer gives a list of Continental thinkers who allowed the taking of interest. The list, which is in approximately chronological order, begins with Calvin, Martyr and Bucer and ends with Ames, Grotius and Salmasius.[26] Salmasius's first work on usury was the *De usuris liber*, published in 1638.[27] Filmer cited this book in his *Observations concerning the originall of government* of 1652, but in the *Quaestio quodlibetica* he did not refer to any specific titles by Salmasius.[28] Clearly, Filmer cannot have completed the preface to the *Quaestio* before 1638, when Salmasius began to publish on usury. Perhaps the reference in the preface to Downam as still alive was simply a mistake. Or perhaps Filmer added to his book over a period of years but failed to update it consistently. We know, for example, that he composed more than one version of *Patriarcha*.[29]

The bulk of the *Quaestio quodlibetica* is directed against Roger Fenton's *A Treatise of usurie* which was published in 1611 and reissued in the following year.[30] The *Quaestio* also has much to say about George Downam's *Lectures on the XV. Psalme*, printed in 1604. Indeed, Filmer claimed that Fenton derived his arguments from Downam. Fenton, he said, was 'little less than a Plagiary', though he was not guilty of usury for he had borrowed freely from Downam 'without paying the interest of one new Argument or Reason'.[31] Filmer mentions Andrewes much more rarely

24. Filmer, *Quaestio quodlibetica*, sig.a4v (Author's preface).
25. Filmer, *Quaestio quodlibetica*, p.135 quotes from Andrewes's *De usuris, theologica determinatio*; the passage occurs in *Opuscula quaedam posthuma* (Oxford, 1852), p.128.
26. Filmer, *Quaestio quodlibetica*, sig. a3v.
27. Claudius Salmasius (Claude de Saumaise), *De usuris liber* (Leiden, Bonaventura and Abraham Elzevier, 1638). It was followed by Salmasius, *De modo usurarum* (Leiden, Bonaventura and Abraham Elzevier, 1639), and *Dissertatio de foenore trapezitico, in tres libros divisa* (Leiden, Joannes Maire, 1640).
28. Filmer, *Observations concerning the originall of government*, in Filmer, *Patriarcha and other writings*, ed. Johann P. Sommerville (Cambridge, 1991), p.214.
29. There are two distinct texts of *Patriarcha*, one dating from 1632 or earlier, the other from 1635-1642: Filmer, *Patriarcha and other writings*, ed. Sommerville, p.viii, xxxiv.
30. Fenton, *A Treatise of usurie*. Fenton's ideas are discussed in David Hawkes, *The Culture of usury in Renaissance England*, p.48-50, 52-53. Hawkes's book is a fine introduction to debates on usury in England between 1500 and 1625. It does not mention Filmer.
31. Filmer, *Quaestio quodlibetica*, p.17-18.

than Fenton or Downam, and he does not refer at all to John Blaxton's *The English usurer; or usury condemned,* which was published in 1634. Later in the century, Sir Josiah Child recommended Blaxton's book as a good guide to the morality of usury.[32] The book is derived largely from the writings of Fenton, Downam and like-minded authors, and provides a convenient summary of their arguments.[33] That Filmer does not cite it may suggest that he had already written most of his own work before it came out, or simply that he had not heard of it. Perhaps Filmer began writing his book at an early date, but added to it later. The statement that Downam is 'now Bishop of London-derry' can be read as implying that he had only recently been appointed to that post. Downam was in fact appointed in 1616. Filmer refers to the Authorised or King James version of the Bible, which was first published in 1611, as 'our new Translation', which fits better with an early than a late date.[34] But none of this is conclusive. All we can say for certain is that Filmer's preface as we now have it dates from 1638 or later, as it refers to Salmasius. The body of the text is unlikely to date from before 1629 as it cites Andrewes' work on usury, published in that year. There is no reason to insist that the *Quaestio* was Filmer's earliest work. He had certainly completed 'A discourse [...] of Government and in praise of Royaltie' (presumably the first version of *Patriarcha*) by 1632, and it may therefore pre-date the *Quaestio*.[35]

Filmer argued that the problem of whether usury is sinful is 'a meer popish question' which had been unnecessarily raised by the idle curiosity of Roman Catholics.[36] His opponents alleged that Scripture banned usury, and that the Fathers of the early church had forcefully endorsed the biblical prohibition.[37] Filmer rejected such claims. A simple-minded and literal interpretation of the Bible might indeed suggest that it forbade usury. But like Locke, and unlike the Filmer of modern myth, he maintained that biblical laws must be 'interpreted according to the rule of *natural reason*', asserting that the 'light of *Nature* must help us in the interpretation of many texts'. Filmer drew on the writings of Richard Hooker to confirm such views – and Locke likewise cited Hooker repeatedly.[38] Nature and reason, asserted Filmer, show that we should not oppress poor people. This, he said, is an eternally binding moral law,

32. Sir Josiah Child, *A Discourse about trade* ([London], A. Sowle, 1690), second set of signatures, sig.A4v.
33. John Blaxton, *The English usurer; or usury condemned by the most learned and famous divines of the church of England* (Oxford, John Norton for Francis Bowman, 1634). Blaxton quotes Downam (p.1-3) and Fenton (p.4) on the definition of usury and much else.
34. Filmer, *Quaestio quodlibetica*, p.78.
35. Filmer, *Patriarcha and other writings*, ed. Sommerville, p.viii.
36. Filmer, *Quaestio quodlibetica*, sig.a4r.
37. For example Fenton, *A Treatise of usurie*, p.35, 49-50.
38. Filmer, *Quaestio quodlibetica*, p.53, 54.

and it underlies Old Testament strictures against usury. The ancient Jews had not banned all lending at interest, he claimed, but only oppressive loans which victimised the poor. The very first biblical texts on usury (Exodus 22:25 and Leviticus 25:35) specified that it was lending at interest to the poor that was wrong, and other passages in Scripture were to be interpreted in the light of these verses. The Bible (Deuteronomy 23:19-20) prohibited Jews from lending at interest to other Jews, but allowed usurious loans to strangers. Filmer noted that some critics of usury claimed that by strangers the Bible meant enemies, but he rejected this, arguing that all non-Jews had been classed as strangers.[39]

Filmer denied that the Old Testament condemned all taking of interest on loans. He also claimed that many Old Testament laws do not apply to Christians. So, even if the ancient Jews had in fact banned usury completely, this would not necessarily mean that seventeenth-century Christians were bound to follow them. It was commonplace to distinguish between three varieties of law established by Moses. Some of these laws, it was widely agreed, were moral, which is to say that they were perpetually binding. Others were judicial, condemning particular crimes and stipulating specific penalties for them. A third category of Mosaic law consisted of ceremonial regulations for use in Jewish religious practices. There was wide consensus among all Christian groups that the ceremonial laws had been abrogated by Christ. There was equally wide agreement that we must continue to observe moral laws, like the prohibitions of murder and adultery. But there was a spectrum of opinion on the judicial laws of Moses. Some Puritans took the line that where possible we should revive the Mosaic criminal law. In 1636 John Cotton drew up a law code for Massachusetts, deriving it largely from the laws of Moses. Cotton strongly advised against usury, citing the usual Old Testament texts.[40] Filmer was far less impressed by Mosaic law. He argued that we ought to take notice of the eternal moral principles which underlie the judicial laws, but that we are perfectly free to reject the laws themselves. The moral principle behind Old Testament pro-hibitions of usury, he declared, was that we ought to relieve the poor and not to oppress them. The ancient Jews did this by banning the taking of interest on loans to the poor. But there was no reason at all, he argued, why we should relieve the poor in the same way as the Jews had done: certainly, the poor should be assisted, but to do so by 'not taking *Usury* of them is not necessary'.[41] So, as long as there was some provision for poor

39. Filmer, *Quaestio quodlibetica*, p.58 (not oppressing poor is a moral law), p.19 (Exodus and Leviticus), p.67-71 (strangers).
40. Jesper Rosenmeier, 'John Cotton on usury', *William and Mary quarterly* 47:4 (1990), p.548-65 (557, 562).
41. Filmer, *Quaestio quodlibetica*, p.61.

relief, interest could licitly be taken even on loans to the poor. It was up to the state to regulate poor relief. Christ's coming had abrogated the Old Testament regulations. Many critics of usury claimed that Christ forbade us to take interest on loans in Luke 6:35. Filmer insisted that the English Bible did not adequately translate that text, and argued that usury was nowhere banned in the New Testament.[42]

The opponents of usury claimed that economic as well as biblical arguments worked against it. The need to pay interest on loans drives up prices, they declared.[43] Filmer challenged this thesis, arguing that 'the dearness of things is caused either by the scarcity of the things themselves, or by the plenty of mony'. Evidently, he proceeded, usury could not cause things to be scarce, 'for it neither eats up corn nor cattle, nor weares out apparell'. Rather, by borrowing at interest merchants are enabled to import scarce commodities from abroad, and to export goods which are plentiful in England but rarer overseas. As for high prices that were caused by an abundance of money, they were no bad thing: 'those places are not the Richest where things are cheapest, for then *Scotland* would excell *England*'.[44] Republicans commonly argued that the prosperity of the Dutch Republic and similar states demonstrated the excellence of popular government. Filmer took a similar line to justify usury rather than republicanism: 'The Lawes of *Venice, Genoa,* and the *Low-countries* (three simply the richest states in *Europe*) do allow thereof [that is, of usury], and yet are free from poor, which perswades that *Usury* is not so hurtfull to a state'. Here, as throughout his discussion, Filmer said nothing at all to suggest that he held the interests of landowners dearer than those of merchants.[45]

Fenton and like-minded authors followed Aristotle and the scholastics in maintaining that money was barren and that taking interest on loans was therefore unnatural. According to Fenton, 'the primitive life was most naturall' when men lived by farming. By 'mans industrie' 'seed cast into the ground' brings 'foorth more into the world then there was before'. But 'the summe of one hundred pounds, turne it and returne it as often as you can, is still the same summe without increase'. Since money does not naturally increase, it is unnatural for a moneylender to take interest on a loan. If one person hires something from another – say a horse, or a house – it is reasonable, argued Fenton, that in addition to

42. Filmer, *Quaestio quodlibetica*, sig.a8r, p.50, 81-83, 135-63. Filmer discusses the translation of Luke 6:35 at p.82-83; the text of the Authorised version says 'lend, hoping for nothing again', but Filmer, following Beza ('who is no friend to *Usury*' (p.82)) argues that the meaning is that we should lend to the poor and not fear that they will fail to repay us.
43. Fenton, *Treatise of usurie*, p.36.
44. Filmer, *Quaestio quodlibetica*, p.44-45.
45. Filmer, *Quaestio quodlibetica*, p.114.

returning the thing, the person who hires it should also pay the owner for the use of it. For the thing hired 'weareth in the using and is worse for the wearing'. Moreover, virtually every thing 'hath some use in it selfe', 'either to feed, or to cloath or to shelter' and so on. The single exception to these rules, Fenton affirmed, is money, for it is not 'of any use to the possessor, but only in dispossessing himselfe of it', and it alone is not 'the weaker or worse for the using'. It is therefore quite unreasonable that money lent by a usurer should 'bring forth' a profit 'unto him without travel, cost, or perill'.[46] Usury, said Fenton, is not only unnatural but also ungodly. Religion and piety, he argued, teach Christians 'to depend upon Gods providence'. Farmers pray 'for seasonable weather' and merchants ask God to deliver them 'from tempest and wracke'. Only usurers refuse to depend upon God's providence at all: 'Of all men the Usurers thinke worst of God, and will least trust him: be it faire or foule, all is one; they will have their money'.[47]

Filmer denied that money is barren, claiming that there is no significant difference between hiring money on the one hand and a horse or a house on the other; he insisted that usurers do not scorn divine providence, argued that usury benefits trade and contended that there is in any case no feasible alternative to it. Money considered as metal might not naturally increase, Filmer said, but 'money considered as it is money, which Art not Nature hath produced, may be allowed an artificial increase or gain, as well as houses, ships, and many other things not natural'. Fenton had argued that we can reasonably be charged for the hire of anything except money. Filmer responded that money was invented to facilitate trade, but that if money were treated as the only commodity that could not profitably be rented out, people would avoid owning it and trade would suffer. Fenton claimed that hire compensates the owner for the deterioration of goods other than money, but that money does not deteriorate and therefore no compensation is due to moneylenders. But this is simply false, declared Filmer, for a horse hired to go on a moderate journey might well be in *better* condition after such exercise than before. If hire ought to be taken only for things that 'are the worse for using', he contended, 'then I believe all the Rent that hath been paid for land since *Noahs* Flood hath been unjustly taken: For it will hardly appear that any Acre of land is worse now than in his dayes; since many Acres are bettered by tillage and maturing, which by lying waste are hurt; and houses also decay for want of inhabiting'. The justification of rent lies in the borrower's gain by the use of the thing rented, and in the owner's loss through foregoing that use. Filmer asserted that this

---

46. Fenton, *Treatise of usurie*, p.91, 93, 94.
47. Fenton, *Treatise of usurie*, p.95.

applies as much to money as to anything else. Despite Fenton's talk of the natural increase of land, 'tillage and pasturage are required' before land becomes useful – a point which of course featured centrally in Locke's famous fifth chapter of the 'Second treatise', where he grounded rights of property upon labour. Money, like land, could be productive if skillfully handled. Filmer argued that there is little difference between renting money and renting land, and noted that the two activities are in fact closely linked, for the price of land rises when interest rates fall.

Far from arguing that landownership was a respectable activity greatly preferable to vulgar commerce, he claimed that 'He that purchaseth land is the greatest *Usurer* in the world' as he makes the largest and surest profit, for if land sells at (say) sixteen years' purchase, after sixteen years the owner receives the full income of the land in perpetuity. Filmer did admit that people ought to use their talents 'to serve God and their Country'. To live idly on usury could be sinful, but that was because idleness, not usury, was a sin. Nor was there any danger that '*Usury* will bring idleness in the world, for if all men be idle there can be no Usury'. The abolition of usury, on the other hand, would make many people idle since they would be unable to borrow capital: 'many must be idle if they borrow not a stock to set them on work'.[48]

Filmer denied that usurers slight God's providence, and insisted that they always take risks in lending money. Fenton and his allies treated it as certain that the usurer would recover both principal and interest. Filmer responded that it was far from certain. Bad weather or shipwreck might prevent the borrower from repaying, and make life troublesome for the lender. Borrowers were also capable of various kinds of fraud to try to evade their debts.[49] Lending money was always a hazardous business. The scholastic tradition on usury – which Fenton, Downam and the rest largely accepted – came to authorise the payment of compensation (interest) to a lender in special cases where he incurs damage (*damnum emergens*) or loss of profit (*lucrum cessans*) as a result of making a loan.[50] In the course of the later Middle Ages and early modern period, commentators extended the range of cases in which lenders were entitled to such

---

48. Filmer, *Quaestio quodlibetica*, p.122 (money as money), p.124 (discommodity of Trade; horse in better condition after exercise), p.125 (rent since Noah's Flood), p.125-26 (justification of rent), p.126 (tillage and pasturage), p.144-45 (interest rates and price of land; greatest usurer), p.'146' = 147 (usury and idleness), p.148 (borrowing a stock).
49. Filmer, *Quaestio quodlibetica*, p.129.
50. Noonan, *The Scholastic analysis of usury*, p.115. The term 'interest' strictly referred to payments made to the lender in such special cases, but it was commonly used (by Filmer and others) to refer more generally to all payments beyond the principal, and it is so used throughout this chapter. An account which stresses the importance of the distinction between interest in the strict sense and usury is Eric Kerridge, *Usury, interest, and the Reformation* (Aldershot, 2002).

compensation. Discussing *lucrum cessans*, the Low Countries Jesuit Leonardus Lessius came very close to justifying the taking of interest by all professional moneylenders.[51] Filmer noted that the scholastic tradition allows the payment of interest to compensate for loss of profit. He argued that 'in all lending a mans gain is hindered', since the lender is prevented for the term of the loan from deploying his money in some profit-making venture. On the scholastics' own account, then, 'Interest is due for all Lending'. His opponents claimed that usury was sinful but they allowed partnerships in which the lender and borrower share profits or losses. Filmer responded that if the lender cannot claim interest at an agreed rate but instead has to take a percentage of the borrower's profits, endless litigation will result: 'It would make all bargaines nothing but sutes in law, no debts should be due but upon proof and witnesses examined'. It was much more practical to contract for interest payments at the customary rate. The value of money, Filmer affirmed, like the value of land and goods, 'is a *humane arbitrary custom*, grounded upon the several necessities or opinions of each particular Nation'.[52]

Filmer observed that his opponents themselves admitted that it could be very difficult in practice to distinguish between usurious and justifiable contracts. Indeed, said Fenton, it was sometimes the intentions of the contractors, and not the contract itself, that made the transaction usurious: 'the poyson of Usurie is in some contracts so closely and cunningly conveied, as the very turne of the intention of the mind may alter the case, to make it iust or uniust, the contract remaining one and the same'.[53] If this were so, replied Filmer, we would have to 'look for a new definition of Usury in the Consciences of men, and not in Dr Fentons treatise'. Filmer suggested that Moses's laws set down no penalty for usury 'because the sinne is determinable only by the judgement of a mans own Conscience'.[54] It was hard for the state to access consciences and so enforce prohibitions of such sins.

The *Quaestio quodlibetica* was one of the most detailed early defences of usury written by an Englishman. It argued that contracts to lend money at interest are morally binding. It nowhere claimed that such contracts threaten the existing social hierarchy and, indeed, said remarkably little about any such hierarchy. It also said little to support the interests of landowners against merchants, and argued that where the law allowed usury, commerce flourished and general prosperity resulted.

---

51. Noonan, *The Scholastic analysis of usury*, p.222, 263.
52. Filmer, *Quaestio quodlibetica*, p.105-106 (all lending involves loss of profit and entitlement to interest), p.100 (nothing but sutes in law), p.132 (humane arbitrary custom).
53. Fenton, *Treatise of usurie*, p.128.
54. Filmer, *Quaestio quodlibetica*, p.143-44, 27.

In Filmer's time, many clerics wholly opposed taking interest on loans, while some – such as William Perkins, William Ames and Andrew Willet – took a more moderate line.[55] None justified usury as trenchantly or at as great length as Filmer. An early defence of lending at interest was 'The lawyers oracion' in Thomas Wilson's *Discourse upon usury* of 1572. This voiced a number of arguments which later featured in the *Quaestio*, claiming that usury could not be unnatural, since God permitted the Jews to practise it towards strangers, declaring that lenders always suffer loss and therefore deserve compensation and contending that only biting or oppressive usury is objectionable.[56] Though Wilson proceeded to try to refute the lawyer's arguments, not everyone thought him successful, for the arguments lived on. Filmer was certainly familiar with Wilson's book, and responded to it in the *Quaestio*.[57] In 1591, Charles Gibbon briefly but forcefully justified usurious loans to the rich.[58] Attacking usury in 1604, George Downam referred to 'a tedious and disorderly discourse written, but not printed in English, in defence of usurie'. Fenton attacked the same manuscript discourse. It does not survive, but evidently its author argued in much the same way as Filmer, for Fenton tells us that it claimed that there was no significant difference between letting a cow for hire and letting money, and that it justified taking interest on loans to the rich.[59] A 'Treatise on usury' reputedly written in 1605 by Walter Howse justified the practice, observing that God permitted the Israelites to lend at interest in some cases.[60]

Filmer was rather unusual among the seventeenth-century writers who debated the morals of usury in being a layman. Sir Francis Bacon ducked the question of the morality of taking interest, arguing that in practice usury was necessary and that it was mere utopianism to speak of abolishing it.[61] Sir Thomas Culpeper in a famous pamphlet of 1621

---

55. Jones, *God and the moneylenders*, p.151, 158. Willet vacillated somewhat: Michael MacDonald, 'An early seventeenth-century defence of usury', *Historical research* 60 (1987), p.353-60 (358).
56. Thomas Wilson, *A Discourse upon usury*, ed. R. H. Tawney (London, 1925), p.234-49 (not unnatural, p.237; lenders suffer loss, p.238; biting usury, p.241-42).
57. Filmer, *Quaestio quodlibetica*, p.92.
58. Charles Gibbon, *A Work worth the reading: wherein is contayned, fiue profitable and pithy questions* (London, Thomas Orwin, 1591), p.26-42. This is a dialogue on 'Whether a reasonable allowance may be taken for lending of monie'; the debate concludes: 'although Usury is prohibited to be taken of the poore, I see no reason it should be remitted of the rich' (p.42).
59. Downam, *Lectures on the XV. Psalme*, p.198; Downam refers to the manuscript discourse again at, for example, p.215, 277, 289, 304. Fenton, *Treatise of usurie*, p.133.
60. Jones, *God and the moneylenders*, p.156-57; the 'Treatise on usury' is in the Bodleian Library, Oxford, MS Rawlinson D 677.
61. Sir Francis Bacon, 'Of usury', in *The Oxford authors: Francis Bacon*, ed. Brian Vickers (Oxford, 1996), p.421-44 (422).

resolved to 'leave the proofs of the unlawfulness of usury to divines', and contented himself with arguing that high rates of interest discourage investment in trade and in agricultural improvements, noting that the industrious Dutch did not tolerate interest rates above six per cent.[62] Later in the century, Sir Josiah Child similarly evaded the moral dimension, and accepted the inevitability of usury, concentrating his efforts on analysing the economic effects of high and low rates of interest.[63] He was responding to Thomas Manley, whose *Usury at six per cent. examined* was a purely economic discussion of the subject.[64] Parliament in 1571 condemned virtually all usury as contrary to God's law, though it only set up legal machinery for punishing those who took interest at more than ten per cent. By 1624, when the rate was reduced to eight per cent, lay perspectives on usury had softened considerably. Religious objections to it were not raised in the Commons' debates on the bill, and it was the House of Lords – where the bishops sat – that introduced a proviso stating that 'no Words in this Law shalbe construed or expounded to allow the practise of Usurie in point of Religion or Conscience'.[65] To say that the law did not positively allow it was, of course, far milder than saying it prohibited it.

The debate on the morality of usury continued long after Filmer wrote the *Quaestio*, and centred on precisely the issues which he discussed, but his book was only rarely cited. It was briefly mentioned in an anonymous pamphlet of 1661, and discussed at much greater length by John Huddleston alias Dormer,[66] a Jesuit priest whose *Usury explain'd; or, conscience quieted in the case of putting out mony at interest* was published in 1695/6.[67] Huddleston took exception to some of Filmer's arguments, and

---

62. Sir Thomas Culpeper, *Tract against usury* (London, William Jaggard for Walter Burre, 1621), in *Seventeenth-century economic documents*, ed. Joan Thirsk and J. P. Cooper (Oxford, 1972), p.6-12 (6-9).
63. Child, *A Discourse about trade*, second set of signatures, sig.A4*v*, A5*r*, *passim*.
64. Thomas Manley, *Usury at six per cent. examined* (London, Thomas Ratcliffe and Thomas Daniel for Ambrose Isted, 1669), *passim*.
65. Quoted in Jones, *God and the moneylenders*, p.62-63. On usury against the law of God, an exception was made for moneylending at interest on behalf of orphans; p.195, 197). In the parliament of 1621, Sir Edward Montague voiced religious objections to usury (p.191).
66. *An Essay towards the deciding of the so much, and so long controverted case of usury [...] By D. C.* (London, John Rothwell, 1661), sig.B1*v*, refers to the *Quaestio*. The attribution to John Huddleston of *Usury explain'd; or, conscience quieted in the case of putting out mony at interest* (London, D. Edwards, 1695/6) is discussed in Thompson Cooper, 'John Dormer (1636-1700)' in *Dictionary of national biography*, 22 vols, ed. Sir Leslie Stephen and Sir Sidney Lee (London, 1885-1901) and in the entry on 'Huddleston [*alias* Dormer, Shirley], John (1636-1700)', revised by Ruth Jordan in the *Oxford dictionary of national biography*; he was rector of the English College at Liège.
67. Richard Capel, 'An appendix touching usury', in *Tentations: their nature, danger, cure: the fourth part. [...] by Richard Capel, sometimes fellow of Magdalen Colledge in Oxford. To all which is added an appendix touching usury* (London, T. R. and E. M. for John Bartlet, 1655), p.288-98,

censured his anti-Catholicism, but on a number of key points he adopted much the same position as the *Quaestio*. He claimed that 'MONY may be LETT' as well as lent, and that there is no significant difference between letting a horse and letting cash. It is perfectly fine, he said, to take interest on money that someone hires from me, provided that the rate does not exceed the legally permitted figure – and even that might sometimes be acceptable.[68] Though Huddleston was a Catholic, his conclusions on usury, and many of his arguments, were close to Filmer's. Yet liberalising tendencies in relation to usury are sometimes linked to Calvinism or Puritanism rather than to Catholicism or to the high church Anglicanism characteristic of Filmer's Tory followers.[69] The next section is about the religious contexts of Filmer's arguments and of attitudes to usury more generally.

Usury, religion and Filmer

Filmer's views on usury, and those of like-minded thinkers, had little to do with any characteristically Calvinist or Puritan principles, though a number of modern scholars have tried to forge such a connection. According to Joyce Appleby, Filmer 'took the line marked out by Calvin and stressed that it was the spirit of the act that counted' in usury.[70] If the moneylender did not intend to live idly or to act uncharitably towards the poor, then he did nothing wrong in collecting interest on money he lent. Benjamin Nelson stresses the revolutionary nature of Calvin's teachings on usury, arguing that everyone 'from the sixteenth to the nineteenth century who advocated a more liberal usury law turned to

---

asserts that 'There is an English *Manuscript* carried about from hand to hand, said to have been written by a great man and a great Clerk' (p.293); the manuscript denied that lending for trade was usury and agued that the lender was entitled to interest even if the borrower made a loss on the trading venture, just as a landlord is entitled to rent even if the tenant made a loss in farming the rented land. Capel calls the author 'This noble writer' (p.295) and says that he granted that you can take rent for a house from a poor man but denied that you can exact interest on lending money to the poor. Since Filmer was not a nobleman and since he permitted taking interest on loans to the poor, it seems unlikely that the manuscript was the *Quaestio*.

68. Huddleston, *Usury explain'd*, p.7, 13, 18, 34 (against Filmer's arguments); p.30, 47 (against Filmer's anti-Catholicism); p.30 (money can be let); p.32 (little difference between letting a horse and letting money); p.43 (usury is taking more interest than law allows). At p.48-49 Huddleston argued that it could be justifiable to take higher interest than the law of the land regularly allowed, if you did so through a triple rather than a single contract: a contract of partnership between yourself and the borrower, a contract insuring the principal, and a contract insuring the interest.

69. It is worth noting that Huddleston's book was condemned by the Catholic Church in 1703: Cooper, revd by Jordan, 'Huddleston [*alias* Dormer, Shirley], John (1636–1700)'.

70. Joyce Oldham Appleby, *Economic thought and ideology in seventeenth-century England* (Princeton, NJ, 1978), p.68.

Calvin for support'. Nelson champions Max Weber's thesis that the spirit of capitalism is connected to the Protestant ethic, and, in particular, to Calvinism.[71] This thesis has, of course, been vigorously attacked, and is rarely maintained in its full form by modern scholars.

Some recent writers have, however, suggested that there is a link between liberalising attitudes towards usury and Protestant or more specifically Puritan thinking. Norman Jones connects the ending of the legal prohibition of usury in England with the development of 'a new understanding of man's relationship with God'. This new attitude, he asserts, grew 'out of the doctrine of solifidianism', and centred on 'the internalization of sin and the demand for freedom of conscience'. As the new view gained ground, Jones tells us, many people came to think that sin was not 'a public concern'. 'Reformed theology', he claims, 'played an important role in these developments, and it was that group of theologians loosely known as Puritans who took the lead in developing these ideas'. They emphasised 'obedience to conscience over obedience to established authority'. In support of his argument, Jones shows that such thinkers as William Perkins and Andrew Willet denied that human laws bind in conscience; he asserts that they 'celebrated the rule of conscience over the rule of positive law', and places Filmer squarely in their tradition.[72] Keith Wrightson similarly contends that some English Protestant moralists 'were engaged in developing an alternative moral theology which placed its emphasis less upon positive law than on the primacy of the individual conscience'.[73] On the other hand, Charles H. George claims that the large majority of English Calvinist and Puritan moralists *opposed* usury, and he refers to 'the reactionary, last-ditch courage of English Calvinism' on this question. According to George, Puritan ideas had little or nothing to do with the softening stance on usury, which stemmed rather from secular and capitalistic thinking: 'the alliance in England of Calvinism and capitalism in this specific regard is a fiction'.[74] Weber himself roundly castigated the view that the 'prohibition of interest' is 'the decisive criterion of the difference between the Catholic and Protestant ethics', and observed that in the sixteenth century the Calvinist churches in France and the Dutch Republic

---

71. Benjamin Nelson, *The Idea of usury: from tribal brotherhood to universal otherhood*, 2nd edn (Chicago, IL, 1969), p.xv-xvi, 235-39, 242-45, 247-50.

72. Jones, *God and the moneylenders*, p.163 (new understanding; solifidianism, sin, and freedom of conscience), p.203 (sin not a public concern; Reformed theology), p.151, 166 (human laws do not bind in conscience), p.158 (celebrated rule of conscience; Filmer).

73. Wrightson, *Earthly necessities*, p.208.

74. Charles H. George, 'English Calvinist opinion on usury, 1600-1640', *Journal of the history of ideas* 18:4 (1957), p.455-74 (469, 471). Kerridge, *Usury, interest, and the Reformation*, similarly stresses the opposition to usury of most of the Reformers, and the continuities between their thinking and that of the medieval scholastics.

campaigned against usurers and often excluded them from communion.[75]

The case of Filmer does nothing to support the idea that it was Calvinism or Puritanism that led to the relaxation of established convictions on usury. Filmer did indeed cite Calvin and some other Calvinists on the question, but he attached little importance to their authority. Filmer's arguments on usury were not based on any distinctively Calvinist doctrines, and the two authors he opposed most vigorously – Fenton and Downam – were themselves Calvinists. The fact that those two broadly agreed on usury with the anti-Calvinist Andrewes – against whom Filmer also wrote – does not serve to confirm the suggestion that Calvinism pointed in any particular direction on the issue. It is very difficult to show that Puritans such as Perkins celebrated the rule of conscience over the rule of positive law, and even if they had done so it is not clear what the implications of this would have been for their position on usury. Many Puritans did indeed deny that *human* laws bind in conscience, but the case against usury rested on the idea that it was against *God*'s law, not against the law of the land. No Puritan ever seems to have used the idea that human laws do not bind our consciences to argue for usury, and it is difficult to see how such an argument could have been mounted.

Filmer (as we saw) claimed that on Fenton's account of usury it would often be difficult to tell from external appearances whether a particular act was usury or not, for according to Fenton some loan contracts would be usurious if the intentions of the lender were evil but not otherwise. But, of course, Filmer's main argument in defence of usury was simply that it is not against *any* law, either of God or (in England after 1571, and more clearly after 1624) of man. He therefore had no need to assert the superiority of conscience to human law, and in fact did not do so, either in the *Quaestio* or elsewhere. Indeed, in *Patriarcha* he placed a very high value indeed on the duty to obey our superiors, even if they command us to do things which look sinful and to which we might therefore conscientiously object. 'The sanctifying of the Sabbath is a divine law', he observed, 'yet if a master command his servant not to go to church upon a sabbath day, the best divines teach us that the servant must obey this command, though it may be sinful and unlawful in the master'. This was very far from Puritan views on the sabbath. Elsewhere, he considered the claim that if a monarch is accused of misgoverning, it is ultimately up to 'every man's conscience' to decide in favour of or against the sovereign. This, said Filmer, would make every man 'his own judge', and would

75. Max Weber, *The Protestant ethic and the spirit of capitalism*, trans. Talcott Parsons (London, 1930), p.201.

bring in 'utter confusion and anarchy'.[76] Filmer was no Puritan pioneer of rights of conscience against human authority.

Perkins and other Puritans sometimes argued that God's law alone binds our consciences. We sin if we disobey God, they said, but not otherwise. If a human law commands us to do something that God has not commanded, then we may with a good conscience disobey, provided that in doing so we show no disrespect for the authority of the magistrate.[77] But they held that our consciences are wholly subordinate to God's laws, both positive and natural. Natural laws applied to everyone, while positive ones had been given by God to particular groups – to the Jews of the Old Testament, and to Christians since Christ's coming. So far from elevating conscience above God's positive laws, Perkins insisted that 'the word of God written in the books of the old and new Testament' 'hath absolute and soveraigne power in it self to bind the conscience'.[78] On this line of thinking, we are wholly *unfree* to decide for ourselves on the question of whether usury is sinful or not. If it is condemned in the Bible then it is sinful, and if not, not. If we are misinformed about what the Bible says, we should take steps to be re-educated. Calvin held that Scripture did *not* condemn all forms of usury, and this is the central tenet on which liberalising Calvinists rested their case for softening the laws on usury.[79] Their case in no way relied on any new Puritan theory of conscience. Perkins and others argued that though human laws do not bind our consciences, God's laws do. They did *not* argue that the state should refrain from enforcing God's laws or that it should leave individuals free to decide whether and how to obey them. As Perkins put it, 'Gods lawes are perfect, and absolute' 'and therefore are to be executed without dispensation, relaxation, or any mitigation'.[80] Of course, some sins were not detectable by human courts, as they were sins of thought or intention which God alone could see and punish. It is difficult for the state to punish me for coveting my neighbour's ox if I go no further than coveting. But in the case of detectable sins, Puritans were rarely bashful about calling on the civil authorities to aid in their extirpation.

76. Filmer, *Patriarcha and other writings*, p.43, 153-54.
77. Attitudes towards the question of whether human laws bind the conscience are discussed in Johann Sommerville, 'Conscience, law, and things indifferent: arguments on toleration from the Vestiarian controversy to Hobbes and Locke', in *Contexts of conscience in early modern Europe, 1500-1700*, ed. Harald E. Braun and Edward Vallance (Houndmills, 2004), p.166-79.
78. William Perkins, *A Discourse of conscience* (Cambridge, John Legate, 1596), p.11.
79. Calvin's various statements are discussed, with documentation, in Nelson, *The Idea of usury*, p.73-82. A key passage is quoted in Filmer, *Quaestio quodlibetica*: 'unto him it did not appear by any testimony of Scripture that all Usury is altogether condemned' (p.26-27); 'Nullo testimonio Scripturae mihi constat usuras omnimodo damnatas esse' (sig.a1r).
80. William Perkins, *Epieikeia, or A Treatise of Christian equitie and moderation* (Cambridge, John Legat, 1604), sig.B2r.

Puritan ideas on conscience played little role in relaxing attitudes towards usury, and had little impact on Filmer. Yet it is true that serious doubts about the unlawfulness of usury spread amongst Calvinists earlier than amongst other major religious groups. This had little to do with any intrinsically Calvinist moral principles, but was connected with the fact that Calvinists and other Protestants found it much easier than Catholics to break with the traditions of the medieval church – Catholic traditions – on matters like usury and lying as well as on religious doctrine. As John Noonan observes, it was only after the mid-eighteenth century that Catholics could safely defend usury with arguments of the kind long employed by some Calvinists and Lutherans. He claims that Charles Du Moulin (or Molinaeus) was 'the first Catholic writer to urge the licitness of moderate usury', and notes that Du Moulin's book was 'placed on the Index'.[81] In fact, when he wrote his *Tractatus commerciorum, et usurarum* in 1542, and when he published it in 1546, Du Moulin was not a Catholic but a Calvinist. Indeed, his work may well have influenced Calvin, either directly or through another Calvinist, François Hotman, who plagiarised the *Tractatus*.[82] Filmer classed Du Moulin among 'the Divines of the reformed Churches' (though he was actually a lawyer).[83] Noonan mentions Du Moulin's 'contempt for scholasticism'.[84] Calvinists, and indeed Protestants in general, argued that much of the Catholic scholastic tradition was valueless or even pernicious. The break with Rome left Protestant groups free to decide how much, or how little, of Catholic tradition to retain in a wide range of areas. Some adopted the old theories, while others rejected them. As Filmer observed, the Lutherans Philip Melanchthon and Martin Chemnitz drew heavily on Catholic scholastics in their own arguments against usury, while Downam and Carleton, who were Calvinists, in turn borrowed from the two Lutherans.[85] Later Lutherans who took a more liberal line on usury include Jakob Andreae, Johann Gerhard and Christoph Besold.[86]

81. Noonan, *The Scholastic analysis of usury*, p.367, 370.
82. See the biographical entry on 'Du Moulin, Charles', in *The Cambridge history of political thought 1450-1700*, ed. Burns and Goldie, p.672; Nelson, *Idea of usury*, p.104-105 (Du Moulin's religion); Jones, *God and the moneylenders*, p.15-16 (date of composition and publication of the *Tractatus*); p. 17 (influence on Calvin, perhaps through plagiarist Hotman). Jones gives the date of publication as 1547, as does Nelson, *Idea of usury*, p.104n, but the correct dating of the *Tractatus commerciorum, et usurarum, redituumque pecunia constitutorum, & monetarum* is 1546. Some later editions of Du Moulin's book include the word 'Contractuum' in the title and the first edition is also sometimes erroneously described as including that word.
83. Filmer, *Quaestio quodlibetica*, sig.a3v.
84. Noonan, *The Scholastic analysis of usury*, p.368.
85. Filmer, *Quaestio quodlibetica*, p.17.
86. Nelson, *Idea of usury*, p.92; Eugen von Böhm-Bawerk, *Capital and interest*, vol.1: *History and critique of interest theories* (South Holland, IL, 1959), p.21.

Catholics could not so easily abandon the scholastic tradition, for to
do so would have been difficult without admitting that some of their
most authoritative theologians had erred on key questions of morality.
The Catholic way, therefore, was to stick to the letter of the old principles
while introducing increasing numbers of exceptions which had the
practical effect of bending if not breaking the traditional rules. As
commerce grew in medieval Europe, the rules on usury were adapted
to take account of commercial realities. From the 1180s the idea developed that a contract is usurious only if the intentions of the contractors
are so, and this could, of course, be difficult or impossible to prove.
Compensation was allowed, as we have seen, for damage incurred, or
profit lost by the lender. Aquinas argued that the compensation had to
be for actual and not merely *probable* damage or lost profit. But the late-
thirteenth-century Franciscan Peter John Olivi went further and
asserted that 'probable profit has a real and measurable existence' within
capital (a term which he employed but did not coin). Distinguishing
productive capital from mere money, he argued that the market was the
best regulator of commercial transactions. It has been claimed that Olivi
and others began an intellectual revolution which led to 'a radically new
image of the world', in which 'a static world of points and perfections'
was replaced by 'a world of lines in constant expansion and contraction'.
This new view of commercial society, it has further been contended, in
turn influenced attitudes towards nature, and paved the way for the
scientific revolution.[87] All this may be true. But the old condemnation of
usury survived the revolution. In the case of usury, as in the case of lying
(for example) Catholics clung doggedly to their traditional rules, while
evolving means of evading the more awkward consequences of those
rules. They condemned all lying but (in some circumstances) allowed the
telling of intentionally deceptive untruths which involved ambiguous
language or mental reservations – and which looked just like lies to many
people. Similarly, they invented the triple contract and similar devices to
permit loans at interest while avoiding usury. Catholicism was no more
hostile than Calvinism towards commerce, but took a different path in
accommodating itself to the needs of traders.

So far, we have seen that Filmer was not a conservative or a traditionalist on usury. In the *Quaestio* he showed no inclination to preserve a
social hierarchy dominated by a landed elite against the assaults of

87. Joel Kaye, *Economy and nature in the fourteenth century: money, market exchange, and the emergence
    of scientific thought* (Cambridge, 1998), p.82, 85, 121, 122, 126-27, 158, 246. More sceptical of
    Olivi's importance and originality are Julius Kirshner and Kimberly Lo Prete, 'Peter John
    Olivi's treatises on contracts of sale, usury and restitution: Minorite economics or minor
    works?', *Quaderni fiorentini per la storia del pensiero giuridico moderno* 13 (1984), p.233-86 (for
    example 275-76, 285).

capitalistic merchants. In what follows we will discover that it is very difficult to sustain the thesis that on broader questions of social and political theory he was a reactionary defender of the ideology of order and the domination of the landed elite over the social hierarchy, while Locke was a progressive.

Filmer and Locke on politics and the family

A number of modern scholars claim that Filmer was a conservative and traditionalist in his social and political thinking. According to Lawrence Stone, he defended 'the ancient argument' that 'the authority of the King and that of a father were directly linked by scriptural authority and the natural laws of hierarchy', while Locke broke with tradition in attacking such notions.[88] Carole Pateman similarly contends that Filmer subscribed to 'classic patriarchalism' while Locke articulated a contractualist version of patriarchal theory and made 'the key theoretical contribution' to the construction of a distinctively '*modern* patriarchy' which 'structures capitalist civil society'.[89] According to Linda Nicholson, Locke was responsible for 'the theoretical separation of the family and the state'. He was, she tells us, 'an early exponent of the modern separation of the familial and the political'.[90] W. H. Greenleaf and J. C. D. Clark contend that Filmerian patriarchalism was underpinned by an ideology of order which portrayed the social hierarchy as natural and divinely ordained, and which stressed the correspondences between human society and other created hierarchies.[91] Filmer, we are told, was a religious thinker and an orthodox Anglican, while Locke was a secularist and heterodox in religion.[92] What follows suggests that much of this case needs drastic revision.

Filmer's political writings contain very few if any arguments based on analogies or correspondences between human society and other hierarchies. It was commonplace in Filmer's day to defend monarchy by observing that the lion is the king of the beasts, that the eagle is the lord of the birds and that a hive of bees is governed by a single ruler. Strikingly, Filmer does not argue in this way. Again, it was often said that social degrees amongst humans are natural and reflect the hier-

---

88. Stone, *The Family, sex and marriage*, p.265.
89. Carole Pateman, *The Sexual contract* (Stanford, CA, 1988), p.21, 25.
90. Linda J. Nicholson, *Gender and history: the limits of social theory in the age of the family* (New York, 1986), p.133, 134.
91. Greenleaf, *Order, empiricism and politics*, p.14-57, 80-94; Clark, *English society 1688-1832*, p.64-92.
92. The importance of Locke's religious heterodoxy is emphasised in Clark, *English Society 1688-1832*, p.280-82, 294.

archical structure of all of creation. Filmer has virtually nothing to say about social hierarchy. He mentions nobles and gentry, especially when he is describing historical events, but although he was obviously aware that such ranks existed, they play no important part in his political theory. For that theory is not at all dependent upon any conception of social hierarchy. Filmer's ideas on political power were *not* hierarchical. He did not argue that political power is or ought to be distributed through the social hierarchy, with the ranks near the top (nobles and gentry) possessing more than those who were baser born, and with the person at the summit – the monarch – possessing more still. Rather, he contended that the sovereign holds absolute power, and the rest of the population – nobles as much as artisans – none at all. The sovereign's authority, he claimed, is the same as the authority which the first father – Adam – had possessed over his family. All sovereigns, including those in republics and democracies, hold 'the natural authority of a supreme father' over their subjects.[93] Rulers ought, indeed, to allow subordinate fathers a large measure of control in their own private families. But the details of this were up to the ruler. Filmer argued that political and fatherly power were identical, not analogous.

Filmer's political works say remarkably little to link him to Anglican attitudes on purely religious questions, or on issues of church government. He said nothing about the claim that the clergy have a divine right to tithes, for example, or that bishops hold their powers *jure divino*. Indeed, it is arguable that his writings made good Tory propaganda on secular questions in 1679-1680 precisely because of his neutral tone on ecclesiastical matters. As we have seen, Filmer rejected the teachings of many Anglican divines on usury. Fenton claimed that the primitive agricultural life was best, but Filmer disagreed. Yet in his politics, we might be tempted to argue, he advocated a return to primitive patriarchalism, and we could conclude that there is a radical disjunction between his economic and political theories. It was not, however, because it was primitive that he supported patriarchalism, but because he believed it was endorsed by Scripture and nature. Filmer used a combination of biblical texts and rational arguments to reject the idea that God had made human consent the foundation of government. Locke likewise deployed Scripture and reason to demonstrate that all government *does* rest on consent, and that God and nature have drawn a strong distinction between the purely domestic power of fathers and the political power of states. It is by no means clear that the Bible was very helpful to either of them in this debate, for its writers were unconcerned

93. Filmer, *Patriarcha and other writings*, ed. Sommerville, p.11, 44.

with seventeenth-century controversies or with the problem of whether government arises by contract.

The argument from reason essentially resolves itself into two connected questions, on both of which Locke took a well-worn line. The first question is whether by nature a father has the power of life and death over the members of his family, while the second is whether there are any key differences between families and states, such that even if fathers *do* naturally have the authority to execute their children, this authority is qualitatively different from political power. Filmer's argument is that fathers have the right of life and death, and that there are no differences between states and families. In the seventeenth century virtually everyone agreed that fathers possess some natural powers within their families and that these powers are independent of the consent of family members. By collapsing the distinction between families and states, Filmer was able to argue that sovereigns similarly have authority independently of any contract with their subjects. By denying that fathers can kill their children and asserting that families are very different from states, Locke was able to argue that consent underlies the authority of political rulers, though not of fathers.

Locke was not at all original in grounding government in the consent of the governed, and the original sovereignty of the people. Such ideas were commonplace among parliamentarians in the English Civil War, and can be traced back through Huguenot resistance theorists to medieval conciliarists. Nor was there anything new in his insistence that domestic and political power are quite different from each other.[94] His claim that fathers are not authorised to execute their children was equally familiar, and was commonplace in the thinking of Thomists. According to Locke, children have 'a Right to be nourish'd and maintained by their Parents'. This right, he argued, created correlative duties in parents. But the authority of parents over their offspring extended no further than was necessary to carry out the obligation to look after them. It was, he declared, no more than was needed to aid them while they were weak and discipline them to receive an education. Locke insisted that fathers have no power over 'the Lives or Goods' of their children, and that once children reach 'the years of discretion' they become fully free from their parents' authority. Parents had no authority whatever to make laws that bound their children 'all the course of their Lives', nor to enforce such laws 'with Capital Punishments'. The power of making laws and enforcing them with penalties up to and including death, said Locke, was 'the proper *power of the Magistrate*, of which the

---

94. Quentin Skinner, *The Foundations of modern political thought*, vol.2: *The Age of Reformation* (Cambridge, 1978), p.348, 156.

Father hath not so much as the shadow'.[95] So political power was very different from parental power, and families were not states.

All of these principles had been expressed long before by St Thomas Aquinas and his followers. Aquinas permitted fathers to punish their erring children only lightly. Locke said that children have a right to be nourished by their parents, and that parents may discipline their children in so far as this aids their upbringing. Aquinas likewise argued that parents have a duty to provide their children with 'nourishment and discipline'. The sixteenth-century Thomist Domingo de Soto claimed that fathers have only limited powers of punishment, and Filmer's older contemporary, the Jesuit Francisco Suárez, insisted that Adam and later fathers did not have the power of life and death over their families, drawing a strong contrast between political and domestic society and basing the authority of rulers on the consent of the ruled, as Locke was to do. Suárez's purpose in this was precisely to rebut ideas of absolute monarchy and to show that kings derive their powers from the people by contract. Filmer attacked Suárez at length in *Patriarcha*. In responding to Filmer, Locke adopted many of the basic tenets of the Jesuit. Later in the seventeenth century the German Protestant Samuel Pufendorf argued that parents have a duty to promote the welfare of their children and have no authority to execute them. Annotating Pufendorf, Jean Barbeyrac took his position to be the same as Locke's, and opposed to Filmer's, as it does indeed seem to be.[96] Underlying the Lockean and Thomist contrast between the state and the family were the teachings of Aristotle, who distinguished domestic from civil authority and economics from politics.

Filmer argued that the first state in the world had been Adam's family, and that Adam had possessed authority over it 'by right of fatherhood'. Adam's power over his subjects had been at once fatherly and political. Later rulers, Filmer contended, were not the literal fathers of their subjects, as Adam had been, but they held the same kind of power as Adam had done, and it was both fatherly and political. Only the sover-

95. John Locke, *Two treatises of government*, ed. Peter Laslett (Cambridge, 1988), I.89-90 (p.207-208 – children's rights and parents' duties); II.65 (p.310-11) – parents have only limited and temporary power over children).

96. St Thomas Aquinas, *Summa theologiae* (Alba, 1962), 2a2ae, q. 65, art. 2; Aquinas, *In decem libros ethicorum Aristotelis ad Nicomachum expositio*, ed. Angeli M. Pirotta and Martini-S. Gillet (Turin, 1934), p.3 (bk I, lectio I, section 4: 'nutrimentum et disciplinam'). Domingo de Soto, *De iustitia et iure* (Salamanca, Andreas a Portonariis, 1553), lib. I, quaest. I, art 3, p. 13. Francisco Suárez, *Tractatus de legibus ac Deo legislatore* [1612] (Naples, 1872), p.164-68 (3:2:3); Samuel Pufendorf, *De jure naturae et gentium libri octo*, ed. and trans. C. H. Oldfather and W. A. Oldfather, 2 vols (Oxford, 1934), 6:2:6 (p.917-19). Pufendorf, *Le Droit de la nature et des gens*, ed. and trans. Jean Barbeyrac, 2 vols (Amsterdam, Henri Schelte, 1706), vol.2, p.169-70.

eign, he said, has full fatherly power in any state. Because fathers do not derive their authority over their children from the latter's consent, but from God and nature, sovereigns ever since Adam have likewise drawn their powers from God and not from the consent of their subjects. He concluded that since sovereigns do not get their authority from the people they are not accountable to the people for how they exercise it.[97] Filmer's equation of political and fatherly authority served the purpose of showing that government does not spring from the consent of the governed. His claim that by nature fathers *do* have the power of life and death over their children had precedent – in Roman law and in the writings of Jean Bodin, Richard Hooker, Marsilius of Padua, William of Ockham and others.[98] But where Filmer parted company with all of these authors was in insisting that there is no conceptual difference between a family and a state. Bodin and the rest claimed that a state must consist of a number of families joined together. Filmer denied this and argued that a single family may be a state, as Adam's family had been. The point of this move was to rebut the idea that government began only when a group of families, or their heads, consented to join together and elected a ruler. For that idea had the implication that kings derive their powers from the consent of the governed. But if Adam's family was a state and if Adam derived his authority from God and nature, by right of fatherhood, then the world's first government was not grounded in consent. So it was false to claim that government always or necessarily sprang from the consent of the governed. Filmer was not the first writer to equate political and fatherly power, but he was one of the first, and certainly the most influential.[99]

On the question of the relationship between the state and the family, then, Locke's ideas were largely traditional, while Filmer's were more innovatory, even if their tendencies were different. Both were making moves in an old and familiar game, but Filmer's moves were the more

---

97. Filmer, *Patriarcha and other writings*, ed. Sommerville, p.6 (by right of fatherhood), p.10-11 (all sovereigns hold paternal power), p.12 (subordinate fathers), p.16, 32 (rulers hold absolute power which is not derived from the people, and are not accountable to the people).

98. Jean Bodin, *Les Six livres de la république* (Paris, Jacques du Puys, 1576), bk 1, ch.4. Richard Hooker, *Of the laws of ecclesiastical polity*, 1:10:4, in *Of the laws of ecclesiastical polity: preface. Book I. Book VIII*, ed. Arthur Stephen McGrade (Cambridge, 1989), p.90. Marsilius of Padua, *Defensor pacis*, trans. Alan Gewirth (Toronto, 1980), p.10-12. William of Ockham, *Dialogus*, third part, tract 1, bk 2, ch. 3; in *Monarchia S. Romani imperii*, ed. Melchior Goldast, 3 vols (Hanover, Thomas Willierius, 1611-14) (facsimile reissue Graz, 1960), vol.2, p.793. A highly influential text in this connection is Aristotle, *Politics*, 1259a40-1259b2, which states that the head of a household governs his wife as a republican magistrate over fellow citizens, and his children as a monarch over his subjects.

99. Johann P. Sommerville, *Royalists and patriots: politics and ideology in England 1603-1640*, 2nd edn (Harlow, 1999), p.31-35.

original. As we have seen, it is sometimes suggested that Locke's theory embodied a 'new worldview', that he 'decisively separated the "political" from the "familial" ', and that in doing so he created a '*modern* patriarchy' which 'structures capitalist civil society'.[100] But Locke's separation of state from family was unoriginal – adding little or nothing to what had been said by earlier Thomists and Aristotelians – and it was calculated to render kings accountable, not to justify modern patriarchy or capitalism. On questions of capital and interest Locke and his opponent Filmer in fact took much the same line. Neither endorsed the ideology of order, and neither was particularly concerned to defend as natural – or to attack – the existing social hierarchy. Patriarchalist royal absolutism and ideas of limited and accountable government were equally compatible with the defence of usury.

100. Nicholson, *Gender and history*, p.137, 1; Pateman, *Sexual contract*, p.25.

John Locke's philosophy of money[1]

DANIEL CAREY

John Locke scored an impressive political victory when he intervened in the debate over English money in the 1690s. The depletion of silver from English coins had become so severe in this period that by mid-decade 50 per cent or more of the weight had been removed by illegal clipping.[2] Two rival solutions to the problem had backing in Parliament: either to devalue the currency, or – as Locke argued – to maintain the existing standard, recalling coins from circulation and re-minting them at full weight. The principles (if not all aspects of the plan) favoured by Locke and his supporters prevailed against strong opposition, and in 1696 what is called the Great Recoinage began.[3]

The deterioration of England's coinage was closely connected to pressures created by financing the war effort against France during the Nine Years' War (1688-1697), which required bullion for remittances to England's armies and allies.[4] This demand encouraged clippers to continue their illegal attack on coin, with the proceeds melted down and exported. Milled money, which began to be produced in 1662, was inscribed at the edges to protect against clipping and counterfeiting, and it provided some defence, but it represented only a small percentage of the circulating medium.[5] Full-weight money – whether milled or

1. I am grateful to Patrick Kelly and Carl Wennerlind for discussion and comments on previous drafts of this chapter. My thanks to Nicholas Mayhew for inviting me to participate in the Winton Institute for Monetary History at the Ashmolean Museum, Oxford, as an associate fellow and to himself and Anthony Hotson for the opportunity to present my research there. I appreciate the support of the Irish Research Council for assisting my work.
2. Patrick Hyde Kelly, 'General introduction: Locke on money', in *Locke on money*, Table 4 (vol.1, p.116).
3. See Li, *The Great Recoinage*; Horsefield, *British monetary experiments 1650-1710*, ch.3-6. Key provisions of Locke's proposal were not followed in the Recoinage, including the fact that the government plan compensated holders of clipped coin and allowed for gradual demonetisation of coins, while Locke wanted them to pass immediately only by weight (since the stamped 'face' value no longer corresponded to the actual silver content). See Kelly, 'General introduction', in *Locke on money*, vol.1, p.31-33, 37, 91. On the advantages and disadvantages of this approach, see Li, *The Great Recoinage*, p.68-69. On the government's fear that this would cause a fall in the price of guineas and stop trade, see Henry Horwitz, *Parliament, policy and politics in the reign of William III* (Manchester, 1977), p.160.
4. See Jones, *War and economy in the age of William III and Marlborough*.
5. For an estimate that milled money amounted to 2% of the total circulation in March 1696

hammered (the older, hand-tooled method of fabrication) – was typically hoarded or melted, leaving lightweight hammered coins as the vulnerable medium of exchange. Attempts in Parliament in the early 1690s to address the situation had failed, but action became urgent in 1694/5 as the loss of silver accelerated and the price of gold in the form of guineas rose to new heights (as an alternative store of value). The proposal for a devaluation was initially set around nine per cent in March 1695 but it increased to 20 per cent by September of the year in connection with the higher market rate of silver.[6] In William Lowndes's famous *Report containing an essay for the amendment of the silver coins*, drafted in September 1695 for the Treasury, Lowndes responded by recommending the retention of the existing alloy and weight of coins while raising the denomination to establish an equivalence with the market price of bullion, thus reducing the incentive for clipping and encouraging holders of full weight coins to dishoard them.[7] Locke had already entered the debate over the worsening coinage in 1692 with the publication of *Some considerations of the consequences of the lowering of interest, and raising the value of money*.[8] He then made a series of briefer contributions in connection with debates in Parliament and at committee level before the appearance of his *Further considerations concerning raising the value of money* (1695). In all of these writings, he resisted plans to devalue the currency.

As Patrick Kelly has remarked, Locke defended a 'new, and in the circumstances revolutionary, doctrine of insisting on the sacrosanctity of the monetary standard'.[9] Whether he was right to do so remains a matter of dispute. Some recent critics have described his economic analysis as an 'embarrassment',[10] containing errors that were 'obvious' to his

---

(including newly minted and old milled money), see Kelly, 'General introduction', in *Locke on money*, Table 1 (vol.1, p.112). On practices of clipping and coining the proceeds, as well as punishment of offenders, see Malcolm Gaskill, *Crime and mentalities in early modern England* (Cambridge, 2000), p.123-99. Gaskill points out that milled money was not invulnerable since milled edges could also be re-engraved after being clipped (p.145).

6. See Kelly, 'General introduction', in *Locke on money*, vol.1, p.20-21, 25.

7. The option of altering the weight and fineness of the coin attracted little support. Generally devaluationists did not favour this approach as their proposals had the advantage of allowing for a revaluation of the coin once the war was over. Kelly, 'General introduction', *Locke on money*, vol.1, p.25, 62.

8. The prefatory letter was dated 7 November 1691 and copies were available before the year's end.

9. Kelly, 'General introduction', in *Locke on money*, vol.1, p.29. See also Sir Albert Feavearyear, *The Pound sterling: a history of English money*, 2nd edn revd E. Victor Morgan (Oxford, 1963): 'The sanctity which Locke attached to the Mint weights was something new' (p.148).

10. Thomas J. Sargent and François R. Velde, *The Big problem of small change* (Princeton, NJ, 2002), p.288.

critics,[11] while Andrea Finkelstein has questioned his grasp of the complex economic factors at stake in the currency crisis.[12] Others, however, have praised his position as a far-sighted intervention to prevent endless cycles of inflation and devaluation.[13] In this chapter I attempt to make sense of Locke's defence of that standard and to show the ways in which his decision, whatever its economic merits, was congruent with convictions held elsewhere in his philosophy. Precisely because a coherent alternative to Locke's position on recoinage existed at the time – however intemperately he characterised it – the subject of money offers a particular insight into the driving motivations of Locke's philosophy.

What emerges, I will argue, is a picture of Locke as committed, above all, to inter-subjectively agreed standards of value. Locke insisted in the case of money on valuing coin according to the existing standard set by law at the Mint, in which an ounce of silver was rated at 5s. 2d. This price was long established and it coincided with an internationally accepted valuation of silver. He condemned any departures from this agreed rating as a form of theft or fraud, whether by allowing lightweight coin to circulate above the value of the silver it contained or by a devaluation. Even though internal or domestic arrangements might facilitate manipulation of the standard in this way, the international acceptance of silver by weight as its true worth gave Locke a solid criterion. His approach to this problem coincides with his convictions about how societies and individuals should regulate themselves more generally, that is, according to received, inter-subjective agreements about meaning and value. This view of Locke contradicts some established interpretations of his work, especially those that assign to him a private theory of meaning. My argument is that although in a number of areas addressed by Locke we have a kind of discretion over the meanings we give to things, a moral imperative exists to respect agreements and adopt settled standards to regulate exchange (whether this occurs between individuals, between the state and its citizens or between different national economies).

11. Joyce Oldham Appleby, 'Locke, liberalism, and the natural law of money', p.49.
12. Finkelstein, *Harmony and the balance*, ch.9. For Nicholas Mayhew, Locke's 'high-minded, though utterly unrealistic, principle that money should be constant thus won the day, and (mis)guided government policy for a century thereafter'. 'Silver in England 1600-1800: coinage outputs and bullion exports from the records of the London Tower Mint and the London Company of Goldsmiths', in *Money in the pre-industrial world: bullion, debasements and coin substitutes*, ed. John H. Munro (London, 2012), p.101.
13. See for example Walter Eltis, 'John Locke, the quantity theory of money and the establishment of a sound currency', in Mark Blaug *et al.*, *The Quantity theory of money: from Locke to Keynes and Friedman* (Cheltenham, 1995), p.4-26. See also Richard A. Kleer, '"The ruine of Diana": Lowndes, Locke, and the bankers', *History of political economy* 36:3 (2004), p.533-56. For a balanced assessment of Locke's economic thought, see Kelly, 'General introduction', in *Locke on money*; and Feavearyear, *The Pound sterling*, ch.6.

Engagement not only with Locke's politics but also his philosophy of language offers an important insight into these issues. Of course his account of signification and meaning in the *Essay concerning human understanding* (1690) has itself been open to dispute, with critics questioning whether Locke adhered to a private theory of meaning or in fact rejected it.[14] I maintain that a parallel exists in the dispute over money. Locke acknowledges in his account of English currency that clipped coins impose no burden as long as they are accepted at face value. In other words, a kind of self-referential (or essentially 'private') system of meaning – the kind that would operate in a closed economy – is viable up to a point. But the thrust of his analysis of money is to establish an objective standard of value in the form of silver by weight that exists independently of individual economies and comes into play through an international market. Similarly, Locke's account of language in some way recognises the possibility of private meaning; however, the focus of his discussion of language is directed toward the goal of achieving stable communication between members of a given society which militates against privacy. The problem of maintaining an agreed standard remains endemic, but Locke does not abandon the attempt to locate one. In several other contexts of Locke's philosophy, including his moral theory and critique of religious enthusiasm, we see a comparable effort to secure a standard beyond the control of individuals, which stabilises meaning and provides protection against various kinds of abuse and manipulation. Locke never detaches himself from a suggestion of voluntarism in these scenarios, which is to say that the rules he proposes are not logically binding but ultimately derive from the will of an authority;[15] nonetheless he searches for shared standards and measures outside the individual and outside an internally functioning economy in order to stabilise the system. The enforcement of the standard would occur through losses imposed on the English economy by counterfeiting, arbitrage and inflation when it tampered with its coinage. Thus the study of Locke's position reveals an important pattern in his thought more generally, while attention to his wider philosophical commitments, in turn, indicates why he adhered so rigorously in his account of money to the notion that coinage has a sacrosanct value constituted by its weight in silver.

14. See Hannah Dawson, 'Locke on private language', *British journal for the history of philosophy* 11:4 (2003), p.609-38; Hannah Dawson, *Locke, language, and early-modern philosophy* (Cambridge, 2007); Michael Ayers, *Locke: epistemology and ontology*, 2 vols (London, 1991), vol.1, p.207-17.

15. On the question of Locke's voluntarism, see Daniel Carey, *Locke, Shaftesbury, and Hutcheson: contesting diversity in the Enlightenment and beyond* (Cambridge, 2006), p.130-31.

Coinage controversies and the problem
of the foreign trader

Locke assigns the value of any coin to the quantity of silver it contains (by weight and fineness), not to the denomination stamped on it. The stamp represents merely a guarantee of value, a 'publick voucher', as he calls it, not the source of value itself.[16] The giving of names to coins, whether groat, penny, crown or shilling, is purely arbitrary, but the silver content is not. Silver constitutes the 'intrinsic' value of the coin.[17] Lightweight coins pose a problem because the denomination no longer corresponds to the vouched silver content which has been filed or shaved away. When they pass as current – in other words, when they are accepted at face value rather than in terms of their actual weight in silver – they deprive the public of 'real value', according to Locke, by the percentage of their reduction.[18]

Although Locke accepts that *'Clip'd* and *unclip'd Money* will always buy an equal quantity of any thing else, as long as they will without scruple change one for another',[19] he regards it as only a matter of time before this arrangement would collapse. Silver by weight as the true standard becomes apparent when attending not to these domestic transactions but to the practice of foreign traders. An outside merchant might temporarily ignore disparities between English clipped and 'weighty' money in circulation, but only until such time as he was ready to 'carry away' his cash. If he could convert his sums into weighty money without trouble, then no problem would arise and he would depart with the amount he contracted for by tale as well as in terms of 'the quantity of Silver he expected for his Commodities, according to the standard of our

16. John Locke, *Some considerations*, in *Locke on money*, vol.1, p.312. For contemporary disagreement with this view, see Barbon, *A Discourse concerning coining the new money lighter*.
17. On the scholastic notion of 'intrinsic value', see Kelly, 'General introduction', in *Locke on money*, vol.1, p.82-83, 86-87.
18. Locke, *Some considerations*, *Locke on money*, vol.1, p.307. Despite the strictness of Locke's definition it is worth bearing in mind that ostensibly 'full weight' hammered coins varied considerably in their actual weight (as they were worked by hand and were difficult to standardise, with heavy coins being candidates for melting down to realise the extra silver content). Even in the case of milled money, according to Isaac Newton's estimate, one quarter of the coins was under- or over their defined weight (making the latter worth melting). See Kelly, 'General introduction', in *Locke on money*, vol.1, p.45.
19. *Some considerations*, *Locke on money*, vol.1, p.319. In *Further considerations* he was more explicit (in *Locke on money*, vol.2, p.469). This point indicates that Appleby is in error when she asserts that 'It was central to Locke's argument to deny that clipped coin ever passed at face value'. 'Locke, liberalism, and the natural law of money', p.66 (see also p.49). He knew very well that this was happening, confirmed for example in his 'Answer to My Lord Keepers queries' (in *Locke on money*, vol.2, p.387). Locke went on to point out that the receipt of lightweight coin by the government in payment of taxes and by landlords encouraged the public to follow suit (*Further considerations*, in *Locke on money*, vol.2, p.469).

Mint'.[20] Once the volume of clipped money in England became so significant that he encountered difficulty substituting heavy for light coin, he would either make contracts for payment specifically in full-weight money or raise the price of his goods. In short, Locke presents two damaging outcomes – on the one hand enabling foreigners to engage in arbitrage, in effect, or on the other, introducing inflation in the cost of commodities to match the diminished silver.

Arbitrage was possible so long as coins of different weights circulated in England, allowing outsiders to make off with heavy pieces. Inflation would be triggered when the source of full-weight money dried up. Clipping created the problem in both cases, with a consequent hoarding of full-weight coins (whether milled or hammered). But this was only one side of the equation. The other side, Locke indicated, was the effect of a negative trade balance which fuelled the demand for silver (he refrained from mentioning the need for wartime remittances as a contributing factor at this stage). Foreign debts had to be settled, ultimately, in specie or bullion;[21] regardless of the form it came in, silver would be valued only in terms of 'quantity' or weight. To meet this need, the heaviest coins at home would be culled (since lightweight coins maintained their pur-chasing power domestically). The pattern would repeat itself as the supply of weighty money became depleted, meaning that the 'Foreign Merchant, or his Factor' doing business in England would raise his prices because he could no longer convert lightweight money into heavy. At this stage people would learn, to their cost, that 'the quantity of Silver [...] buys Commodities and Pays Debts, and not the Stamp and Denomi-nation which is put upon it'.[22]

By 1695 it became clear that a full scale recoinage was necessary, an expensive and disruptive undertaking. The question was whether to use the current Mint standard as the basis for the recoined currency or to devalue it at the same time. Locke presented a series of arguments against devaluation in *Further considerations* at a critical stage of public and parliamentary debate, but he had already made his position known in 1692 in *Some considerations* when different alternatives remained in play. A simple re-rating of the currency might have been sufficient at that stage (rather than a recoinage), with two possible methods of doing so –

---

20. Locke, *Some considerations*, in *Locke on money*, vol.1, p.319-20.

21. For the purposes of his argument in *Some considerations* Locke ignored the system of bills of exchange for making payments, but he understood how it operated, as he makes clear in *Further considerations*, in *Locke on money*, vol.2, p.421. On bills of exchange in this context see Jones, *War and economy*; and Stephen Quinn, 'Gold, silver, and the Glorious Revolution: arbitrage between bills of exchange and bullion', *Economic history review* 44:3 (1996), p.473-90.

22. Locke, *Some considerations*, in *Locke on money*, vol.1, p.322.

enhancing a single coin in value (say, a crown or shilling) or the entire run of coins proportionally. Having stated that the latter option (a complete re-rating) was the plan under serious contemporary consideration, Locke spent some time refuting the single-coin alternative. While addressing this target was somewhat beside the point, it allowed Locke to establish the fact that manipulating the coinage in this way would run into difficulties exposed by patterns of international exchange. Thus the capacity to regulate the system of value did not really exist at a domestic or internal level but belonged in an external or international space where silver content alone prevailed.

Locke gave a recent historical example of a failed attempt to alter the rating of a single coin that he had noted in France during his travels in the 1670s. By edict, Louis XIV ordered the re-rating of 4-sols pieces such that 15 of them became equivalent to a French crown, even though 15 of the 4-sols coins contained substantially less silver than the crown (the silver écu).[23] The king tried to restrict the circulation of these debased coins to the 'Inland parts of his Kingdom' because he knew that making them current in seaports would encourage outsiders to bring base coins into France. Yet this too failed: 'They were still Imported; and, by this means, a great loss and damage brought upon his country. So that he was forced to cry them down, and sink them to near their intrinsick Value.'[24] As a result, any internal inconsistency was rectified, however harsh the consequences, by an external force, and the intrinsic silver content again governed the coin's value.[25]

If England took this approach it would encounter the same problem and thereby invite 'Foreigners to fetch away your Money without any

23. For the text of the edict of 8 April 1674, see Pierre Clément, *Les Questions monétaires avant 1789, et spécialement sous le ministère de Colbert* (Paris, 1870), p.52. These coins are also referred to as 4 sous pieces.

24. Locke, *Some considerations*, in *Locke on money*, vol.1, p.308. On these events see Pierre Clément, *Histoire de Colbert et de son administration*, 2 vols (Paris, 1874), vol.1, p.386-97. The context is described in Frank C. Spooner, *The International economy and monetary movements in France, 1493-1725*, 2nd edn (Cambridge, MA, 1972), p.191-92. For an extended contemporary assessment, see François Le Blanc, *Traite historique des monnoies de France: depuis le commencement de la Monarchie jusques a present* (Paris, Jean Jombert, 1690), p.393-97. Le Blanc described the measure as 'ruineuse pour le public' (p.393) and remarked on the position of foreigners, who computed value according to 'bonté interieure' (p.395, 397), and either ceased their trade or took advantage of the situation by exchanging light for heavy money. He also cited counterfeiting and a flooding in of light money as a consequence (p.395-96).

25. See also Locke's account of what happened in Portugal, in *Further considerations*, in *Locke on money*, vol.2, p.418. The Portuguese example and the French 4-sols are both mentioned by Abraham Hill in his anonymous *Letter about raising the value of coin* (London, Randal Taylor, 1690), p.2. Hill, treasurer of the Royal Society, shared with Locke the distinction of being asked for his advice on the coinage crisis by the Lords Justices (who presided in William III's absence during war) in 1695.

Commodities for it'. This they could do through an elaborate counterfeiting scheme imagined by Locke:

> For if they find that Two-Penny weight of Silver, marked with a certain
> Impression, shall here in England be equivalent to 3d weight mark'd with
> another Impression; they will not fail to stamp Pieces of that Fashion; and so
> Importing that base and low Coin, wil here in England, receive 3d for 2d, and
> quickly carry away your Silver in exchange for Copper, or barely the charge
> of Coynage.[26]

In the scenario Locke sketches out, half-groats (worth 2d.) bearing a
certain impression would be recoined (presumably with a copper alloy)
by the English Mint and then given a new stamp, making them pass by
public authority for 3d., despite having no more silver in them than 2d.
coins formerly possessed.[27] According to Locke, foreigners would seize
the opportunity and counterfeit these new coins and bring them into the
country, realising a premium in the process because they would get 3d.
worth of goods for the mere expense of 2d. in silver (and whatever
copper and coinage expense they laid out). However hypothetical this
possibility remained, it reinforces the existence of a standard, demon-
strating that English manipulation of its currency would open the door
to theft and arbitrage due to the overvaluation of the coin in terms of its
actual silver content.

The arbitrage opportunity requires two separate markets in order to
work; hence the privileged position of the outsider as someone with
ready access to these distinct locations. Locke positions such figures as
exposing a standard of value that transcends the state. For the purposes
of his argument, Locke implicitly denies that English nationals, who
remain within the country and routinely ignore the difference between
the value of the coin in tale and its value in silver, would have the same
chance. In fact, they could have exploited the situation just as easily so
long as they had access to markets beyond national borders in which to
operate.[28]

---

26. Locke, *Some considerations*, in *Locke on money*, vol.1, p.308. In 1695, Charles Davenant
    affirmed the possibility that foreign traders could counterfeit light money 'and thereby
    traffic here at ye same advantage'. 'A memorial concerning the coyn of England', in *Two
    manuscripts by Charles Davenant*, p.46.
27. Locke's French example shows that such a re-rating need not have involved recoining the
    currency or even restamping it, but merely a revaluation by proclamation. Recoining the
    half-groats in the manner Locke describes would have been both costly and time
    consuming; he may have introduced this imagined episode for rhetorical effect.
28. Quinn, 'Gold, silver, and the Glorious Revolution', focuses in part on the career of one
    such arbitrageur, the London goldsmith-banker Stephen Evance. Locke would have seen
    such a figure simply as a 'factor' of the foreign merchant (*Some considerations*, in *Locke on
    money*, vol.1, p.322). Quinn's account shows that the arbitrage arrangement was complex,
    involving trading between gold, silver and bills of exchange. See also Larry Neal and

The question arises whether Locke used the foreign trader in a generic way or to refer in coded language to Jews. He made an interesting comment on this subject in September 1695 when plans for a full-scale recoinage were underway. In an unpublished piece prepared at the request of Sir William Trumbull,[29] during the height of parliamentary debate, Locke addressed the merits of a proposed tax to compensate holders of clipped coin and asked whether this plan would invite 'the Jews and other forainers' to send 'great sums of light mony to power in upon you and soe carry away all the profit of the tax from your own innocent people'.[30] Jews are not the only 'foreigners' to benefit in this instance. The inflow that he anticipated on this occasion was not counterfeit coin but lightweight English money sourced from abroad, invited in by allowing holders of it (as the legislation later enacted approved) to redeem it at face value and receive a ticket for the missing 'value', paid for by a special tax.[31] The related problem was the failure to demonetise the currency immediately, as Locke strongly recommended, so that it would pass only by weight. In the lag time before light money was no longer accepted (pushed back to 4 May 1696), a further invitation was effectively being made to outsiders to flood England with bad coin so they could make off with any good money in circulation. Locke antici-pated that this would happen in discussion with his colleagues in the 'College' in December 1695.[32] He asked (in an unpublished manuscript), 'What if forrainers Jews or others have ready or will provide for you a good Stock of clipd Money Do you thinke your weighty money melted down into bullion may be worth the takeing for it at 50 percent profit or what profit great their conscientious sheers please?'[33] The implication is

---

Stephen Quinn, 'Markets and institutions in the rise of London as a financial center in the seventeenth century', in *Finance, intermediaries, and economic development*, ed. Stanley L. Engerman, Philip T. Hoffman, Jean-Laurent Rosenthal and Kenneth L. Sokoloff (Cambridge, 2003), p.20-23.

29. Trumbull, promoted to secretary of state in May 1695, made this request in his capacity as a Treasury commissioner (a post he retained until November 1695).

30. John Locke, 'A paper given to Sir William Trumbull which was written at his request September 1695', in *Locke on money*, vol.2, p.370.

31. See Li, *The Great Recoinage*, 117-19. The cost was paid for by a window tax (supplemented by a tax on paper when this was found to be insufficient).

32. The 'College' was a designation adopted in Locke's correspondence, referring to himself, John Freke and Edward Clarke (one of the Junto Whig managers in the House of Commons), as members of a like-minded group strategising over the issue of the recoinage and other parliamentary political matters in the period from January 1695 to March 1696. See Patrick Kelly, '"Monkey business": Locke's "College" correspondence and the adoption of the plan for the Great Recoinage of 1696', *Locke studies* 9 (2009), p.139n.

33. Bodleian Library MS Locke b.3, p.81 (contractions expanded), endorsed 'Qs sent to the Colledg 9 Dec 95'. Benjamin Furly wrote to Locke from Rotterdam in October 1691,

that full-weight coin that had been sent out of England to pay debts could be clipped and then sent back under these circumstances.

Having demonstrated the mistake of enhancing a single coin, Locke moved on in *Some considerations* to reject the more pressing concern of a prospective across-the-board devaluation of the currency (of the kind advocated later in Lowndes's *Report*). He stated emphatically that doing so would '*rob* all *Creditors*' by the amount of the devaluation since they would receive payment in coin of diminished value. He had in mind landlords whose rents would be watered down, those with money out on loan and others who had made 'Bargains' in stated amounts of money.[34] Furthermore, the newly rated coin would enjoy no additional purchasing power in the market and therefore represented no gain.

This mistaken approach somehow assumed that denomination constituted the source of value. To proceed on this basis was to assign meaning to something grounded only in internal conviction, in which value becomes a baseless fancy. Locke wonders what would put a stop to the endless raising of names:

> If it be good to raise the Crown Pieces this way One twentieth this Week, I suppose it will be as good and profitable to raise it as much again the next Week. For there is no reason, why it will not be as good to raise it again another One twentieth the next Week, and so on; wherein, if you proceed but 10 Weeks successively, you will by New-years-Day next have every Half-Crown raised to a Crown [....] And if you please to go on in this beneficial way of raising your Money, you may by the same Art bring a Penny-weight of Silver to be a Crown.[35]

His *reductio* serves its purpose rhetorically, but he positions the advocates of 'raising' the value of money as if they sought to enhance a full-weight coinage rather than one with a significant percentage of silver already missing from it.

Locke's remark makes it clear that in his view we are not entitled to endow things with value according to self-generated standards or subjective criteria. The value comes from elsewhere, and is 'intrinsic' to silver by weight. Locke emphasises the impact of a devaluation on the price of commodities, the defrauding of creditors and the prejudice to crown revenue, but he also returns again to his trope of the foreigner,

---

commenting on the outflow of bullion from London. Using some rather extravagant figures, he stated that three London bankers made 20 per cent on silver they sent over. 'If then 3 Bankers sent to one man [in Amsterdam] 29 millions [in shillings] it may easily be thought that the Jews, and all the rest sent double, 58 millions'. *The Correspondence of John Locke*, ed. E. S. de Beer, 8 vols (Oxford, 1976-1989), vol.4, p.318.

34. Locke, *Some considerations*, in *Locke on money*, vol.1, p.309-10. See also Hill, *A Letter about raising the value of coin*, p.2.

35. Locke, *Some considerations*, in *Locke on money*, vol.1, p.311.

external to the system, who detects the cheat. The change of valuation cannot remain a 'secret concealed from Strangers',[36] and they will therefore raise the price of their wares in line with the percentage increase in the value of the currency. As one of Locke's supporters put it: 'Foreigners were not imposed upon by our Mistakes: They considered not the Nominal, but the Real Value of our Coin; and sold us their Commodities too at proportionable Rates. But especially they taught us the true Estimate of our imaginary Riches, by the course of Exchange between their Money and ours'.[37] In this analysis, the worsening exchange rate told the story, coupled with a rise in prices. The problem is precisely the imaginary nature of the wealth created by false denominations detached from the standard.[38]

Locke considers a second form of intervention to raise the value of coin, this time in relation to gold. The market establishes a ratio between the two metals. If by legal means the rate of guineas vis-à-vis silver is raised by five per cent, then foreigners exploit the opportunity yet again. They send over gold, and in Locke's words, 'fetch away our Silver at 5 per Cent. profit, and so much loss to us'.[39] Conversely, if the rating of gold goes down relative to silver, then the same thing happens in reverse: 'For then strangers would bring in Silver, and carry away your gold, which was to be had here at a lower rate than any where else'.[40] As he clarified in his *Further considerations*, adjustments in these ratios 'would do well enough, if our Money and Trade were to Circulate only amongst our Selves, and we had no Commerce with the rest of the World',[41] but the moment we enter into international trade, the problem is exposed. In the case of overvalued gold, the foreign merchant makes off with as much as thirty per cent profit (the guinea having risen from 21s. to 30s. or more at the height of the coinage crisis).[42] By exploiting the overvaluation, foreign

---

36. Locke, *Some considerations*, in *Locke on money*, vol.1, p.313.
37. *A Review of the universal remedy for all diseases incident to coin: with application to our present circumstance. In a letter to Mr. Locke* (London, A. and J. Churchill, 1696), p.13. Hill likewise emphasised the reckoning of overseas debts according to 'intrinsick Goodness, and not [...] the image or Superscription' on coin, which meant that 'our Alteration of the Value of our Coin is not regarded by Foreigners' (*A Letter about raising the value of coin*, p.1).
38. For the response of Locke's contemporary critics see Kelly, 'General introduction', in *Locke on money*; Li, *The Great Recoinage*; Horsefield, *British monetary experiments*; Appleby, 'Locke, liberalism, and the natural law of money'.
39. Locke, *Some considerations*, in *Locke on money*, vol.1, p.323.
40. Locke, *Some considerations*, in *Locke on money*, vol.1, p.324. This account is in fact closer to the kinds of arbitrage that actually occurred at this time. See Quinn, 'Gold, silver, and the Glorious Revolution'.
41. Locke, *Further considerations*, in *Locke on money*, vol.2, p.469.
42. R. J., *A Letter of advice to a friend about the currency of clipt-money* (London, A. and J. Churchill, 1696), a work circulated by Locke among his neighbours in Essex, explained that silver was being sent to Holland to buy gold and then reimported, where it would be brought to the

merchants settled their accounts in England with gold from their own country. In fact they might as well be paying in money 'coin'd and clip'd beyond Sea' that lacked a huge amount of its silver content: for 'thus we lose near One third in all our Exportation, while Foreign gold Imported is received in Payment for Thirty Shillings a Guinea'.[43] Once more, an external intervention serves to correct a system of value that might otherwise be viable internally. Whatever we may fancy, no law can introduce a lasting proportion between the two metals, which will always vary according to the market. If, for example, we set the par at fifteen ounces of silver to one ounce of gold when the market rate in other countries has it at sixteen to one, Locke asks, 'Will they not send hither their Silver or fetch away your Gold at One sixteen loss to you?'[44]

Although the rising price of gold in England was directly related to the deterioration of the silver coinage, the problem Locke describes was in fact endemic in a bimetallic system where the bullion prices of the two fluctuated in international markets. Any variation between them would create the potential for arbitrage, as he makes clear, an issue exacerbated when setting by law the rate at which gold would be received at the Mint.[45] To the extent that legal authority has a role to play, Locke confines it to stamping gold coin to ensure only its weight and fineness, rather than assigning it a fixed price relative to the unit of account.[46] But Locke's strategy of leaving it to the market to determine the relative value of the two metals is only a partial solution. He assumes that England's market rate will equalise with the rate in other countries and thus cut arbitrage out of the equation. But internal factors specific to the English economy would have a bearing on the price ratio in the country, as well as international developments in exchange rates and foreign devaluations,[47]

Mint to coin guineas. Sixteen ounces of silver coined at the Mint would result in £4 2s. 8d., whereas the same sixteen ounces, having purchased an ounce of gold abroad, would make four guineas at the Mint. At the current valuation of 30s. per guinea this would make them worth £6 in silver. By this means, he reckoned, 'all our new Money, and all the Silver in the Kingdom was like to have been melted down, and carried away' (p.18).

43. Locke, *Further considerations*, in *Locke on money*, vol.2, p.469. The money stock of gold increased in England from £6.5m in 1693 to £7.7m in 1698, with an additional £1.5 million in foreign coin (mainly gold), out of a total money stock of £23.2m in 1698. See Kelly, 'General introduction', in *Locke on money*, vol.1, p.66, and Table 1 (vol.1, p.112-13).

44. Locke, *Some considerations*, in *Locke on money*, vol.1, p.327.

45. For a discussion of this issue focusing on the mid-eighteenth century, see Pilar Nogués-Marco, 'Competing bimetallic ratios'.

46. Locke, *Some considerations*, in *Locke on money*, vol.1, p.327-28.

47. Furly described previous Dutch experience of losing gold due to English and French overvaluation in a letter to Locke of 2 January 1691. *Correspondence*, vol.4, p.182-83. See also Furly to Locke 15 October 1691 (p.319). Hill described the problem of differing valuations of gold and silver in 1690 in *A Letter about raising the value of coin*, p.2.

making it an open question what proportionality would result at any given time (as he elsewhere suggests).[48]

The real problem with gold is that it represents a rival standard to silver. This prompts Locke, in his reiteration of first principles, to state that 'it is in the Interest of every country, that all the current money of it should be of one and the same Metal; That the several Species should be all of the same Alloy, and none of a baser mixture: And that the Standard once thus settled, should be Inviolably and Immutably kept to perpetuity'.[49] By giving gold a fixed rating at which it was received, a situation developed in which rival standards vie within one another in the same system. Gold had become another form of measurement intruding on the province of silver as the legal money of the country.[50] Locke's statement calls attention to the role that a standard plays in his thinking on the subject, and the necessity that the standard should remain settled and permanent. He resisted the conclusion that a devaluation would simply recognise an existing state of affairs by re-rating the coin. For him, the move represented an abandonment of a standard rather than an introduction of a new one. As for clipped coins, their circulation created a predicament in which "tis no wonder if the price and value of things be confounded and uncertain, when the Measure it self is lost'.[51]

The politics of money

Despite Locke's vituperations against devaluation, such a course of action had a number of advantages. The consequences would have been less deflationary,[52] and the degree of economic disruption less severe, while also making English goods more attractive as exports and discouraging imports. Given Locke's preoccupation with the balance of payments, this option might therefore have attracted him. At the same time, his quantity theory of money could have made the deflationary

---

48. Locke observes that since there are 'no two things in Nature, whose proportion, and use does not vary, 'tis impossible to set a standing regular price between them'. *Some considerations*, in *Locke on money*, vol.1, p.328. The rising price of gold was also caused by a shift in world silver/gold ratios. In 1692, Locke put it at 15.5:1 and in 1695 at 16:1.
49. Locke, *Some considerations*, in *Locke on money*, vol.1, p.329.
50. For Locke, '*Money* is the *measure* of Commerce, and the rate of every thing, and therefore *ought to be kept (as all other measures) as steady and invariable as may be*. But this cannot be, if your *Money* be made *of two Metals*, whose proportion, and consequently whose price, constantly varies in respect of one another' (*Some considerations*, in *Locke on money*, vol.1, p.326).
51. Locke, *Further considerations*, in *Locke on money*, vol.2, p.430.
52. Lowndes's scheme would have reduced the total coin in circulation by *c*.16% compared to *c*.30% under Locke's plan, with a parallel drop in prices. For these calculations, see Horsefield, *British monetary experiments*, p.30-31.

impact of his proposals more apparent to him.[53] For Locke the main
force counteracting the contraction of the money supply was the expectation of a return to circulation of previously hoarded coin, although the
evidence suggests that this process did not take place rapidly.[54] Thus, the
alternative proposal to the one put forward by Locke was not as dubious
as he made it out to be. To understand why these considerations did not
prevail with Locke, leading him instead to defend the existing monetary
standard as sacrosanct, we can benefit from a wider analysis of the
interrelationship between money, politics, and language in his philosophy. In this section I consider his political argument.

As Constantine George Caffentzis has pointed out, Locke's identification of money with silver leads to the conclusion that silver's value in
terms of property corresponds to its weight; the political responsibility
of government to preserve property is paramount and therefore militates against a devaluation, which would unjustly transfer property by
allowing debtors to repay in 'light' or raised values of silver. As Locke
puts it in *Further considerations*, such a plan represents 'a publick failure of
Justice, thus arbitrarily to give one Man's Right and Possession to
another'.[55]

There is no doubt that Locke placed enormous emphasis, especially in
his *Further considerations*, on the defrauding of landlords and creditors
that would occur if a devaluation went forward, and on his particular
interpretation of the property vested in silver. He reasoned that contracts had been executed according to the legal valuation of silver in
which an ounce was worth 5s. 2d. A devalued currency would allow
debtors to repay with lightweight money, in effect, and thereby violate
their contracts.[56] The express duty of government was to uphold property, as he made clear in *Two treatises of government* (1690), which made
tampering with the standard an abuse of power. In case we are in any
doubt about money's status as property and its inclusion within the

---

53. On Locke's inconsistency in relation to deflation, see Douglas Vickers, *Studies in the theory
   of money 1690-1776* (1959; New York, 1968), p.70-72. Constantine George Caffentzis, *Clipped
   coins, abused words, & civil government: John Locke's philosophy of money* (New York, 1989), points
   out that as Locke understood coin, the country would be no poorer or richer by restoring
   the legal weight of the currency (p.40); actual riches consisted of no more than the silver
   itself, which made the assertion of deflation problematic since prices had been inflated by
   artificial values placed on clipped coin.
54. See Kelly, 'General introduction', in *Locke on money*, Table 1 (vol.1, p.112-13).
55. *Further considerations*, in *Locke on money*, vol.2, p.416.
56. Davenant, who opposed devaluation, argued that if such a plan were implemented a law
   should be enacted at the same time to 'break all past Contracts, that relate to Letting land'
   so that landlords could recoup their losses. 'A memorial concerning the coyn of England',
   in *Two manuscripts*, p.24.

category of things that must be secured by the magistrate, Locke made matters clear in a statement in the *Letter concerning toleration* (1689):

> *Civil Interests* I call Life, Liberty, Health, and Indolency of Body; and the Possession of outward Things, such as Money, Lands, Houses, Furniture, and the like. It is the Duty of the Civil Magistrate, by the impartial Execution of equal Laws, to secure unto all the People in general, and to every one of his Subjects in particular, the just Possession of these things belonging to this Life.[57]

Money, like other 'outward things' that formed part of civil interests, unquestionably required the protection of government.

But evidence that Locke himself presents suggests that his premise about contracts being made on the basis of full-weight coin was far from straightforward. He admits in *Further considerations* that 'our clip'd Money retains amongst the People (who know not how to count but by Current Money) a part of its legal value, whist it passes for the satisfaction of legal Contracts, as if it were Lawful Money'. The king was prepared to receive light coin in taxes and 'the Landlord for his Rent',[58] which makes it difficult to allege that any fraud was taking place since the exchange was acceptable to both parties. Locke still insists that these transactions merely amount to treating light money *as if* it were legal.

However, Locke's normative claim about contracts being executed in terms of full-weight coin was much more problematic than he allows. In the first instance, he ignores an important feature of the currency. In fact, in the 1680s the silver content of coins had already depreciated from their full weight by figures ranging from *circa* eleven to nineteen per cent.[59] The process accelerated in the 1690s, but substantial deviation from the standard was already a reality. The more likely scenario was that for some time contracts had priced in the loss of silver. If so, then Locke's revaluation scheme actually defrauded *debtors* by forcing them to repay in full-weight coin, when their agreements had been made on the basis of lighter money.[60] Lowndes clearly believed that since the

---

57. John Locke, *A Letter concerning toleration*, trans. William Popple (London, Awnsham Churchill, 1689), p.6.

58. *Further considerations*, in *Locke on money*, vol.2, p.469.

59. See the figures in Jones, *War and economy*, Table 7.5 (p.232-33). Similar figures are given in Quinn, 'Gold, silver, and the Glorious Revolution', Table 4 (p.481). A higher level of depreciation is reported in sources quoted by Feavearyear, *The Pound sterling*, p.120. See also Gaskill, *Crime and mentalities*, p.186-87. Contemporaries recognised this situation. In a work published posthumously in 1675, Rice Vaughan (d. *c*.1672) noted that silver coin in circulation was lightweight. *A Discourse of coin and coinage*, p.70-72.

60. Henry Layton made this accusation against Locke, complaining that he exercised care to protect the position of creditors and lenders but did not concern himself with the plight of borrowers who in recent years had taken out loans in lightweight coin but would now be forced to repay in heavy money, possibly doubling their financial burden. See

money now 'commonly Applied' in payment of 'Rents, Revenues and Debts' was substantially lightweight, then his proposal imposed no 'imaginary Loss' on creditors; in fact, he would be *adding* silver to the coin used in payments (by devaluing it only by 20 per cent and not by a figure closer to the actual loss of silver content of coins in circulation).[61] The key point is that determining where the property actually lay was a much more complicated question than Locke allowed.[62] More decisively against Locke's view, research by David Fox has shown that an aggrieved creditor would not have been able to enforce a contract in law which demanded repayment in full-weight coin.[63] Since the early seventeenth century (and possibly well before) English legal decisions were based on a nominalist understanding of money not on a valorist one – in other words, the unit of account was what mattered, and unless and until a proclamation or act of Parliament declared otherwise then coin at face value would have to be accepted by a litigant.[64]

The merits of Locke's argument may run into difficulties on this issue, but he held on to the criterion of silver by weight as the object of legal bargains all the same. Caffentzis has emphasised the grounding of Locke's position in his natural law theory as set out in *Two treatises of government*. In Chapter V of the 'Second treatise' ('Of property'), Locke took occasion to explain the origins of money and its transformative effects. The putting of value on gold and silver created the potential for accumulating property since these metals served as an imperishable

---

Observations concerning money and coin (London, Peter Buck, 1697), p.13, noted in Appleby, 'Locke, liberalism, and the natural law of money', p.58.

61. Lowndes, *Report*, p.81. See Kepa Ormazabal, 'Lowndes and Locke on the value of money', *History of political economy* 44:1 (2012), p.157-80 (162). I would add that Lowndes gave Locke a convenient out here by saying that five shillings coined on his proposal 'will and ought to go further' than five *clipped* shillings, due to the extra silver in them (p.81). Thus he conceded that purchasing power depended on silver content rather than the stamp, and it would have been easy for Locke to step in and remark that on his own plan, which 'added' yet more silver to the depleted coins (by returning them to the current legal standard), the purchasing power of coin would be extended further still.

62. Even in the best case scenario where clipping did not occur, hammered coins as well as milled money varied in weight, while wear and tear reduced their silver content, which makes the standard to which Locke appeals notional at best.

63. D. Fox, 'The *Case of Mixt Monies*: confirming nominalism in the common law of monetary obligations', *Cambridge law journal* 70:1 (2011), p.144-74.

64. Fox states, 'Locke was mis-describing the legal effect of money debts as contracts for the delivery of certified quantities of silver. The legally proclaimed values of coin were their essential values for the purpose of discharging debts valued in the money of account' ('The *Case of Mixt Monies*', p.157). Locke's position is closer to the much older tradition of various glossators commenting on the Digest and Code of Justinian. On these authorities, see Wolfgang Ernst, 'The glossators' monetary law', in *The Creation of the ius commune: from Casus to Regula*, ed. John W. Cairns and Paul J. du Plessis (Edinburgh, 2010), p.219-46 (esp.227-36).

store.[65] Where use value alone had once prevailed, accumulation of wealth now became possible; land also rose in value because its productive potential could be translated into a lasting form. According to Locke, consent for these developments occurred in the state of nature. Caffentzis concludes that according to Locke's principles, 'The civil government cannot by its authority create value any more than it can create the consent required for the social contract. (For it is this value and consent that creates civil government.) The function of government is to guard and preserve the foundation of value and consent: silver and property'.[66]

Silver as a store of value would indeed represent property on this account, but is the state really incapable of intervening significantly in these matters? Two features of Locke's argument suggest that it can. First, after noting in the 'Second treatise' that the assignment of value to gold and silver takes place in the state of nature, Locke promptly points out a contrast with the era of civil government: 'in Governments the Laws regulate the right of property, and the possession of land is determined by positive constitutions'.[67] Property may be sacred, but the determination of who holds it is evidently subject to civil legislation. Second, a significant difference exists between money in the state of nature and money as it is configured by governments. Whereas Locke speaks in the 'Second treatise' of gold and silver indiscriminately – both function as a store of value that enables the accumulation of property – he is explicit in his major economic works, *Some considerations* and *Further considerations*, in declaring that only silver counts as the standard of value (as we have seen). Gold is a form of wealth (or 'Treasure' as Locke calls it),[68] but it should not intrude on the unique status of silver because this creates a damaging competition between rival standards. Locke cannot appeal to the state of nature as marking the occasion for this distinction between the two precious metals, so it must belong to the period of government. This makes perfect sense, of course, because he is discussing the role of silver as the unit of account, a position it occupies only by virtue of public authority.[69] The relevance of this is that it evidently affords governments the scope to introduce important changes relating to money, unconstrained by the limited provisions in the state of nature.

65. John Locke, *Two treatises of government*, ed. Peter Laslett (Cambridge, 1988), II.50 (p.301-302). Before that time, interestingly, 'intrinsick value' was equated solely with use value (II.37 [p.294]).
66. Caffentzis, *Clipped coins, abused words, & civil government*, p.107.
67. Locke, *Two treatises*, II.50 (p.302).
68. *Further considerations*, in *Locke on money*, vol.2, p.424.
69. After Locke's death, Newton, as Master of the Mint, would effectively switch England to a gold standard.

As the government establishes the unit of account (and corresponding silver weight and alloy) favouring only one of the two metals agreed as valuable by common consent, it is difficult to see how the argument of the 'Second treatise' on its own would provide an adequate foundation for the principles described in Locke's writings on money. Nor does Locke appear in a strong position to rule out innovation in setting the value of money strictly on the basis of the 'Second treatise'.

In fact, Locke acknowledges the capacity of the state to create value to the extent that it set the Mint price for silver at 5s. 2d. in the time of Elizabeth I. But he confines its current role to providing a stamp to guarantee the weight and fineness of coin. The reason why it cannot intervene any longer is because legal contracts have been made according to the publicly announced valuation, and property is predicated on it.[70] This argument would apply even if the decision to devalue only had internal repercussions. But it clearly gains strength from knowing that such a manipulation (justified potentially on the grounds of 'absolute necessity'[71] under crisis conditions) would add nothing to the purchasing power of coin because the value of silver resides in an internationally accepted standard in which the weight determines the price in exchange.

Money, language and mixed modes

Some crucial philosophical issues come into relief when we consider Locke's account of money in conjunction with his views on language. In particular, money constitutes a 'mixed mode' in Locke's system. Mixed modes draw together ideas, both simple and complex, to form new concepts, but they have no physical referent in the world to stabilise their meaning.[72] Rather, their meaning corresponds to definitions supplied by individual language users who must employ them with care and consistency. Without these words, the richness of our social and intellectual life would be radically diminished, but they suffer from constant threats of abuse, changes of usage and conflicts of interpretation.

Mixed modes constitute an area of potential linguistic instability because individuals have a right to define them according to their own internal archetypes. This entitlement means that the capacity of others to intervene and correct their usage is highly circumscribed if not completely non-existent. According to Caffentzis, Locke's philosophy of money represents an attempt to counter Lowndes's position because

---

70. *Further considerations*, in *Locke on money*, vol.2, p.415.
71. *Further considerations*, in *Locke on money*, vol.2, p.415.
72. In the case of money, pointing to an object like a physical coin would not in itself explain its meaning.

Lowndes would have reduced money to the status of a mixed mode.[73] Lowndes's endorsement of devaluation would shift the accepted definition of money, but Locke's privileging of silver – according to Caffentzis – gives him a way to resist Lowndes. Silver is a substance, and because it is a substance Locke can treat it as resilient against improper manipulation.[74]

Locke's dilemma is really much deeper. We can start with the fact that silver's status as a substance does not in itself transform the situation, for two reasons. Mixed modes, as Locke makes clear, are complexes of ideas and in certain instances they include ideas of substances or substance equivalents.[75] Thus the mere reference to silver is insufficient to avoid the 'reduction' of money to a mixed mode. More to the point, neither Lowndes nor Locke's critics, like Nicholas Barbon, advocated the elimination of silver from the coinage altogether; the contest was over its rating in terms of the unit of account (whether 5s. 2d. per ounce or 6s. 3d.). In this context, Locke was defending silver according to its current legal weight against efforts to introduce an alteration. Locke actually remarked in *Further considerations* that the weight set for the coin in the past was relatively unimportant – it might have been a fifth higher or a fifth lower than at present without making much difference – but it did matter how long the standard had been in place. 'The Harm comes by the change, which unreasonably and unjustly gives away and transfers Mens properties, disorders Trade, Puzzels Accounts, and needs a new Arithmetick to cast up Reckonings, and keep Accounts in'.[76] We have already seen that the 'transfer of property' argument is more contentious than Locke would admit, which makes his case dependent on a number of practical considerations militating against devaluation: the disruptive impact on trade and the 'puzzling' of accounts by requiring new computations.[77] Lowndes had accumulated a series of examples to indicate that changes of valuation in silver had occurred frequently in English history, so Locke is really making an essentially conservative and pragmatic argument rather than one that rests on absolute and incontrovertible principle.

Locke himself draws an instructive analogy between language and money in Book III of the *Essay* where we get a clear sense of his priorities, yet we can also recognise the limited room within his system for

73. Caffentzis, *Clipped coins, abused words, & civil government*, p.105, 114.
74. Caffentzis, *Clipped coins, abused words, & civil government*, p.114-15.
75. Locke is explicit about this in *An Essay concerning human understanding*, ed. Peter H. Nidditch (Oxford, 1975), III.xi.16. Subsequent references are given in the text.
76. *Further considerations*, in *Locke on money*, vol.2, p.463.
77. For an elaborate statement of the proposed new reckonings, see Lowndes's *Report*, p.62-67.

invalidating alternative schemes of language use or monetary theory. He creates a structure in both spheres in which an opposition exists between internally self-regulating systems of meaning and others based on inter-subjective standards or measures of value. Locke's preference for the inter-subjective and external may be obvious, but uncertainty remains about whether he can compel acceptance of his favoured option and invalidate the alternative. In the *Essay*, Locke remarks:

> For Words, especially of Languages already framed, being no Man's private possession, but the common measure of Commerce and Communication, 'tis not for any one, at pleasure, to change the Stamp they are current in; nor alter the *Ideas* they are affixed to; or at least when there is a necessity to do so, he is bound to give notice of it. (III.xi.11)

He positions language as a common possession and words as a system of measurement. His monetary metaphors suggest that changing the stamp, where language and meaning, word and idea, have a settled relationship or currency, is improper. Yet even here Locke acknowledges that circumstances of necessity may require a change, in which case language users have a responsibility to provide notification.

Locke found these principles used against him with considerable irony in a response to his *Essay* by Edward Stillingfleet, his most redoubtable critic, in 1698. Locke had described words as public, not private, and he censured those who changed their 'stamp' at will. Stillingfleet now accused him of doing just that. According to Stillingfleet, Locke's way of philosophising meant that 'our old Words must not now pass in the current Sense; but then it is fit they be *called in*, and *new stampt*, that we may have none but *New milled Words* to talk with'. He positioned Locke as someone who departed from the standard with his novel usages: 'I am utterly against any *Private Mints of Words*; and think those Persons assume too much Authority to themselves, who will not suffer common Words to pass in their general Acceptation; but will set such Bounds and Limits to the Sense of them, as suit best with their own Speculations.'[78] For Stillingfleet, words should pass in their ordinary acceptation, not according to the private fancies of philosophers. On this account, Locke became the figure who departed from the standard and exploited the slippery potential of language for his own ends.

Locke was evidently stung by this remark and came back with his own reply. He parried the 'dazling Metaphor' of a mint and new milled words that Stillingfleet 'delighted' in, partly by treating the issue literally. No word or phrase, through all the changes in the language since Saxon

---

78. Edward Stillingfleet, *The Bishop of Worcester's answer to Mr. Locke's second letter* (London, J[ohn]. H[eptinstall]. for Henry Mortlock, 1698), p.24-25.

times, ever had 'its Authority from the Great Seal, or [was] passed by Act of Parliament', nor did any public mint for words exist. On the contrary, words, he said, 'are offer'd to the Publick by every *private* Man, Coined in his *private Mint*, as he pleases'.[79] The source itself was not important: ''tis the receiving of them by others, their very passing, that gives them their Authority and Currancy'.[80] What makes this remark important – apart from the fact that he contradicts the dictum about not changing the meaning of words in the *Essay* – is that he articulated here the key insight of his opponents in the coinage controversy, namely that what gives meaning to money is precisely its acceptability, conferred on it by the stamp or denomination, which makes it pass as current.[81] Thus, for them, to 'raise' the coin was not objectionable but rather a thoroughly appropriate and conventional course of action.

Locke, however, offered a crucial clarification on the subject of currency lest Stillingfleet (or advocates of devaluation, for that matter) mistake him. Money did indeed circulate by authority on the basis of the stamp provided at the 'publick *Mint*'; but the purpose of the stamp was to vouch 'its intrinsick Worth', that is, in terms of silver. As he concluded: 'This use of the publick Stamp would be lost, if private Men were suffer'd to offer Mony stamp'd by themselves'.[82] In short, he disallowed self-authorisation in the sphere of money. An economy run on its own internal denomination of values would effectively replicate the private minting of coin if it did so without reference to silver content. Something objective and external, intrinsic and inalienable, needed to anchor the situation.

The predicament with respect to money becomes clear when we attend to the implications of the fact that it comes under the category of mixed modes in Locke's analysis of language. Mixed mode terms are especially difficult to police because they depend, ultimately, on definitions supplied and superintended by individuals.[83] Locke calls them 'voluntary Combinations' of ideas which differ from ideas of substances

---

79. *Mr Locke's reply to the Right Reverend the Lord Bishop of Worcester's answer to his second letter* (London, H[annah]. C[lark]. for A. and J. Churchill, 1699), p.129-30. In support of this, Locke quoted apposite lines from Horace's *Ars poetica* (ll. 55-59) to show that among the Romans – jealous of usurpations of public privilege – any changes in the 'signification or credit of any word by publick use' always began in 'some *private Mint*', a point reinforced by *Ars poetica* (ll. 70-72), which showed that '*private Mints of Words* were always Licensed'. Contra Stillingfleet, someone who offered new milled words to the public from his own mint was therefore not 'so bold an Invader of the publick Authority' (p.130-31).

80. *Mr Locke's reply*, p.130.

81. See for example Barbon, *A Discourse concerning coining the new money lighter*, p.34.

82. *Mr Locke's reply*, p.130.

83. On this point see Paul Guyer, 'Locke's philosophy of language', in *The Cambridge companion to Locke*, ed. Vere Chappell (Cambridge, 1994), p.141.

because 'the essence of each Species' is 'made by Men alone, whereof we have no other sensible Standard, existing any where, but the Name it self, or the definition of that Name'. In the end, we have 'nothing else to refer these our *Ideas* of mixed modes to as a Standard, to which we would conform them, but the *Ideas* of those, who are thought to use those Names in their most proper Significations' (II.xxxii.12).[84]

These comments explain a great deal about Locke's approach to his discussion of money. In his prefatory letter to *Further considerations*, Locke remarked on the 'Mysterious Business of Money', bedevilled by 'hard, obscure and doubtful Words, wherewith Men are often misled and mislead others'.[85] Locke clearly wanted to present himself as someone who used words in their 'proper signification', enabling others to rectify their language and thinking about the issue and to 'conform' themselves to his notions accordingly.[86] Consistent with the fact that so many of the key terms under discussion represented mixed modes (like money, coin or interest), Locke concentrated to a large extent on offering definitions.[87] But Locke's guidance in the matter is not philosophically binding. Mixed modes remain 'voluntary collections' precisely because no pattern fixes them; they vary considerably from person to person in the absence of a 'standing rule to regulate themselves and their notions by, in such arbitrary ideas' (III.ix.7).

Locke provides a number of different examples of mixed modes. As Nicholas Jolley observes, they appear to be 'hybrids of natural and non-natural properties, whether normative or institutional'.[88] The majority of them relate to concepts and events whose meaning is partly moral and social. However much they refer to things occurring in the world, their meaning exceeds simple denotative reference. Locke includes words describing moral 'actions', such as murder and sacrilege (III.ix.7), incest and adultery (III.v.3), abstract concepts like justice, cruelty, liberality, gratitude, glory (II.xxxii.10-11) and hypocrisy (II.xxii.2), and what might be called social 'events' such as processions (III.v.13) or triumphs (II.xxii.8).

Money counts as a mixed mode because it likewise includes reference to something that exists physically but whose meaning is not contained or completed by that reference; to understand it fully we would have to take account of its role as a socially instituted practice and its normative

---

84. For discussion of Locke's position on species in this context, see Daniel Carey, 'Locke's species: money and philosophy in the 1690s', *Annals of science* 70:3 (2013), p.357-80.
85. *Further considerations*, in *Locke on money*, vol.2, p.403.
86. Locke comments in the *Essay*, III.xi.11: 'The proper signification and use of Terms is best to be learned from those, who in their Writings and Discourses, appear to have had the clearest Notions, and apply'd to them their Terms with the exactest choice and fitness.'
87. On the advantages and disadvantages of Locke's definitional approach in economic matters, see Vickers, *Studies in the theory of money 1690-1776*, p.52-53, 60.
88. Nicholas Jolley, *Locke: his philosophical thought* (Oxford, 1999), p.159.

function, as Locke does in his discussion. Locke attempts to introduce an unvarying standard that would stabilise the meaning of money through his appeal to silver by weight, but it is not clear that he can limit the definition of the term in such a way as to rule out a different one, in which money was not understood as a fixed quantity of silver but rather as the unit of account, subject to periodic variation – for example, according to the bullion price of silver.

If we consider other examples of mixed modes cited by Locke, specifically moral terminology, an interesting pattern emerges in which Locke searches for an external standard or measure that certifies meaning. Potentially such words would be subject to disputed definitions on Locke's account of mixed modes, but he provides a limit in this case. As Locke puts it in the *Essay*, 'where God, or any other Law-maker, hath defined any Moral Names, there they have made the Essence of that Species to which that Name belongs; and there it is not safe to apply or use them otherwise' (IV.iv.10). The definitions come, then, from an external source; either God or government sets their meaning. In his unpublished essay 'Of ethick in general' (*c.*1689) Locke elaborates on the point that such terms are not subject to the whim of personal definitions: 'these notions or standards of our actions not being Ideas of our own makeing, to which we give names, but depend upon some thing without us & soe not made by us but for us & these are the rules set to our actions by the declard will or laws of another who hath power to punish our aberrations'.[89] The importance for Locke of possessing a determinate, external standard could not be more clear.

Locke's aspiration in the case of money to locate an equivalent fixed standard becomes more intelligible in light of these remarks. On the one hand, he acknowledged that economies could run themselves on the basis of internally adopted names and measures for their currency, that is, as a fiduciary system in which a nominal value is assigned to coins in excess of their silver content. This situation developed in England when clipped coins circulated by tale, that is, according to the face value and not by their weight in silver. They were accepted not only in ordinary commercial transactions,[90] but also, importantly, by the Exchequer in payment of taxes.[91] But as Locke presented it, such a practice ('internal'

---

89. John Locke, 'Of ethick in general', in *Writings on religion*, ed. Victor Nuovo (Oxford, 2002), p.13.
90. See Appleby, 'Locke, liberalism, and the natural law of money', p.46, with references to contemporary sources on this subject.
91. See Locke, 'Guineas', in *Locke on money*, vol.2, p.363-64. Locke maintains that the state's continued acceptance of lightweight coin was responsible for keeping up the internal purchasing power of the depleted currency. Noted by Kelly, 'General introduction', in *Locke on money*, vol.1, p.26.

to the country) was fundamentally mistaken and unsustainable. The operation of an external, independent standard of value becomes clear when we attend to the foreign merchant who exploits the disparity between the face value and actual weight of silver in the coin. This arbitrage opportunity reveals that the standard is not in the possession of England as an individual country to alter as it sees fit but exists independently in an international market. Locke's impulse then is to adhere, above all, to silver as the standard by its weight.

Locke favours not only inter-subjective agreement, but agreements made in reference to a standard or rule. From one perspective, the acceptance of lightweight coin within the English economy would constitute an instance of an agreement made inter-subjectively, but the problem, for Locke, is that this occurs without tying it to an external standard to regulate the situation. We find in a number of other contexts Locke's search for such a standard. For example, in *Two treatises of government*, Locke regards reason as 'the common Rule and Measure', or the 'Rule betwixt Man and Man, and the common bond whereby humane kind is united into one fellowship and societie'.[92] Reason not only provides rules but it also serves as a ruler, a system of measurement which people share between themselves. That is why it creates a 'common bond', a way of bringing disparate human beings into social relationships. Similarly, when Locke tackled the problem of religious enthusiasm in a chapter added to the *Essay* in 1700, he had recourse to two different external standards for evaluating the testimony of those who allege divine inspiration: their claims must either conform to Scripture, which he called 'the written Word of God without [i.e., outside] us', or alternatively, to 'that Standard of Reason which is common to us with all men' (IV.xix.16). As he remarked, if reason were not allowed to test these assertions 'by something extrinsical to the Perswasions themselves; Inspirations and Delusions, Truth and Falshood will have the same Measure, and will not be possible to be distinguished' (IV.xix.14). Locke consolidated his reply to enthusiasm (which he began composing, incidentally, in the midst of the coinage crisis) by arguing that "tis not the strength of our own Perswasions which can by it self give [something] that Stamp' of divine authority (IV.xix.16). When he addressed himself to English coinage he similarly rejected the view that coins could be stamped with a self-authorised value independent of a standard, represented by their silver content.

The continuity in Locke's philosophy in embracing a standard, free from manipulation by individuals, suggests the importance to him of securing a stable reference point and measure for language use, moral

---

92. Locke, *Two treatises of government*, II.11 (p.274), II.172 (p.383).

terms and also money. This explains his strategy on the recoinage question in the midst of reasonable alternative choices. Far from contenting himself with a 'private' system of meaning, Locke struggled to find some way of anchoring usage inter-subjectively. For an economy like England's this meant not succumbing to the temptation of creating 'fictitious' values that might have worked internally but which, once exposed to international exchange, would quickly crumble. The foreign trader, profiting from the situation, had an important lesson to teach an English audience.

The Great Recoinage of 1696: Charles Davenant and monetary theory

CHARLES LARKIN

In 1695 the English currency was in a state of distress and a small number of eminent persons were invited to address the crisis. John Locke and Isaac Newton were among the most prominent members of this distinguished group, which included Sir Christopher Wren, John Wallis, Gilbert Heathcote, John Asgill, Sir Josiah Child and Charles Davenant.[1] Davenant (1656-1714), who provides the focus of this chapter, was a political arithmetician and economic policymaker from 1686 to 1714. His work on the recoinage informs our understanding of the debate and offers an important glimpse into the economic world of the 1690s as it moved from a specie monetary-base driven view of policy to one founded on financial instruments.[2] The recoinage plan put forward by Locke and his supporters (in most if not all its principles) was eventually adopted. Davenant proposed an alternative in two unpublished contributions, 'A memorial concerning the coyn of England' (1695) and 'A memoriall concerning creditt' (1696), which describe the functioning of the English credit system at the cusp of the Financial Revolution.

The Financial Revolution itself is more than just the institutional developments, such as the creation of the Bank of England in 1694, that took place during the last part of the seventeenth century and the early part of the eighteenth century in England.[3] The emergence of new financial instruments fundamentally changed the way that commerce was viewed. The English monetary system was no longer based only on the coins of the realm, but was now something much broader, incorporating paper money, bills of exchange and various financial instruments that underwrote merchants, the military and the state itself.[4]

1. See Kelly, 'General introduction', in *Locke on money*, vol.1, p.25. A selection of the contributions appears in Li, *The Great Recoinage*, p.183-200, 217-36.
2. The monetary base is considered as that part of the money supply that consists solely of notes and coin in circulation. It is sometimes termed high-powered money. Notes during the 1690s would have had several sources, so a precise measure of the monetary base is therefore difficult.
3. Dickson, *The Financial Revolution in England*.
4. This new financial world developed gradually, beginning with the financial transactions that supported the Florentine woollen trade in the fifteenth century. This innovation

The key impetus for these innovations was to enable the state to develop the financial resources necessary to sustain a protracted war with France (the Nine Years' War, 1688-1697).[5]

The economic crisis of the 1690s, caused by related pressures associated with this war and the problem of England's silver coin, which was severely depleted by clipping, had to be addressed by Parliament and the Treasury. Although the Bank of England was the first bank to be designed from the beginning as a financial arm of the state, it was limited in its functions insofar as it lacked the financial capacity to act as a lender of last resort and the legal authority to regulate the monetary sector of the economy. This means that in the 1690s the response to the situation took place through temporary commissions, such as the one served on by Locke, Newton, Davenant and their colleagues.

In 1696, facing these monetary difficulties, England made the fateful decision to recoin all its silver currency. This choice eventually led to the economic policy that created the famed British Gold Standard and subsequently the International Gold Standard. Thus it was a moment of lasting significance. Yet the story behind the recoinage has been told in what can be considered a rather limited way. J. R. McCulloch, the first to describe the importance of this period, in 1856, framed the question of recoinage as a debate between John Locke, Lord Somers, acting on behalf of the king, William Lowndes of the Treasury and Isaac Newton, future Master of the Mint.[6] Despite his giving prominence to these individuals in the debate, all the figures asked to give their advice presented the Lords Justices (the regency council which governed in William III's absence on campaign) with options for improving the monetary situation of England. This chapter will focus primarily on Davenant's contribution, addressed to the Lord Treasurer, Sidney Godolphin, who secured Davenant's participation.[7]

The currency crisis resulted from developments in the international bullion market and institutional neglect, causing such a significant deterioration of silver-based coins in circulation that the state felt that it was forced to respond.[8] As financial instruments became more ad-

---

over time was transformed into the system of finance that drove Venice, Amsterdam and Antwerp.

5. Brewer, *The Sinews of power*; Niall Ferguson, *The Cash nexus: money and power in the modern world, 1700-2000* (London, 2001).

6. J. R. McCulloch, 'Note on the re-coinage of 1696-1699', in *A Select collection of scarce and valuable tracts on money*, ed. J. R. McCulloch (London, 1856), p.261-65. Newton became Warden of the Mint in 1696 and Master in 1700.

7. Kelly, '"Monkey business": Locke's "College" correspondence', p.154.

8. Li, *The Great Recoinage*; Horsefield, *British monetary experiments 1650-1710*; William Shaw, *The History of the currency 1252 to 1894* (London, 1895); William Shaw (ed.), *Select tracts and documents illustrative of English monetary history 1626-1730* (1896; London, 1935).

vanced, and with a greater breadth and depth of institutions to support them, money became much more complex than simply precious metal coins (specie) in circulation. Yet specie still defined money and wealth in the minds of many policymakers and economic thinkers (tantamount to bullionism)[9]. Given this, it was natural for the policy response to the difficulties facing the silver coin of England to be considered from a purely specie point of view. Nonetheless, a solely specie-approach to monetary policy was no longer advisable due to the developments in financial instruments since the 1660s. This chapter will consider the development of monetary theory and policy as it attempted to react to market and institutional developments.

First, I will discuss the monetary system as it existed in 1690s England. This can be broken down into two analytical issues, one being the poor state of silver coin necessitating the recoinage, and the other being the disequilibrium in the price ratio between silver and gold. Second, I will discuss the traditional view of the Locke, Lowndes and Newton debate. Third, I will assess Davenant's role in this debate and his importance in the development of monetary thought. Finally, I will explain some of the effects of the recoinage. While the preoccupation of Enlightenment thinkers with money and political economy is widely recognised, insufficient attention has been given to the recoinage controversy in the 1690s as a crucible for developments in reflection on the nature of credit and the function of the circulating medium.

The institutional context – money and the economy in 1690s England

Today monetary policy is a function of the Central Bank. The policies of the European Central Bank are quite clear, with the predominant model of the Taylor Rule explaining many changes in monetary policy.[10] Despite the numerous financial instruments that make up the money supply, the monetary base or high-powered money is relatively simple to understand and account for in the market. In the early modern period the monetary base was specie – gold and silver – but the bimetallic specie standard proved very difficult to maintain.

9. Bullionism is the confusion of specie money (gold and silver) with the wealth of the nation. The so-called 'mercantilist' authors are commonly associated with confusing bullion with the national wealth. The wealth of a nation comes from its output and in modern terms is described in Keynesian national income terms: Gross Domestic Product/ National Income (Y) = Consumption (C) + Investment (I) + Government Expenditure (G) + the Trade Balance (Exports (X) – Imports (M)).

10. An explanation of the Taylor Rule can be found in Athanasios Orphanides, 'Taylor rules', in *The New Palgrave dictionary of economics*, 2nd edn, ed. Steven N. Durlauf and Lawrence E. Blume, 8 vols (Houndmills, 2008), vol.8, p.200-204.

Monetary systems that are based on specie are significantly different from systems of fiat money now in use.[11] The essential component of a specie standard is that the market price of precious metals is kept at a parity level (or so close to it that transaction costs eliminate profits) vis-à-vis the Mint price of the coin.[12] The public acceptance of coins required that they be fairly consistent in weight, and despite fabrication limitations the coinage was largely adequate. However, in the 1690s, the effects of clipping the coinage had resulted in the specie system being strained as the face value of the coinage did not correspond to the actual metal content. These complications led to the eroding of confidence in the coin and the rising of transaction costs.

As the coinage deteriorated, the ability to judge coins as full weight, genuine or counterfeited became more difficult. Questioning of the validity of the coinage introduced higher transaction costs. Simultaneously it lowered government revenues as coins of low weight were returned to the Treasury for tax purposes. William Lowndes writes in his *Report containing an essay for the amendment of the silver coins* (1695) how the revenues of the Crown had been significantly reduced by lack of bullion.[13]

The English economy, like almost all economies of the late seventeenth century, was intimately linked to its bullion-based currencies. A corruption of the coinage was not only potentially inflationary, but also destructive to the very fabric of the economy and political establishment at large. The coinage problem had its origins in the coin being the monetary base of a specie system. Given that precious metals had a market price, coins could be clipped or shaved and the silver or gold gained could be melted into bullion and sold. Even when clipped, the coin could still circulate, since it would not have been perfectly round or correctly stamped in the first place. This was the basic problem of the 1690s: as the bullion market price of silver rose, there were profits to be made from clipping the coinage. The invention of milling at the edges in

11. The US dollar, UK sterling, the Japanese yen and the euro are the primary examples (in fact all modern currencies, though many small currencies are 'pegged', that is, linked to one of the larger currencies in a *de facto* or *de jure* fashion).
12. The coin would be defined as having a certain precious metal content (measured in carats, like the metal content of modern jewellery, 24 carats indicating purity) and that metal would be mixed with a baser metal such as copper, nickel or tin. The stamp on the coin would ensure that the coin would not have to be assayed upon receipt, since the Mint, by the sovereign stamp, ensured the fineness of the precious metal in the coin. The process of clipping the coin undermined the stamp of the state, since there is obviously *less* precious metal content in the coin. Even the routine process of wear and tear will result in the coin's value coming into question.
13. See the table indicating the deficiency in weight of coin as measured at the Treasury in William Lowndes, *A Report containing an essay for the amendment of the silver coins*, p.159.

1662 had provided some assistance with the problem but coins in this form were not produced in great volumes and were typically hoarded. Thus the continued use of handicraft methods for the fabrication of the coins (as opposed to mechanical devices powered by horses or water-wheels) meant that milling remained of little use. Although milling was designed to prevent clipping, coins produced with minting errors remained in constant circulation and it became difficult to discern clipped coins from coins that were carelessly produced. This enabled the coins to be clipped with little ability to stop the process. As more and more coins were clipped, the face value of the existing body of coins came into question, raising transaction costs. By 1696 over 50 per cent of the precious metal content of the coinage was removed.[14]

This problem becomes even more difficult to solve in a case where there are two precious metals used for money. While England used both gold and silver in the 1690s, it was the silver coin that was being clipped. This was due to the ratio of gold to silver being upset by the high Mint price of gold and the high bullion price of silver. Though this is a simple problem to grasp theoretically, it again is difficult to solve in practice.

In 1696 England was at war with France. The war was largely fought on the Continent, and King William III and his armies required a constant flow of remittances from London. This created arbitrage opportunities. As the specie prices rose and fell on the international bullion markets, individuals could melt down clippings and sell them abroad for money if the price disparity were great enough. An example in the 1690s would be to clip silver coin, melt it into bullion and sell it on the Continent for gold coin, where silver fetched a higher price than in England. This gold coin would then be shipped back to England where the Royal Mint was paying a higher price for gold than other countries. This gold would be sold to the Mint for silver money and the arbitrageur would make a profit. The result would be a drain of silver and an oversupply of gold.

The bimetallic specie standard requires that the Mint price of specie and the bullion market price of specie of both silver and gold should be equal or sufficiently close that transaction and transport costs eliminate all arbitrage profits. If this delicate balance was disturbed between the market to Mint price and the price ratio of silver to gold, it could result in the coined currency being altered for profit-making purposes (that is, if gold's Mint price rises and silver's bullion price rises, this would result in gold flowing into the Mint and being coined and silver coinage leaving circulation to be sold on the bullion markets). This would typically involve clipping the coin (or in extreme cases actually fully melting down coins), thereby debasing the monetary standard. Such a scenario would

14. Jones, *War and economy in the age of William III and Marlborough.*

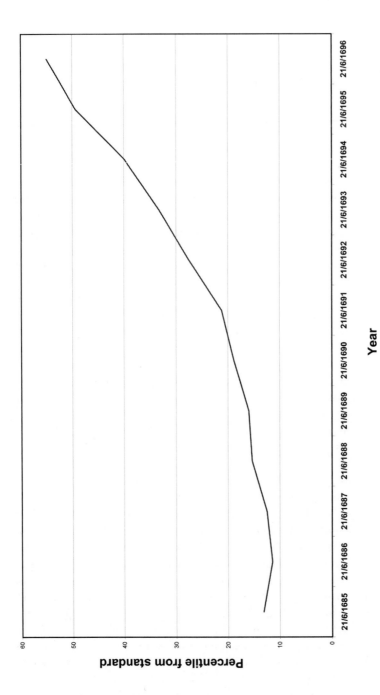

Figure 1: Deficiency of silver metal content.

have debilitating effects on the economy, resulting from rising trans-action costs and reduced liquidity as the face value of the coin came into question and more specie left the monetary base.[15]

The coinage problems in 1696 provide an example of this type of imbalance. Dutch silver had a higher bullion price than the English Royal Mint's price for silver. This caused silver to flow out of England into Holland to gain the arbitrage profit. England, on the other hand, had a very high Mint price for gold. Continental gold bullion (paid to the English sellers for their silver bullion) was imported into England and sold to the Royal Mint. The result of this was that silver coinage became scarce and gold coinage became plentiful.

Thus there was an added incentive to clip the silver coin and export it as bullion abroad. Clipping the coin resulted in a problem for the economy at large as it undermined the face value of the coin, increasing transaction costs of doing business. Second, it was debilitating to the collection of taxes to fund the war, as remittances required full-weight (unclipped) coin. William Lowndes in his submission to Parliament on the state of the coin in England found that the weight of the coin entering the Treasury from tax collection was almost half what it should have been. As seen in Figures 1, 2 and 3 (p.88, p.90, p.91), the fiscal situation was quite poor. As England exported more specie to pay remittances and incurred more foreign denominated debt the economy came under greater and greater stress.

The corruption of the coinage made covering the cost of remittances extremely difficult.[16] The problem of the coin rapidly became not just economic but one of military logistics, as funds to supply William's army were being slowed by monetary constraints in England. The war with Louis XIV was at a stalemate: any weakness, financial or otherwise, could result in the Anglo-Dutch alliance being defeated. William could not afford this and the Commission's brief was to find a rapid solution to the problem.

Clipped coinage and silver outflows together created a liquidity problem for the economy. As Thomas Sargent and François Velde, and Angela Redish have found, until the advent of the steam press and low cost methods of coin and paper money production, small change was a scarce commodity.[17] The silver outflow only made this problem worse in England. Between 1694 and 1696, silver's bullion price rose, resulting in silver coins being clipped and the clippings melted and sold on the

15. For further information on this monetary system see Angela Redish, *Bimetallism: an economic and historical analysis* (Cambridge, 2000).
16. Lowndes, *Report containing an essay for the amendment of the silver coins*, p.87-90.
17. Sargent and Velde, *The Big problem of small change*; and Redish, *Bimetallism*.

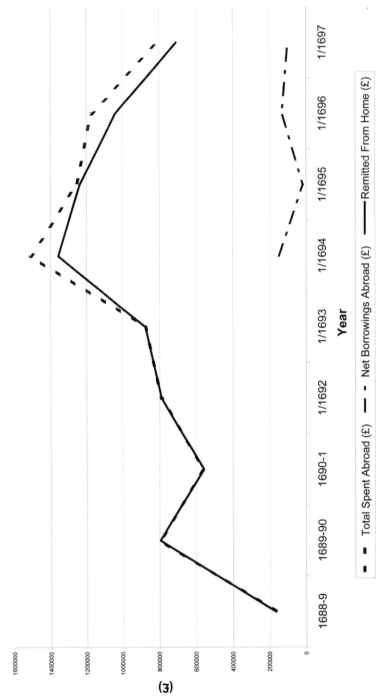

Figure 2: English remittances to troops and allies abroad, 1688-1697.

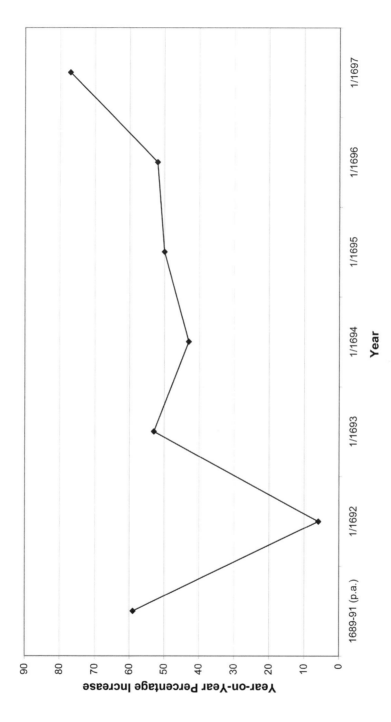

Figure 3: Borrowings.

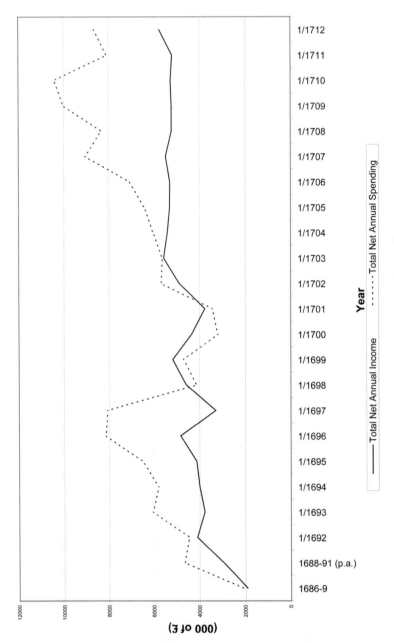

Figure 4: Government income and expenditure.

bullion market. As this process of clipping expanded, the quantity of small denomination coins was reduced (both in the sense that they were lighter post clipping, and because more and more of them were being melted outright into bullion), and a liquidity problem emerged. Sargent and Velde state that the liquidity problem at the small-denomination end of the market increased transaction costs and made transactions between individuals more difficult.

The question of the Recoinage was framed within this economic context. The Commission existed to find a solution to a problem that was obviously becoming an economic, political and military liability. Money to most persons (and Locke states this explicitly in *Some considerations of the consequences of the lowering of interest, and raising the value of money* (1692)) was silver coin. Gold was also in circulation, but as a high denomination coin (30s. in mid-1695) it was used by few individuals, similar to a €500 note today.[18] In order to find a solution to the looming remittance problem and the liquidity crisis facing the economy, Lowndes, Locke, Newton, Davenant and others were asked to find a quick method of correction.

The proposals varied greatly. Within the structure of a specie standard, one possibility was to change the weight of the coin by increasing or decreasing metal content. A second potential solution was to change the face value of the coin and maintain the present metal content. Locke desired to bring the coinage back to its original face value and metal content. This was consistent with his social contract philosophy – the state had an obligation to maintain property, and this property included coinage. Lowndes proposed a considerable devaluation as a method of finding a rapid solution. Davenant, drawing on his experience as an economic policymaker as one of the commissioners for excise and his expertise in political arithmetic, was behind the idea of maintaining the status quo and supporting the expansion of England's credit system. In his two manuscripts, 'A memorial concerning the coyn of England' (1695) and 'A memoriall concerning creditt' (1696), which were rediscovered and edited by Abbot Payson Usher in 1942, Davenant outlines the idea of an economy that does not require a perfectly functioning specie system to survive. In doing so, Davenant provides a view of the beginnings of the Financial Revolution in late seventeenth-century England, and in this description he outlines the importance of credit in the monetary system. His input into the policy discussion on Recoinage was not accepted, but it enriched the debate and confirmed his position as an important contributor to the origins of the Classical School of Economics.[19]

18. See Sargent and Velde, *The Big problem of small change*, for more on this topic.
19. To quote Keynes: '"The classical Economists" was a name invented by Marx to cover

Specie-focused policy – the debate between
Locke and Lowndes

The position put forth by Lowndes, speaking on behalf of the Treasury, was that devaluation of the coin was by far the best course of action for the Crown, maintaining the face value of the coin but establishing a much lower precious metal content. The breakdown, due to clipping, of the linkage between the intrinsic and extrinsic values of the coin is at the heart of the problems facing England's money in the 1690s. Lowndes's proposal did attempt to correct this problem, and by bringing the face value into line with the current (much reduced) metal content by law he expected the problem of silver outflows and gold inflows to stop.

Lowndes set out his ideas and those of the Treasury principally in his *Report* (dated 12 September 1695).[20] The *Report*, which argued its case in part by offering a history of English currency since the time of William the Conqueror, drew the conclusion that the English silver coinage should be devalued by 25 per cent. The nominal value (that is, extrinsic value) of the Crown piece would be raised from 5s. to 6s. 3d. and all other silver coinage in proportion. As silver coins would now have a higher face value, or Mint price, the incentive to sell silver bullion would be eliminated. This was a course of action that would solve some of the immediate problems facing the Crown, but not the long-term questions, such as the bimetallic ratio.

Lowndes began his discussion by stating that the standard fineness of the coin should be maintained. This statement prepares the ground for his solution of devaluation. The devaluation would be considered sizeable even by modern standards. He explains his rationale in this way:

Ricardo and James Mill and their *predecessors*, that is to say for the founders of the theory which culminated in the Ricardian economics. I have become accustomed, perhaps perpetrating a solecism, to include in "the classical school" the *followers* of Ricardo, those, that is to say, who adopted and perfected the theory of the Ricardian economics, including (for example) J. S. Mill, Edgeworth and Prof. Pigou' (John Maynard Keynes, *The General theory of employment, interest, and money* (New York, 1936), p.3) [original emphasis].

20. Research by Patrick Kelly ('General introduction', in *Locke on money*) indicates that the Chancellor of the Exchequer at the time, Charles Montague, was responsible for commissioning this work. Montague was Chancellor for the entire Recoinage and was the sponsor of the Recoinage Acts in Parliament. The basis for this assertion is the similarity of the Lowndes report with the Fourteen Resolutions of the Scobell Committee. Montague was the moving spirit behind these points and a fervent supporter of devaluation; he attempted to press for a resolution of Parliament in spring 1695 with the support of Godolphin. The political machinations of the time, most especially the desire of the king to maintain the monetary standard, and the price of reconciliation between the Montague and Wharton faction and the Shrewsbury and Somers faction following a leadership challenge, meant that the devaluation proposal had to be abandoned.

The Value of the Silver in the Coin ought to be Raised to the Foot to Six Shillings Three Pence in every Crown, because the Price of Standard Silver in Bullion is Risen (from divers necessary and unnecessary Causes, producing at length a great scarcity thereof in *England*) to Six Shillings Five Pence an Ounce: This Reason (which I humbly conceive will appear irrefragable) is grounded chiefly upon a Truth so Apparent, that it may well be compared to an Axiom even in Mathematical Reasoning, to wit, *That whensoever the Extrinsick Value of Silver in the Coin had been, or shall be less than the price of Silver in Bullion, the Coin hath been, and will be Melted down.* [original emphasis][21]

Despite the logical position that if the price of bullion is higher than the face value of the coin, bullion will be exported (be it in the form of clippings from coins or in bars of silver) his devaluation was too radical for the Parliament to adopt.[22] The problem was that Lowndes's plan would have resulted in the removal of silver from the monetary system, as there were no provisions in his plans to alter the gold to silver ratio or to reduce the fineness of the specie. Silver was considered to be the true currency of England; gold was secondary.

There were errors in Lowndes's analysis of the benefits of the devaluation of the silver currency. One of the most striking of these errors, and, interestingly, one that continues to this day, was that he viewed devaluation as a panacea for international payments problems. Lowndes stated: 'It is hoped that the Exchange to *Holland*, (which by the way had risen a little of late) may by the Success of some good Designs on Foot (though the War should continue) be kept at a stand, at least from falling much lower.'[23] He further defended his position by stating that there was a

21. Lowndes, *Report containing an essay for the amendment of the silver coins*, p.38.
22. The question of its reasonableness as a monetary policy must also be addressed. Lowndes's proposal was effectively a devaluation of the currency. As modern economists are aware, the policy of devaluation has long-run negative welfare effects, even if there are some positive effects to creating a temporary, artificial competitive advantage. Lowndes accepted that a *de facto* devaluation of sterling had occurred as a result of the loss of silver content of coins in circulation through clipping. Horsefield, *British monetary experiments*, and Li, *The Great Recoinage*, both address this question within the context of financial instruments and policy debate. The alternative, to restore the silver content of the currency to face value, would set in motion a process of deflation. Deflation also has welfare implications. In welfare terms, a devaluation typically results in domestic inflation, improved short-run external competitiveness, and an increase in the debt burden on firms and individuals that have borrowed in foreign currency. Inflation results in the decrease in the burdens on domestic currency borrowers at the expense of lenders. Those that hold foreign currency loans are placed under extreme stress and may be faced with the need to restructure debt or default. The impact is that it benefits domestic borrowers. Following a deflationary course of action benefits lenders at the cost of borrowers. Deflation also dampens consumption and begins to encourage a vicious cycle of thrift that slows credit and economic growth. Such welfare considerations were not mentioned in such clear terms but the relative impact of the state of the coin was a cause of concern for lenders. Davenant expands this discussion to include liquidity considerations.
23. Lowndes, *Report containing an essay for the amendment of the silver coins*, p.72-73.

distinct need for a reliable base of specie for the smooth running of the domestic economy. Though devaluations had been used in the past, the scale of the devaluation in the Lowndes proposal was radical, in the sense that a 25 per cent devaluation was unprecedented. But his *Report* was also insightful, in that it provided a corpus of monetary history of England to inform his side of the debate. Locke worked diligently to discredit the proposal, and eventually won the day.

Locke and Lowndes shared a common vision despite their different approaches to the recoinage; they both saw silver as the true money of England and gold as a distant second. They also both believed that the monetary system needed to be grounded in specie.

Locke felt that since silver was paramount, it was the link between the intrinsic and extrinsic values of the coin that required the greatest defence. This reflects his understanding of the currency system both philosophically and empirically. He was resolutely against the idea of devaluation and had powerful support from King William as well as friends such as Lord Somers and Sir William Trumbull. (Somers was one of the principal members of the Whig administration and an ardent opponent of the devaluation proposal put forward by Lowndes.) Locke was also driven by his ideas on property and social contract. For Locke, the state had a responsibility to its citizens to provide a sound currency. In debasing the currency, the state would effectively renege on its responsibility to ensure that property (which was defined as money in this situation) be maintained to the standard that the citizenry expected, that is, its true weight and measure. The state's role in the production of money was to issue a stamp of value that served at the same time as a statement guaranteeing that the extrinsic and intrinsic value of the coin coincided with what the Royal Mint specified in production. The state ensured that the silver content of the coin was equal to its face value; Locke therefore felt that the debased coin must be returned to its original intrinsic value, as that was the promise made by the stamp of value. This entailed recoining according to the existing standard.

Locke apparently had difficulty reconciling the guinea situation with contemporary problems of the *de facto* bimetallic currency. The *de jure* currency of England was silver. Locke approaches this problem from the point of view that *only* silver exists as legal tender. This complicates his analysis and causes him to reject the interplay between gold and silver in international markets.[24]

Arbitrage opportunities created by the war had allowed for a complex market to develop between silver, gold and bills of exchange. It was clear that silver was leaving the country at an alarming rate. Lacking in Locke's

24. Kelly, 'General introduction', in *Locke on money*.

analysis was the price-specie-flow mechanism: the price-specie-flow-mechanism is a long-run adjustment mechanism for the effects of specie exports and imports. An excess of imported goods results in specie exports in the short run. This loss of specie causes the money supply of the country to be reduced. The reduced money supply causes a reduction in the price level. This conclusion follows from an early version of the quantity theory of money. The theory had its origin in the Spanish authors in the mid-1500s and the School of Salamanca, so would have been readily accessible in the late seventeenth century.[25]

The Quantity Theory[26] holds that with a lower quantity of money, consumption will be reduced (given that money supply must equal money demand), but with unchanged levels of output of goods and services prices are lower. The reduction of prices as a result of the outflow of specie is the key to the long-run adjustment mechanism. The lower prices subsequently result in the increase in exports, as the home country gains a competitive price advantage. Additionally, there will be a reduction in the level of imports as they become less competitive vis-à-vis domestically produced output. With the combination of cheaper domestic goods and more expensive imports (reducing demand), the result was less foreign exchange demanded at each spot rate. This system would bring about the natural adjustment of a country's price level and specie level as a result of specie imports and exports.[27] Though Locke did understand the concept of the quantity Theory of Money he did not link it to the price-specie-flow mechanism. Such a link would not be made until Richard Cantillon's *Essai sur la nature du commerce en général* (1755; composed between 1728 and 1730) and David Hume's *Political discourses* (1752).[28] Implementation of this theory would have been revolutionary in the late seventeenth century since it represented a stark departure from the balance of trade theory that specie inflows via a constant balance of payment surplus were desirable.

Locke's economic epistemology is another potential pitfall in his analysis. When Locke expanded upon his position that the coin should be restored to its original state at the expense of the public he made clear that silver was the true currency of England:

25. See Bernard W. Dempsey, 'The historical emergence of quantity theory', *Quarterly journal of economics* 50:1 (1935), p.174-84; and Earl J. Hamilton, *American treasure and the price revolution in Spain, 1501-1650* (Cambridge, MA, 1934) for more discussion of the formation of the Quantity Theory. On Locke's understanding of the theory, see Kelly, 'General introduction', in *Locke on money*, vol.1, p.84-86.

26. Here described in modern terms of MV = PY [money supply × the velocity of money = price level × national output (GDP)].

27. Charles Poor Kindleberger, *International economics*, 3rd edn (Homewood, IL, 1963).

28. Murphy, *The Genesis of macroeconomics*, p.89, 105-12.

Money is the *measure* of Commerce, and of the rate of everything, and therefore *ought to be kept (as all other measures) as steady and invariable as may be.* But this cannot be, if your *Money* be made *of two Metals*, whose proportion, and consequently whose price, constantly varies in respect of one another. *Silver*, for many Reasons, is the *fittest* of all Metals to be this measure, and therefore generally made use of for Money. But then it is very unfit and inconvenient, that *Gold*, or any other metal, should be made current Legal Money, at a standing settled Rate.[29] [original emphasis]

Locke had decided that the best course of action for the government was to maintain the standard of money and restore the clipped and worn money to its original status. The maintenance of parity between the seal and the actual intrinsic content was the key to running a viable monetary system, as Locke emphasised:

Only this I will confidently affirm, *That it is the Interest of every Country, that all current Money of it should be of one and the same Metal; That the several Species should be all of the same Alloy, and none of a baser mixture: And that the Standard once thus settled, should be Inviolably and Immutably kept to perpetuity.* For whenever that is alter'd upon what pretence soever, the Publick will lose by it.[30] [original emphasis]

The focus on the scholastic concept of intrinsic value was vitally important to Locke's understanding of money. Intrinsic value is a passive power, a quality which enables one object to affect another, whereas exchange value is a relative quality and can only be considered secondary.[31]

Money exists through common consent; it is part of that compact whereby society has allowed itself to be *regulated* by the law of nature. The maintenance of money's extrinsic and intrinsic value is part of that regulation. This is not a literal contract or in any way explicit, but a tacit agreement. As Kelly observes:

Consent, for Locke, is concurrence in a mutually beneficial course of action, arising as it were in the form of spontaneous intellectual assent once the advantages of an arrangement become apparent. In the *Second Treatise* men consent to the adoption of money, since by permitting the accumulation of the surplus product and facilitating the division of labour money makes possible a more advanced standard of living.[32]

---

29. Locke, *Some considerations*, in *Locke on money*, vol.1, p.326.
30. Locke, *Some considerations*, p.329.
31. To look at it from the point of view of pure scholastic thought, the *valor impositus* on silver comes from its function as the medium of exchange; the *valor intrinsicus* of money is the product of the common consent of all to acknowledge this medium of barter or exchange universally. Locke firmly plants himself in the category of a neo-scholastic natural law theorist by embracing this epistemological construct.
32. Kelly, 'General introduction', in *Locke on money*, vol.1, p.87-88.

Locke's understanding of money is only part of his approach to the Recoinage. While Lowndes presents the historically proven and traditional policy option of devaluation (though on a scale never attempted before, which was the ultimate downfall of his proposal), Locke abandons this familiar and somewhat pragmatic approach. Locke differs from Davenant, however, in so far as he does not understand the importance of credit to the English monetary system and consequently to the economy. In addition, Locke's methodology is highly distinctive. Economics, for Locke, exists as part of the field of *praktikê* and not as part of a Baconian experimental science. *Praktikê* he defined in the *Essay* as

> The Skill of Right applying our own Powers and Actions, for the Attainment of Things good and useful. The most considerable under this Head, is *Ethicks*, which is the seeking out those Rules, and Measures of humane Actions, which lead to Happiness, and the means to practise them. The end of this is not bare Speculation, and the Knowledge of Truth; but Right, and a Conduct suitable to it.[33]

Davenant's analysis, however, is the product of 'Political Arithmetick', a fundamentally different epistemological method. Davenant viewed things from a Baconian, pragmatic perspective. He followed the empirical tradition that he had learned from the writings of Sir William Petty (who is frequently cited in Davenant's published works) but he was also willing to innovate in science, even to introduce intellectual inconsistencies, subject to the pragmatic needs of the moment, something that was made clear during his time as a Commissioner of Excise. This is not to deny the empiricism that is the cornerstone of Locke's thought, but this empiricism is applied in the context of an understanding of economic issues which retains a more traditional mercantilist and scholastic character.

Locke's proposal won out, therefore maintaining the *de facto* bimetallic system and bringing the coin back to full weight through the recoinage. The system remained legally bimetallic but over time market forces and transactions preference caused a shift from silver to gold as being the dominant monetary coin, something that none of the participants expected. It was left to Newton to compensate for this shift during his various roles at the Mint.[34] The problem was created by Locke's resolute position that the linkages between what money passes for in the market and what the silver content of that money was would ensure the

---

33. Locke, *An Essay concerning human understanding*, IV.xxi.3 (p.720).
34. This was because Newton was the only member of the advisory body to be placed in a position where he could significantly alter monetary affairs. Newton was made Warden in 1696 and Master in 1700. As Master of the Mint he changed the price of the guinea many times over his tenure to stop the outflow of silver coin.

functioning of England's monetary system. His final thoughts related to the devaluation supported by Lowndes's proposal, where he predicted that Lowndes's recommendation would result in the complete elimination of all the milled money of England as well as the already corrupted stamped money.

A swift solution to the problem of recoinage was extremely important to King William, as political and military considerations were pressing. The decision was made to recoin at the existing legal standard. The advice of the Lords close to the king was that recoinage should not be undertaken as a royal decree but under the auspices of Parliament. In the king's speech on 23 November 1695, he mentioned the ill state of the coin and the need to expedite a solution to this problem, though he gave no indication of the precise plan.[35] The Commons began to formulate a general position on recoinage during the month of December. By the 10th of December a resolution was proposed that followed the spirit of Locke's thinking, if not all of his provisions.

In January 1696, Godolphin took over the Commons' proposal and the Earl of Rochester essentially created a new bill.[36] The first coinage bill was passed on 13 January 1696: the 'Act for Remedying the Ill State of the Coin of the Kingdom' took effect on 17 January 1696.[37] It was decided that by the 4th of May clipped coins would cease to be considered legal tender, and by the 24th of June they would no longer be acceptable as a form of payment for taxes.

The proposals of both Locke and Lowndes had explicitly ignored the problem of gold and the bimetallic question. The action or rather inaction of Parliament and the ensuing confusion over the gold situation made this issue even plainer. In a letter signed 22 September 1698, Locke wrote to the Lords Justices as a Commissioner of Trade, imploring the government to solve the continuing problem of guineas which he had neglected in his proposal on recoining silver. The recommendation was to lower the guinea to 21s. 6d. from the current price of 22s., although this was not enacted until 1699 on the advice of Newton, when the Bank of England refused guineas at 22s.

Following this painful monetary contraction, Newton had come to the understanding that as long as the price of silver bullion was higher than that of the legal rate of the coinage there would be no natural inflow of silver into the Mint, because it would be more profitable to sell silver on the bullion market. According to Ming-Hsun Li:

---

35. Henry Horwitz, *Parliament, policy and politics in the reign of William III.*
36. Rose, *England in the 1690s: revolution, religion and war.* Rochester was another powerful member of the Tories.
37. Li, *The Great Recoinage.*

It appears that gold had been over-valued all along since the recoinage of 1696-1699 [....] Although the price of guineas was reduced to 21s 6d apiece during 1699-1717 and to 21s thereafter, the overvaluation of gold still existed in England up to 1760 at least. In 1702 and 1717 Newton had observed that while a guinea was only worth 20s 5d to 20s 6d on the European Continent, it was accepted in England at no less than 21s 6d, the difference being 4 to 5 per cent. It was therefore most advantageous to ship gold to England and to bring it to the mint to be coined.[38]

The further instructions left to the Commons by King William and Lord Somers were to consider the price of guineas, whose price fluctuations were already resulting in exchange rate difficulties and a scarcity of small denomination coinage.[39] At 30s. per guinea and with the price rising rapidly there was an acute need for the overvaluation of gold to be resolved. 'The Act for taking off the Obligation and Incouragement for Coining Guineas for a certain time therein mentioned' (5 March 1696) addressed the problem by immediately lowering the price of guineas from 28s. to 26s., subsequently to 25s. and finally to 22s.

Ultimately, Locke's errors and the confusion over the future value of guineas were problems solved by Newton. The outflow of silver coins continued after the recoinage was completed, while gold inflows and the coining of gold increased. The value of the guinea to the public was 21s. 6d. and it was received at that rate for all payments. McCulloch suggests that

It appears, however, from the best attainable information, that this valuation of 21s. 6d. was really equivalent to a premium of 10d. in favour of the Guinea, it being worth only about 20s. 8d. of the new Coins. And in consequence of this marked, though unintentional preference of Gold, it was used, to the exclusion of silver, in all considerable payments; while the new Coins of the latter, being not only under-valued but in excess, immediately began to be exported.[40]

The premium on bullion still drew silver out of the country and the ratio between silver and gold had not been modified sufficiently to ensure the retention of a bimetallic system. Newton, unlike Locke, felt that passing

38. Li, *The Great Recoinage*, p.167. Future commentators stated that the real problem was a lack of devaluation of silver. The reduction in the price of the guinea was politically problematic since it was disadvantageous to important parts of the state apparatus, due to the main holders of gold coin being the government and the Bank of England. In addition England was engaged in several wars between Spain and France between 1702 and 1721, which further complicated this monetary correction. 'Both [Richard] Cantillon and [John] Conduit suggest that the right course to take should have been a devaluation of the silver standard. The latter recommended that the devaluation be about 4 per cent' (Li, *The Great Recoinage*, p.172).

39. Horwitz, *Parliament, policy and politics in the reign of William III*.

40. McCulloch, 'Note on the re-coinage of 1696-1699', p.263-64.

the clipped silver coin by weight was an impractical approach. His position fell between those of Locke and Lowndes: he proposed that the coin be brought back to its mandated full weight in stages.

By 1702, 21s. 6d. was an overvaluation of the guinea by 9d. (3.49 per cent) and had resulted in a surplus of gold coinage over the previous thirteen years.[41] Newton realised the mistakes of the past and to rectify the situation he made a final decision on the future of sterling late in his tenure at the Mint – a Proclamation issued on the reduction of the value of the guinea from 21s. 6d. to 21s. (a fall of 2.32 per cent), and a final gold-to-silver ratio decided at 1:15.212 gold to silver. Still, Newton's final intervention to correct the errors of 1696 was for nought. There was still an overvaluation of the guinea of 4d. or 1.58 per cent. Sterling became *de facto* mono-metallic from 1717 to 1816, with the silver stock of coinage becoming entirely secondary coins, well-worn and of little importance.[42] The Earl of Liverpool legalised this situation with the recoinage at the close of the eighteenth century.

Davenant and a financial-instrument based point of view

Charles Davenant, an advanced economic thinker and astute prac-titioner of the method of political arithmetic, had many ideas on recoinage and monetary theory that deserve exploration. His relative neglect in the context of the debate on recoinage has been due to a number of factors. Waddell has commented on Davenant's reputation as a Tory 'pen for hire' and his extreme desire to regain the patronage and power he lost with the end of the Stuart monarchy. This has traditionally caused some concern about his integrity.[43]

Davenant's two statements to the Commission were not printed at the time, and the main trace of the debate in his better-known works appears in his continued references to the Recoinage and insistence that it was a detrimental decision for many years after 1696. Though Davenant's logic is not always watertight, he is still able to demonstrate to the reader clear conclusions, based on a method of analysis that helps to draw them together.

Unlike Lowndes, Davenant approached the questions of the Great Recoinage from the point of view of deductive science. Davenant first set out his theories on money and credit and then proceeded to provide an answer to the questions that were posed to him by Lord Godolphin. This section of the chapter will address Davenant's background and will set

41. Li, *The Great Recoinage*.
42. McCulloch, 'Note on the re-coinage of 1696-1699', p.264.
43. D. Waddell, 'Charles Davenant (1656-1714) – a biographical sketch', *Economic history review* 11:2 (1958), p.279-88.

out his monetary theories and their influence on his approach to the problem of recoinage.

Davenant, it is important to note, was from the first against the idea of the recoinage and felt that devaluation would only result in inflation and a worsening of the exchange rate with Holland. Unlike both Locke and Lowndes, he was of the mind that the recoinage should be delayed as long as possible, at least until the completion of the war, and should under no circumstances be rectified by devaluation.[44] His most pressing concern was that the war with France made England vulnerable; to engage in such a risky action as a comprehensive recoinage would only result in disaster. He believed that as the problem had existed for so long a delay until the end of the war would not significantly exacerbate the situation. The central precept to which Davenant continuously returned was the need for a base of money in which there was confidence, but the draft horse of the monetary system of England was to be found, he insisted, in credit, not bullion. Credit was more flexible and able to absorb real and monetary sector shocks better than specie.

Davenant was one of the bridging individuals in the history of economic thought. He was a student of the school of 'Political Arithmetick'. This was a method of analysis designed to assist in the running of government and the creation of policy. Davenant subscribed to the philosophy of Sir William Petty, whose *Political Arithmetick* appeared posthumously in 1690 (only five years prior to Davenant's writing on the state of the coinage and money of England), after having been developed and practised much earlier in the 1670s.[45]

Davenant was a civil servant during the period of 1686 to 1714, though this was not a continuous position. The law had never provided him with a sufficient income so that in 1678 he became a commissioner of excise.[46] Davenant was elected MP during the reign of James II for St Ives in Cornwall in 1685. He was later returned to Parliament as MP for Great Bedwyn in 1698 and again in 1700.

The Glorious Revolution of 1688 resulted in his removal from the commissioners of excise. As his career in government came to a dramatic halt his own personal fortune, derived from his father, Sir William Davenant, Poet Laureate and general in the army of Charles I, was

---

44. Charles Davenant, 'A memorial concerning the coyn of England' (1695), in *Two manuscripts by Charles Davenant*, p.28-29 and 62-63.

45. The most notable exercise in this mathematical method came in the Davenant-King Law of Demand, which was one of the first formulations of the law of demand in the history of economic thought.

46. Julian Hoppit, 'Davenant, Charles (1656-1714)', in *Oxford dictionary of national biography* (Oxford, 2004); D. A. G. Waddell, 'The career and writings of Charles Davenant (1656–1714)' (Doctoral dissertation, University of Oxford, 1954).

obliterated. A personal loan of £30,000 made by Davenant (and two partners) to the Crown was defaulted on, resulting in monetary difficulties that plagued Davenant for the rest of his life.[47]

On the accession of Queen Anne in 1702, Davenant returned to political favour and negotiated through the Lord Treasurer Godolphin in 1703 a post as secretary on the Commission on the Union of Scotland and England and a diplomatic post in Frankfurt for his son Henry.[48] In June 1703 he obtained the lucrative position of Inspector-General of Exports and Imports. Davenant took this to be a position of advisor to the English Government on economic policy and his *Report to the commissioner for public accounts* (1712) includes a statement of the most economically favourable policies to develop trade and increase the wealth of the nation in addition to the comprehensive and well-devised statistics developed by Davenant.

In his position as a policymaker in the 1680s Davenant distinguished himself as an economist. Though he took many of his ideas from figures like Petty, he advanced upon their methods of political arithmetic and modelling. Davenant designed his theories and policies around his circular model of wealth and trade, his theory of credit, and his statistical analysis of the *de facto* economy,[49] which will be elaborated below. As a practitioner he not only illustrated his ideas but also developed and refined them, ultimately using them to form economic policy and advice for England.[50]

Unlike Locke or Lowndes, Davenant saw money not as bullion but as credit.[51] One finds through inspection of Davenant's writings that, although he recognised the importance of accumulating specie as a concern of the state, he differed from the mercantilist view by arguing that this was not the principal aim of economic activity.[52] Davenant began his discussion with a statement that the position of public credit had consistently improved since 1667.[53] He further developed the credit

---

47. Hoppit, 'Davenant, Charles (1656-1714)'; Waddell, 'The career and writings of Charles Davenant (1656-1714)'.
48. Waddell, 'The career and writings of Charles Davenant (1656-1714)'.
49. Brewer, *The Sinews of power*, p.78.
50. Davenant's financial problems and political concerns resulted in a life-long friendship with James Brydges (the future first Duke of Chandos). This friendship would be an important part of his access to the government and involvement in policy decisions. See Godfrey Davies and Marjorie Scofield, 'Letters of Charles Davenant', *Huntington library quarterly* 4:3 (1941), p.309-42.
51. This is not immediately apparent from his works, where he tends to be less than consistent.
52. The main reason for his interest in specie may be a direct result of the economics of war, when gold and silver were the only medium of exchange (true even as recently as World War II).
53. An interesting note comes in his comment that trade between nations took place even in the absence of specie, an indication of the move of the economy towards a more fiat-based

system as a circulating system of flows, much like Sir William Petty's description,[54] but noted that there were failures preventing the circulation of credit throughout the whole of England.

Davenant, like Petty, considered money to be an important factor in the economic system and understood that lack of access to money, or for that matter credit, damaged the economy, led to unemployment and impaired the nation's productivity.[55] Credit was needed as trade expanded and England was exposed to competition from the rest of world. The core principles that guided Davenant's ideas came from an interpretation of money as something that is used as a means of exchange rather than as the definition of wealth. He made this point of view clear in the following statement:

> for gold and silver are the measure of wealth, all things [are] dear or cheap as that sort of wealth is wanted or abounding. And in all countries of the world where money is rare and scarce, the product of the earth is cheap; as for instance, in Scotland, Ireland, the Northern Kingdoms, Germany and most parts of Asia and America [....][56]

Davenant's theory of money was steeped in the concept of monetary flows, originating through the wealth that trade provides (which he calls the foundation of credit). Money was part of the economy. It was the measure of the economy; it was a source of growth by providing a basis for credit, but contrary to the claims of Smith and others in their

---

monetary system. He outlined that those who desire to charge high rates of interest are doing damage to the public good and to the government. Due to this failure of policy, the monetary system must be regulated in such a manner that the government finds it easy to gain access to credit and at a reasonable rate of interest.

54. Sir William Petty outlines his views on money and the circular flow of income model in his *Quantulumcunque concerning money* (1682) published in 1695 (London, A. and J. Churchill). Petty's ideas, techniques and data are repeatedly cited by Davenant, elaborated upon and used as part of his arguments relating to trade and monetary policy as well as assisting in his work on the law of demand. See Murphy, *The Genesis of macroeconomics*, p.36-40, for a brief summary of Petty's monetary thought. On Davenant in comparison to Petty see Schumpeter, *History of economic analysis*, p.212-13; Luigi Cossa, *An Introduction to the study of political economy*, trans. Louis Dyer (London, 1893); John Creedy, 'On the King-Davenant "Law" of demand', *Scottish journal of political economy* 33:3 (1986), p.193-212; A. M. Endres, 'The functions of numerical data in the writings of Graunt, Petty, and Davenant', *History of political economy* 17:2 (1985), p.245-64; Endres, 'The King-Davenant "law" in classical economics', *History of political economy* 19:4 (1987), p.621-38; Lars Magnusson, *Mercantilism: the shaping of an economic language* (London, 1994); Miles Ogborn, 'The capacities of the state: Charles Davenant and the management of the Excise, 1683-1698', *Journal of historical geography* 24:3 (1998), p.289-312; Stephen M. Stigler, 'Jevons on the King-Davenant law of demand: a simple resolution of a historical puzzle', *History of political economy* 26:2 (1994), p.185-91; and Aspromourgos, *On the origins of classical economics*.

55. Murphy, *The Genesis of macroeconomics*, p.38-39.

56. Charles Davenant, *The Political and commercial works of that celebrated writer Charles D'Avenant, LL.D.*, ed. Sir Charles Whitworth, 5 vols (London, R. Horsfield *et al.*, 1771), vol.1, p.160.

polemics against the mercantilists, it was not the economy itself. Davenant took the idea of monetary flows and brought it to a new level by applying concepts based upon a theory formulated from observations and political arithmetic to outline feasible policy recommendations.

Money, to Davenant, was a tool of economic growth and a signal of stability. The use of economic factors (fiscal policy, monetary policy, currency, taxation) as tools in policy-making was a giant leap from previous English authors in the direction of modern economics. Prior writers used money as the object of policy; the law was the agent and catalyst of change. Davenant went further – he used money and credit as the agent and catalyst of change for the objective of expanding output and employment. Davenant went beyond Petty by applying theory to reality directly, by trying to make a scientific study of the natural laws of the market and then to use these laws to change the final outcome of the market over time. By understanding the actual mechanisms that govern the economy he took a radical new step in policy-making away from the earlier position of legally imposing order on 'disorder'. The old method of coinage laws and the proposal of Lowndes and Locke attempted to alter the monetary system without regard to the context within which it functioned. Davenant advocated using the forces of natural law to bring a more favourable order[57] on what he knew to be either an unfavourable order (high unemployment/low output) or legally induced 'disorder' (laws governing commerce distorting the market mechanism towards an inefficient outcome).

Though Davenant's work in its published form illustrates an astute mind, the place where his monetary ideas find their most coherent and powerful representation is in his unpublished manuscripts, 'A memorial concerning the coyn of England' (1695) and 'A memoriall concerning creditt' (1696). Davenant's work relies heavily on the use of biological analogy, a key aspect in the terminology of later authors in the description of the economy and the monetary system. His views on money and trade in the 'Coyn' manuscript show how Davenant understood the nature of a money economy and that money is not the wealth of the economy but only a part of the general system, yet an integral and necessary part of that system. In his comments on the problems with the specie money of England during the Nine Years' War he made an important connection between the actions of trade and the sustaining of a stable economy and political establishment:

57. Or to be more economically correct – Pareto-optimal equilibrium. There can exist multiple equilibria; one can be low unemployment with high output and the alternative equilibrium point can have high unemployment/low output. Both exist and both can be stable; it is just that one does not want to exist in the high unemployment/low output equilibrium.

This Commerce of Money does not only arise from Trade but often from Warr, When a Prince has an Army to pay in Forreign Parts, that does require greater Summs then the Balance of Trade with that Countrey can answere, Trade and Money are in their Nature so mixed one with the other that it Seems Impossible to consider them apart with any Effect conducive to those Ends proposed by the Government

Trade and Money are like Blood and Serum, which tho Different Juices, yet runn through the veines mingled together

And this present Corruption of our Coyn is like a dangerous Ulcer in the Body Politick which is never to be thoroughly Cured by applying Remedies to the Part, but by mending the whole Mass of Blood which is corrupted.[58]

The basic idea of a price-specie-flow mechanism is hinted at in the works of Davenant but not fully outlined or described. Davenant, though successful in splitting money from specie and in his descriptions of money substitutes, does not go so far as to develop this theory. In addition, he outlined the principal concerns and uses of money, although he does fall into some of the commonly held errors of his day. This may reflect some of his focus on practicality of application, something he developed during his time as a commissioner for excise.[59]

Davenant stated his monetary assumptions as his introduction to his response to Godolphin's questions on recoinage:

That the Importers who cannot Satisfie their Ballance with Commodities must do it with Money or with Bullion

That if the Merchant can get more by sending money or Bullion then Goods he will make his Returnes by Money or Bullion.

That Gold and Silver tho. they are the measures of Trade are themselves but a Commodity

That the Nation which is not Superior in Trade can never Sett the price upon Bullion [....]

That whatever price any Countrey setts upon its own Coine it will be Esteemed with other Nations but at its Intrinsick value

That in the Naturall Course of Trade each Commodity will find its price.[60]

Davenant illustrates the separation between the basic commodity concerns of specie flows and the overall economic well-being of the state, insofar as he does not see bullion movements as explicitly damaging:

Tis true that gold and silver tho' they are the Measures of Trade, are themselves but a Commoditye, and may be Trafficted and exported, either Coined or uncoined like other Commodityes without any Damage to ye publick.

But this holds onely in Countreys which have means of inviting Bullion to

58. Davenant, 'A memorial concerning the coyn of England', in *Two manuscripts*, p.8.
59. Ogborn, 'The capacities of the state: Charles Davenant and the management of the Excise, 1683-1698'.
60. Davenant, 'A memorial concerning the coyn of England', in *Two manuscripts*, p.12-13.

them, as well as occasions to carry it abroad, and cannot hold in that Countrey which carryes it out only to pay a dead loss, or a dead expence.[61]

Davenant stated that, despite all concerns, trade was still the most important aspect of the English economy. He made the important statement of the need for trade and that England existed as a 'price-taker': a small open economy in late seventeenth-century Europe. As he maintained: 'we are a Tradeing Nation, all our Interests are closely linked with the Interests of Trade. The product of our Land must be guided and ruled by our Forreign Commerce, Almost whatever our Soile produces must be valued here at the Price which the Luxury or Necessities of other Nations put upon it.'[62]

The question that Davenant attempted to address in his manuscript on 'Coyn' was whether the effects of an edict-driven change in the value of the coin would be felt by the economy of England. Davenant stated that this change would have no effect. He saw the adjustment as natural and near instantaneous, resulting in no disruption of the flow of trade. The intrinsic value of the specie would remain the same, an ounce for an ounce, whereas the change in the extrinsic value of the currency would be dealt with by changes in the prices of commodities. 'No man can buy by one valuation of Mony, and sell by another.'[63] He expanded:

> And since all these things are so necessary to the Being or well being of Life, they must be had at what ever Rate they Cost: Nor can Law Interpose in this Matter with any effect, for in the Naturall Course of Trade, Each Commodity will find it's [sic] Price.[64]

Davenant had a well-developed view of the market for capital, both physical and liquid, in addition to his hypotheses on the nature of specie flows. The rental rate of capital, or the price of that capital, was illustrated in a quite 'classical' fashion. The idea of the tenant-landlord relationship as described by Davenant has much in common with Cantillon's view of the circular flow of income.[65] In addition to utilising his own calculations to make his point throughout this section of 'Coyn', Davenant clearly illustrated the rationale behind the hiring of capital and the letting of capital, which was similar to the Marshallian descrip-

61. Davenant, 'A memorial concerning the coyn of England', p.39.
62. Davenant, 'A memorial concerning the coyn of England', p.17.
63. Davenant, 'A memorial concerning the coyn of England', p.21.
64. Davenant, 'A memorial concerning the coyn of England', p.21.
65. This idea, with its extension to trade between nations, finds its clearest statement in 'Coyn': 'For as We have Observed before, The Commerce of Money by Exchange goes in a Circle, and a Debt in Flanders may be paid by Commodities sold in Turkey or in Spain. And if this Trade had proceeded in its usual Course, We might during this War have kept a great part of Our Money still in the Kingdome' (Davenant, 'A memorial concerning the coyn of England', p.58).

tion of investment. The only modern aspect lacking in his description of the functioning of the rental rate of capital was his exclusion of risk:

> In Letting Land for Rent, as in other Bargains the mutall [sic] worth of each, are compar'd together and Consider'd. The Tenant takes the Land because it brings forth such Commodities, as in the Market will yield him such a price, wherewith to sustain himself and to Pay his Rent. The Landlord lets it because it yields such Commodities, and he thinks with such Rent to Maintain his usuall Port, and manner of Liveing.[66]

Davenant used this definition to illustrate that the rental price of capital cannot be dictated by law, most especially if that rate is below the market clearing equilibrium, as no individual will knowingly take a loss on their capital or produce even if the state attempts to compel them to do so by force. Should the state impose such controls it would be detrimental to the overall economy as it would precipitate a breakdown in the economic and legal contracts between tenants and landlords. This breakdown would spread from the real economy to the monetary economy, notably credit markets.

Credit is extremely important in Davenant's economics. He argues 'That the greatest part of Trade, both fforreigne and Domestick, is allwayes carryd on by Creditt'.[67] This position on the creation of credit was further developed by Davenant when he came to describe the state of English commerce, as the transactions were performed via credit and bills of exchange:

> as the publick deals with the people by giving Tallyes or Bank Bills, for Goods and Money, so the people deal among themselves by assigning or transferring to one another those or such like securityes, which have no existence but in Credit, publick or private by which the bulk of Trade is carryed on; The Species rarely Intervening; Just the same thing being practiced in Holland, and in severall States of Italy.
>
> These sort of securityes are already equall to the running Cash, and if the supplyes to be given hereafter consist (as tis likely they will) in Credit upon remote ffonds they will far surmount it and grow the governing Wealth of ye Kingdome. If soe, and that they continue to hold their present esteeme there is no reason to believe, but by their help the domestick Trade of the Nation may be carry'd on in whatsoever condition the Coyne remaine.[68]

In 'A memoriall concerning creditt', Davenant again provided a more developed look at his theory of credit than what is afforded in his later works. This piece has two very useful aspects for students of Davenant or of any late seventeenth-century monetary theorist – first, it provides a portrait of the functions of credit and money and, second, it includes an

66. Davenant, 'A memorial concerning the coyn of England', p.23.
67. Davenant, 'A memorial concerning the coyn of England', p.25.
68. Davenant, 'A memorial concerning the coyn of England', p.45.

invaluable description of the functioning of the wartime English monetary sector. The necessity of money (be it paper or specie) and credit in
the economy was clearly stated by Davenant, and was similar to the view
of money that Hume would later take in his *Political discourses* (1752).[69]
Hume felt that money oils the wheels of commerce and that without it
commerce would grind to a halt. Petty stated that it was the fat on the
body-politick.[70] In his mention of the necessity of money and credit
Davenant continued with this line of thought:

> If there should be a want of Species, and of Credit, there must happen a
> generall decay in the fforraigne Trade and Manufactures of the Kingdom.
> The spring and originall of all our Commerce abroad, arises from the
> Materialls that our soil produces, and those Commodityes which from
> thence are manufactured. If the stock of 30. Millions formerly running in
> Credit be much diminished, and if the species of mony be likewise wanting
> to carry on the Minuter business in ye Market, and for payment of labouring
> men and Artificers, the Manufactures of the Nation must stand still, and if
> We have not Goods to export, we must expect no Importation, but such as
> shall be destructive to us. Numbers of men, Industry, Advantagious situation,
> Good ports, skill in Maritime affaires, with a good Annuall Income from the
> Earth, are true and lasting Riches to a Country; But to put a Value upon all
> this, and to give life and motion to the whole, there must be a quick stock
> running among the people, and alwayes where that stock increases, the
> Nation growes strong and powerfull; and where it visibly decayes, that decay
> is generally attended wth publick Ruin.[71]

Davenant had bridged the gap between the 'mercantilist' and 'classical'
world in this statement.[72] He later stated in his manuscript that the
government should not default on its loans, as this would undermine
confidence in the credit of England.[73] If the public were to lose faith in
the sustainability of the debt held by the state, then the entire system
would 'sink all Sort of Credit, and with it's [sic] ruine, hazard the very
being of the Government'.[74] This was similar to the predictions of

---

69. 'Money is not, properly speaking, one of the subjects of commerce; but only the
    instrument which men have agreed upon to facilitate the exchange of one commodity
    for another. 'Tis none of the wheels of trade: 'Tis the oil, which renders the motion of the
    wheels more smooth and easy.' David Hume, 'Of money', in *Political discourses* (Edinburgh,
    R. Fleming for A. Kincaid and A. Donaldson, 1752), p.41.
70. William Petty, 'Verbum sapienti' [1664], in *The Economic writings of Sir William Petty*, ed.
    Charles Henry Hull, 2 vols (Cambridge, 1899), vol.1, p.113. See also Desmedt, 'Money in
    the "Body-Politick"', for further discussion.
71. Davenant, 'A memoriall concerning creditt', in *Two manuscripts*, p.72.
72. Davenant took a view that was different from most of his contemporaries. He felt that the
    economy was governed by natural law, and that to intervene in the economy would be a
    contravention of the natural order. This was a policy that later became the hallmark of
    Adam Smith.
73. Davenant, 'A memoriall concerning creditt', p.77-79.
74. Davenant, 'A memoriall concerning creditt', p.78.

modern macroeconomists with respect to unsustainable debt in developing countries (and developed countries as well). If there is a falter in confidence capital flight takes place. This results in a credit crunch that undermines the real economy as well as destroying the monetary sector.[75]

Davenant's final monetary innovation was his outline of how a money-substitute system would work in England, under the auspices of the early notes of credit and bills of exchange that initiated the development of the paper money system. As Davenant's concern at the time was the maintenance of the paper money system that flourished in wartime England, he outlined the functioning of that system. Seeing the specie standard slowly being corrupted over the 1690s, Davenant observed that economic activity continued due to the ability of financial instruments to provide liquidity and capital in the circumstances of a compromised, traditional specie system. Davenant's view of this new monetary system, which was to become the foundation of the Financial Revolution, is summed up as follows:

> To make those Credits pass Currently from hand to hand (and so become in the nature of a new Stock in the Nation, where with the People may trans-act their Bargaines) they must be Secured upon Solid and Substantiall Fonds, In the Same Manner for Debts hereafter to be contracted, Such Talleys as are proposed to go in Payment of the Army, the Fleet, Ordnance, Civil List or for Stores, or for repayment of Money acctually to be lent should be placed upon Such Fonds as will every Year Clear off the Interest, and a certaine proportion of the Principall. If Such Fonds can be found out and Sett afoot the Tallies Struck thereupon will be as so much new Stock in ye Kingdome and because they carry Interest with them, may perhaps in time be more esteemed then money it selfe, and if Tallies can obtaine their former Esteeme and value, Paper Credit of all kinds will revive of Course.[76]

Providing one of the earliest and clearest statements on the nature of paper money functioning in an economy, Davenant showed himself to be a master theorist. The interesting part of this statement on the monetary system is that Davenant described an empirical reality; paper credit became an integral part of the monetary system as specie flowed out of England and alternative methods were required to engage in efficient trade. The Bank of England was still quite new and lacked the ability to weather a significant crisis. It became more and more apparent that the costs of the war with France were finally beginning to compromise England's economic viability. As Dickson has shown, the structures that were to dictate eighteenth-century finance were already in

75. Ben S. Bernanke and Cara C. Lown, 'The credit crunch', *Brookings papers on economic activity* 1991:2 (1991), p.205-47.
76. Davenant, 'A memoriall concerning creditt', p.97.

place.[77] Davenant perceived these new structures, and his views on credit and the monetary sector were descriptions of the first creaking motions of this new engine of economic growth.

The considerable treatment of Davenant's monetary theory above is by no means complete; what has been described are the basic concepts that he had regarding money and credit in England in the 1690s. Davenant was able to see how new developments in public finance and private credit markets had changed the economy of England. New fiscal and financial instruments were altering the character of the established specie-driven system and therefore changing the internal dynamics. Gold and silver coin were very important but only as a monetary base, and money's definition was expanding to include other media. Davenant's proposals enable the reader to understand this development process and provide insights into why his proposal was rejected and Locke's accepted. The movement away from a pure specie system to a modern financial architecture was difficult for policymakers to understand. Davenant was one of the of the few who did, though the influences of political patronage and a lack of understanding of monetary economics resulted in his ideas being considered only by Lord Godolphin, who, despite his rank in the Commons, was not in favour with the king.

The aftermath – institutional difficulty and economic collapse

The monetary effects of the demonetisation of clipped/lightweight coins in 1696 were not limited to the problems of the transactions demand for money. Demand for hard cash rose as a crisis of confidence gripped depositors in the Bank of England.[78] Already weakened by losses due to the exchange rate depreciation of 1695 and the management of Continental remittances to William's army since 1694, the Bank had little hope of sustaining itself in the presence of a considerable bank run. The demonetisation had destroyed all the remaining confidence in English coinage and depositors of the Bank of England demanded that their bills be honoured in specie.[79] The result was a classic credit crunch – as the demand for specie payments outstripped supply the run became a self-

---

77. Dickson, *Financial Revolution*.
78. Horwitz, *Parliament, policy and politics in the reign of William III*.
79. As Davenant had stated in his recommendations, the base of credit was specie, but that specie was now being altered, causing a crisis in confidence. The Bank of England's bank run was a result of the recoinage, as depositors attempted to exchange the notes of the Bank for hard currency. The ensuing credit crunch was consistent with Davenant's predictions.

fulfilling prophecy and the Bank of England was faced with collapse. Rose states:

> On 6 May, two days after the final demonetization of the clipped coin, a run on the Bank by cash-hungry depositors jeopardized its liquidity. Nor was the Treasury able to help the Bank in its hour of need, for the state's cash reserves remained locked up in the demonetized clipped coinage. Faced with the prospect of imminent financial collapse, the Bank swallowed a bitter pill. In early July it reneged upon its commitments to Continental creditors. At a stroke, confidence in English credit evaporated, leaving the army paymaster in Flanders penniless. Not until October was the Bank able to resume remittances to the army, and then only thanks to a substantial loan from a worried Dutch government.[80]

As the monetary sector continued to contract violently, the bimetallic situation further worsened. The price of the guinea had risen too high and was causing additional stress on the Mint and on the monetary and real sectors of the economy. Newton, as Warden of the Mint, was responsible for the maintenance of the bimetallic standard; therefore he proposed a series of price changes to keep the newly coined silver from leaving England. Newton proposed a price ceiling on guineas fixed at 22s. This legislative action was to become only one subject of the great outcry in the government over the mishandling of the recoinage. As the king left for war in the spring of 1696 the country was in the grip of a liquidity crisis (one of the first 'modern' economic crises) and the inadequacy of the measures implemented by the government to retain the old standard was becoming rapidly apparent. As seen in Figures 1-4 (p.88, p.90-92) the state of the national accounts, borrowings and coinage was deteriorating. Borrowing supported the war effort by 1695, revenues were falling short and the intrinsic metal content of the coinage had fallen to new lows. This grave situation was to be remedied by the Recoinage Act, but as William departed, it was more than apparent that the worst was yet to come. The Mint was terribly unprepared for the Act and Newton had only £700,000 of new milled coin on hand to reissue as £4.7 million had been brought to the Exchequer at that stage for transfer.[81] The lack of preparation was the result of a prior policy of staff reduction at the Royal Mint in London when mass quantities of new coinage were not required.[82]

The monetary collapse that ensued not only damaged the credibility of the Bank of England, but also resulted in the creation of new systems of

---

80. Rose, *England in the 1690s*, p.141.
81. Horwitz, *Parliament, policy and politics in the reign of William III*.
82. Mint facilities were still recovering from the disruptions of the republican period and the lack of additional mints beyond the Tower. (Li, *The Great Recoinage*, p.68-69, 135, 177.)

payment.[83] Bank of England notes had ceased to be a viable alternative to specie as the Bank defaulted and its bills were being heavily discounted. One statement by a correspondent of the Duke of Beaufort is telling on how grave the situation in London had become by 5 May 1696:

> at this time all money is refused unless it be new money or very broad [that is, heavy or full weight], of which there is but little stirring. I was forced to enter my name in a book to pay for my dinner, for they choose rather to trust than take even passable sixpences. The Exchequer has a double guard these two days, and the common people begin to grow a little mutinous.[84]

The failure of silver as a medium of exchange left a gap that was filled by the guinea. It became the principal transactions currency during the recoinage, despite the fact that it was an extremely high denomination of anywhere between 22s. and 30s. in 1696. The demand on guineas and gold completely changed the market for silver bullion in England, with the price of gold and the price of guineas rising rapidly. This resulted in a gold inflow into England and a continued silver outflow. The eventual effect of this preference for gold was that it would take over the position of silver as the principal currency of England. Gold inflows to England dominated the concerns of the dealers on the Continent and guineas rapidly became the standard means of payment. By 1717, when Newton was still Master of the Mint and Davenant and Locke were both long dead, the quantity of silver coinage had all been reduced to small change. Newton continued to alter the Mint price of the guinea throughout his administration due to its persistent overvaluation. The problem was not fully rectified until his final reduction of the Mint price of the guinea to 21s. By this time the quantity of gold coined was far outstripping that of silver, and in 1717, £15,186 of gold was coined and only £948 of silver.[85] There still existed a slight overvaluation of the guinea and as stated above only small denomination silver remained in circulation. This *de facto* status of gold as the readily accepted means of exchange and store of value created a mono-metallic standard, the famous British Gold Standard.

The Great Recoinage was an example of early modern economic policy at work. The objective of the Great Recoinage was to correct the problems of a debauched silver specie coin system. England's clipping and subsequent recoinage enabled it to continue with the war, and gain a

---

83. This was important since it undermined confidence in Bank of England notes, causing the domestic bank run and eliminating the trust that foreign lenders had in the institution, as the risk profile of the Bank of England rose following default.

84. Letter of 5 May 1696, quoted in Horwitz, *Parliament, policy and politics in the reign of William III*, p.180.

85. Li, *The Great Recoinage*, p.148.

respectable peace with France. The importance of the Great Recoinage is that it advanced economic theory and strengthened the monetary system and institutions of England by forcing the major thinkers in England to find novel solutions to a potentially devastating monetary problem and, despite the initially inadequate solution, the gold standard was created and enabled a stable currency to exist until the French Revolutionary Wars and Napoleonic era.

The recoinage had been ill thought out and the proposals of both Locke and Lowndes were destined to result in an outflow of silver. The recommendation of devaluation submitted by Lowndes was rejected and the silver-specie focused policy of Locke was adopted. This resulted in an overvaluation of guineas and continuing arbitrage of silver bullion out of the country. The monetary effects of the Bank of England default were substantial: England's economy calcified for most of 1696, resulting in massive unemployment, poverty and civil unrest.[86]

To treat the recoinage as only the product of Lowndes's and Locke's minds is insufficient. They led the debate, with Newton left to execute the plans of the government. Newton's errors in the valuation of guineas gave England a *de facto* gold standard. The monetary ideas that were created and expanded upon during the recoinage formed the foundations of eighteenth-century monetary thought. Lord Godolphin, who usually is thought to have considered only the opinions of Locke, Lowndes and Newton, also gave some attention to the ideas of many of those on the Commission, such as Charles Davenant. The Bank of England, paper credit, bills of exchange, the role of silver and gold, the need for specie, and the ideas of free trade and the favourable balance of trade were all put to the test in these writings. As sterling was recreated as a mono-metallic gold-based currency and the Bank of England regained the respect and power it lost in the 1696 default, monetary theory advanced. Crises have the ability to strengthen surviving institutions and encourage innovative financial instruments. England's financial system was able to weather the wars of the early eighteenth century due to the discipline and lessons of this difficult period. In the area of economic theory, the writings of Davenant began a debate on the future of paper credit and economics that would continue throughout the eighteenth and nineteenth centuries. Later publications like Daniel Defoe's periodical *Mercator* (1713-1714) and Charles King's *British merchant* (1721) discuss Davenant's contributions on the theory and measurement of trade and money. In the nineteenth century, Whewell, Jevons and Wicksteed drew heavily on Davenant's data and theories (though a

---

86. Horwitz, *Parliament, policy and politics in the reign of William III*.

thought must be given to Gregory King, whose data Davenant used for his writings).[87]

The ideas and commentary of Davenant illustrate the rapid development of monetary theory at the time of the Recoinage. The Recoinage served the purpose of correcting the problem of clipping but inadvertently created the British Gold Standard. Davenant's work on coin and credit makes all the more apparent the depth of the 'Financial Revolution' described by Dickson and casts light on the importance of the Great Recoinage in the history of Britain, the development of sterling and the history of economic thought.

87. William Whewell, 'Mathematical exposition of some doctrines of political economy, second memoir' [1850], in *Mathematical exposition of some doctrines of political economy* (New York, 1971); W. Stanley Jevons, *The Theory of political economy* (London, 1871); Philip H. Wicksteed, 'On certain passages in Jevons' theory of political economy', *Quarterly journal of economics* 3:3 (1889), p.293-314. See also Schumpeter, *History of economic analysis*, p.209-15; Stigler, 'Jevons on the King-Davenant law of demand'; G. Udney Yule, 'Crop production and price: a note on Gregory King's law', *Journal of the Royal Statistical Society* 78 (1915), p.296-98; Endres, 'The functions of numerical data in the writings of Graunt, Petty, and Davenant'; Endres, 'The King-Davenant "law" in classical economics'; and Creedy, 'On the King-Davenant "law" of demand'.

'Mysterious politicks': land, credit and Commonwealth political economy, 1656-1722[1]

JUSTIN CHAMPION

> A man is a spirit raised by the magic of nature; if
> she does not stand safe, and so that she may set
> him to some good and useful work, he spits fire,
> and blows up castles; for where there is life, there
> must be motion or work; and the work of idle-
> ness is mischief, but the work of industry is
> health.
>
> James Harrington, *Oceana* (1656)

Republican historiographies: land, credit, and liberty

The debate about the nature and political identity of post-regicidal
republicanism in England continues. Ever since the powerful intervention of J. G. A. Pocock in *The Machiavellian moment*, the intellectual
genealogy and subsequent ideological afterlife of the canon of commonwealth writers of the 1650s (Milton, Harrington, Sidney, Ludlow) has
been shaped by the tradition derived from the Florentine civic humanism most readily exemplified in Machiavelli's *Discorsi*.[2] The intellectual
authority of James Harrington's understanding of the relationship between political power and the distribution of property drew from these
intellectual sources. Harrington's legacy, Pocock claimed, ensured that
post-Restoration republicans ('neo-Harringtonians') were concerned
with the corrupting qualities of institutions such as standing armies,
the court and still later the agencies of central government, rather than
the tyranny of kings. Civic virtue was threatened by the corrosive

1. I am very grateful to Daniel Carey for suggesting this topic to me, and indeed for his
   patience and advice in the preparation of the contribution. Sam Barnish, Nicola Pullin,
   Richard Alston, Steve Pincus, Mike Braddick, Mark Jenner and Andrew Seltzer all offered
   helpful suggestions and insights.
2. J. G. A. Pocock, *Virtue, commerce, and history: essays on political thought and history, chiefly in the
   eighteenth century* (Cambridge, 1985); J. G. A. Pocock (ed.), *The Political works of James
   Harrington* (Cambridge, 1977); Pocock, *The Machiavellian moment*; Pocock, 'Early modern
   capitalism: the Augustan perception', in *Feudalism, capitalism and beyond*, ed. Eugene
   Kamenka and R. S. Neale (London, 1975), p.62-83.

influence of mercenaries, placemen and commercial luxury, rather than the illegal passions of tyranny. Succinctly, Pocock described the republican project (especially after 1689) as a language rather than a programme, one aimed at cultivating communal virtue, in place of an armed and independent republic. Developing these themes, subsequent historians have stressed the idiomatic quality of republican discourses in place of any commitment to fundamental reform of monarchical institutions. In adapting to the political conditions of a vibrant and robust Protestant monarchy, the development of new and powerful financial interests and an increasingly effective and functional state apparatus, 'republicanism' became a respectable and backward-looking ideology of a landed and virtuous political elite. Captured by oppositional elements in the 1720s and 1730s, commonwealth ideology became an element of the politics of nostalgia, rather than a practical political prospectus. As Jonathan Scott has put it, there was a 'retreat from political centre stage, a retreat from the struggle to run the country'.[3]

Recently this vision of the successful transformation of republican ideology from regicidal concerns to civic politeness has been challenged from a number of quarters. Examining the anticlerical dimensions of the later commonwealth writers suggests that the commitment to fighting institutional tyranny and mental slavery were still a potential threat to the status quo of the confessional state. Destroying the legal dominance of priestcraft, establishing a measure of civic toleration and reforming the theological foundations of the universities, were key practical programmes advanced by serious politicians after 1689.[4] Republicans like John Toland, the third Earl of Shaftesbury, Viscount Robert Molesworth and earls Stanhope and Sunderland adapted their commonwealth principles to the pressing demands of modern politics. A further substantive engagement with the intellectual afterlife of republicanism has been advanced by Steve Pincus who suggests that the canonical texts of men like Harrington and Milton were fundamentally out of kilter with progressive elements within political and economic culture.[5] Put simply,

3. Jonathan Scott, *England's troubles: seventeenth-century English political instability in European context* (Cambridge, 2000), p.495; see also J. G. A. Pocock (ed.), *The Varieties of British political thought, 1500-1800* (Cambridge, 1993); and essays by Blair Worden in *Republicanism, liberty, and commercial society, 1649-1776*, ed. David Wootton (Stanford, CA, 1994): 'Marchamont Nedham and the beginnings of English republicanism, 1649-1656', p.45-81; 'Harrington's "Oceana": origins and aftermath, 1651-1660', p.111-38; 'Republicanism and the Restoration, 1660-1683', p.139-93; 'James Harrington and "The Commonwealth of Oceana", 1656', p.82-110.

4. This is the broad theme of my *Republican learning: John Toland and the crisis of Christian culture, 1696-1722* (Manchester, 2003).

5. See Steve Pincus, 'Neither Machiavellian moment nor possessive individualism: commercial society and the defenders of the English commonwealth'. See also Mark Jurdjevic,

the agrarian dimension of republican ideas of political economy meant that men like Harrington (and those influenced by him) were incapable of coming to terms with the new dynamic commercial society. Accepting Pocock's description of Harrington's celebration of agrarian values, but disputing Harrington's centrality in commonwealth thinking, Pincus claims that a cadre of other 'commonwealth' thinkers 'invented a new ideology applicable to a commercial society, an ideology that valued wealth but also the common good'. The aristocratic idiom of the backward-looking civil history of property was at odds with developing institutions of commerce, credit, finance and state-building. The forward-looking writers, who perceived the fundamental transformations in the nature of the economy, argued not simply that there was a nexus between land and political power, but more broadly between 'wealth' and power: this was an insight 'that constituted a new political economy'.[6]

Pincus's engagement is vigorous and provoking: it certainly raises some important issues regarding the pragmatic dimensions and reception of Harringtonian ideology which have not been addressed by the current historiography. At the core of his arguments are two related claims: that Harrington and like-minded men misconceived the agrarian nature of the society they lived in ('They thought they lived in an agrarian society, which, they believed, should always remain an agrarian society'), and that the society they misunderstood was a 'newly emerging commercial society'.[7] Both arguments are plausible, but open to debate. The question of the commercial nature of seventeenth-century English society and of contemporary perceptions of this transformation is complex.[8] The connection between economic change, contemporary awareness of change and the historical accounts of that process is not immediately obvious. Despite some important work on economic ideology, on the development of fiscal and financial institutions and the intensification of domestic and international trade, it is not clear that it is accurate to describe England as a 'commercial society'. There is a profound danger that historians of the economy, in applying modern conceptions of economic theory, may by default impute anachronistic perceptions to contemporaries. As D. C. Coleman remarked three dec-

---

'Virtue, commerce and the enduring Florentine republican moment: reintegrating Italy into the Atlantic republican debate', *Journal of the history of ideas* 62:4 (2001) p.721-43; and Eric Nelson, *The Greek tradition in republican thought* (Cambridge, 2004).

6.　Pincus, 'Neither Machiavellian moment nor possessive individualism', p.708, 720. But now see Pincus, *1688: the first modern revolution*, esp. ch. 12.

7.　Pincus, 'Neither Machiavellian moment nor possessive individualism', p.725, 707-708.

8.　Muldrew, *The Economy of obligation: the culture of credit and social relations in early modern England*; Wrightson, *Earthly necessities: economic lives in early modern Britain*.

ades ago, most of the so-called 'economic' writings of the period were in fact determined by political priorities rather than detached observation.[9] At a deeper discursive level, Keith Tribe's work on land, labour and economic discourse suggests that there is a fundamental Whiggism in suggesting that key concepts like rent, credit or land have any connection with modern economic categories.[10] Taking this into account, it may well be more plausible to suggest that when Harrington described the relationship between land and political power, he was engaging in a predominantly social and political discourse, rather than a specifically economic one.

After 1642, as a number of works have established, there was an intensification of institutional structures which, combined together, has been branded as a process of 'state-building'.[11] Political thinkers, like Harrington and his followers, reacted to this process, perhaps without being completely conscious of its trajectory. One implication of Pincus's account is that republican political theorists, because they were wedded to an essentially agrarian account of society, were handicapped from adjusting their arguments to the pragmatic demands of the time. As Jonathan Swift noted in 1710, times had changed, 'So that *Power* which, according to the Old Maxim, was used to follow *Land*, is now gone over to *Money*'.[12] Hostile to credit, fearful of the moneyed interest and nostalgic for the senatorial values of antiquity, the republican project was marginal, conservative and impotent. Driven by a persistent anxiety (especially after 1689) that developing economic forms and government institutions would disrupt or distort the perdurable stability of political and most importantly social structure, republicanism became an idiom of cultural dissent rather than a tool of political action.[13] Those republicans who did thrive in the political environment of the post-revolutionary period did so by abandoning the core commitment of a Harringtonian devotion to agrarian values. The *locus classicus* of this revision was John Toland's edition of Harrington's works in 1700, which lauded the Bank of England as equivalent to 'the Temple of Saturn among the *Romans*'.[14] That a republican could defend the idea of public

9.   See D. C. Coleman, 'Mercantilism revisited', *Historical Journal* 23:4 (1980) p.773-91.

10. See Keith Tribe, *Land, labour and economic discourse* (London, 1978).

11. See Michael J. Braddick, *State formation in early modern England c.1550-1700* (Cambridge, 2000); Braddick, 'The early modern English state and the question of differentiation, from 1550 to 1700', *Comparative studies in society and history* 38:1 (1996), p.92-111.

12. Jonathan Swift, *The Examiner* 13 (2 November 1710). Quoted in Paul Langford, *Public life and the propertied Englishman, 1689-1798* (Oxford, 1991), p.58; see in general on the commonplace acceptance of Harrington's insight in the eighteenth century 'The propertied mind', p.1-70.

13. Dickson, *The Financial Revolution in England*, p.35.

14. John Toland, dedication 'To the Lord Mayor, Aldermen, Sherifs, and Common Council of

credit, in the form of one of the central institutions of the 'Financial Revolution', seems to confirm the general view that the more sophistic- ated thinkers reshaped Harringtonian principle for practical relevance.

By examining more closely the arguments devoted by Harrington, Toland and later authors to the consideration of the relationship between land, credit and political personality, it will be possible to establish that republican attitudes to political economy were much more subtle and robust than has commonly been assumed. The case of Toland is germane to the issue, both because of his role as transmitter of Harrington's ideas to the eighteenth century, but also, as we will see, because of his personal interests in banking, credit and property. Much has been written about the connections between Toland's political and religious ideas, concentrating, in particular, on the heterodox and irre- ligious intentions of his public and scribal works.[15] Less precise attention has been devoted to his more straightforwardly political and economic writings. Amongst his private papers (and reproduced in the posthum- ous printed collection of his work) is a letter (probably written to Molesworth *c.*1720) detailing 'The Scheme, or practical model, of a national bank'. As already noted, Toland had included a eulogy to the Bank of England in his edition of Harrington's works, indicating that he appreciated the financial function of credit. In the 'Scheme', as Toland acknowledged in the accompanying letter, he was drawing from a manuscript treatise ('little in bulk but big with matter') written by an unidentified gentleman who had died in 1708. His purpose in bringing the revised document to light was to make a contribution to the proposal for setting up a Bank of Ireland: as he put it 'I see no reason why I should not be suitably gratified, whether they may think fit to follow my whole plan [...] or that they may only take proper hints, and accommodate such parts of it as they please to their own project'. His version of the 'Scheme' was the 'only practicable one in that Kingdom, and the only honest and secure one in any other'.[16] Coming in the immediate context of the crisis of public credit provoked by the collapse of the South Sea Company shares, this seems a remarkable project for Toland to have been engaged

London', in *The Oceana of James Harrington and his other works*, ed. John Toland (London, [John Darby], 1700), p.iii. See Pincus, 'Revolution in political economy', in Pincus, *1688: the first modern revolution*, p.366.

15. See Champion, *Republican learning*.

16. John Toland, 'The Scheme, or practical model, of a national bank', in *A Collection of several pieces of Mr John Toland, now first publish'd from his original manuscripts*, ed. Pierre Desmaizeaux, 2 vols (London, J. Peele, 1726), vol.1, p.449. The scribal version of the document is British Library Add Mss 4465 f.39-42 (internally paginated, 1-5). On the context, see Ryder, 'The Bank of Ireland, 1721: land, credit and dependency'.

in. What it does illustrate is that republicans were perfectly capable, and sufficiently motivated, to think politically about money.

Toland had, very early in his career, exhibited an interest in the nature of money and financial theory. In 1696, he had translated (from the Italian) the sixteenth-century Florentine Bernardo Davanzati's *A Discourse upon coins* (originally 1588) as a contribution to the debate prompted by the crisis of specie and Recoinage, produced, and scribally circulated, while he was part of the circle around John Locke. The work was calculated to support arguments about the relationship between the value of coin and the level of production, as well as to curry favour with Locke. In common with the 'mass of economic writings' prior to the mid-eighteenth century, including Locke's work on the subject, as Patrick Kelly puts it, it was 'a response to specific economic difficulties rather than the fruit of disinterested inquiry'.[17] The work traced the origins and function of coin back to early antiquity: it was a device to enable and encourage 'human commerce or traffick' within and between nations. The essential definition of money was 'Gold, silver, or copper coin'd by Publick authority at pleasure, and by the consent of nations made the price and measure of things, to contract them the more easily'. Rejecting the analogy that money was the sinews of war and government, Davanzati suggests, 'it may be more properly stil'd the second blood thereof'. Circulation of money (like blood) 'preserves alive the Civil body of the Commonwealth'. Counterfeiting, monopolising, simony, usury and debasing the coinage thus damaged the community. Confirming Toland's republican sentiments, the text vilified those who corrupted the specie for private advantage, contending that 'the Publick must be in charge of maintaining this blood in the commonwealth, as they pay the souldiers, and the salaries of magistrates for the preservation of Liberty and Justice'.[18] The themes of the active circulation of money to invigorate the commerce of a commonwealth premised upon public credit and trust were repeated in his and other people's later work.

Toland's theological indiscretion soon compromised his intimacy with Locke, but there were others in his milieu who would have been expert sounding boards for thoughts about money, finance and commerce. Friendships with merchants and financiers like Sir Robert Clayton and Sir Theodore Janssen meant Toland was familiar with the world of business and financial investment. Although not much has been made of the point, it is significant that a commonplace contemporary attitude to

17. Kelly, 'General introduction', in *Locke on money*, vol.1, p.1. On Toland's translation of Davanzati, see p.34-35. A very lightly annotated copy of the work belonging to Locke is in the Goldsmith's Library, Senate House, London, at GL. 1696 [3274].

18. Bernardo Davanzati, *A Discourse upon coins*, trans. John Toland (London, J. D. for Awnsham and John Churchil[l], 1696), p.9, 12, 18-19, 24.

the idea of banks was that they were implicitly republican institutions. Harrington himself had remarked in 1658 that 'Where there is a Bank, ten to one there is a Commonwealth'.[19] The example of the bank of Amsterdam and the thriving commercial success of the Dutch republic prompted similar assumptions from the 1660s through to the 1690s. While it is a historical fact that the eventual institutional permanence of the Bank of England has become identified with the 'Financial Revolution', it would be wise to exercise caution about such proleptic assumptions. Just as the institution of a Protestant monarchy was persistently contested, and could have potentially failed, so too there were constant challenges to the legal existence of the Bank of England. As J. Keith Horsefield's insufficiently-cited work on British monetary experiments between 1650 and 1710 has shown in considerable detail, there was a cornucopia of rival suggestions regarding the constitution, function and political implications of creating a national bank.[20] The writings of men like Samuel Hartlib, William Paterson, Robert Murray and John Broughton were sensitive to the public social and political consequences of new initiatives. The controversy over the 'battle for the banks' in the 1690s was rehearsed in the 1700s and 1710s as the legislative arrangements underpinning the Bank of England were revisited.[21] The relationship between civil society, political constitution and public credit was one that was contested rather than simply constructed. Rival schemes for creating a system of public credit, which would secure the debt prompted by increased government expenditure, were manifold. Republicans were ideologically capable and indeed did offer imaginative proposals alongside many others.

The origins of Toland's 'Scheme' lay in the debates of the 1700s. Importantly, while acknowledging the centrality of public credit to the well-being of the nation, the thrust of the 'Scheme' proposed a rival 'national' bank to that of the current Bank of England. Clearly Toland's commitment to either existing institutions like the Bank of England or potential new innovations was determined by his perception of their contribution to public virtue. Such a bank, premised on the creation of 'immense credit, on real not imaginary foundations', was intended to generate wealth, security and trust. Unlike the current Bank of England, where a defective constitution allowed private interests to profit,

---

19. James Harrington, *The Prerogative of popular government* (London, [G. Dawson] for Tho. Brewster 1658), p.17; *The Oceana of James Harrington and his other works*, ed. Toland, p.247.
20. See J. Keith Horsefield, *British monetary experiments 1650-1710*.
21. See Dennis Rubini, 'Politics and the battle for the banks, 1688-1697'; Pincus explores the ideological dimensions of this debate in considerable detail in *1688: the first modern revolution*, ch. 12. But see also Sir John Clapham, *The Bank of England: a history*, esp. vol.1, p.3, 61, 81, 90.

Toland's 'Scheme' was intended for public 'advantage', convenience and 'great benefit'. Perhaps reflecting his intimacy with the battles within elite Whig circles, he adjusted his initial eulogy of the Bank of England. Its creation, on reflection, had been built on 'narrow foundations' which created suspicion because the 'private management' was not subject to 'any inspection, check, or controul from the supreme authority'.[22] Mercenary stock-jobbers and projectors would be disappointed by his proposal, while the design would be of great 'service to the Nobility and Gentry', but also provide the government with 'ten or twelve hundred thousand pounds at low interest'. Such method and discipline would raise and advance the 'Kingdom to a degree of Plenty, Wealth, and Power, far superior to all preceding ages'. These would not be 'airy riches but real effects'. It was then a product not of subscriptions and investment but 'a prudent and honest appointment of state'.[23] The 'Scheme' was an act of *'political Art'* based not on *'visionary calculations, or private, mercenary, and temporary Views'*, but on *'easy methods, truly natural, public, and perpetual'*.[24] The proposals were to create a bank which neither borrowed nor lent money, but encouraged the secure circulation of money and honest business transactions.[25] The perceived function of the bank was then to facilitate the efficiency of commerce, without generating a credit which threatened the distribution of political power.

Like many banking projectors before him, Toland modelled his plan on the example of the Bank of Amsterdam: much of the 'Scheme' was an outline of its constitution and function adapted to English circumstances.[26] The essential character of this financial institution was that it 'open'd its books with bare walls, without any cash at all'. Since such a bank only had the custody, not the disposal, of 'other men's cash', it would not fall prey to what Toland called 'mysterious politicks'. The overwhelming theme of Toland's suggestions was that a 'national' bank would bring combined benefit to the public, to individuals and even the government (since it would facilitate the collection of revenue and other fiscal processes). The scheme followed the original conception of the Dutch bank, which was to handle deposits, the transfer of money payments and the exchange of currency in a secure environment. All transactions (commercial and fiscal) above a fixed sum were to take

---

22. Toland, 'Scheme', in *A Collection of several pieces*, vol.1, p.451, 450.
23. Toland, 'Scheme', in *A Collection of several pieces*, vol.1, p.453, 454, 455.
24. Toland, 'Scheme', in *A Collection of several pieces*, vol.1, p.448.
25. Toland, 'Scheme', in *A Collection of several pieces*, vol.1, p.470.
26. See Toland, 'Scheme', in *A Collection of several pieces*, vol.1, p.455-65; see J. G. van Dillen, 'The Bank of Amsterdam', in *History of the principal public banks*, ed. J. G. van Dillen (The Hague, 1934), p.79-123. It is worth comparing Toland's discussion with his friend Sir Theodore Janssen's *A Discourse concerning banks* (London, James Knapton, 1697), esp. p.1-2, 3-4.

place through the bank (at a small administrative cost): there was no process for creating credit. It was to be 'so constituted, as that every man shall at first sight perceive his security and advantage in it; and immediately trust it, without the least hesitation or doubt'.[27] This conception of the financial role of a national bank (as described here) is quite distinct from that developed by the Directors of the Bank of England in the course of the eighteenth century. The 'Scheme' described by Toland was intended to offer what we could call commercial banking services – credit extension, deposit-taking and payments processing – administrative functions which would enable more effective and secure commercial transactions. Such a vision of the role of the bank was compatible with the republican commitment to developing *industria* and *opificium*: it saw banking as another institution which would reinforce the commonwealth, rather than provide a speculative investment opportunity for those with surplus money. Like Sir George Downing, Toland saw an opportunity in the application of Dutch models to English circumstances. Such a bank would create a robust credit, which even if threatened with 'any sudden fright or consternation' was like a 'living and inexhaustible spring, [which] wou'd flow out again, and florish as before'.[28] This evidence suggests that the republican attitude to credit and the function of money within a political community was more sophisticated than the current historiography allows. There was, for example, a very precise distinction between credit which benefited the public, and that which advantaged private interest, as well as between a real and imaginary credit. The corrosion of Toland's initial optimism about the possibilities of the Bank of England did not extend into a universal hostility to all public financial institutions. Like all public institutions, of course, the Bank might be subject to shifting virtue. The force of his later recommendations was to address the potential for corruption by careful regulation. The ability of republicans like Toland to adapt to changing circumstances can be illustrated from the reaction to perhaps the greatest crisis of credit of the period.[29]

Republicans and the South Sea Bubble

On 8 December 1720, King George I addressed the sixth session of the fifth Parliament of Great Britain, promising an urgent inquiry into 'the

27. Toland, 'Scheme', in *A Collection of several pieces*, vol.1, p. 452.
28. Toland, 'Scheme', in *A Collection of several pieces*, vol.1, p.452. See Jonathan Scott, ' "Good night Amsterdam": Sir George Downing and Anglo-Dutch statebuilding', *English historical review* 113 (2003), p.334-56.
29. See Julian Hoppit, 'Attitudes to credit in Britain, 1680-1790', *Historical journal* 33:2 (1990), p.305-22; Hoppit, 'The myths of the South Sea Bubble', *Transactions of the royal historical society* 12 (2002), p.141-65.

most effectual and speedy methods to restore the National Credit, and [to] fix it upon a lasting foundation'.[30] The catastrophic consequences of the financial disaster of the South Sea Bubble hit London in late summer.[31] Initial hopes were invested in the possibility of a parliamentary remedy to the difficulties. Robert Walpole's exploitation of the crisis to reinforce his own dominance of the Ministry (exchanging commitments of political loyalty for 'skreening' malpractice) was derailed by angry and passionate interventions in the Commons' debates. The scolding tirades of the wild-eyed Jacobite, William Shippen, focused on the criminal mismanagement of the crisis. This implicated not just those in the South Sea Company, but also those above them, at the 'helm', who had abused the 'trust reposed in them'. Shippen's interventions, while moving, were tainted with Jacobite disloyalty.[32]

Of much more consequence was the speech of Robert Molesworth, a man whose commonwealth and Hanoverian credentials cast no reproach on the motivation for his complaints. As his own writings on tyranny had established, he was accomplished at forensic analysis of political corruption.[33] Before considering proper remedies, he declared, enquiry into the 'cause and nature of the distemper' was vital. Applying a commonplace homology between the body politic and natural, he insisted that 'they ought to imitate skilful surgeons, who, in order to cure a wound, begin with probing it, and, when they find it necessary, make incisions and scarifications to get the venomous core out of it, before they apply healing plaisters'. Mere 'empirics', applying palliatives, would 'make the sore rankle and fester, and endanger the life of the patient'. If using the tools of political anatomy would be appropriate to exposing the criminals, applying the lessons of the Roman republic would be suitable for punishing them. The example of the ancient Roman treatment of parricides was most pertinent: as Molesworth pointed out there was no law against the crime 'because their legislators supposed no son could be

---

30. William Cobbett, *Parliamentary history of England*, 36 vols (London, R. Bagshaw, 1806-1820), vol.7, p.679.
31. The literature on the South Sea Bubble is substantial: the standard account is John Carswell, *The South Sea Bubble*, revd edn (Stroud, 1993); see also Malcolm Balen, *A Very English deceit: the secret history of the South Sea Bubble and the first great financial scandal* (London, 2002); for a recent study, see Helen J. Paul, *The South Sea Bubble: an economic history of its origins and consequences* (New York, 2011). For a robust financial analysis see Richard Kleer, ' "The folly of particulars": the political economy of the South Sea Bubble', *Financial history review* 19 (2012), p.175-97. I am very grateful to Daniel Carey for drawing my attention to these recent works.
32. Cobbett, *Parliamentary history*, vol.7, p.682.
33. See Justin Champion, 'Introduction', in Robert Molesworth, *An Account of Denmark, with Francogallia and Some considerations for the promoting of agriculture and employing the poor*, ed. Justin Champion (Indianapolis, IN, 2011), p.ix-xxviii.

so unnaturally wicked, as to embrue his hands in his father's blood'. One convicted of such a heinous crime would be 'thrown alive, sewed up in a sack, into the Tyber'. His concluding remark noted 'that as he looked upon the contrivers and executers of the villainous South Sea Scheme, as the parricides of their country, he would be satisfied to see them undergo the same punishment'.[34]

Despite Walpole's rear-guard advice that precipitate action and 'odious inquiries' might exasperate the distemper (and 'render all remedies ineffectual') the Commons was galvanised into the appointment of a Committee of Secrecy in the second week of January 1721. Chaired by the Irish Whig Thomas Brodrick and empowered to send for papers, persons and records, the Committee included the 'True Whig' voices of Molesworth and Lechmere.[35] Delivering seven reports to Parliament between February and June 1721, this committee was a constant irritant to Walpole's project of protecting leading ministers and courtiers from exposure. The first report published revelations of active corruption in the issue and pre-sale of stock, as well as evidence of fictitious entries and poorly executed cover-ups. The resolutions of the Commons in response were clear cut and unambiguous: the initial 'notorious breach of trust' was compounded by fraud calculated to enrich specific men. Revelation of bribery of MPs was attacked as exposing 'corrupt, infamous, and dangerous practices, and highly reflecting on the honour and justice of parliaments, and destructive of the interest of his majesty's government'.[36] The fraudulent conspiracy, in benefiting private men, had injured public credit and damaged the constitution. From February 1721, Parliament attracted over seventy petitions and addresses from concerned boroughs, JPs, counties and corporations around the nation. These expressions of complaint and anxiety underscored the sense of conspiracy and public injury – with a recurring vocabulary of impostures, confederacy, delusion, treachery, cunning, ambition and dissimulation. As the mayor and burgesses of Leicester complained, such individuals had 'propagated lies and forgeries, [and] so imposed upon the honest credulous people, as to draw all their ready money and treasure into their infamous hands'. The men of New Sarum decried the 'insatiable covetousness and ambition, supported by the base arts of

---

34. Cobbett, *Parliamentary history*, vol.7, p.683.
35. See *House of Commons journals*, 11 January 1721, p.399. Molesworth was nominated with 267 votes; Brodrick with 334. See Cobbett, *Parliamentary history*, vol.7, p.694, for the full membership. For a discussion of Irish investment in the London market, see Patrick Walsh, 'Irish money on the London market: Ireland, the Anglo-Irish and the South Sea Bubble of 1720', *Eighteenth-century life*, forthcoming, 2014). I am very grateful to the editor of this issue, David O'Shaughnessy, and to the author for allowing me a view of this important paper pre-publication.
36. Cobbett, *Parliamentary history*, vol.7, p.742.

fraud and dissimulation'. According to those in Exeter, the private ambition of 'wicked men' had 'imagined, contrived and almost compassed the death of the Commonwealth, if the loss of money, trade and credit, may be so called'. The 'trust reposed in them for the common good' had been abused. 'Mysterious contrivances, insidious schemes, and delusive overtures' had compromised the 'public faith'. 'National credit' had always been 'esteemed sacred and inviolable', but had been destroyed by 'secret confederates' and 'so vile and artful a conspiracy'. Echoing the republican language voiced by Molesworth, the County of Warwick had condemned the 'avarice and rapine of a set of parricides'. The recurrent demand was 'that public justice may be applied to public roguery'.[37]

There was, without doubt, a persisting republican idiom and vocabulary in the political discourses articulated during the crisis of 1720-1721, whether delivered in parliament (by men like Molesworth), composed in addresses and petitions or in printed pamphlets. When the Duke of Wharton reflected that 'the government of the best princes was oftentimes made intolerable to their subjects by ill ministers' he used the example of Sejanus, who, as he put it, 'made a division in the imperial family, and rendered the reign of the emperor Claudius odious to the Romans'. Stanhope, who detected the slur cast against himself, responded with the example of the great republican patriot Brutus, who 'in order to assert the liberty of Rome, and free it from tyrants, sacrificed his own degenerate son'.[38] The fracture within the Whig ministry, combined with the political consequences for those implicated in the commercial crisis, was represented in public discourse by the application of republican history – the leading oppositional journal carried *Cato's letters*, while one of the most successful pamphlets described deliberate parallels between contemporary politics and the Catiline conspiracy. Thomas Gordon's *The Conspirators; or the case of Catiline* (ten London editions in 1721; two other editions) exposed these parallels: 'our circumstances may be like those of old Rome when the plot of Catiline was set on foot'. Citing classical Roman sources and the commentaries of Machiavelli, Gordon delivered an incisive republican analysis of the nature of conspiracy.[39] Sallust's account of the Catiline conspiracy was used to explain the subversion of the constitution, drawing out a specific parallel between the Roman conspirators and

---

37. Cobbett, *Parliamentary history*, extracts from 'Several remarkable petitions for justice on the authors of the present calamities', vol.7, p.760-80.
38. Cobbett, *Parliamentary history*, vol.7, p.705-706.
39. Thomas Gordon, *The Conspirators; or the case of Catiline*, 9th edn (London, J. Roberts, 1721), p.iv, vi, ix-x, xiii, 1, 3, 5, 8-9, 10-12, 22.

contemporary politicians.[40] The language of Cato and the Catilines was an idiom for understanding contemporary political structures and conduct. Whereas the Romans had been corrupted by gold, eighteenth-century contemporaries had been contaminated by paper stocks.

What Richard Steele succinctly called the 'crisis of property' created a political opportunity for the display of republican anxieties about the changing relationship between political power and social and economic structures. At the core of the debate was a contested idea about the nature and function of 'credit' within the polity. While for many the mess of the 'Bubble' was a predictable consequence of corrupt credit, this was not to imply necessary hostility towards all forms of public credit. As Steele acutely suggested, 'that plain word credit carries with it everything that is valuable amongst men'. When public credit was compromised all would suffer, 'the Landed Man will be impoverished, the Soldier disarm'd, as certainly as the Merchant is beggar'd'.[41] Credit tied the community and the government together in a bond of trust. The 'supposed honesty and justice of the government' rested on 'its disposition to support and maintain the legal rights of its creditors'.[42] Modern historiography has viewed this hostility to the corruption of the South Sea Bubble as the last hurrah of the republican moment. The bitter invective against stock-jobbers, the monied interest and financial institutions, betrayed the backward-looking and anti-commercial identity of their ideology.[43] That Molesworth threatened to throw the South Sea directors and their conspirators into the Thames is emblematic of this tradition. In this view then, Cato and Catiline were fundamentally out of kilter with the commercial culture of the eighteenth century.

Republican polemic against the crisis of 1720 displays the considerable political anxieties about the functional nature of credit and wealth in eighteenth-century society. Before categorising such commentary as conservative, it will be worth returning to the contemporary arguments to tease out what could be called republican *analysis* from republican *prescription*. The underpinning polemic against the Bubble was not contrived against 'credit' *qua* 'credit', but against the corrupt exploitation of credit for private advantage. Public credit was laudable; private credit was potentially problematic. Even men of unimpeachable republican

40. The copy of the work in the British Library [Call-mark 518.e.21(2)] interestingly has MS annotations indicating the parallels between the Roman cast and contemporary figures: Hortensius is Walpole, Jugurtha is King George and Caius Cornelius Cathegus is 'Crag': Gordon, *The Conspirators*, p.10-11, 25, 28.
41. Sir Richard Steele, *The Crisis of property* (London, W. Chetwood *et al.*, 1720), p.21.
42. Cobbett, *Parliamentary history*, vol.7, p.908, quoting *A Letter to a Member of Parliament* (London, s. n., 1721).
43. The *locus classicus* is Pocock, *Machiavellian moment*, p.468-78.

credentials like Molesworth and Toland had a more complicated understanding of credit and commerce than is commonly appreciated. This
complexity can be traced to Harrington. Significant evidence, which
allows an appreciation of this distinction between the public and private
dimensions of credit, is the text which survives in John Toland's archive:
'The secret history of the South-Sea scheme'.[44] As noted, the work was
not by Toland, 'but it was found among his MSS, and is enlarged and
corrected throughout with his own hand'.[45] It has performed an
interesting historiographical role in modern accounts of the Bubble,
being used as a reliable source for the narrative of events and intentions
of the actors by both John Carswell and P. G. M. Dickson.[46]

Modelled on a literary and historical parallel between the account
given by Livy of the conduct of Appius Claudius and the *decemvirs*
(*c.*450 BC) and the conspirators in the South Sea Company, the work
intended to make public the 'dark contrivances of those men'. As any
reasonably well-read eighteenth-century republican would have known,
Machiavelli's *Discorsi* on these passages of Livy represented the exemplar
of Appius and the *decemvirs* as telling a story both about the dangers of
tyranny and an anatomy of the Republic's fall.[47] Like the Romans, the
modern *decemvirs* were the 'idols of the people; and, as the distributors of
those fancy'd blessings they were showring upon them, little less than
ador'd'. In the figure of Appius, the 'Secret history' referred to the
machinations of Sir John Blunt, regarded as the ringleader of the
conspiracy against the public. Working with a 'Cabinet Council' of other
South Sea figures (Grigsby, nicknamed the 'negromancer', and Knight
being the most prominent), Appius cultivated a dictatorial control over
the operations of the company: together they aimed to 'make their
power perpetual'. Just as in ancient Rome, the conspirators acted 'till by
their urgent and violent proceedings, they had almost overturned the
Commonwealth'. The development of the Bubble over the course of the
spring and summer of 1720 was understood through two corrupt political strategies. First, Appius exploited 'the general madness of those
days' and effectively 'bewitch'd people by false appearances'. Secondly,

44. The manuscript was apparently originally preserved in Toland's papers (but not in the
    modern archive), and subsequently published by Pierre Desmaizeaux in his 1726 edition
    of Toland's works: 'The secret history of the South-Sea scheme', in *A Collection of several
    pieces of Mr John Toland*, vol.1, p.404-47. Unfortunately the printed edition gives no hint of
    what additions Toland may have made.
45. 'Secret history', in *A Collection of several pieces*, vol.1, p.404n.
46. See Carswell, *The South Sea Bubble*, which notes that it was 'written by someone in the
    confidence of a director who was not a member of the inner ring, and is extremely hostile
    to Blunt' (p.272); Dickson, *The Financial Revolution*, p.94-95.
47. See Livy III.34-58, Machiavelli, *Discourses on Livy*, I.35 (p.76-77); I.40 (p.85-89); I.41 (p.90);
    I.42 (p.90-91); I.45.1 (p.93).

the 'cabinet council' worked by stealth, 'skulking in some by place or Tavern in the night, and often shifting from one house to another'. The people, the other South Sea Company directors, leading ministers and members of parliament were all deceived 'by the juggles and artifices of this cunning projector'. The conspirators were able to exploit the company's constitution, to manipulate parliamentary business, and to 'intoxicate the minds of people' with the guiding motto of 'the more confusion the better'.[48]

The republican analysis of the South Sea Bubble focused not on the moral threat of credit and speculation run wild, but on the confederacy of deceit. The 'Secret history' presented the crisis as an instructive case-study in how 'credit' (of different sorts) operated in public society. The issue was not simply the financial relationship between lender and borrower, but the question of the political or social credit which created and underpinned public reputation. The 'conjuror', Appius, at the height of his power had been irresistible: despite the anxieties and doubts of many he acted without opposition because, 'whilst a man has authority in a society, 'tis the hardest thing in the world to carry anything against him, if he will determinately oppose it. All bodies politic, and particularly mercantile Companies, may be safely appeal'd to for the truth of this observation'.[49] In an audit of responsibility, the root source of corruption lay in the contrivance of the original scheme by the inner cabal, rather than any necessary and latent deformation in the commercial world. Understood in this light, the current preconception that republican figures like Molesworth and Toland were hostile to the 'Bubble' because it represented a fundamental threat to the agrarian foundations of their political ideology seems imprecise. Without doubt Molesworth was an outspoken and passionate voice arraigned against the fraudulent actions of the malefactors, but his hostility was provoked not by any visceral or principled objection to such financial schemes. What he objected to was selfish, private and deceitful people who betrayed the public. His objection was political rather than economic.

A similar trait can be observed in the polemic of *Cato's letters* (rumoured to have been a representation of Molesworth's views),[50]

---

48. 'Secret history', in *A Collection of several pieces*, vol.1, p.404, 405, 406, 411-12, 417, 419, 431, 438.
49. 'Secret history', in *A Collection of several pieces*, vol.1, p.441, 444.
50. Evidence that Molesworth was intimate with the production of the periodical can be seen in the Spencer Mss, University of Kansas, Mss G23, f.28, John Trenchard to William Simpson [29 October 17**] reporting a conversation with Norton, owner of the *London journal*, that Toland had 'brought a paper signed Cato from Ld Molesworth to him to be inserted in his journal'. See also letters at f.32 noting that Molesworth 'was and would be Cato, and that all the world knew him to be Cato', pointing out the hint evident in the verses engraved in his electioneering 'effigie'. I am very grateful to Richard Clement,

despite this work being regarded as one of the staples of the republican polemic against commercial culture. Composed mainly by John Trenchard and Thomas Gordon, *Cato's letters* complained bitterly against the 'dirty race of money-changers' who sacrificed the public good for 'private advantage': the Bubble was regarded as an episode where 'honesty and industry' were exploited by the 'dull cunning of inferior rogues, void of bravery, void of abilities'.[51] Invoking Harrington's arguments about the connections between property and politics, Cato noted that the principle that 'every man, who has a share of property, having a proportionable share of power' had been compromised by a 'conspiracy of stock-jobbers' who had planted the seeds of anarchy.[52] Industry was discouraged and 'credit undone' by such practice.[53] Very carefully and deliberately the journal drew a contrast between proper 'publick credit' and the corrupt practice which 'destroys all property', associated with the 'cannibals of credit'.[54] Those false politicians in the ministry who failed to expose the crimes turned human life into a 'masquerade' and civil society into 'a mock-alliance between hypocrisy and credulity'.[55] In a similar vein to the narrative of the 'Secret history', Cato lamented how 'self love beguiles men into false hopes': credit easily degenerated into credulity and delusion. Men were 'ever the prey of craft, and ever caught with shadows'.[56] By December 1722, after the full extent of the catastrophe was manifest, Cato devoted an entire issue to the analysis of 'public credit and stocks', which took as its premise the cultural power of the notion of credit.[57]

As was noted in the journal, words and concepts were powerful because they captured public esteem and veneration. Unfortunately this meant that there was no consistency in use and application: 'their meanings will be varied as often as those in possession of reverence and popular applause have occasion to make different uses of them'. The word 'credit' was an example which had endured extreme abuse, and, as a consequence, the public had been subjected to mischief. Producing a

---

Librarian of the Kenneth Spencer Research Library, University of Kansas for providing copies of the Trenchard-Simpson correspondence.

51. *Cato's letters*, ed. Ronald Hamowy, 2 vols (Indianapolis, IN, 1995), vol.1, p.42, 43 (no.2, 12 November 1720). See also Ronald Hamowy, '*Cato's letters*, John Locke, and the republican paradigm', *History of political thought* 11:2 (1990), p.273-94.
52. *Cato's letters*, vol.1, p.44 (no.3, 19 November 1720 [written by Gordon]).
53. *Cato's letters*, vol.1, p.47 (no.4, 26 November 1720 [written by Gordon]).
54. *Cato's letters*, vol.1, p.47, 49 (no.4, 26 November 1720 [written by Gordon]); *Cato's letters*, vol.1, p.51 (no.5, 3 December 1720 [written by Gordon]).
55. *Cato's letters*, vol.1, p.53 (no.5, 3 December 1720 [written by Gordon]).
56. *Cato's letters*, vol.1, p.55, 56 (no.6, 10 December 1720 [written by Gordon]).
57. *Cato's letters*, vol.2, p.753-61 (no.107, 15 December 1722 [written by Trenchard], 'Of publick credit and stocks').

republican lexicon of the variety of uses, Cato distinguished a positive mercantile definition which emphasised the moral probity of the individual from an account which underscored deceit and neglect. The good merchant and tradesman (importantly like the good gentleman) 'is said to be in good credit, when his visible gains appear to be greater than his expences; when he is industrious, and takes care of his affairs; when he makes punctual payments, and the wares he sells may be depended on as to their goodness and value'. This was a credit that one could trust. Similarly a gentleman was said to have 'great credit who lives within his income, has regard to his character and his honour, is just to his word and his promises'. The point was that 'all these will be trusted for as much as they are worth, and sometimes more, at the lowest price for the goods which they buy, and at the lowest interest for the money which they borrow'. In contrast, projectors, shufflers, gentlemen who over-mortgaged their estates, those who 'perpetually' borrowed money, could not be trusted.[58] Cato, then, understood 'credit' to be ultimately a social quality, a relationship between men, reputation and conduct, rather than a purely financial or economic facility. This analysis, derived from the conduct of individuals, was applied to the function of credit in the nation and the state.

The nation was said to have high credit when it consisted of 'great numbers of wealthy subjects' of good trustworthy character and an 'affluent trade' composed of the commodities and labour finding a 'ready vent, and at a good price'. Without trust this system of trade and profit was compromised, thus driving up interest and prices. In the same way, the 'credit of a state' (also known as 'publick credit') was preserved by 'doing strict justice to particulars': this consisted of being exact in payments, 'not altering the nature of property', and not to 'put the stamp of public authority upon base and counterfeit metals'.[59] Trust was the cement that bonded individuals to their neighbours, but also underpinned the integrity of the political community: it was the interest of all men, nations and governments to preserve their reputations for honesty. In the business of buying and selling, lending and borrowing, just like the operation of government, the successful infrastructure was built out of honesty and trust. Unfortunately, as Cato continued, this positive credit had been corroded by a 'new-fangled and fantastical credulity'. As a consequence of these corruptions, 'poor, innocent, industrious and unwary, people have been delivered into the ravenous and polluted jaws of vultures and tigers'. Such conduct had inverted the 'oeconomy and policy of nations': individuals, courts and parliaments

58. *Cato's letters*, vol.2, p.754 (no.107, 15 December 1722 [written by Trenchard]).
59. *Cato's letters*, vol.2, p.755 (no.107, 15 December 1722 [written by Trenchard]).

had been compromised, 'as if the business of government was not to protect people in their property, but to cheat them out of it'. Cato was in no doubt that a system of public and private credit was absolutely essential to the successful functioning of a community: 'that its commodities should sell at a good price, and find a ready vent; that private men should be able safely to trust one another; that lands should find ready purchasers, good securities, money at low interest; and that mortgages should be easily transferable'. Inventing new forms of property 'of a precarious, uncertain, and transitory value' contaminated honest credit.[60] A conspiracy 'by constant juggles and combinations' to elevate this form of credit against true 'public securities' would eventually destroy good government by shifting the 'greatest part of the property of a kingdom [...] into the hands of but a few persons, who will then undoubtedly govern all the rest'.[61] Faction, conspiracy, knavery, juggling, intrigue, corruption – keywords in a language of republican political analysis – were the pejorative terms used to condemn the Bubble.

The important point to reinforce here is that Cato, the cynosure of republican polemic, did not object to credit *per se*, but to the corruption of credit. The South Sea Bubble was an exemplar, not of the fundamental dangers of modern commerce and credit, but of the distortion of those practices. The Bubble was transgressive credit in the sense that in place of promoting virtue, trade, and trust, it produced knavery and deceit: 'It taints men's morals, and defaces all the principles of virtue and fair dealing, and introduces combination and fraud in all sorts of traffick'. Cato underlined this negative transformation in remarking that 'It has changed honest commerce into bubbling; our traders into projectors; industry into tricking'. The resolution of the crisis was to be found not in destroying commerce and credit but reinforcing its public integrity: honest political intervention was the best means to achieve this 'and to do all in our power to increase trade and publick wealth [...] and to become once more a free, rich, happy, and flourishing people'.[62] This recommendation of commerce sits uneasily with commonplace historiographical accounts of republican ideology.

Elsewhere in *Cato's letters* it is clear, however, that these attitudes were regarded as compatible with Harringtonian accounts of property as the '*first Principle of Power*'. Succinctly outlining the arguments derived from *Oceana*, Cato explained that property was the natural foundation of political power, and that by consequence 'every man will have his share of it in proportion as he enjoys property, and makes use of that

60. *Cato's letters*, vol.2, p.757, 758 (no.107, 15 December 1722 [written by Trenchard]).
61. *Cato's letters*, vol.2, p.759, 758 (no.107, 15 December 1722 [written by Trenchard]).
62. *Cato's letters*, vol.2, p.760, 761 (no.107, 15 December 1722 [written by Trenchard]).

property'. Variation in the form of government followed the pattern of distribution and alteration in the 'balance of property'; indeed the secret of politics was 'nicely to watch and observe this fluctuation and change of natural power, and to adjust the political to it'.[63] The current formation of property determined that the 'well poised' monarchical establishment was appropriate to the best preservation of liberty. The idea of an agrarian law was simply implausible because no one 'can ever get enough power to turn all the possessions of England topsy-turvy, and throw them into average'.[64]

In all these discussions in defence of property, Cato did not lay undue emphasis upon the agrarian nature of property. Although the Harringtonian analysis initially claimed that the distribution of land shaped the contours of power, the category of 'property' in *Cato's letters* was more inclusive. Land was important, but mercantile riches were part of the natural foundations of power. As he explained, 'all men are animated by the passion of acquiring and defending property' because property conferred independence and, therefore, liberty. Even those men dependent upon others aimed, by acquisition of property, to achieve 'an agreeable independency'.[65] Liberty was both a cause and effect of property; in consequence, only free governments which preserved property by application of consensual law were happy and secure. This property might be acquired by possession of land, trade and commerce and labour. As Cato explained, ownership of land and estates was one of the most effective ways of annexing power through the creation of dependence by others, but it was not the only source of political personality: other kinds of riches were capable of generating morally estimable forms of independence.[66] That republicans in 1720 had a more capacious and flexible understanding of the nature of property which included commercial riches is not only evident from their writings on the subject but is also manifest in their economic behaviour.

Honest investment in credit: Molesworth and Toland buy company shares

Amongst John Toland's unpublished private papers remains a rather curious and little-noticed fragment. Dated 21 September 1720 (in London) it appears to be a financial agreement between Toland and a man tentatively identified as Jean de Fonvive. The latter was a publisher

---

63. *Cato's letters*, vol.2, p.607, 609, 610 (no.84, letter of 7 July 1722 [written by Trenchard]).
64. *Cato's letters*, vol.2, p.614 (no.85, 14 July 1722 [written by Trenchard]).
65. *Cato's letters*, vol.1, p.483 (no.68, 3 March 1721 [written by Gordon]).
66. *Cato's letters*, vol.2, p.614-16 (no.85, 14 July 1722 [written by Trenchard]).

(of French Protestant extraction) who had produced a successful news-letter since 1694.[67] De Fonvive was a business partner with Richard Baldwin, and a sometime correspondent of Robert Harley in the early 1700s; he and Toland may have encountered one another through dealings in the booktrade, political collaboration or both. There is no other record of contact or interaction between the two men in either Toland's manuscripts or printed works. The contract outlines an agree-ment for transactions between four individuals: Robert Molesworth, John de Fonvive, Robert Knight and Toland himself. What it indicates is that Toland, acting in the name of Molesworth, agreed to purchase £1000 worth of stock in the Third Money issue of June 1720 (when the speculation was at its zenith) from Robert Knight. De Fonvive advanced the money for this transaction in return for a half share of any profits. This fragment raises some interesting issues. Both Toland and Molesworth, although they later exhibited extreme prejudice against the Bubble, initially considered investment in stock an acceptable undertaking. The relationship with Knight is surprising too, given his central role in the fraud and subsequent flight from the parliamentary investigation in 1721. This was not a deal struck with a minor player, but with one of the central conspirators.[68] Compounding this involvement in the speculative project, the exchange of credit and trust between de Fonvive and Toland indicates (on both sides) an experienced relation-ship between trustworthy partners. The sum involved (£1000) was not a trivial investment, even in a context where remarkable capital gains were expected. That de Fonvive thought the persistently impecunious Toland a safe partner for such an enterprise is probably testimony to the delusions the South Sea scheme inspired, but more possibly to his assurance that Molesworth was a reliable bet.

In fact, the transaction that the contract describes was even more complex. Writing to Toland on 25 June 1720 (eight days after the Third Money subscription referred to in the note), Molesworth (responding to Toland's offer of service in the subscriptions) indicated his interest: 'I shou'd be glad enough to [...] get a little money, (which I need to pay off

---

67. The full document reads: 'Whereas Mr John Toland had a subscription of one thousand pounds in the third money subscription to the South Sea under the name of the right honourable the Lord Viscount Molesworth and that of John de Fonvive made the first payment of one thousand pounds upon condition that the said Mr Toland and I should go halves on the profit. I do hereby acknowledge that the said Mr Toland had delivered to me an order of the said Lord Molesworth upon Robert Knight Esq Treasurer of the South Sea Company, to deliver me the receipt or receipts and order or orders, and then the said subscriptions shall be sold and disposed of with our mutual consent according to our agreement and the usual custom upon the exchange. Witness my hand the day and year above said.' BL Add Mss 4295 f.36.
68. See Carswell, *South Sea Bubble*.

some debts) in any honest Project'. Clearly worried that he had missed a good opportunity, Molesworth recommended Toland should consult (on his behalf) with Sir Theodore Janssen, 'whose judgement and honesty is to be relied on'. Honest investment was acceptable. Molesworth rather immodestly noted that 'I have good credit, having never yet, I thank my stars, forfeited it in any one instance'. This sense of public credibility did not, however, sit uncomfortably with Molesworth's sense of his own political identity. Far from simply being focused on the South Sea prospect, his letter continued to outline other projects: of the rival scheme launched by the Hamburg Exchange he wrote, 'I do not understand what it is; but if I cou'd do it and become one of the undertakers, without any great risk (or subscribers), you may speak to Sir A*** of it.'[69]

This correspondence reveals unexpected detail. The mention of Sir Theodore Janssen is significant, for he was one of the leading investors in the country, an MP, former Director of the Bank of England and sometime Director of the South Sea Company. One of the serious financial casualties of the Bubble, Janssen had much of his own private wealth sequestered by Parliament, as well as being expelled as an MP in punishment.[70] As an international financier and a member of the Board of Trade Janssen may have been an unusual friend for Toland and Molesworth to have, although his staunch commitment to religious toleration (he voted for the repeal of the Occasional Conformity and Schism Acts) may have been just cause. That Toland was regarded by Molesworth as a broker between himself and Janssen reveals a further dimension; by implication the letter suggests that Toland was accustomed to introducing new opportunities for investment to the Irish peer. Molesworth and Toland were entangled in the speculation of 1720: it seems that they actively sought out opportunities. Molesworth justified this involvement explicitly, 'I am desirous of having my small oar in the public boat, and not to obstinately to refuse profit. Since the Nation is a sharing, I have contested long enough, and may now without imputation come in for my part of it'. The profit was public and national; participation in a collective dividend was (in his view) only a just desert for political service and commitment. The only problem Molesworth saw was that, as he put it, 'I believe I am too late for any signal gain'.[71]

69. *A Collection of several pieces of Mr John Toland*, vol.2, p.463. It has not been possible to identify Sir A.

70. It is likely that whereas Molesworth used his political influence in the Commons against certain Directors retaining personal estates he supported Trenchard's motion to allow Janssen to retain £50,000 of his capital (which was carried by 134 votes to 118). See Cobbett, *Parliamentary history*, vol.7, p.827, 830-34; *House of Commons journals*, XIX, p.425-6, 524; XXI, p.172, 245; Romney Sedgwick, *The House of Commons 1715-1754*, 2 vols (London, 1970), vol.2, p.262.

71. *A Collection of several pieces of Mr John Toland*, vol.2, p.463.

Toland's response to this letter (composed on the same day) under-scores the intimacy between republicans and speculation. Noting that he had actually been to the South Sea house (and indeed had written his last letter from that place), Toland explained that Janssen 'has generously kept his word with me' and presumably secured him stock in the third subscription. More than that, he had added a further promise, 'that on the next such occasion, about three months hence, he'll procure me the liberty of another subscription'. This was almost certainly the origin of the deal with de Fonvive: Toland explained that 'any body else laying down the money, and on that score going halves for the profit' was commonplace. Rather sheepishly (perhaps especially so in the light of Molesworth's previous letter rueing the missed opportunity of invest-ment) Toland admitted that he had used Molesworth's name ('ever auspicious to Liberty') to secure the subscription. Here was republican virtue being turned to speculative purposes. Demand for the Third Money issue had been furious. The directors had tried to limit it by insisting that 'none except a Parliament-man shou'd subscribe for a thousand pounds'. With the collusion of Janssen, Toland explained they 'put in your name for mine, as being sure you wou'd not take it ill, since there was no time for asking your leave'.[72] Toland denied both that this was sharp practice (it was simply a case of taking an opportunity when it presented itself), but also that it did not compromise Molesworth's 'judgement' since many other parliament men in the Lords and Com-mons had subscribed even though they had opposed the scheme.

At this point we might pause to ponder whether this letter is a piece of hypocritical disingenuousness. *Post-facto*, Toland apologised for his potentially damning breach of etiquette while simultaneously justifying his acuity in taking advantage of the circumstances. Contrary to what might be expected from the editor of Harrington, Toland could barely restrain his excitement at the prospect of capital gain. 'I was offer'd a thousand pounds advantage three hours after the thing was done, and thirteen hundred this very day', he proudly boasted. Janssen advised him to sit tight, assuring him that 'at the opening of the Books it will be worth a great deal more'.[73] Molesworth, independently of these transactions, had invested £3000 in the Third Money subscription and £500 in the Fourth.[74]

There is evidence, then, of Toland using a variety of forms of credit available to him in this episode. Clearly, like Molesworth, he saw no ideological conflict in exploiting the opportunities as they were

72. *A Collection of several pieces of Mr John Toland*, vol.2, p.464, 465.
73. *A Collection of several pieces of Mr John Toland*, vol.2, p.465.
74. On Molesworth's money, see Dickson, *Financial Revolution*, p.168.

presented. He was, without much sign of remorse, capable of both borrowing a large sum of money for the speculation, but also invoking the reputation of his patron to secure the transaction. He was also unafraid of accepting the counsel of a financial expert (Janssen): as he explained in these matters, 'You may easily guess I will be govern'd by him'. This may strike the casual observer as evidence of an acquisitive nature out of kilter with the supposed land-based commitments of true republicans. The complexity of Toland's position is best betrayed by his own words of justification: as he reasoned, 'Another such job will make me as easy and independent as I desire, without ever Stockjobbing more'. Just as the comments in *Cato's letters* had conjectured, all men sought out independence, and wealth was a means to this end. Toland anticipated that with his profits he might 'by an annuity of two or three hundred pounds, tho' the purchase of land is got up to thirty years, and, if things go on at this rate, will mount much higher'.[75] Purchase of land would provide the security and independence necessary to allow the pursuit of intellectual and political agendas. In aiming to invest the profits in land, Toland was not alone. A majority of the South Sea directors invested their capital gains in land: such was the trend that by mid-1720 the price of land was greatly inflated.[76] Toland's intimacy with both Molesworth and Janssen was not compromised by the disaster of the bursting Bubble. Toland's understanding of friendship was shaped by constancy of political commitment: as he wrote to the disgraced Janssen in 1721, 'I have known you for many years, not only under as fair a character as any Merchant in London, but likewise a most zealous friend to the British Constitution'. Only when a friend became an enemy to the 'Liberty of our Country' would all ties 'be dissolv'd, and all obligations cancell'd'. Clearly anxious to ensure that Janssen was innocent of the fraud, Toland noted that the financier had 'condemn'd the too great power that was lodg'd in a few hands, and the arbitrary use they made of it', a theme that was writ large in the 'Secret history'. As Toland remarked, because Janssen had expressed his 'uneasiness at almost everything from a little before the third subscription' it was evident he was 'rather imprudent than criminal'. Toland's urgent advice was to co-operate with the parliamentary enquiry and 'to clear your self with the soonest' by speedy and frank confession of all he knew.[77]

Political commitments then formed the basis of this friendship with Janssen, and allowed it to survive the embarrassment of the crisis. Indeed Toland acted on behalf of Janssen in his moment of disgrace,

---

75. *A Collection of several pieces of Mr John Toland*, vol.2, p.465.
76. Dickson, *Financial Revolution*, p.146.
77. *A Collection of several pieces of Mr John Toland*, vol.2, p.466-67.

recommending that the Frenchman seek out Molesworth (who was leading the process of 'doing justice to the Public') and to be as 'candid as his integrity and your case requir'd'.[78] Appealing to Molesworth's good nature in this matter was probably an optimistic expectation, but it gives an insight into the limits and dimensions of republican hostility to finance. Such a meeting did in fact take place on 18 January 1721, with other members of the committee of investigation present. Toland was keen, even in the aftermath of Robert Knight's flight from the country (an act which necessarily placed pressure on those directors left in the country), to reassure Janssen that he was able and willing to offer him service and support. Significantly, amongst Toland's papers (and reproduced in the posthumous collection) was a copy of 'A letter written in the name of a member of the House of Commons to another member', which was essentially a defence of directors like Janssen who had been excluded from the inner cabinet of conspirators, but yet were bearing the brunt of the blame.[79] Toland persisted in his loyalty to Janssen, who was after all, in one view, merely a failed speculator. There is probably much more to be explored regarding the cultural and intellectual commitments of the financier: evidence of the inventory of his library, for example, suggests his reading matter was diverse and heterodox. Certainly he owned works by Bayle, Spinoza, Machiavelli, Milton and Locke, as well as a full range of modern erudition and, intriguingly, a copy of the Koran.[80] His involvement with a London-based Whig club in the early years of George I's reign places him in radical circles, as did his marriage to the sister of the Whig MP, Anthony Henley.[81] Cosmopolitan, politically committed, and (even after 1721) a wealthy man, Janssen was a powerful friend for the republican Toland. It is intriguing, then, that in the very last letter Toland wrote (to Molesworth) he gratefully noted that Sir Theodore had visited him in his rather lowly lodgings in Putney and arranged payment of some necessary living expenses.[82]

78. *A Collection of several pieces of Mr John Toland*, vol.2, p.467.
79. See *A Collection of several pieces of Mr John Toland*, vol.2, p.469-75. An account is also given in *The Case of Sir Theodore Janssen, one of the late directors of the South-Sea company* (London, s. n., 1721).
80. For details of the books (and his investments in publications) see *Sir Theodore Janssen, Kt Bart his particular and inventory* (London, Jacob Tonson, Bernard Lintot and William Taylor, 1721), esp. p.10-14.
81. See Elspeth Veale, 'Sir Theodore Janssen, Huguenot and merchant of London *c.*1658-1748', *Proceedings of the Huguenot society of Great Britain and Ireland* 26:2 (1995), p.264-88; see Henry Horwitz (ed.), *London politics 1713-1717: minutes of a Whig club 1714-1717* (London, 1981), p.34; for a broad context, see also François Crouzet, 'The Huguenots and the English financial revolution', in *Favorites of fortune: technology, growth, and economic development since the Industrial Revolution*, ed. Patrice Higonnet, David S. Landes and Henry Rosovsky (Cambridge, MA, 1991), p.221-66.
82. *A Collection of several pieces of Mr John Toland*, vol.2, p.494.

It is patently clear that Toland's unimpeachable republican credentials did not stop him from either dabbling in financial speculation, or in having a close association with a monied man of international reputation. His own investments (presumably directed by insider advice from Janssen) were not successful in the long term. Writing to Barnham Goode in late October 1720, he accepted the caprice of fortune with the tranquillity of a 'pantheist' and acknowledged that the best course was to 'leave this national affair to the consideration of the Parliament, which alone can address its own mistakes'.[83] Other contemporaries mistakenly were convinced Toland had profited enormously from his business venture. A person only identified as 'Gargan' wrote from Hanover in the autumn of 1720 congratulating Toland on his windfall investment. Interestingly Gargan had been (mis?)informed of Toland's financial well-being by John Lambert, one of the directors of the South Sea Company who had wide international business interests (and indeed had speculated in the French bubble inspired by John Law earlier in 1720). According to Gargan, Lambert (whose estate was reduced to a mere £5000 by Parliament) claimed that Toland's 'grand souscription' would return 'quelques milliers de livres sterling'.[84] As a consequence Toland was, Gargan believed, in a favourable position to pay off his debts. He explained that his own ever-growing expenses and extended family commitments meant he was keen to see the sum settled; to this end he included an account of the outstanding amount (which in fact dated back to 1708, so included a calculation of interest at 6 per cent). Appealing to Toland's justice and honesty, Gargan suggested he pay either by 'lettre de change' or by the intermediary of a Mr Cairns.[85] It is unlikely that this particular debt was paid off, but the letter throws light on how far someone like Toland was embedded in a culture and network of credit and debt. He was able to draw on connections in England and on the Continent; that Janssen, Lambert, and Gargan were intimate with his financial affairs indicates he was both familiar and creditworthy in these circles. This was a republican entangled in the world of money and credit, not one who stood aloof from such contamination.

John Toland had a complicated attitude towards money. All his life he was in financial difficulties: politicians, printers, friends and patrons were all approached to settle him in some security. Intimate with men and women of considerable wealth and status, he must have found the inequalities between his own condition and theirs uncomfortable (although he regarded these differences of status stoically as mere

83. BL Add Mss 4295 f.39.
84. BL Add Mss 4295 f.37; Cobbett, *Parliamentary history*, vol.7, p.834, shows Lambert's estate of £72,508 reduced to £5000.
85. BL Add Mss 4295 f.38, gives full details of the original debt and the outstanding amount.

'accidents in life'). It is clear that many of his wealthy associates did spontaneously give him money: one, hearing of his indisposition by accident, dispatched a servant with 'a very affectionate Letter, and five Guineas inclos'd in it'. Certainly he held only a thinly veiled contempt for the 'rich' (or 'muck-worms') whose taste and judgement was blinded by the 'love' of money.[86] As he explained to Harry Collins (a man of considerable wealth himself), for such men 'Money is the sole object of their affection, and whatever is so to any man, in that he places his chiefest happiness: so that 'tis natural for him not to consent any way to its diminution, but to endeavour by all means possible the increase of it'. It was better to distinguish 'the use of mony from the abuse of it'. The person who 'makes it his servant and not his mistress' would recognise that, using money to do service to his friends 'to relieve the poor and needy, or to promote undertakings of public benefit' would have more pleasure than someone who 'saves and hoards over and above the rules of prudent foresight'. This was not to suggest that each person ought to ignore the 'main chance' and reject the opportunity to 'preserve his estate clear and intire' (to do so would be regarded neither as 'generosity nor charity, but prodigality and profuseness'). An individual of sound understanding, and a 'liberal mind', would recognise the medium between 'what he can spare, and what he ought to lay up'.[87] Money in this perception was an instrument of friendship and sociability; using it created dependence and duty, as well as freedom and comfort. As Toland recognised, the distribution of wealth was not simply a question of merit and charity: the five guineas he had received were given in such a way that it made 'a deeper impression upon me, than if another had presented me with five hundred guineas in a disobliging way'. As he put it (with the bitter taste of rejection in his mind), 'the circumstances of giving are sometimes no less disobliging, than those of denying'.[88]

Rethinking republicanism and money

It may by now be apparent that the relationship between republicanism and political economy – or between a commitment to republican forms of political liberty and institutions and land, credit and money – was much more complicated than the current historiography has suggested. A plausible response may be that the case-study of Toland and Molesworth is an idiosyncratic one; each man, for contingent reasons, may have compromised his public commitments to 'republican' core principles. Alternatively it may be that the historiographical reading of

86. *A Collection of several pieces of Mr John Toland*, vol.2, p.447, 446.
87. *A Collection of several pieces of Mr John Toland*, vol.2, p.445, 446.
88. *A Collection of several pieces of Mr John Toland*, vol.2, p.447.

the nature of 'republicanism' has glossed over some of the complexities, in particular, of James Harrington's works. Here the example of John Toland, however eccentric he may be classified, is seminal because of his role in the publication of the canonical edition of Harrington's works in 1700. The modern editor of the works has insisted that the 1700 edition crystallised a neo-Harringtonianism which 'now became part of the ideology of the "landed interest", or it might be more accurate to say, of those whose aim it was to constate such an "interest" as against its "monied" opposite'.[89] The purchase of this achievement was to have established that political liberty and autonomy were only preserved by property in the form of land, rather than the more mobile forms of money and finance. Republican political theory was premised upon a conception of civic personality which was in turn based on an agrarian rather than a mercantile theory of property. Central to this republican vision was the insistence that property conferred political independence, and given the right sort of civil institutions, would deliver virtue. By the early 1700s, as Pocock describes it, the definition of property as land was 'opposed more urgently than [Harrington] had ever found necessary to property in other forms – office, credit, and commerce'. The neo-Harringtonians had developed an account of the political function of modern forms of property which created new types of dependence on the central institutions of government, on public credit and most disastrously on the market.[90] Pocock did however sound a note of caution in remarking that there was a 'dimension of ambiguity' about Toland's 1700 edition, most manifest in the dedication of the work 'To the Lord Mayor, Aldermen, Sherifs, and Common Council of London' and the fulsome praise of the Bank of England. Like the commonwealth publicist, Marchamont Nedham, Toland made these editorial interventions as part of a tactical 'shifting game' calculated for contingent political objectives and personal influence.[91] There is more to say, especially in the light of Toland's attitudes to money, about this edition and its role in the formation of late republican attitudes to land, credit and commerce.

The material context and presentation of the volume casts some further light. The publication was planned over a period of years in the late 1690s: a letter from William Simpson to Toland noted that the former exclusionist Whig and City of London Alderman, Sir Robert Clayton, had proposed (unsuccessfully) raising money from other city men to support the costs of the volume. Toland had known Clayton's son at Oxford, and had extended his intimacy to the father after the son's

89. Pocock, 'Historical introduction', in *The Political works of James Harrington*, p.138.
90. Pocock, 'Historical introduction', p.145.
91. Pocock, 'Historical introduction', p.142.

death in 1698. It is possible that Clayton may have considered using his electoral influence on behalf of Toland's candidature for the House of Commons at this time too. In writing a letter of condolence, Toland commended Clayton's reputation as a man who had 'rais'd your fortune solely by your own merit and industry (without losing your honor or reputation by any indirect and criminal methods of growing rich)'. Clayton had served his country in the 'most publick capacity' in both Parliament and city. Indeed his magistracy in the 'greatest, freest and most powerful City in the world' had brought universal esteem.[92] It was precisely these qualities, in the exact language of the private letter, which were praised in the dedication to the volume of 1700: Toland saw no impropriety in anchoring Clayton's industrious, commercial and Whig reputation to the status of Harrington's writings. An agreement was signed with the printer John Darby in July 1699 to 'reprint upon very good paper'. It is notable that Toland bore the cost of the publication (agreed in the first instance at £30), paying off the initial debt between March and June 1700, although there is evidence in this manuscript that further money was paid for subsequent copies. Some of Toland's friends (Shaftesbury and Benjamin Furly being the most obvious) helped in distributing the works in England and on the Continent.[93] The sociability which enabled the production of Harringon's works was urban and commercial, as well as entrenched in a republican political tradition.

The most obvious indication of Toland's revisionist reading of the cultural purchase of Harrington's ideas can be seen in the frontispiece of the volume. This is a deeply textured, multi-layered presentation of republican tradition and its connection with religious and national identity in the British Isles. Martial symbols rest upon a classical monument portraying a tradition of republican political legislators (controversially) from Moses to William III. The central figure of 'Liberty' holding the stave of manumission and a Phrygian cap establishes the core political value of the volume. Importantly the pillars of the political architecture (so in a Harringtonian sense, those foundations which support the superstructure of the state) rest upon foundation stones labelled 'commercio' and 'opificio', accompanied by representations of city and rural scenes. Given the supposed antagonism between land and credit, or between countryside and city, the choice of terms here is instructive. 'Commercio' is straightforward, indicating trade, business and mercantile activity: the building delineated could be a bank, a grand

---

92. *A Collection of several pieces of Mr John Toland*, vol.2, p.21-22 (letter to Sir Robert Clayton dated 4 December 1698). See Robert E. Sullivan, *John Toland and the deist controversy: a study in adaptations* (Cambridge, MA, 1982), p.283, n49; Margaret Jacob, *The Newtonians and the English Revolution, 1689-1720* (Hassocks, 1976), p.120-21, 221.

93. BL Add Mss 4295 f.10.

marketplace or an exchange. Its elevation to the status of dual foundation is significant. The other term – 'opificio' – labelling the agrarian scene of animals grazing, is more challenging. *Cultura, terra, rusticus, ager* might have been a more appropriate root for a label that emphasised the land-based themes in Harrington's notion of property determining dominion. 'Opificio' suggests a collection of ideas loosely associated with making, fabrication and artisan labour and industry, rather than a sense of land-based agricultural cultivation. That the frontispiece represents a political architecture resting on the dual foundations of countryside and city, on commerce and cultivation, is a deliberate reading of Harrington's suggestions; it is one out of kilter with the modern understanding.

This process of rereading is evident in Toland's editorial contributions to the volume. Dedicating it to the Lord Mayor, aldermen, sheriffs and Common Council of London, Toland celebrated London as the 'largest, fairest, richest and most populous City in the world', and, as he concluded, all built on the foundation of freedom. Liberty was 'the true Spring of its prodigious Trade and Commerce' which had created an empire of colonies and factories 'in *Europe, Asia, and Africa*: hence it is that every Sea is cover'd with our Ships, that the very Air is scarce exempted from our Inventions, and that all the Productions of Art or Nature are imported to this common Storehouse of Mankind'. The admirable citizens of London had 'so high a degree of Riches and Politeness, that for their stately Houses, fine Equipages, and sumptuous Tables, they exceed the port of som Foren Princes'. Whether in cities, towns or the countryside, citizens lived happy in secure enjoyment of 'Life and Property'. The 'Power and Freedom' of the city was embodied in the Bank of England: this financial institution, which rendered public credit secure, was also commendable because it 'coms the nearest of any Government to Harrington's Model'. Toland expressed his belief that the Bank's existence (at that point limited by statute) would be 'render'd perpetual'.[94] The dedication rather artfully reworks the 'government' of the City of London into a Harringtonian model of the 'Rules of good Polity'.[95] It is not too fanciful to suggest that Toland's commendations of the forms of constitution evident in the government of London ('a new Rome in the West') were a substitution for dealing with the issue of the political identity of the national establishment. If there was a republican form of government extant in London, then the nation's liberty was safe.

94. Toland, dedication 'To the Lord Mayor, Aldermen, Sherifs, and Common Council of London', p.i-iii.
95. Toland, dedication 'To the Lord Mayor, Aldermen, Sherifs, and Common Council of London', p.vi.

A commercially dynamic metropolis was an acceptable and convenient surrogate for republican aspirations in 1700.

There is no space here to discuss how Toland refashioned common-wealth political theory to incorporate the rule of kings, or as he put it, 'the secret of so happily uniting too [sic] seemingly incompatible things, Principality and Liberty'.[96] Toland was convinced that republication of Harrington's works would perform a 'Public Good' in providing learned reading for gentlemen keen on imitating the '*Roman* Patricians' they resembled.[97] We should take this suggestion seriously: it is not plausible (especially given statements in the preface) that Toland believed reading Harrington would turn England into a republic, but he undoubtedly did think there was some constructive point for his broader political agenda. Just as they read Plato's *Republic*, or travel literature, for education and diversion, so they could profitably absorb counsel about the nature and function of politics from *Oceana*. It was possible then to use Harrington's works as an instrument of analysis rather than a prescriptive text. These writings explained both how politics worked, as well as offering counsel on how it worked 'best'. According to Toland (and most subsequent commentators), one of the central analytical achievements of Harring-ton's work was the perception that there were 'natural' foundations to political processes encapsulated in the principle that empire followed dominion. In Toland's words, Harrington pointed out that there were 'in Societys [sic]' natural causes producing their necessary effects, as well as in the Earth or the Air'. This discovery meant that the causes of civil conflict were not provoked by faction but by natural distemper prompted by distribution of the 'national balance' of property. Toland illustrated the principle that '*Empire follows the Balance of Property*' by pointing out that the man who had £1000 per annum could command and influence more servants than someone with £100.[98]

Harrington had claimed that 'Domestic Empire' was founded upon the ownership of property 'real or personal, that is to say, in Lands, or in Mony and Goods'. The distribution of landownership was taken to be the key determinant in the shaping of political power, although it was acknowledged that this would not apply 'in a City that has little or no Land, and whose Revenue is in Trade'.[99] Throughout his writings, Harrington expressed a preference for thinking about land rather than other financial or mercantile forms of property. Indeed, in a phrase cited a good deal he appears to have been hostile towards (or at least

96. Toland, 'The Preface' to *The Oceana of James Harrington and his other works*, p.viii; see Champion, *Republican learning*, part 2.
97. Toland, 'The Preface' to *The Oceana of James Harrington and his other works*, p.ix, x.
98. Toland, 'The Preface' to *The Oceana of James Harrington and his other works*, p.xvii, xviii.
99. *The Oceana of James Harrington and his other works*, p.39.

unconvinced by) communities where power was shaped by non-agrarian wealth: he stated, 'As for Dominion personal or in Mony, it may now and then stir up a Melius or a Manlius, which, if the Commonwealth be not provided with som kind of *Dictatorian* Power, may be dangerous'. Effective property, he argued, 'is requir'd that it should have som certain root or foothold, which, except in Land, it cannot have, being otherwise as it were upon the Wing'. However (and rather confusingly) he recognised that in some places where mercantile wealth far outweighed land (the examples are Holland and Genoa), 'the balance of Treasure may be equal to that of Land'.[100] The perception was that land, in the first instance, provided the best material resource for the business of government, in particular for the important commission of supplying an army. Citing the aphorism that 'an Ox knows his Master's Crib', Harrington noted that an 'Army is a Beast that has a great belly, and must be fed; wherfore this will com to what Pastures you have, and what Pastures you have will com to the balance of Property, without which the public sword is a mere name or spitfrog'.[101] The experience of furnishing the military during the 1640s and early 1650s unmistakably had an impact on generating this wisdom.

Harrington's writings betray an admiration for and eulogy of the political culture produced by landed society. The insistence that 'Tillage bringing up a good Soldiery, brings up a good Commonwealth' underpinned the idea that the amount of land owned determined an individual's freedom: 'for where the owner of the Plow coms to have the Sword too, he will use it in defence of his own'. As in ancient Rome where the consuls were called from the plough, so in England (citing Aristotle's Latinised dictum 'agricolarum democratica respublica optima') 'Husbandry, or the country way of Life' was the 'best stuff of the Commonwealth'. The turbulence of 'city life' in Athens was contrasted with the stability of a land-based polity: even the 'Urban Tribes' of Rome were 'of no reputation in comparison of the Rustics'. The exception of Venice, where the gentleman rulers were 'wholly addicted to City Life', was only successful because every one else was excluded from government. In the city 'Ambition' was 'everyman's trade', whereas in the country 'the Plow in the hands of the owner finds him a better calling'.[102] The most explicit theoretical consequence of this admiration was Harrington's suggestion that the way to avoid distempers and conflict within a commonwealth was to manage the stable distribution of landed property through *leges*

100. *The Oceana of James Harrington and his other works*, p.40.
101. *The Oceana of James Harrington and his other works*, p.41.
102. *The Oceana of James Harrington and his other works*, p.34-35; note that the Latin citation from Aristotle is left out of the 1700 edition; see James Harrington, *The Common-wealth of Oceana* (London, J. Streater for Livewell Chapman, 1656.), sig.B1*v*.

agrariae.[103] Drawing from historical evidence Harrington identified the agrarian law as a device for halting the chain of conflict which underlay the cycle of changes in the forms of polity. To reinforce his point a number of rhetorical objections were raised against the benefits of an agrarian law which, for example, might limit the inheritance patterns of land to portions worth £2000 per annum. Such an agrarian law was unnecessary, dangerous, insufficient to 'keep out Monarchy', ruins families, destroys industry and lastly would be impossible to introduce without conflict. However, contradicting Aristotle and Machiavelli, Harrington insisted that agrarian legislation was a necessary antidote to the corrupting poison of internal conflict. By analogy with the natural function of the Nile, he noted that the land where the river 'wanders in one stream, is barren; but where it parts into seven, it multiplys its fertil shores by distributing, yet keeping and improving such a Propriety and Nutrition, as is a prudent Agrarian to a wellorder'd Commonwealth'.[104]

The proposed agrarian legislation was calculated to create stability ('a fixation' in his words) of constitutional form.[105] Contrary to the views of recent commentators it was not regarded by him as a device for dampening the economic vitality of the community.[106] Agrarian legislation would positively encourage 'industry': as Harrington speculated in prophetic mode, 'Who knows how far the Arms of our Agrarian may extend themselves? and whether he that might have left a Pillar, may not leave a temple of many Pillars to his more pious memory?' Some might devote themselves to trade, others would cast their 'thoughts upon the Commonwealth' and have leisure to serve the public. Unlike the effects in Sparta and Laconia, the function of an agrarian in Oceana would 'multiply' money. Such increase might bring problems of covetousness, as did Lysander's 'bringing in of the golden spoils of *Athens*, [which] irrecoverably ruin'd that Commonwealth'. The hope was that 'in time every Citizen will have his *Villa*'.[107] Despite this fundamental concern with the distribution or management of landownership, Harrington was sensitive to the value of trade and commerce – what he called 'industry'. He calculated that 'the revenue of Industry in a Nation [...] is three or

103. For detailed discussion see, *The Oceana of James Harrington and his other works*, p.101-11. See also the debate in John F. H. New, 'Harrington, a realist?', *Past & present* 24 (1963), p.75-81; C. B. Macpherson, 'Harrington as realist: a rejoinder', *Past & present* 24 (1963), p.82-85; John F. H. New, 'The meaning of Harrington's agrarian', *Past & present* 25 (1963), p.94-95. The question of whether the seventeenth-century understanding of the function of *leges agrariae* in antiquity was accurate is discussed in Ronald T. Ridley, '*Leges agrariae*: myths ancient and modern', *Classical philology* 95:4 (2000), p.459-67.

104. *The Oceana of James Harrington*, p.103, 108.

105. *The Oceana of James Harrington*, p.106.

106. See Pincus, 'Neither Machiavellian moment nor possessive individualism'.

107. *The Oceana of James Harrington*, p.108, 109, 111.

fourfold greater than that of the mere Rent'.[108] The agrarian would cause 'their industry to flow with milk and hony'. As Alan Cromartie has elegantly pointed out, 'Harrington actually favoured the growth of a commercial civilisation'.[109] Not only would this bring prosperity, but it would also allow the expansion of a leisured class who could devote their virtuous energy to the public interest. Husbandry and agriculture had a priority in providing the 'Bread of the Nation', as he explained: 'we are hung upon it by the teeth; it is a mighty Nursery of Strength, the best Army, and the most assur'd Knapsac'. Building on this basis, industry, the 'principal nerve of a Commonwealth', had potential to develop manufactures and merchandise which might challenge the supremacy of the Dutch.[110] To later men like Toland and Molesworth, these hints of commendation in the canonical text provided justification for a republican appreciation of the intimate relationship between *commercium* and *opificium*.

Many of Harrington's immediate contemporaries were unconvinced by his claim that 'imperium fundatur in dominio'. His critic Matthew Wren expressed his doubts in the most simple manner: 'For what is propriety, but riches? And riches are confest to be power.' To draw a distinction between power and property was to design a 'new Lexicon to express those things we knew before'. Power was power: disposable power in the form of money was more immediately useful than 'a large possession in lands'. He continued, 'It is not to be doubted but that a Revenue sufficient to maintain a Force able to bear down all Opposition, does equally conduce to Empire, whither it arises from the Rents of lands, the Profits of ready moneys, the Duties payable upon Manufactures and Traffique, or any other kind of Income'.[111] In particular Wren thought the example of the agrarian laws unpersuasive: while the case of ancient Israel and Lacedaemon seemed to support Harrington's arguments, the predominance of wealth in non-agrarian forms militated against its application to the British Isles. As Wren explained, Lycurgus's agrarian was designed for moral purposes, 'not so much to attain an equality in the Frame of Government, as to drive into Exile Riches, and the Effects of them Luxury and Debauchery'.[112] Applied to the conditions of seventeenth-century society agrarian legislation would be

---

108. *The Oceana of James Harrington*, p.166.
109. Alan Cromartie, 'Harringtonian virtue: Harrington, Machiavelli, and the method of the *Moment*', *Historical Journal* 41:4 (1998), p.987-1009 (999).
110. *The Oceana of James Harrington and his other works*, p.178.
111. [Matthew Wren], *Considerations on Mr Harrington's common-wealth of Oceana* (London, Samuel Gellibrand, 1657), p.14, 16.
112. Wren, *Considerations*, p.78.

inappropriate because it was ineffective at regulating the expansion of money and wealth displayed in the commercial success of London.

Harrington took up this challenge explicitly in subsequent works, acknowledging that commerce was often a means by which the balance of property was altered (a 'natural revolution'). In his response, Harrington considered in some detail the cases of Israel, Holland and Genoa and how the relationship between landed and moneyed property was moderated by agrarian laws. In ancient Israel a ban on usury supplemented the agrarian law. As a comparative exercise between the cases of Canaan and Yorkshire illustrated, Harrington was aware of the potential power of money, but in the context of England, he judged that it was secondary to the magnitude of land. As he explained, 'Now if we imagin *Yorkshire* divided as was *Canaan*, into six hundred thousand lots, or as was *Laconia*, into thirty thousand; a *Yorkeshire* man having one Thousand pounds in his purse, would, I believe, have a better estate in Money then in Land'. In such a case, to keep the balance determined by property, usury and money 'must of Necessity be forbidden'. Fortunately, in Harrington's judgement, in a territory of the magnitude of England, the land was not 'overballanced by money' and therefore there was no need to manage the equilibrium of such wealth. This was not to dismiss the benefits of commerce: as he underscored, 'in a Countrey where Merchandise is exercised, it is so far from being destructive, that it is necessary'. Money must not be left to 'rust unprofitably in private purses'.[113]

The perceived antagonism Harrington is alleged to have displayed towards commerce, money and finance needs revision. His writings show an awareness of the significance of trade, a reasonable understanding of the nature of revenue and a measure of insight into the business of lending and borrowing. It is accurate to say that Harrington laid primacy on the determining function of landed property (especially in the English context) but this should not imply that he was either ignorant of or indifferent to the influence of other forms of property. A conviction that ownership of land was the dominant mode of property in England shaped his interpretation of structures of political power, but it did not necessarily exclude the consideration that other modes of property might exercise power in different circumstances. In the case of Harrington's own perceptions, the general principle, 'imperium fundatur in dominio', by default meant that the balance of power was shaped by land ownership; later interpreters could quite plausibly take 'property' to be a much more capacious category without compromising the intellectual claims of the principle. Harrington's property principle was a tool of analysis that could, with imagination, pertain to a number

---

113. Harrington, *Prerogative*, p.14-15; *The Oceana of James Harrington and his other works*, p.245-46.

of alternative circumstances. The application of an agrarian balance was a specific prescription to remedy what he saw as fundamental disjunction between property and the superstructure of political institutions. The tool of analysis might easily be detached from the pragmatic recommendations.

It would not be an exaggeration to suggest that, while later seventeenth-century republicans subscribed to the belief that landownership was a primary determinant of political power, they were also utterly uninterested in the prospect of enacting agrarian legislation. Walter Moyle, for example, one of the most learned republicans of the later period, in his long manuscript essay on Roman government used Harrington's approach, 'the natural transmigration of dominion', to explore the 'great revolution' behind the fall of Rome, but showed no inclination to call for the application of such historical lessons to his own political culture.[114] Toland's contributions to the 1700 edition (the citation of the commercial cultural milieu represented by Sir Robert Clayton, and the presentation of the frontispiece) suggest that he had a reasonable expectation that contemporaries would perceive the relevance of Harrington's ideas to their own context. That this did not include agitation for a redistribution of landed property is evident from even the most cursory survey of his political writings.

An insight into the process which saw Harrington's very deliberate appreciation of landed property evolve into a defence of a more capacious understanding of property can be seen in Toland's *The Art of governing by partys* (1701), an analytical account of the causes of conflict in contemporary political culture. Delineating how the rival interests of party (provoked by an opposition with tyrannous intentions) caused distempers in social, political and even economic institutions, Toland (despite using Harringtonian tools of scrutiny) included a profound and impassioned defence of public credit. Ideological division had surfaced in rivalry between the New and Old East India Companies, which had 'miserably divided the Capital City of this Nation'.[115] This not only compromised the integrity of particular commercial activities, but also ruined public credit because the financial arrangements were 'a manifest violation of the public Faith'. As Toland explained, public credit in England was underpinned by the security of Parliament. If this trust was

114. See Caroline Robbins (ed.), *Two English republican tracts* (Cambridge, 1969) p.231, 233-39 (on agrarian legislation). See also the manuscript version, The National Archives PRO 30/24/47/4, which includes references to the classical sources.

115. Toland, *The Art of governing by partys* (London, Bernard Lintott, 1701), p.120; Henry Horwitz, 'The East India trade, the politicians and the constitution: 1689-1702', *Journal of British studies* 17:2 (1978), p.1-18; Robert Walcott, 'The East India interest in the general election of 1700-1701', *English historical review* 71 (1956), p.223-39.

broken by deceitful private interest, liberty would be threatened: 'this is the certain way to bring us at one Stroke under that Slavery we have ever so barvely [*sic*] resisted'.[116] The defence of public credit was a republican pursuit.

Toland saw an intimate connection between the private property of individual citizens and the trust placed in public institutions which secured that property. If the national institutions were not creditable, 'no body will ever part with their mony again to the Government on any terms, be the premiums never so great or temting'. Historical experience showed that conspirators (Manlius, Catiline and Julius Caesar are the examples given) had destroyed 'all public Faith' in order to enrich themselves on the dissolution of government.[117] The textual authority deployed to expand on this theme, Cicero's *De officiis* 2.21, is significant in terms of examining how a republican understood the nature of property.[118] Toland quoted Cicero's words *in extenso*, but carefully presented them in order to support the point that the function of government was to protect the property and estates of private men. It was, according to Cicero (in Toland's rendering), the 'principal care of him, who is at the head of the government, that every one be secur'd in his property, and that the estates of privat men be not diminish'd under pretence of a public good'. Government and cities were constituted chiefly for 'this very reason'. As Toland commented, this implied that the credit of the Treasury ought to be maintained with as little cost to the people as possible. Expenses of state should be frugal and moderate: the squandering of public money must be avoided. More powerfully, he called attention to Cicero's hostility to the *populares* who had proposed agrarian laws.[119] Here it seems apparent that Toland was quite prepared to abandon one of the central planks of Harrington's approach.

Agrarian legislation threatened the foundations of government by destroying equity; it was 'essential to a community or city that it be free, and not under any doubts or fears about the safety of their possessions'. Any sort of activity which spoilt 'credit' damaged the reputation of government; swift settlement of debts, inexpensive taxation and the preservation of property was the virtuous business of government. The usage of the word *fides* in Cicero's text (translated by Toland as 'credit') denoted trustworthiness or good reputation rather than simply financial probity.[120] Eighteenth-century use by men like Toland invoked both

116. Toland, *Art of governing by partys*, p.124, 125.
117. Toland, *Art of governing by partys*, p.124, 127.
118. Toland, *Art of governing by partys*, p.128-34.
119. Toland, *Art of governing by partys*, p.30.
120. See Cicero, *On Duties*, ed. M. T. Griffin and E. M. Atkins (Cambridge, 1991), p.95-98, esp. p.97n4 and p.xlvi.

senses of the word. Toland's deployment of Cicero's polemic against the *leges agrariae* betrays the aristocratic culture celebrated elsewhere in his interpretation of Harrington's texts. Cicero's conception of the nature and function of landed and other forms of property was firmly embedded within his broader republican political thinking. Reflecting the lack of a formal system of credit in the ancient world, for Cicero it was a fundamental belief that real estate was the premise of a secure political identity. As a consequence agrarian laws threatened, by enforced redistribution, to distort the natural balance of political power. This meant, as Julia Annas has noted, 'nobody could be a stronger supporter of the institution of private property than Cicero'.[121] Cicero's defence of the sanctity of private property was a justification of the economic foundations of senatorial power: land gave wealth, which was a necessary platform for a successful political career. In a phrase Harrington may have applauded, J. M. Carter argues that Cicero believed 'land was an essential political commodity'.[122] Just as in Harrington's work, Cicero can be read as celebrating the political culture derived from land-ownership, at the same time as demeaning commerce and trade. Certainly passages in *De officiis* (1.151) exhibit a manifest condescension towards those who earned a living in commercial or manufacturing sectors. By contrast, as Cicero remarked, 'there is no kind of gainful employment that is better, more fruitful, more pleasant and more worthy of a free man than agriculture'.[123] Of course here, like Harrington, the Roman did not intend to imply that actually tilling the soil was virtuous, but that managing a large estate provided ample opportunity for 'industry' and virtue.

Cicero's attitudes to riches, other than land-based wealth, were influenced by his Stoicism. The accumulation of wealth for its own end, or for avarice, was unacceptable. Riches, in any form, should never be allowed to compromise the exercise of virtue. Extravagance, luxury and the accumulation of wealth, for any other purpose than a moral end, was wrong. Compounding such moral damage those, like Crassus, who used their wealth for fomenting political and social unrest, were condemned. One of the key concepts, grafted on to this Ciceronian celebration of the political value of land, was that of 'industria' or

121. Julia Annas, 'Cicero on Stoic moral philosophy and private property', in *Philosophia togata*, ed. Miriam Griffin and Jonathan Barnes (Oxford, 1989), p.151-73 (170).
122. See J. M. Carter, 'Cicero: politics and philosophy', in *Cicero and Virgil: studies in honour of Harold Hunt*, ed. John R. C. Martyn (Amsterdam, 1972), p.15-36 (33). See also Neal Wood, *Cicero's social and political thought* (Berkeley, CA, 1988), esp. p.105-19; G. E. M. de Ste Croix, *The Class struggle in the ancient Greek world from the archaic age to the Arab conquests* (London, 1981), p.122, 125.
123. Cicero, *On duties*, p.58-59.

improvement. The moral worth of land was not passive: Cicero's own biography displays a man immersed in property deals and financial transactions. One of the ways a landowner was meant to expand his virtue was by the creditable improvement of his estate. The works of Xenophon and Cato delivered advice on best conduct – the industrious development of villas, fishponds and farms, as well as an acute sense of the variety of ways of maximising rental income were all practical ways in which a man like Cicero might improve his status morally, politically and economically.[124] It was this aristocratic yet active conception of property that informed the culture of republican attitudes to property, whether land-based or commercial, in the 1700s. Harrington's own writings had venerated not only land, but gentility in its management. Gentlemen, the natural aristocracy of virtue, were a leisured class who could devote their lives to public good. As Harrington rather extravagantly put it, 'if any man has founded a commonwealth, he was first a Gentleman'.[125] Republican attitudes to property and land were not simply conceptual but had profound practical application to the conduct of life. Late in his life, in correspondence with Molesworth, Toland imagined himself as Atticus writing to his friend and patron Cicero.[126] Like the great Roman senator, Molesworth had retired to his estate to write, commented Toland, 'that excellent work, wherein you have made such progress, and which seems to resemble so nearly Cicero *de Republica*, [which] will be a nobler task, and more useful to mankind, than any Senatorial efforts'.[127]

Molesworth, industry and estate management

Contrary to the view that Molesworth's republican commitments conformed to traditional 'neo-Harringtonian' conceptions, an exploration of his political and economic practice, in particular attitudes to estate management, allows a fuller view of the later evolution of this ideology. As will be argued, despite his unimpeachable Harringtonian credentials, Molesworth was fully engaged with the commercial and improving economic life of his culture. Following the commonplace premise of Harrington's thinking, Molesworth emphasised the role of

124. See Wood, *Cicero's social and political thought*, p.112-13, 117, 118-19; Elizabeth Rawson, 'The Ciceronian aristocracy and its properties', in *Studies in Roman property*, ed. M. I. Finley (Cambridge, 1976), p.85-102 (esp. 94-97); P. Walcot, 'Cicero on private property: theory and practice', *Greece and Rome*, 2nd series, 22:2 (1975) p.120-28 (esp. 122-24); Nicholas Purcell, 'The Roman *villa* and the landscape of production', in *Urban society in Roman Italy*, ed. T. J. Cornell and Kathryn Lomas (London, 1995), p.151-79.
125. *The Oceana of James Harrington*, p.56.
126. BL Add Mss 4465 f.36.
127. *A Collection of several pieces of Mr John Toland*, vol.2, p.492. The work referred to here does not survive in either Molesworth's printed œuvre or private papers.

landownership as a platform for virtuous public service. Yet, like many of his republican friends, Molesworth was more than capable of adapting this ideology to the circumstances of eighteenth-century commercial society. In Molesworth's public and private writings it is possible to see this process of adaptation, as agrarian nostalgia was eschewed for discourses of progress and improvement. Nevertheless, land was at the core of his beliefs, and having 'Estates in the Kingdom' was a prerequisite for political citizenship (in particular membership in the Commons). Such property should not be 'fleeting ones, which may be sent beyond Sea by Bills of Exchange, by every Pacquet-Boat, but fix'd and permanent'. Those merchants, bankers and 'money'd' men ambitious of senatorial position 'shou'd also have a competent, visible *Land Estate*'. While some contemporaries argued that moneyed status was preferable to those whose estates were encumbered with debts and mortgages, Molesworth remained unconvinced. His underlying principle was that those with estates would have the same interest as the rest of the country when it came to 'publick taxes, gains and losses'.[128] Despite this apparent conservatism, Molesworth's broader vision of economic life was an active one. So, for example, general naturalisation was regarded as a good device for increasing the population and thereby stimulating trade. Expanding the number of workmen in any town would enable the community to 'thrive'; as a consequence, 'the greater will be the *Demand* of the Manufacture, and the *Vent* to foreign Parts, and the quicker *Circulation* of the *Coin*'. Decrying the restrictive practices of many town corporations where commerce was entangled in complex bye-laws, Molesworth argued that the new villages which had grown up unincorporated were 'more liberal' in their regulatory structures and by consequence deserved parliamentary representation. Such better-peopled and more 'industrious' places were preferable to wastes and deserts like Old Sarum.[129]

Following Harrington's insights, Molesworth argued that the moral character of a community, and its constituent individuals, was shaped by the 'form of government', and that this was closely bound to the distribution of property. Molesworth had famously conducted his own Harringtonian analysis of a disordered commonwealth in the much reprinted and translated *An Account of Denmark* (1694).[130] Manners and customs were moulded by the experience of the institutions and laws of a nation: liberty was cultivated by the land. In his writings, through his parliamentary career and evident in his stewardship of his own country

---

128. Molesworth, 'The translator's preface', in François Hotman, *Franco-Gallia: or, an account of the ancient free state of France*, 2nd edn (London, Edward Valentine, 1721), p.xix.
129. Molesworth, 'The translator's preface', in Hotman, *Franco-Gallia*, p.xxiii, xxiv.
130. See Molesworth, *An Account of Denmark*, ed. Champion.

estates in England and Ireland, Molesworth embodied republican ideals of the industrious gentleman, stalwart in defence of public liberty, hostile to tyranny, yet active in nurturing improvement. He defended this vision consistently post-1689: his edition of the monarchomach Calvinist writer François Hotman's *Franco-Gallia*, prepared in 1705, first published in 1711 and republished in 1721 with additions and a new preface, is testimony to this durability of political commitment. A consistent defender of 'civil rights', Molesworth conceived of his political career as supporting the continuity of the liberty of the 'ancient free state': he hoped 'that my Friends, Relations and Children, with their Posterity, will inherit their Share of this inestimable Blessing, and that I have contributed my Part to it'.[131] Unlike many modern accounts, Molesworth's perceived no discontinuity between the commonwealth ideologies of the 1650s and the 1700s: the core principle of a consti-tution, where 'the Good of the *Whole* is taken care of by the *Whole*', made the question of whether a monarchy existed irrelevant; as he put it, 'the having a *King* or *Queen* at the Head of it, alters not the Case'.[132] Such a community, committed to universal liberty, independent of religious confession, would encourage all to use their 'Body, Estate, and Under-standing for the publick Good'. The ambition of such a community was to provide the grounding for improvement so that each could 'securely and peaceably enjoy *Property* and *Liberty* both of *Mind* and *Body*'. By such provision, individuals and community gained: as he clarified, 'The Thriving of any one *single Person* by honest Means, is the Thriving of the *Commonwealth* wherein he resides.'[133] In this conception, the purpose of political society was to enable a flourishing and industrous community.

Benefiting the public was the point of economic and fiscal policy. Molesworth, for example, defended the potential of 'Parliamentary Credit' which would promote 'all *publick Buildings* and *High-ways*, the making all *Rivers Navigable* that are capable of it, employing the *Poor*, suppressing *Idlers*, restraining *Monopolies* upon Trade, maintaining the Liberty of the *Press*, the just *paying* and *encouraging* of all in the publick Service'.[134] Far from decrying the burdens of taxation to support such government initiatives (especially in the costly business of Continental war), Molesworth insisted that 'no true *Englishman* will grudge to pay Taxes whilst he has a Penny in his purse'. Since the cost of government was managed in a frugal manner, a citizen who 'sees the publick Money well laid out for the great Ends for which 'tis given', would contribute

---

131. Molesworth, 'The translator's preface', in Hotman, *Franco-Gallia*, p.v.
132. Molesworth, 'The translator's preface', in Hotman, *Franco-Gallia*, p.viii.
133. Molesworth, 'The franslator's preface', in Hotman, *Franco-Gallia*, p.xv.
134. Molesworth, 'The translator's preface', in Hotman, *Franco-Gallia*, p.xxxiv.

according to his abilities.[135] Notwithstanding this commitment to the virtues of landed property and its political culture, Molesworth was optimistic about the benefits of an industrious nation.

Molesworth's extensive correspondence also reveals a man who, while predisposed to place primary value on the political function of a landed aristocracy, also appreciated the contributions of commerce and industry. Molesworth spent most of his life in pursuit of financial security, both for himself and his extensive family. Ever hopeful of government office which would bring secure income, he was repeatedly disappointed. His sons, themselves on the margins of government, were anxious that their own places might be not compromised by their father's fierce reputation for 'true noble Roman courage, that neither rewards or threatenings can change'. It must have been doubly galling to Molesworth that his fatal decision to invest in South Sea stock resulted in further debt: as he commented, 'I am forced in my old age, when I expected ease and idleness, to turn my own receiver and manager again'. A frugal man (he only drew £25 per month 'for all expenses relating to myself in England', allowing his wife to manage the rest of the family estate), he regretted the folly of investing in South Sea stock, especially since he had borrowed the £2000 he invested. He acknowledged that this was for purely speculative ends: he had 'hopes of that stock's further rise, and in order to cheat some other buyer, fancying that it would not die in my hands'. The price fell only two days after he had purchased them: as he lamented 'I was rightly served for going against my own judgement'.[136] Other members of his immediate family invested too. Daniel Pultney, writing to John Molesworth (12 June 1720 n.s.), congratulated him on his gains, but hoped he would be 'moderate in your desires and be contented with a hundred thousand pounds'.[137] Certainly such profits would allow candidature for the next parliament. Molesworth's daughter, Mrs Tichborne, had dabbled too in hopes of securing the fortune of herself and her children from the uncomfortable dependence on the court. While her father acknowledged that her behaviour had been prudent and honest, she lamented being unable to 'buy a little plate and furniture, which I want sadly'.[138] The prospect of 'imaginary riches' had tempted, it seems, many in the Molesworth connection.[139]

It was a common theme of the correspondence carried out amongst Molesworth, his sons and their friends that the best remedy for the

---

135. Molesworth, 'The translator's preface', in Hotman, *Franco-Gallia*, p.xxxv.
136. Molesworth's extensive correspondence is calendared in *Historical Manuscripts Commission: report on manuscripts in various collections* (hereafter *HMC*), vol.8 (London, 1913), p.350.
137. *HMC*, p.287.
138. *HMC*, p.288-89.
139. *HMC*, p.296, 301-303, 312-13, 350-51.

current crisis was 'improvement' of trade. Daniel Pultney put it most succinctly when he insisted that 'we must put a stop to all sort of gaming in stocks, encourage trade and manufacture, industry and frugality'. Molesworth's management of his own domestic economy reflected these values too. The 'sheet anchor' of the family was his Irish estate, where he and his wife had undertaken virtuous 'projects of good husbandry'. Late in his life he wrote in some considerable pique against the charge that he had been extravagant in matters of estate improvement in Yorkshire (the rumour that he had spent thousands was spread about by 'envious fools'; as he explained, 'I never exceed above 150*l*. per annum, whatever you may hear to the contrary'). He admitted he had spent a considerable amount on digging a canal that had profited him only by £300; he continued: 'There is neither bench, statue, fountain of stone, stairs, urn or flower-pot here as yet, so that you may judge that mere grass, trees and hedges cannot cost much.'[140] The evidence of his correspondence with his wife, sons and daughters suggests that Molesworth was a landowner with a keen eye for opportunity and development of his agrarian resources. So, for example, throughout his papers there is a recurring concern with the rental potential of his estates in Yorkshire and Ireland. The decision to adjust the nature of property-titles from freehold to twenty-one-year leases marked (according to his son) 'a way of improvement, which it never was before'. In the same instance, he encouraged the trade in Philipstown (in King's County (Offaly), Ireland) by collaboration with two 'master manufacturers' (who happened, much to the disgust of the local cleric, to be Quakers). One of these, John Pym, employed the poor to spin his wool 'to the great satisfaction of all the country and increase of the market'. Even towards the end of his life, Molesworth had a vision for how estate improvement would pay for the family's debts. As he summarised the state of play, 'the selling of woods, the setting out of St. Patrick's well land, the Alnage revenue, and the improvement of Philipstown and Swords are groundworks to raise a new estate from'.[141]

Attentiveness to the potential exploitations of new rental agreements was matched by a forensic attention to detail over the rights and privileges of his estates. Neighbours who threatened to enclose his land, tenants who took advantage of mowing allowances and people who exploited short-term rental rates for their private advantage and at damage to the integrity of the land, were all dealt with. In such circumstances Molesworth was keen to 'vindicate our right'. Molesworth's dedication to his estates was not purely driven by personal interest. Good management of tenancies set at a reasonable price would benefit

140. *HMC*, p.357.
141. *HMC*, p.286, 350, 357, 369-70.

both landlord and tenant: severe measures would have beneficial effects. Replacing 'unimproving idle people' with 'better tenants' would ensure the land was more productive. Certainly Molesworth did not take the matter of fixing the rate of his rents lightly; he was aware of the benefits of the different forms of lease holding and researched the historical fluctuation of costs over four decades. He was also profoundly aware that his relationship with individual tenants necessarily involved their dependence on him. In one instance Molesworth was explicit in this regard. He explained to his wife that he was quite against making 'leases in parchment', preferring to let his tenants remain 'tenants at will'; as a consequence 'they are so already at their own will, and it is but just they should be so at ours'. The point in refusing a material copy of the leases was not 'to turn out or raise the rents upon good tenants, but to keep them in awe and hinder them from destroying our estate'. Here is an insight into the forms of dependence that Harrington theorised in his account of empire following the balance of property.[142]

Molesworth had an intimate understanding of the politics and economics of his relationship with the land, his tenants and the status it conferred. He did, upon occasion, even turn his hand to the plough (something no self-respecting Roman senator would have considered). He was able to calculate the potential financial benefits of renegotiating rentals, but also to consider mortgaging his lands to raise ready cash to ensure his son's embassy in Turin was a success. Molesworth was a man who certainly took enormous delight and pride in *opificium* in relation to his estates. His correspondence is teeming with references to specific arboreal projects, agrarian developments and piscatorial undertakings.[143] Clearly a man expert across a range of areas of horticultural and natural knowledge, the pride taken in improvement is evident in the remarks about developments on the Yorkshire estate of Edlington: 'all the coarse, rough, unimproved land is taken in and under fine grass or tillage, a deal of new closes and hedging and building, and repairs, and planting the town street full of new industrious tenants, the commons taken in and turned to the best profitable land.'[144] Here the language of improvement, industry and profit illustrates the core values of a republican understanding of the function of landed property. Constantly anxious about the need for money to support his sons in their careers, Molesworth bemoaned that 'all our care and industry cannot set us at

---

142. *HMC*, p.230-31, 239, 241, 249, 250.
143. For an excellent discussion of his achievements see Finola O'Kane, *Landscape design in eighteenth-century Ireland: mixing foreign trees with the natives* (Cork, 2004).
144. *HMC*, p.257.

ease in the world'. Despite these moments of despair, it seems he did continue compulsively to project improvements for common benefit.[145]

Molesworth also theorised his experience and applied its lessons to the decay of gentlemanly cultivation in Ireland. Echoing both Cicero and Harrington, it was fundamental to his convictions that '*Agriculture* is not only a science, but the most useful one to Mankind'. The ablest statesmen, philosophers and poets had devoted considerable efforts to elucidating the best principles of agricultural practice, 'knowing it to be that whereon the Life and well-being of the Community depends'.[146] Fundamental to this project was the need for 'honest and improving Tenants' which would enable the gentry to undertake two sorts of cultivation, of the soil and of their minds. Good tenants would allow gentlemen the leisure to improve their 'natural Parts' by reading; the counter-example was the experience of the Irish gentry who were forced (in order to avoid the destruction of their estates by bad tenants) to 'manage their own Lands, and turn their own Husband-men'.[147] Such low employment and mean company meant that the gentry became 'degenerate by degrees; the best Education of many of their Sons, reaching no higher, than to know how to make the most of a Piece of Land'. Molesworth made it very explicit that this relationship with the land was no training ground for republican virtue. An understanding of 'the Business of Parliament, the Duty owing to ones Country, and the Value of Publick Liberty' could not be cultivated 'under such a cramp'd and low Education'. Such a gentry class would grow 'narrow Spirited, covetous and ungenteel'.[148] One remedy was to create 'schools for husbandry' in each county, which would not only teach the best principles of agricultural conduct but also good manners. Thriving and industrious farmers would produce more food and thereby alleviate the poverty of the nation. Reform of the clerical distortion of agricultural practice (in particular tithes and saints days) would create yet further opportunities. Molesworth's scarcely disguised anticlericalism mixed with his economic notions when he declared, 'I wish all the Saints Days were let slip, with all my Heart, and that People might be left at liberty to keep open Shop, plow, reap and follow their lawful Trades on those Days; they would serve God better, and their Country and private Families, than now they do.'[149]

It is not clear, then, that later seventeenth- and eighteenth-century

145. *HMC*, p.248, 283.
146. Robert Molesworth, *Some considerations for the promoting of agriculture, and employing the poor* (Dublin, George Grierson, 1723), p.4.
147. Molesworth, *Some considerations*, p.10, 28.
148. Molesworth, *Some considerations*, p.29.
149. Molesworth, *Some considerations*, p.39-40.

republican attitudes to the land produced a necessarily conservative ideology. Molesworth combined a veneration for the idea of cultivation (indeed the book he recommended as a standard guide to husbandry was written in the sixteenth century) with a new eye for what we could call the modernisation of the landlord-tenant relationship, as well as a keen perception of the national function of an industrious husbandry.[150] The classical authors on the role of agriculture (Xenophon and Cato) un-doubtedly provided a model for Molesworth's conception of his relation-ship with the land, but his prescriptions, aspirations and actions suggest he was capable of adjusting these perceptions to the imperatives of eighteenth-century society. John Toland, too, drew inspiration from classical traditions and Harringtonian sources, but also had a keen understanding, and indeed experience of (and participation in), the function and benefits of a variety of financial and commercial insti-tutions.

The interpretation of the later republicans as a bewildered group of nostalgic aristocrats more comfortable in their country libraries than in the bustle of urban and commercial society does not mesh well with the evidence of the life and ideas of Toland and Molesworth. Speculating in financial projects, proposing new schemes for a public banking system, debating the role of the circulation of coin, innovating progressive and commercially driven estate management programmes, are activities that sit uncomfortably with the commonplace representation of republican ideology after 1689. The point is that men like Toland and Molesworth lived their republican commitments. The ability to subscribe to a set of principles and attitudes did not preclude a pragmatic adjustment of those ideas to the pressing demands of circumstance. Toland and Molesworth needed to live and to eat, as well as being driven to attempt to reform the political context they operated within. It is unreasonable to imagine that their commitment to a set of principles – about the nature of liberty, the absolute priority of public good, the fundamental hostility to clericalism and persecution, the veneration of ancient re-publics, the devotion to a culture of agrarian values – somehow by default handicapped the potential efficacy of their politics. For these men, Harrington's belief that political power followed the distribution of economic wealth within a community was a compelling instrument of political analysis which could be applied in a variety of different histori-cal circumstances. The fact that his perception implied that the most dominant form of wealth was agrarian did not discount the application

150. Molesworth recommended Thomas Tusser's *A Hundreth good pointes of husbandrie* (London, Richard Tottel, 1557), which achieved twenty-one editions (expanded under various titles), with the last being printed in 1848.

of the insight to other contexts where commerce was more profound: even he acknowledged that, as we have seen.

The ability of these pamphleteers and politicians to adapt and adjust contemporary republican discourses is useful evidence of how textual traditions were absorbed, understood and made into individual beliefs. Exploring how Toland's and Molesworth's republican values were placed under stress during the crisis of the Bubble gives us a useful case-study for assessing how amphibious their principles and commitments were. One perspective suggests that these processes of engagement enabled republican ideas from the 1650s to evolve to function successfully in a set of changing historical contexts and political environments. The survival of a republican tradition born in the regicidal context of 1649, and then shaped by the events of 1689 and 1714, was a process of ongoing adaptation to fundamental changes in political ecology, as such values had to be accommodated to the rule of monarchy rather than simply a retreat into nostalgia and respectability.

Berkeley and the idea of a national bank

PATRICK KELLY

The establishment of a national bank – whose primary function would be the issue of paper money – is widely known to have been the keystone of the proposal for the stimulation of the Irish economy propounded by George Berkeley in his work *The Querist* of 1735-1737.[1] Berkeley believed that such a bank would prove the salvation of the Irish economy (speaking of it as 'the true philosopher's stone' (III.132) and 'more beneficial even than a mine of gold' (II.23). Despite the notorious failures of the South Sea Bubble and John Law's Mississippi Company, the project could, given honesty and good-will, be effectively established by the Irish parliament. By careful analysis of the strengths and weaknesses of recent banking schemes in both Europe and America, the inherent risks could be avoided and the benefits obtained for Ireland, the nation which above all others required the boost to its economy that a national bank could uniquely provide (I.199-201, 204, 223; II.129, 275). As George Caffentzis has shown, Berkeley devoted more than two-and-a-half years to furthering the establishment of an Irish national bank, preparing the ground by the sequential publication of the three parts of *The Querist* each year from 1735 to 1737. Shortly before the opening of the biennial session of the Irish parliament in the autumn of 1737 he issued specific proposals for the establishment of a bank in *Queries relating to a national bank, extracted from The Querist* and followed this up with extensive lobbying of members of both Houses, both personally and

---

1. Citations from *The Querist, containing several queries, proposed to the consideration of the public* are taken from the three parts of the anonymous first edition published separately in Dublin (R. Reilly for G. Risk, G. Ewing, and W. Smith, 1735-1737), and identified in the text in the form 'I.000'; 'II.000'; and 'III.000', respectively. Most modern commentators have relied on the shorter second edition of 1750, to which Berkeley set his name, and which thus has claims to be regarded as the authoritative version. Since, however, much of the excluded material relates to banking, the 1750 edition is inappropriate for examining Berkeley's views on this particular subject. A useful table of correspondences between the queries in the two editions is to be found in Joseph Johnston, *Bishop Berkeley's Querist in historical perspective* (Dundalk, 1970), which prints the sequentially numbered 595 queries of the 1750 edition, followed by the omitted queries from each of the three original parts of 1735-1737, together with Berkeley's two other works on banking, 'The plan or sketch of a national bank' (1737), and the unpublished 'The Irish patriot or queries upon queries' (1738).

through allies such as Thomas Prior, Samuel Madden and the Perceval brothers.[2] In the event, all this activity proved of no avail: Berkeley failed even to have the matter raised in parliament – perhaps not surprisingly given the 1721 Lords' resolution stating that any peer advocating a banking scheme would be 'a Betrayer of the Liberty of his Country', and a similar vote from the Commons.[3] The extent of Berkeley's frustration can be gauged by the extraordinarily bitter language of 'The Irish patriot or queries upon queries' (written in early 1738, though not published until 1930) as for example: 'Whether it be not our great comfort and security that we can now cry out upon all occasions, "*Poor Ireland! Beggarly Ireland!*" But if Ireland once became rich, what cry could we cry?'[4] Never again did he attend a session of the Irish House of Lords of which, as a bishop of the established church, he was an *ex officio* member. Caffentzis has further argued that Berkeley sought to revenge himself on the group of libertines and freethinkers, whom he believed were chiefly responsible for the attitudes that had brought about the sinking of his proposal, in his attack on the Blasters, entitled *A Discourse addressed to magistrates and men in authority: occasioned by the enormous licence, and irreligion of the times* (Dublin, 1738).[5] These literary fusillades did little, however, to assuage his anger. A dozen years later when Berkeley came to publish a shortened, single-volume version of *The Querist* (largely shorn of his detailed bank proposals) in 1750, his re-aroused frustration found expression in even more savage denunciations of Irish parliamentarians in *Maxims concerning patriotism*.[6]

2. C. George Caffentzis, 'The failure of Berkeley's bank: money and libertinism in eight-eenth-century Ireland', in *The Empire of credit: the financial revolution in the British Atlantic world, 1688-1815*, ed. Daniel Carey and Christopher J. Finlay (Dublin, 2011), p.229-48.
3. *Journals of the House of Lords* [Ireland], 8 vols (Dublin, William Sleater, 1779-1800), vol.2, p.720; *The Journals of the House of Commons of the kingdom of Ireland*, 19 vols (Dublin, George Grierson *et al*, 1795-1800), vol.3, p.289. See further Michael Ryder, 'The Bank of Ireland, 1721: land, credit and dependency', esp. p.569.
4. Berkeley, 'The Irish patriot', §23. See also §28: 'whether the whole and sole duty of an Irish patriot be not [...] always to suspect the worst?', and §34: 'Whether it be possible to contrive any scheme for the public good which shall not suppose or require common honesty and common sense in the execution thereof; and whether this be not an unanswerable argument against all projectors?'. The work was published by J. M. Hone as 'A manuscript of Bishop Berkeley' in *The Times literary supplement*, 13 March 1930, p.21, and in a version corrected by R. J. Best in the *TLS*, 3 April 1930, p.295. It is reprinted in Johnston, *Bishop Berkeley's Querist*, p.210-13. Sir Geoffrey Keynes, Kt, *A Bibliography of George Berkeley Bishop of Cloyne: his works and critics in the eighteenth century* (Oxford, 1976), p.88.
5. See further Caffentzis, 'The failure of Berkeley's bank', p.235-38, 241-42.
6. *Maxims concerning patriotism* (Dublin, s. n., 1750). See esp. §7: 'It is impossible that a man who is false to his friends and neighbours should be true to the public', and §9: 'A man who hath no sense of God or conscience: you make such a one guardian to your child? If not, why guardian to the state [that is, an MP]?' The title page appeared with the ascription 'By a Lady'. Luce suggests that Berkeley's wife, Anne, may have had some share

What has not received detailed consideration, however, is what precisely Berkeley understood by the national bank, how he intended it to be established and to operate and how in practice he sought to protect the Irish national bank from abuses of the kind which had destroyed the Law's Mississippi Company in France and the South Sea Company in England.[7] Besides the interesting technical aspects of Berkeley's proposals on bank security and note issues, the bank project also illuminated his views on social, economic and political reform. This emphasis is apparent from his earliest economic contribution, *An Essay towards preventing the ruine of Great Britain*, written in 1721 in the aftermath of the Bubble, which stressed the need for public spirit, along with industry, frugality and religion in achieving public well-being.[8] It further brought out his understanding of the operations of the economic process in giving concrete form to the responsibility of the legislature in directing the economy, and showed how he envisaged public prosperity as inseparable from the happiness of the mass of the population (II.169).

To understand Berkeley's ideas on the national bank, it is necessary to start from his general economic principles and how these should be applied in Ireland. The need for such a prerequisite was made clear by Berkeley himself in prefacing the reprint of his letter describing 'The plan or sketch of a national bank',[9] published immediately before the 1737 session of parliament, with a selection of general queries taken from the three parts of *The Querist*, under the title *Queries relating to a national bank, extracted from The Querist. Also the letter containing a plan or sketch of such bank. Republished with notes.*[10] But before considering these principles, a word is in order about the inherent difficulties in interpreting

---

in it. Arthur Aston Luce, *The Life of George Berkeley, Bishop of Cloyne*, intro. by David Berman ([1949], London, 1992), p.180-81.

7. Constantine George Caffentzis, *Exciting the industry of mankind: George Berkeley's philosophy of money*, has much of importance to say about Berkeley's views on banking, but the topic is only considered rather sporadically in this brilliant and thought-provoking study.

8. See Patrick Kelly, 'Industry and virtue versus luxury and corruption: Berkeley, Walpole, and the South Sea Bubble crisis', *Eighteenth-century Ireland / Iris an dá chultúr* 7 (1992), p.57-74 (esp. 71-73).

9. This had originally appeared in the newspapers (for example, *Dublin Newsletter*, 2-5 April 1737) in the form of a letter 'To A. B. Esq. on the plan of a national bank', shortly after the publication of *The Querist*, part III. It was published again in *Queries relating to a national bank, extracted from The Querist. Also the letter containing a plan or sketch of such bank. Republished with notes* (Dublin, George Faulkner, 1737), under the title 'The plan or sketch of a national bank. To A. B. *Esq.*', p.34-40.

10. *Queries relating to the national bank* reprinted some 188 unnumbered queries, taken in roughly equal measure from each of the three parts published in 1735-1737. These are identified in Johnston's edition (in *Bishop Berkeley's Querist*) by the letters 'S. Q.' preceding the number of the relevant query.

Berkeley's ideas arising from the format adopted in *The Querist*, namely a series of sometimes randomly linked rhetorical questions, totalling 895 in the three parts of the first edition. The number of queries in the single-volume edition of 1750 was reduced to 595 – a total of 345 queries having been excised from the 1735-1737 version, and 45 new ones added. It is noteworthy that the majority of the rejected queries related to banking, while none of the new material added in 1750 deals with this topic.[11] Though the query format has advantages in presenting general issues of economic policy, its disadvantages are very much to the fore when it comes to discussing the technical details of bank management. However, Berkeley was a practiced and skilful writer, as much at home in the higher journalism of Steele's *Guardian* as in his philosophical treatises,[12] and one must accept that the repetition, contradiction and ambiguity of the format were deliberate. As III.88 puts it: 'Whether, in order to make men see and feel, it be not often necessary to inculcate the same thing, and place it in different lights.' Clearly his intention was as much to provoke his readers to think about the problems which he presented for their consideration, as to have them adopt his solutions (I.315). On the other hand, the comment in III.129 as to 'these ten or dozen last queries being easily transformed into Heads of a Bill' reminds us that some queries, at least, were voiced as practical proposals and should put us on our guard against too fanciful or elaborate a reading of *The Querist*. Moreover, in 'The plan or sketch of a national bank' (first published as a letter in Dublin newspapers in the spring of 1737) Berkeley dropped his tentative, interrogative approach in favour of a straightforward exposition of his plan in ten direct proposals for the national bank – counter-pointed by a series of brief expository footnotes.[13]

Ireland and the 'true idea' of wealth

Berkeley's economic principles were sketched out in the opening forty queries of the first part of *The Querist*, and it was not, incidentally, till

---

11. A proportion of the rejected queries owed their omission to repetition between the three parts of the first edition. More significant exclusions included much of the general discussion of banking in I.209-67; the history of banking in II.28-66; the discussion of Law's scheme in II.67-125; consideration of objections to the national bank likely to be raised in parliament in III.14-128; and the role of the national bank in facilitating an alteration of the Irish monetary standard in III.133-64. Also omitted was the extensive cross-referencing between queries that was such a feature of the original edition.
12. On Berkeley's contribution to *The Guardian*, see Luce, *Life of George Berkeley*, p.62 and 62n.
13. This outline plan is further considered below, p.169-70.

I.199 that he even raised the matter of a bank.[14] In these forty queries he set forth his ideas on the nature of wealth; its origins in human industry; the objective of full employment for the populace; the function of money in stimulating economic activity; the primacy of will or opinion in getting men to labour, and the need to motivate this will through arousing the appetite to consume. Given the absence in the early eighteenth century of any conception of the optimisation of resources or establishment of equilibrium through hidden harmony or the design of nature, Berkeley accorded a crucial role to public authority in bringing about the necessary conditions to promote full employment.[15] Central to this directive role was the provision of an adequate circulating medium without which industry would not be set in motion and natural resources would not be exploited.

To make effective policy prescriptions it was necessary to understand the basis from which one must start by determining the true nature of wealth and the true nature of money (and later, when discussing the national bank, the true nature of credit).[16] In place of the traditional mercantilist identification of wealth with gold and silver, Berkeley argued in favour of what satisfies real human needs, namely 'plenty of all the necessaries and comforts of life' (III.260). Since this 'real wealth', unlike gold and silver, was the direct creation of human industry, it could be provided from internal resources quite independently of foreign trade: 'Might we not put a hand to the plough, or the spade, although we had no foreign commerce?' (I.115). Freed from the obsession with maximising the national stock of gold and silver through a foreign trade surplus, the crucial question in creating the wealth necessary to sustain the Irish population became how to stimulate the industry of all the inhabitants of the state so as to advance the common welfare (II.162, 378). In terms of individual motivation, industry could only be 'stirred' by awakening the will to labour, which in turn depended on creating an appetite for the product of labour, that is, stimulating the desire to consume – if only at the basic level of eating beef and wearing shoes (I.5, 11, 20; II.188). Such a perception was particularly relevant in Irish conditions, where Berkeley saw that there was a level below which sheer

14. The account of Berkeley's general economic ideas is a somewhat amended version of Patrick Kelly, 'The politics of political economy in mid-eighteenth century Ireland', *in Political ideas in eighteenth-century Ireland*, ed. S. J. Connolly (Dublin, 2000), p.105-29 (123-25).

15. It is this focus on the primary role of the state (or in Ireland's case the legislature, see further n.45 below) in directing the economy that, for all his rejection of specie fetishism, anchors Berkeley firmly in the mercantilist paradigm.

16. Berkeley, *The Querist*, I.48; III.148; I.5-8, 23; II.100, 140. See II.117: 'without having a proper regard to the use, or end, or nature of things'.

misery and despair inhibited any desire to improve the individual's position (I.66).

Although wealth was derived solely from human industry, unless the product of industry could be exchanged it remained incapable of giving rise to further activity in the economy (III.186-87). What was needed was a means of transferring and exchanging the power over the industry of others represented by the product of labour; that is, its value must become able to circulate in the market through being symbolically represented by money (I.33, 37). For Berkeley money primarily consisted of power over the labour product of others through its capacity to function as 'a ticket or counter' (I.23), and at this level there was little distinction between money and credit.[17] This concept of money as a ticket was not, as some have suggested, to be understood as equivalent to the neutral, inert function of money in exchange favoured by the classical economists, but rather represented the mercantilist conception of money as an active independent variable in the economic process.[18] This important distinction was made clear in III.89, where Berkeley speaks of the 'true and just idea' of money being 'a ticket, entitling to power', in addition to serving 'to record and transfer such power'.

Berkeley was by no means the first writer to propose the adoption of a paper currency as a means of overcoming the shortage of specie in a given country. What was novel was his linking of a paper money solution to the problem of economic growth with the creation in Ireland of what was virtually a closed economy (I.133, 135). This in turn depended on the perception of the inherent difference between Ireland and more developed economies such as those of Holland and Britain. In Ireland's case, the export of raw agricultural produce in return for luxury imports deprived the bulk of the population of basic foodstuffs and prevented them from ever becoming productive members of society: as I.177 asked, 'Whether the quantities of beef, butter, wool, and leather, exported from this island, can be reckoned the superfluities of a country, where there are so many natives naked and famished?' Retaining these commodities at home would enable the unemployed masses to combine their labour with Ireland's natural resources so as to satisfy their needs (I.120, 172), which would be transformed into effective demand through the adoption of paper money. This would in turn bring them into the market

---

17. It is not true that Berkeley simply equated money and credit, as some earlier commentators suggested. *The Querist*, II.172, 174, and 188-89 make clear his understanding of the need for different forms of circulating medium in different levels of transaction, with copper, silver, gold, and paper all having their proper places in an efficiently functioning currency system.

18. As III.318 expresses it: 'Whether the immediate mover [...] be not money, [whether] paper, or metal?'

economy, where their wants would provide further stimulus to set an expanding cycle of production and consumption on its way (I.113).

Before turning to the proposals dealing specifically with the national bank, it is perhaps worth underlining the astonishing boldness of Berkeley's approach to the solution of Ireland's economic problems. In a manner analogous to his solution to the problem of perception in rejecting matter in favour of the sole reality of what is perceived, the famous '*esse* is *percipi*' of *A Treatise concerning the principles of human knowledge* (1710),[19] Berkeley stood on its head the apparently insoluble problem of the Irish economy, namely its inability to provide a living for its starving masses. The very needs of the people now became the motor to transform the economy, and the technical key to bringing this about lay in the adoption of paper money to transform their real physical needs into economic demand. Ironically the only contemporary economic thinker to show anything approaching such audacity of vision was the person against whom so much of *The Querist*'s critique of recent banking practices was directed, namely John Law.[20]

Credit and the merits of public versus private banks

The essence of Berkeley's scheme for a national bank in Ireland was, as already mentioned, contained in the ten proposals which constitute 'The plan or sketch of a national bank' (published together with *Queries relating to a national bank, extracted from The Querist* (1737)).[21] The bank was to be established by parliament's setting up a fund of £100,000 through means of a tax on wine, and undertaking to make good any deficiency in the projected yield. The choice of wine as the subject of the tax was far from an arbitrary one. For Berkeley and his associates, wine typified the luxurious self-indulgence of the gentry which endangered the very existence of their poorer fellow subjects – 'swilling their guts in the blood of their country', as his friend, Samuel Madden, melodramatically put it.[22]

On this security parliament was to authorise the creation of £100,000

---

19. George Berkeley, *A Treatise concerning the principles of human knowledge*, ed. Jonathan Dancy (Oxford, 1998), p.104 (pt.1, §3).
20. See further below, p.174-80.
21. See note 9 above. 'The plan' is printed in Johnston, *Bishop Berkeley's Querist*, p.205-207, and in *The Works of George Berkeley, Bishop of Cloyne*, vol.6, p.185-87. The ten proposals were an amplification of *The Querist*, III.118-28, which III.129 had suggested might 'be converted into the heads of a bill'. Berkeley's detailed bank proposals were first set out in I.230-77.
22. Samuel Madden, *Reflections and resolutions proper for the gentlemen of Ireland* (Dublin, R. Reilly for George Ewing, 1738), p.20. See Berkeley's strictures on wine, I.155-6; II.239. However, III.117 suggested a sumptuary tax on gold and silver thread in clothing as an alternative fund for the bank, while III.118 made clear the choice was up to parliament, together with an undertaking to make good any shortfall below £100,000.

in bills ranging from one to twenty pounds. These notes would then be issued both to individuals in return for depositing specie, or securities in the form of land or goods, as well as to the Revenue in return for government securities.[23] The bank would open an office in Dublin with 'a Treasurer, Cashiers and other Officers' responsible for issuing the notes, valuing securities offered for mortgage, safeguarding the cash and being generally in charge of 'managing [...] this Bank as other Banks are managed'.[24] Overall supervision would be ensured by twenty-one visitors, one third drawn from the Great Officers of State, and one third appointed by each house of parliament, the personnel changing by ballot every second year. The visitors as a body would carry out quarterly inspections, but a quorum of three might visit the bank at any time. Note issue was to be strictly controlled: no notes could be issued without express parliamentary authorisation, that is, there would be no 'running notes' such as had proved so successful in the Bank of England, and the bank's officials would not have the discretion as regards the issue of extra notes, that Berkeley thought had been such a major weakness of Law's scheme.[25] Forging the Bank's notes would be prosecuted as a felony, that is, subject to the death penalty.[26] Finally, any profits from the bank would accrue to the public (which alone was to bear the cost of establishing the bank), and would be applied at parliament's discretion to finance public works and establish new forms of manufacture and industry. Berkeley concluded by reminding his readers that it would be for parliament to decide, after due debate, the precise details of implementing the proposals for the structure and management of the bank.

Though very much to the point as regards the establishment and functioning of the bank, this bare outline does little, however, to explain how Berkeley reached his conclusions; what his views were on the potential of a national bank; and the ways in which he sought to avoid the abuses that had so spectacularly undermined recent banking ventures in Europe and America. For Berkeley the primary function of the national bank was the issue of paper money, which as we have seen had such a key role in his scheme for transforming the Irish economy. A

23. Berkeley did not see the nascent Irish public debt as potential capital for his bank. I.226 specifically attacked a proposal for establishing a bank on the basis of funding the state debt in the anonymous *A Proposal for the relief of Ireland, by a coinage of monies, of gold and silver; and establishing a national bank* (Dublin, s. n., 1734).

24. Berkeley, *Queries relating to a national bank* [...]: *also the letter containing a plan or sketch of such bank*, p.36 (§5); Johnston, *Bishop Berkeley's Querist*, p.205.

25. For 'running notes', see Sir John Clapham, *The Bank of England: a history*, vol.1, p.36-37; for further discussion of Berkeley's analysis of Law's failure, see below, p.175-76, 178-80.

26. Interestingly, a number of these proposals were directly copied from Law's scheme, particularly the arrangements for inspecting the bank, and the penalty for forgery. See II.79, 94, also below, p.176.

properly regulated issue of paper credit (together with adequate provision for small change) would stimulate trade and industry; turn the Irish poor from wretched, starving idlers into contented, well-fed workers able to provide for themselves and their families (I.225, II.129, 315); establish an active public-minded gentry, serving as promoters of activity in their own localities (I.196; II.243-45); and lead Britain to value her hitherto despised colony as a junior partner in a flourishing empire (III.74, 77). It was thus the political medicine so urgently needed for the ailing Irish nation (III.107), recommended not so much by dogmatic theory as by successful experience in other states (II.14; III.19). Ever practical-minded, Berkeley was, however, well aware that his project might appear 'an Atlantis or Eutopia' (I.313) to those who failed to consider matters as they truly were. He therefore stressed that in regulating the economy, legislators would need more than 'a vulgar share of knowledge' and would have to make it their 'study to understand the true nature and interest of mankind, how to guide men's humours and passions, how to incite their active powers, [and] how to make their several talents co-operate to the mutual benefit of each other, and the general good of the whole' (II.170).

Berkeley's discussion of banking covered several fields, firstly the benefits and advantages of banks to what he termed the nation, which in his usage was frequently the equivalent of a word and concept so familiar to us but which did not exist at that time, namely the economy.[27] Next he considered the strengths and weaknesses of various types of bank in a discussion of polarities between the concept of the bad, namely the private bank subject to a whole range of risks and hazards, and the good, that is the national bank, which would be constituted so as to avoid these various risks (I.223, 287). As he expressed the problem in III.58, the question was not a choice between relying on money (that is, specie) or on credit to stimulate the economy, but whether public credit should be preferred to private. This black-and-white presentation of the choice between public and private banks owes much to the crisis created in the Irish economy by the failure of Burton and Falkiner, Ireland's largest private bank in 1733.[28] Berkeley was haunted, one might indeed say obsessed, by the possibility of multiple private bank failure, which he saw as threatening the utter destruction of the Irish economy (I.210; II.7, 8, 10), asking 'Whether a view of the precipice be not sufficient, or whether we must tumble headlong before we are aroused?' (II.146). At a different

27. See I.17, 22, 67, 121, 197, 229, 282; II.236; III.11, 51, 294. Instances of Berkeley's employing 'nation' in an exclusively political sense are rare in *The Querist*, for example II.153.
28. The presentation of the argument in such stark either/or terms possibly owed something to the influence of Machiavelli, whose rhetorical strategies were extolled in *An Essay towards preventing the ruine of Great Britain* (London, J. Roberts, 1721), in *Works*, vol.6, p.82.

level he offered a quasi-metaphysical justification of the national bank, where the bank is seen as encapsulating the 'spirit', or active principle of his later metaphysics, which alone could stimulate industry or activity in the nation.[29] The national bank also represented the positive virtue of wealth created through human labour as opposed to the harmful dimension of gaming and financial speculation, or stock-jobbing, that Berkeley from his earliest piece of economic writing, the 1721 *Essay towards preventing the ruine of Great Britain*, saw as threatening not merely economic well-being but public morality and even political freedom.[30] In mobilising the whole resources of the nation as the stock of the national bank, Ireland would also be maximising the vital ingredient of public spirit and thereby banishing the spectre of national bankruptcy (I.251; III.51). Finally, the national bank as the creation of the legislature (which III.318 characterised as the soul or will of the nation) would ensure that the power of the whole community would be directed to the objective of securing national well-being. Despite this panegyric to the national bank we should, however, be wary of seeing Berkeley as an advocate of unrestricted economic growth; Berkeley's economic goals remain moderate and firmly geared towards social and religious ends, the fulfilment of a particular, essential but nonetheless subordinate part of the creator's plan for mankind (II.112-18).[31]

Minimising banking risk, with particular attention to John Law

Berkeley's analysis of banking rested on what he took to be the self-evident assumption that banks were essential to the economy as the creators and maintainers of credit (II.25). This necessity was all the more acute in the case of Ireland where the ill-functioning currency system already depended on private bankers' notes for half the current circulating medium (I.201, 208).[32] Private banks, however, were subject to a whole range of risks that could largely be avoided in the case of a

---

29. In Berkeley's later philosophy, Spirit represents the active principle; see further Caffentzis, *Exciting the industry of mankind*, p.138-39.

30. See Kelly, 'Industry and virtue versus luxury and corruption', p.71-72.

31. See Berkeley, *Alciphron: or, the minute philosopher*, 2 vols (Dublin, G. Risk, G. Ewing, and W. Smith, 1732): 'in order to make a nation flourish it is not enough to make it wealthy, without knowing the true end and happiness of mankind, and how to apply wealth towards attaining that end' (*Works*, vol.7, p.80).

32. See *The Querist*, I.35. This is probably too high a proportion. David Bindon, *Some reasons shewing the necessity the people of Ireland are under, for continuing to refuse Mr Wood's coinage* (Dublin, 1724), p.11, had estimated bankers' bills at £150,000 and specie at £500,000; while Thomas Prior, *Observations on coin in general. With some proposals for regulating the value of coin in Ireland* (Dublin, A. Rhames for R. Gunne, 1729), p.45, put the specie at £400,000 and stated 'Bankers notes we have in good plenty'.

well-managed national bank, starting with hazards affecting the individual banker, such as general economic conditions, the banker's financial skill and acumen, his personal probity, and the basic question of mortality (I.247, 252). A further shortcoming of private banks was their secrecy with regard to the creation of credit, which being equivalent to minting money was too great a power to entrust to private hands (I.31, 272; II.27). This monopoly was all the more undesirable as private bankers tied up large amounts of specie as vault cash, thereby depriving the nation of a very significant part of its potential circulation.[33] In the opening queries of the first part of *The Querist*, Berkeley wrote as if it were the duty of the state to ensure that individual citizens had adequate money or credit to enable them to participate in the economic process: 'Whether the public aim in every well-governed State be not that each member, according to his just pretensions and industry should have power?' (I.8). Though this notion seems to point directly to the need for a state or public bank, it is not a suggestion which Berkeley explores further in relation to the national bank, other perhaps than in the rather cryptic allusion in II.111: 'as the aim of industry is power, and the aim of the bank is to circulate and secure this power to each individual [...]'.

However, Berkeley did attempt to conciliate the private bankers (who had such extensive influence over Irish monetary policy in the 1720s and 1730s) by pointing out that their numbers had greatly increased in England since the foundation of the Bank of England and that they too stood to benefit in particular through being able to turn to the national bank as a lender of last resort (I.211, 258, 259).[34] Indeed so vital was the function of banking for the economy that where there was no public bank, private banks would still be desirable despite the serious risks they presented (II.26; III.48). But Berkeley did not accept the argument that, failing the establishment of a national bank, parliament should underwrite their liabilities to obviate the calamity of multiple bank failure.[35]

Much of *The Querist*'s discussion of banking was devoted to the question of how to establish a banking system secure from such risks through the strict separation of functions and the rigid observance of guidelines – advice by no means without relevance in today's troubled banking world. In accordance with Berkeley's usual procedure in determining practical matters of this kind, the best guide as to what to conserve and what to

33. See 'The Irish patriot', §3; its claim that a single banker held more than £100,000 in specie, however, strains credulity. See previous note.
34. For the bankers' predominant influence in leading the government to reject the revaluation of gold and the issue of copper in 1729, see Archbishop Boulter to Lord Carteret, 25 and 30 April 1730: *Letters written by his excellency Hugh Boulter, D.D., lord primate of all Ireland*, 2 vols (Dublin, George Faulkner and James Williams, 1770), vol.2, p.3-6.
35. See 'The Irish patriot', §33; Johnston, *Bishop Berkeley's Querist*, p.212.

avoid was provided by comparison of banking practices in other countries: 'Whether, having considered the conveniences of banking and paper-credit in some countries, and the inconveniences thereof in others, we may not contrive to adopt the former, and avoid the latter?' (I.223).

For Berkeley the truly public bank was one that is 'not only established by public authority as the Bank of England, but a bank in the hands of the public, wherein there are no shares: whereof the public alone is proprietor, and reaps all the benefit' (I.222). Banks which purported to be public banks but were in practice merely multi-owner private (that is, joint stock) banks, with state backing and a misleading designation (such as the Bank of England and the Bank of Scotland), might be suspected of subordinating the public interest to that of their shareholders (I.216, 223). Indeed, in the case of the Bank of Genoa, the secrecy inherent in this kind of private 'public' bank had provided the shield for a conspiracy which nearly overthrew the state (I.211). By contrast, true public banks such as those found in Venice, Hamburg and Amsterdam contributed to both economic prosperity and the political stability of the states that established them (I.200; II.29, 36, 52). The Amsterdam bank had developed unintentionally out of the management of the state debt in the past and, like the Bank of Venice, had its books open for state inspection (II.48, 51). The Bank of Hamburg was controlled by the public independently of the state and was required by law to maintain secrecy in regard both to individual accounts and its total deposits; despite this, its credit had remained strong throughout 'the North' (II.55-6, 63-4). All three were, however, banks which primarily provided *compte-en-banque* transfer facilities for their depositors, which greatly reduced the need not only for cash but even bank notes in large scale transactions (II.30, 131).[36]

Berkeley's most extended analysis of banking abuses was directed at the writings and business ventures of John Law, taking in not only his activities in France from the foundation of the General Bank in 1716 to the collapse of the enlarged Mississippi scheme in 1720, but also the land-bank scheme which he had proposed for Scotland in his early pamphlet, *Money and trade considered, with a proposal for supplying the nation with money* (1705).[37] The main factors to which Berkeley attributed the collapse of Law's Banque Royale (the state-owned successor of the General Bank,

---

36. Despite the advantage of the *compte-en-banque* facility, Berkeley advised against attempting to introduce it at the same time as the issue of notes against land and security. See further below, p.176.

37. John Law, *Money and trade considered, with a proposal for supplying the nation with money* (Edinburgh, Heirs and Successors of Andrew Anderson, 1705). Scarcely any reference to Law's French project survives in the 1750 edition of *The Querist* (for example I.283; II.107), the extensive coverage in II.67-125 being dropped in its entirety.

restructured in 1719) were its seemingly uncontrolled issue of notes –
what he termed 'the untimely, repeated, and boundless fabrication of
bills' (II.88), and the merging of this bank with the Company of the Indies
in 1719. The merger pushed up the price of shares in the new conglom-
erate to a height wholly unwarranted by the company's trading potential
by means of 'an imaginary foundation of some improvement to the stock
by trade' (I.221; II.90, 95).[38]

Here, and in other instances, Berkeley constantly reiterated the
danger of 'stock-jobbing' (by which he meant financial speculation
without regard to the promotion of 'industry') as a major threat to
banking stability, referring to the mass hysteria brought about in France
'by the arts of designing men', resulting in a 'sort of enthusiasm which
takes the place of reason, and is the most dangerous distemper in a state'
(II.104-105). In preventing the risk of stock-jobbing it was essential, above
all, to eliminate a link between the national bank and any form of trading
company. Once a bank had shareholders, it would be tempted to engage
in speculative ventures intended to increase the value of its shares at the
expense of facilitating the real economy of goods and services, which was
the true purpose of the national bank (I.220, 273; II.106-10, 140). Despite
the serious risks, Berkeley was confident that the problem of maintaining
an appropriate level of notes in circulation would not prove insurmountable in a true national bank where the absence of shareholders
obviated the desire for speculative ventures (II.287). However, such had
been the strength of Law's bank, that even after the over-issue of notes
and the merger of bank and trading company, its notes succeeded in
retaining parity with specie until the royal edict reducing their value in
May 1720 fatally compromised its prospects. Although the edict had
been rapidly withdrawn, it proved henceforth impossible to overcome
the impact of this measure on the bank's credibility (II.98-99). Ultimately
for Berkeley the real problem of both Law's Mississippi venture and the
South Sea Company was that the intentions of their promoters had been
fraudulent from the very start, 'calculated for the public ruin' as III.286
puts it, but the danger of a thing's being abused was no reason for
concluding that a national bank could not be trusted in the hands of the
honest and competent (I.199, 220, 276).[39]

38. Berkeley may have had the opportunity to discuss Law's career with the latter's one-time
    associate and later rival, the Irish banker and economist, Richard Cantillon, who was the
    next door neighbour of his friend Philip Perceval in Albemarle Street. See Patrick Kelly,
    'Anne Donnellan: Irish proto-bluestocking', *Hermathena* 154 (1993), p.39-68 (42). In the
    absence of substantial evidence, this possible link between the two most distinguished
    early eighteenth-century Irish economists remains, alas, a matter of conjecture.
39. See Berkeley's comment on the South Sea directors in his 1721 *Essay*: 'the modern
    unexampled attempt of men easy in their fortunes, and unprovoked by hardships of any
    sort, in cool blood and with open eyes, to ruin their country' (*Works*, vol.6, p.80).

Vehement though his condemnation was of Law's shortcomings, there was also much which Berkeley sought to emulate in Law's French banking practices – despite the failure to implement them properly. In particular he was impressed by Law's elaborate security arrangements, such as keeping triplicate registers of bank notes issued; having multiple key holders for chests containing specie, bills and printing plates; the limitations on the sums to which individual cashiers had access; and the detailed regulations for supervision and inspection of the bank (II.75-83, 94).[40] He also approved Law's provision for offices in the provinces as well as the capital; the care always to have specie at hand to pay notes on demand;[41] and making the bank's notes acceptable for tax payments (II.84-86, 132, 68; III.127). On the other hand, Berkeley believed that the rapid success of the Law system had gone to the directors' heads (II.109), and he deplored the haste with which the scheme developed, speaking of 'the slow steps and discreet management which a bank requires' (II.66). For this reason, a *compte-en-banque*, or book transfer facility for depositors, should only be introduced once the note issue system of the national bank was solidly established in Ireland (II.134). Other practical details which Berkeley considered were the need for fire-proof buildings (II.136), keeping duplicate records of the *compte-en-banque* accounts in different locations (II.135) and the practice followed both in Venice and Amsterdam of periodic suspension of dealings to make up accounts – the forerunner of bank holidays (II.34, 45).

A further question raised for Berkeley by Law's failure was whether a national bank was compatible with the absolute power of the French monarchy, to which his answer was definitely no (II.66, 107). An effective national bank required a mixed constitution, where if skilfully and cautiously introduced it would gradually win approval, and become in time a vital adjunct to the constitution proper (II.111, 139). He also spoke of other political risks associated with state banks, though without specifying what it was that he feared (III.37). One possibility was the danger of a loan from the bank reducing the government's dependence on parliament for additional revenue (I.217), a risk to which Sir John Perceval (or Percival) had drawn Berkeley's attention at the time of the 1721 bank project.[42] Another may have been fear of the bank's being able

40. Berkeley's knowledge of these provisions seemingly derived from the original letters patent establishing the General Bank in May 1716; see details in Antoin E. Murphy, *John Law: economic theorist and policy-maker*, p.154-55. Berkeley may have acquired a copy when in France with George Ashe in the autumn of 1716; Luce, *Life of George Berkeley*, p.75.

41. That is, while Law's notes could still be exchanged for specie (*The Querist*, II.69); constant provision for specie to redeem notes was also observed in Venice (II.31).

42. Perceval to Berkeley, 9 November 1721. Printed in Benjamin Rand, *Berkeley and Percival: the correspondence of George Berkeley, afterwards Bishop of Cloyne and Sir John Percival, afterwards first*

to exercise corrupt influence in elections and in parliamentary proceedings as a result of its monopoly over the money supply.[43] Remarks in 'The Irish patriot or queries upon queries' (1738) suggested that a wide range of similar concerns had been exploited by Berkeley's critics to block parliament from discussing his bank proposals in 1737.[44] By contrast the most notable feature of Berkeley's national bank was its dependence on the legislature, both as its initiating and conserving authority, and as the guarantee that the power represented by the bank's notes would be exercised exclusively for the benefit of the public (I.203; II.111; III.65). As 'The Irish patriot' also made clear, his critics had serious misgivings as to the wisdom in Irish conditions of entrusting such far-reaching powers to the legislature. Despite the reservations voiced elsewhere in *The Querist* as to the ignorance and lack of public spirit of some Irish legislators (I.182), Berkeley thought such suspicions absurd: where else could public trust be reposed, if not in the legislature? (II.45; III.49).[45] However, there were limits to this confidence, for Berkeley insisted that no member of the legislature should be allowed to participate in the management of the bank; their role was to provide inspection and supervision (I.224, 231). He also flattered MPs by recalling their support for a national bank in 1721, and suggested that they could be relied upon to respond to a proposal intended solely for the public good (II.251-52). There could be no reason to suppose that the legislature, the government, or even 'our fellow-subjects of Great Britain' could ever have any motive to harm the public (III.64-69). Indeed, so far-fetched were some of the objections that it might be asked whether the opponents of the bank even believed their own arguments (III.67). In this confidence and optimism Berkeley manifested a very different spirit to Swift, who raised a black flag on his cathedral steeple at the final implementation of a revaluation of gold by the Irish administration in August 1737, after two decades of debate.[46]

Earl of Egmont (Cambridge, 1914), p.184. On 21 October 1721, Perceval had expressed fear of the bank's facilitating the long-term funding of the Irish state debt, such as was introduced in 1733 (Rand, *Berkeley and Percival*, p.181).

43. Ryder, 'The Bank of Ireland, 1721', p.571-78. As Ryder points out, many of the fears voiced by the opposition to the 1721 bank echoed those raised over the Bank of England in the 1690s.

44. Johnston, *Bishop Berkeley's Querist*, p.212.

45. In the absence of any concept of 'the hidden hand', mercantilists generally looked to 'the statesman' to direct the economy. However, given the suspicion of British statesmen, and their subordinate administration in Dublin, going back to the later- seventeenth-century English acts against Irish cattle imports and Irish woollen exports, the Irish legislature was, by default, the only institution capable of commanding sufficient trust to perform this function in Ireland. See further, Kelly, 'Politics of political economy', p.120.

46. Irvin Ehrenpreis, *Swift: the man, his works and the age*, 3 vols (Cambridge, MA, 1962-1983), vol.3, p.860.

However, Berkeley also sought to exploit less creditable motives such as popular religious prejudice and xenophobia by asking: 'Whether we may not hope for as much skill and honesty in a Protestant Irish parliament as in a Popish Senate of Venice?', and implying that Irish legislators were no less enlightened than the phlegmatic Dutch (II.37). Such suggestions fitted in with his contention that it was necessary to persuade people to adopt beneficial measures not merely by pointing to self-interest but also by exploiting their prejudices (III.131).

Note issue management and the valuation of Irish money

Berkeley's concern with the technical management of the bank was primarily directed to maintaining the value of notes issued, which he seems to have considered the most difficult task facing the directors (II.123). The major concern was to match the circulating medium with the needs of trade (II.124, 269), though he also appreciated that competing sectors in the economy had different interests in relation to the volume of notes issued. Too small a circulation of paper money would harm the interest of landowners, while too large a one would damage the interests of commerce (II.245).[47] Here too Law provided Berkeley's chief cautionary example, not only in relation to what had happened in France but also with regard to his projected Scottish banking scheme of 1705, whose defects had perhaps been magnified in hindsight by the Mississippi debacle.[48] This discussion over note issues also brought out Berkeley's familiarity with the shortcomings of various American paper money issues of the day, not least in Rhode Island, where he had spent the years 1729-1731. His concern was not so much with the lack of proper regulations, as with the failure of colonial legislatures through self-interest or negligence to enforce what they themselves had laid down (I.212, 275, 286). These shortcomings included failure to withdraw notes from circulation when the period authorised for the initial loan had elapsed, failure to sell the mortgaged lands of those who had defaulted on interest payments, and the creation of new note issues while earlier ones still remained outstanding (II.275). All these practices had occurred in Rhode Island in the 1720s and 1730s, where the result had been a severe depreciation of the notes. However, Caffentzis has argued that this did not damage people in Rhode Island so much as it did the residents of neighbouring colonies, who, having acquired the notes at close to par,

47. See Law, *Money and trade considered*, p.89-90.
48. Berkeley's benefiting from hindsight is particularly apparent in his charge that Law had failed to make sufficient precautions against the over-issuing of notes, but see *Money and trade considered*, p.86-90, *passim*.

were in effect fraudulently forced to write down the debts of the Rhode Islanders.[49]

Berkeley's anxiety to prevent an excessive issue of notes (which he had diagnosed as a prime cause of the collapse of Law's bank) was reflected in the extensive list of controls which he recommended for the bank. Most importantly, the legislature should impose an absolute ceiling on the volume of notes issued, a course of action which he accused Law of having failed to see the need for in 1705 (I.215). Persons mortgaging lands should not be permitted to take bills for more than half the value of their securities, and no individual loan should exceed a fixed maximum (II.235, 239).[50] To prevent unauthorised note issue by bank personnel, there should be strict separation of cash keeping and managerial functions (I.238). However, increased prosperity would cause the value of land to rise as the bank's operations got underway, and particular care would be needed to prevent this rise distorting the value of securities pledged against notes (I.240-43).[51] Berkeley also emphasised the importance of allocating the notes on a pro rata basis throughout the country, calling for an equal share for Ireland's four provinces, and internal allocation within the provinces in proportion to the Hearth Money returns (I.233-34). The even distribution of credit throughout the country to be achieved by this means accorded with Berkeley's belief that an equal distribution of wealth would best promote the well-being of the nation, which was the ultimate goal of *The Querist* (I.275).[52] Moreover, a multitude of small active enterprises was preferable to a few large ones both in agriculture and industry (I.56, 104). Berkeley further sought to maintain the value of the notes by having them accepted for all forms of revenue payment, and by willingness to redeem them for specie on demand, as well as having the bank ensure an adequate supply of silver money for small transactions (I.249; II.68).[53] His lowest denomination note was to be one pound (I.236). Interestingly, this was considerably higher than had been the case of American bills, especially in Rhode

49. See further Caffentzis, *Exciting the industry of mankind*, p.93-95.
50. The need for a ceiling on notes and only lending a portion of the value of the pledge are both raised in Law, *Money and trade considered*, p.85-86.
51. The reference in II.243 to the desirability of regular land sales in order to offset this expected rise in prices is puzzling, unless Berkeley has in mind the sale of pledges from defaulting borrowers. See II.212.
52. See query 214 in the second edition of *The Querist* (which is not in the first edition): 'Whether as seed equally scattered produceth a goodly Harvest, equally so an equal Distribution of Wealth does not cause a Nation to flourish?'
53. This would seem to dispose of Caffentzis's claims that Berkeley's paper money was inconvertible, and the money to be produced by the proposed Irish Mint was 'of purely token value that would make Wood's [coin] look substantial'. See C. George Caffentzis, 'Hume, money, and civilization; or, why was Hume a metallist?', *Hume studies* 27:2 (2001), p.326; *Exciting the industry of mankind*, p.6.

Island (where over 80 per cent had been below five shillings), presumably a consequence of the much greater shortage of specie in the colonies compared with Ireland.[54] While he agreed with Law that people would not borrow from the bank to have the money lie idle (III.94), Berkeley did not believe that this alone would be sufficient to prevent an excessive note issue. The danger was that it might be in the bank's short-term interest (as it had been in France in 1719-1720) to issue a greater volume of notes than the economy required, in order to boost its shares. The end of money being to encourage activity, promotion of a sterile monetary circulation was not only economically but also potentially politically dangerous to the nation (I.220, 283). Despite the serious risks, Berkeley was, ultimately, confident that the problem of maintaining an appropriate level of notes in circulation would not prove insurmountable in a true national bank where the absence of shareholders would prevent it engaging in speculative ventures (I.221).

A final area of technical concern for Berkeley was the relation between the volume of bank notes issued and the circulation of specie, as he feared that an excessive note issue would provide an opportunity for draining the country of its silver currency (I.246). This in turn brings up another of the monetary problems discussed in *The Querist*, namely the question of re-rating both gold and silver coin to take account of changes in international specie prices, where he saw an important role for the national bank in easing the process of transition (III.133-64). Disparities between Irish and European values were widely recognised as a major factor in the chronic ill-functioning of the Irish currency system, silver being consistently undervalued throughout the eighteenth century, both in Britain and Ireland, and gold overvalued in Ireland till the revaluation of August 1737.[55] In the case of adjusting disproportionate values for specific sorts of coin (such as Portuguese *moidores*) in relation to the overall value of either gold or silver moneys, Berkeley saw the matter as merely correcting a discrepancy which afforded a premium for private bankers to import over-valued pieces into Ireland (III.137). However, as regards altering gold and silver values in relation to the Irish money of account, particularly restoring the link which existed in the 1690s with the English sterling standard, Berkeley both strongly advocated change (I.27-28), and at the same time voiced reservations over the likely consequences, inquiring 'whether a public benefit ought to be obtained by unjust methods [...]?' (III.143).[56] His concerns recalled (*mutatis mutandis*) Locke's objection to

---

54. Caffentzis, *Exciting the industry of mankind*, p.93.
55. For Ireland's currency problems in the early eighteenth century, see Kelly, 'Politics of political economy', p.110-12.
56. Berkeley was also strongly in favour of establishing an Irish Mint (I.101; III.302), appreciating, like David Bindon, *An Essay on the gold and silver-coin currant in Ireland* (Dublin, E.

altering the English monetary standard in the 1690s, on the grounds that it would entail a violation of existing contracts requiring payment of specific quantities of gold and silver for debts and fixed charges such as rents.[57] Though re-introducing the English monetary standard was desirable in the long run, Berkeley feared that doing so would impose an additional, perhaps even intolerable, burden on tenants and debtors (III.146, 156, 162).[58] This burden might be substantially reduced by using the bank's notes to offset the expected short-term specie hiatus (III.145), which had proved such a problem during the English recoinage of 1696-1698.[59] However, Berkeley concluded his discussion of the role of the bank in easing the implementation of a change in the monetary standard by stating that the general arguments in favour of the bank would stand on their own merits independent of the re-rating question (III.163) – presumably because he did not wish to prejudice opponents of altering the monetary standard against his bank scheme.

The choice of a land bank model

By way of conclusion, I wish to refer to a question posed by the national bank proposal which Berkeley failed to make sufficiently clear, namely why the model to be adopted in Ireland should have been a land bank. Though of importance in itself, the question also brings out the difficulties in elucidating Berkeley's ideas that arise from *The Querist*'s format, as well as the extent to which his proposals were determined by political and broader cultural considerations, as opposed to purely economic ones. At first sight the proposal for a land bank seemingly conflicted with the evidence of banking practices in other countries, which Berkeley held up as the criterion for determining how to proceed in Ireland. None of the successful instances of national banks in Venice, Amsterdam and Hamburg, which Berkeley cited as examples to his readers, had been land banks. Moreover, English opinion remained prejudiced against land banks at this time, following the unsuccessful experiments of Nicholas Barbon, John Asgill and Hugh Chamberlen in the later seventeenth century – to say nothing of the connection with Law's proposed 1705 scheme for Scotland.[60]

Dobson, 1729), p.4, the unnecessary difficulties caused by the lack of coins adapted to the Irish money of account (III.295-96).

57. For Locke's views, see my 'General introduction' in *Locke on money*, vol.1, p.88-89.

58. While Locke's concern had been for the loss to landlords and creditors through the devaluation of the monetary standard, Berkeley's sympathies were with the increased amounts of gold and silver which tenants and debtors would have to pay as a result of a revaluation.

59. Kelly, 'General introduction', in *Locke on money*, vol.1, p.64-66.

60. See further, Murphy, *John Law*, p.45-66. Asgill by this time had acquired a particularly

The notion of a land-bank model (indubitably the most important idea which Berkeley had derived from Law) only emerged at a later stage in Berkeley's call for the establishment of an Irish national bank. He had first spoken of the bank's credit being 'supported by public funds, and secured by parliament' (I.204), later going on to refer to 'a particular fund for public use in answering bills and circulating credit' (III.121; see I.230). Only in I.243 did he refer to 'our visible security in land', and contrast this favourably with the security of the Bank of Amsterdam. The Irish national bank was further commended as a bank of land and paper, the one retaining its value because it could not be taken out of the country, and the other because it had, so Berkeley asserted, no value outside the country and thus would not be liable to be exported (II.148). This dual basis of the bank's credit should engender confidence that the public would not be in danger of becoming bankrupt, as long as the notes were offered to borrowers of good security (I.248). As we have seen, so great was Berkeley's fear of multiple bank collapse that even this condition proved insufficient to satisfy him, for he finally claimed that the ultimate guarantor of the stability of the national bank was that the whole stock of the nation would be at its disposal (III.51-52, 84).

However, this emphasis on the need for landed security, particularly the requirement of backing of the bank's notes by twice their value in land (II.239), is hard to reconcile with Berkeley's famous 'ticket' theory of money, which was an explicit repudiation of the notion that money either possessed intrinsic value or was a pledge in the Lockean, or Aristotelian sense (I.23). As Joseph Schumpeter pointed out over half a century ago, Berkeley's recurring emphasis on the fact that the whole stock of the nation would provide the security for the truly national bank seemingly rendered the need for the backing of its notes with intrinsic value superfluous.[61] Finally the emphasis on the closed economy (I.113-18), which seems to be an essential factor in Berkeley's plan for the issue of paper money in Ireland, further removed the need for external backing of the national bank's notes.

By way of answer to this conundrum, one can make various suggestions, some primarily economic, others more broadly political – though none perhaps entirely convincing considered in isolation. In the Ireland of the 1730s, the shadow of the South Sea Bubble and Mississippi affair, to say nothing of more recent Irish bank failures, particularly such as Burton and Falkiner in 1733, lay so heavily over banking in all its

---

unsavoury reputation in Ireland on account of his unorthodox religious views, which could scarcely have recommended him to Berkeley. See Richard L. Greaves, 'Asgill, John (*bap.* 1659, *d.* 1738)', in *Oxford dictionary of national biography*.

61. Schumpeter, *History of economic analysis*, p.288-89.

manifestations that security was of exceptional concern to the public. In contrast to paper, land was tangible, solid and reassuring and above all the *visible* manifestation of security to which I.243 alluded (and Berkeley's philosophical preoccupation with the primacy of the visual scarcely needs recalling). Since the later seventeenth century, Country ideology had contrasted the volatile, mysterious nature of financial capital like stocks and paper money with the immovable solidity of land. After the crashes of 1720 had rendered financial instruments even more suspect, banks – as the Irish experience of 1721 had shown – sought to give tangible reality to credit by linking it to the moral and political worth of land.[62] A land bank might be expected to persuade the landholders – who made up the majority of members of both houses of the Irish parliament – that something of the durability and moral worth of land itself would rub off on a bank whose credit rested on landed property. Moreover, a form of bank which privileged landowners as borrowers could have been expected to have an additional appeal for such legis-lators.[63] On this level, the apparent contradiction between the emphasis on land as the basis for credit and the apparent logic of Berkeley's theory of money may thus be accounted for as a further example of his assertion that one must take account of people's prejudices in attempting to bring about economic progress (III.131).

Beyond this effort to ground the bank's credibility in such a reassuringly familiar asset as land, there seem to have been two further reasons for Berkeley's advocating the land-bank model for the Irish national bank. The first was the directive role which Berkeley envisaged landowners taking in the development of the Irish economy, and the second an assumption derived from Berkeley's experience in America that land banks were particularly suited to underdeveloped economies with inadequate supplies of specie such as Britain's colonies – presum-ably including Ireland. Berkeley saw it as of key importance that land-owners should take a lead in the stimulation of the Irish economy, particularly at a local level, where agricultural improvement, labour-intensive industries and a high consumption of native-produced com-modities would prove vital. In place of being the drones of the Irish

---

62. Ryder, 'Bank of Ireland, 1721', p.572-78. According to Louis Cullen, 'Landlords, bankers and merchants: the early Irish banking world, 1700-1820', in *Economists and the Irish economy from the eighteenth century to the present day*, ed. Antoin E. Murphy (Dublin, 1984), p.31-33, until the late 1720s, Irish private bankers mainly serviced the needs of landlords, with merchant houses such as Swift and La Touche and Kane being slow to emerge. Berkeley's correspondence with Prior in the 1720s and 1730s reveals dealings with both these banks, along with others.

63. While Berkeley seems to have envisaged the bulk of borrowers being landowners, he did speak of linen, wool and hemp being used as pledges to enable the poor to borrow from the bank (I.267), though he does not follow up on this point.

economy whose luxury imports deprived their poorer neighbours of their very livelihoods, enlightened landowners would use the paper money issued by the national bank to launch the much-needed transition from stagnation to activity at a local level (I.196; II.243-45). Moreover, Berkeley's reference to American experience of paper-money issues would seem to imply that land banks were particularly suited to un-developed, as opposed to more advanced, economies (I.275, 286), though unfortunately he did not expand further on this topic. While a land bank appeared to Berkeley best suited to Irish conditions, one may surmise that for him the form of the national bank, so long as it was truly national in being owned by the public as opposed to private shareholders, mattered less than its function. Its ultimate justification was to facilitate the whole exertion of the faculties, intellectual and corporeal, of a united people, by putting spirit into the national economy, thereby stimulating individual activity and promoting the well-being of the population. As II.129 asked, 'Whether, all things considered, a national bank be not the most practicable, sure, and speedy method to mend our affairs, and cause industry to flourish among us?' (II.112-16), a conclusion very much in keeping with Berkeley's overall pragmatic, Aristotelian (household model) approach to economic matters.

Adam Smith on money, mercantilism and the system of natural liberty

RYAN PATRICK HANLEY *and* MARIA PIA PAGANELLI

On first glance, the study of Adam Smith's understanding of money would seem to be an unrewarding pursuit. In an early draft of *The Wealth of nations*, Smith himself insisted that with regard to the nature, origin and history of money, he had 'little to say that is very new or particular'.[1] Yet modern readers should take care not to be misled by Smith's modesty. For while Smith's understanding of money is indeed derivative of several previous accounts, it plays a crucial role in his development of one of the conclusions for which he is most famous today: the superiority of the system of natural liberty to mercantilism. In what follows, we argue that Smith's theory of money is a central component of his argument staking out this claim.

We start with an exposition of different ways in which social order was conceived in the eighteenth century as a way of setting in context Smith's preference for a social order predicated on natural liberty. We then suggest that his theory of the origins and evolution of money is intended to illustrate the superiority of this natural order to institutions which infringe upon natural liberty. By examining his critique of three proto-monetary policies of his day, we present Smith's understanding of how intervention in the monetary order damages society. We then turn to the role of his theory of money in his critique of one particular proto-monetary policy, mercantilism, which Smith himself regarded as an illustration of the dangers of intervention. Here we argue that his demystification of the mercantilist monetary fallacy was intended as further support of his argument for the superior beauty and order of the system of natural liberty. We end with an examination of the role of the 'science of the legislator' in promoting the realisation of this system. Based on this analysis we conclude that despite the seeming unoriginality of Smith's conception of money, his analysis lies at the heart of the

---

1. Adam Smith, 'Early draft of part of *The Wealth of nations*', in *Lectures on jurisprudence*, ed. R. L. Meek, D. D. Raphael and P. G. Stein (1978; Indianapolis, IN, 1982), p.575. See David Laidler, 'Adam Smith as a monetary economist', *Canadian journal of economics* 14:2 (1981), p.186; and Douglas Vickers, 'Adam Smith and the status of the theory of money', in *Essays on Adam Smith*, ed. Andrew S. Skinner and Thomas Wilson (Oxford, 1975), p.483-84, 503.

fundamental project of *The Wealth of nations*: the demonstration of the advantages of a system of natural liberty over the artificial order established by the mercantilist system of eighteenth-century Britain.

Theories of order and Smith's theory of money

A brief review of the fundamental categories of the eighteenth-century debate over man's capacity to create social order will help establish a context for understanding Smith's preference for a natural system of liberty, as exemplified in his theory of the nature and origins of money.[2] Enlightenment deliberations over the nature and development of social cohesion took different forms. Jonathan Israel remarks on the genealogy of an 'unprecedented intellectual turmoil which commenced in the mid-seventeenth century, with the rise of Cartesianism and the subsequent spread of "mechanical philosophy" or the "mechanistic world-view"', which fed into the onset of the Enlightenment.[3] Brian Singer has described the conception of social order associated with mechanistic philosophy as challenging the notion of something 'given from without by a divine Other, as subjected to a sphere of transcendence that alone provides it with its form, finality and meaning'. On this account, 'The social order is given to be accepted on faith. The divinity appears at the origin of society, and His presence is manifested in the continued, orderly existence of that society.'[4]

---

2. The literature on this topic is of course extensive. On eighteenth-century ideas of social cohesion, see, among others, Carl L. Becker, *The Heavenly city of the eighteenth-century philosophers* (1932; New Haven, CT, 1974); Ernst Cassirer, *The Philosophy of the Enlightenment* (1951; Princeton, NJ, 1979); Roger Chartier, *The Cultural origins of the French Revolution*, trans. Lydia G. Cochrane (Durham, NC, 1991); Chiara Continisio, 'La "politica" aristotelica: un modello per la convivenza ordinata nella trattatistica politica italiana dell'Antico Regime', *Cheiron* 11:22 (1994), p.149-65; Joachim Fest, *Der zerstorte Traum: vom Ende des utopischen Zeitalters* (Berlin, 1991); Michel Foucault, *The Order of things: an archeology of the human sciences* (1970; New York, 1994); Daniel Gordon, *Citizens without sovereignty: equality and sociability in French thought, 1670-1789* (Princeton, NJ, 1994); Jonathan I. Israel, *Radical Enlightenment: philosophy and the making of modernity, 1650-1750* (Oxford, 2001); Arthur O. Lovejoy, *The Great chain of being* (1936; Cambridge, MA, 1982); Robert Nisbet, *History of the idea of progress* (New York, 1980); Roy Porter, *The Creation of the modern world: the British Enlightenment* (New York, 2000); Brian C. J. Singer, *Society, theory and the French Revolution* (New York, 1986); Franco Venturi, *The End of the Old Regime in Europe, 1768-1776: the first crisis*, trans. R. Burr Litchfield (Princeton, NJ, 1989); Franco Venturi, *The End of the Old Regime in Europe, 1776-1789*, trans. R. Burr Litchfield, 2 vols (Princeton, NJ, 1991) (translations of *Settecento riformatore*, vol.3. *La Prima crisi dell'Antico Regime (1768-1776)* [1979]; vol.4, *La Caduta dell'Antico Regime (1776-1789)*, vol.1, *I Grandi stati dell'Occidente* [1984], and vol.2, *Il Patriottismo repubblicano e gli imperi dell'Est* [1984]). On their influence on economics, see William Oliver Coleman, *Rationalism and anti-rationalism in the origins of economics: the philosophical roots of 18th century economic thought* (Aldershot, 1995).
3. Israel, *Radical Enlightenment*, p.14.
4. Singer, *Society, theory and the French Revolution*, p.13-14.

An alternative understanding of philosophy introduced a different account of social order and its origins. This view 'sought to sweep away existing structures entirely, rejecting the Creation as traditionally understood in Judeo-Christian civilisation, and the intervention of a providential God in human affairs'.[5] As a result, social order was reconceived as a human construct, the consequence of rational deliberation. Political society itself was seen by the contractarians as a reasoned agreement among human beings to create an ordered system capable of advancing their collective interests and well-being. One particularly important consequence of this conception was the conclusion that reason and creation render men able and morally obliged to improve the society that they created. Such a position in time served to justify several philanthropic and utopian projects to combat social ills such as poverty, unemployment and social inequality.[6]

Of course this emerging view of man's capacity to shape social order did not go unquestioned, but faced a variety of reactions from moderate to extreme. William Coleman has explored the 'anti-rationalism' of the eighteenth century,[7] and most relevant for us is a version of a moderate 'rationalist' Enlightenment, in which the world is seen as a system, even if not, admittedly, the 'system of hierarchy' favoured by Cartesian rationalists. Rather it is a system of 'mutual interdependence'.[8] The moderate reaction particularly sought to stake out a middle ground between the theological understanding of order as divinely ordained and the anti-theological view that sought to deny any role for providence and harmony.

One significant moderate position of importance as a precursor to Smith's was taken by Montesquieu. In *The Spirit of the laws* (1748), Montesquieu presented morals and laws as man-made rather than God-given, but neither consciously nor rationally constructed. Society is therefore a result of human conduct, though it cannot be said to be its conscious result. Laws are context-specific and emerge from individual interests, and yet, without a conscious intention, they generate a stable social order. Bernard Mandeville also made an analogous point before Smith. In *The Fable of the bees*,[9] Mandeville maintains that from private

---

5. Israel, *Radical Enlightenment*, p.11.
6. See Fest, *Der zerstorte Traum*.
7. Coleman notes: 'To anti-rationalists our only source of knowledge is the reports of our senses (where "senses" include not only the five "external" senses but also our feeling and appetites). The intellect cannot constitute a fundamental source of knowledge, since the "mind's eye" can only see what was previously deposited there by the senses' (*Rationalism and anti-rationalism*, p.4).
8. Coleman, *Rationalism and anti-rationalism*, p.65.
9. Mandeville initially published the poem under the title *The Grumbling hive: or, Knaves turn'd honest* in 1705. In 1714 he reprinted the work together with a commentary as *The Fable of the bees: or, Private vices publick benefits*; he added further sections in editions of 1723 and 1724.

vices public virtues are achieved, claiming that a functioning and prosperous social order is not the consequence of a conscious design but the unintended result of self-interested individual actions.

We share the view that sees Adam Smith and Montesquieu as examples of moderate 'anti-rationalism'. Smith's published works, *The Theory of moral sentiments* (*TMS*)[10] and *The Wealth of nations* (*WN*), though on seemingly different topics, are both grounded in a common understanding of society: namely that it may function and thrive without any conscious human design.[11] *The Theory of moral sentiments* describes how it is not reason, but our senses, emotions and passions that generate canons of behaviour that keep society together and promote both individual and social moral flourishing. *The Wealth of nations* is an enquiry into the ways in which our individual interests, emotions and passions, rather than reason, generate economic phenomena and forces at the macro level that sustain the economy and facilitate individual and social material prosperity.

On Smith's account, the human mind may aspire to understand the social order, and yet the weakness of human reason is such that even the limited process of trying to grasp it seems daunting.[12] Attempts to change this order through rational intervention would be unlikely to bring success. Nevertheless, Smith leaves some space for what he calls the 'science of a statesman or legislator' (*WN* IV.intro.1) to promote the enrichment of the entire nation.

Consistent with the view that successful social institutions are not the product of conscious rational design, Smith presents the origin of money as a natural social occurrence and not as a conscious human creation. It is on this claim that our analysis of Smith's theory of money will focus, rather than aspiring to provide a comprehensive account of his understanding of money.[13] His fundamental claim in this regard is that money

10. Smith [1759]; *The Theory of moral sentiments*, ed. D. D. Raphael and A. L. Macfie (1976; Indianapolis, IN, 1982). References in the essay to Smith's works are given parenthetically to the Glasgow edition as republished by the Liberty Fund according to the standard paragraph numbering system of this edition. *WN = An Inquiry into the nature and causes of the wealth of nations; TMS = The Theory of moral sentiments; LJ = Lectures on Jurisprudence.*

11. The question of whether the lack of human design implies a divine design or no design at all is beyond our scope here. Furthermore, this ambiguity has been widely discussed in the literature on Smith and still has not reached agreement. For a treatment of this literature, see Leonidas Montes, *Adam Smith in context: a critical reassessment of some central components of his thought* (New York, 2004).

12. For a detailed account of this view, see Coleman, *Rationalism and anti-rationalism.* For an account of the difficulties in understanding the physical order, see Eric Schliesser, 'Wonder in the face of scientific revolutions: Adam Smith on Newton's "proof" of Copernicanism', *British journal for the history of philosophy* 13:4 (2005), p.697-732.

13. For such accounts, see Jacob H. Hollander, 'The development of the theory of money from Adam Smith to David Ricardo', *Quarterly journal of economics* 25:3 (1911), p.433-41; and

is in fact an epiphenomenon of commerce, a social institution that developed in an attempt to decrease the inconveniences of the double coincidence of wants and barter. Barter, he explains, is a human propensity that originally afforded incentives to specialise and to further trade. Those engaged in trade then needed to find a means of exchange that 'few people would be likely to refuse in exchange for the produce of their industry' (*WN* I.iv.2). Precious metals frequently began to be used as money and, in time, Mints were founded to make easier their weighing and assaying (*WN* I.iv.7), and eventually the weight and fineness of these metals came to be stated on them as well (*WN* I.iv.9). Thus presented, the history of money is not the result of the rational design of a particular individual, but rather of the interactions of a multitude of individuals over time who collectively developed a mechanism to render simpler those transactions intended to further the pursuit of their self-interest. The same forces that generate social, moral and economic order thus also generate money.

Smith's critique of proto-monetary policies

Smith's critical analysis of what might be considered the proto-monetary policies of his day, like his theory of money itself, is consistent with his view that social and economic growth is not the product of conscious design. Thus, his analysis further develops his claim that the order generated by individuals in the course of pursuing their private interest generally produces more desirable results than do schemes of particular individuals to improve the economy or social order.[14] He continually reminds his readers that a market order ought to be preferred to a constructed order, both in the best and in the worst case scenario of the latter. The best case would be the situation that would obtain under what we would call a benevolent dictator. Smith claims that even the most well-intended legislator cannot outperform the invisible hand of the market, insisting that natural ordering is a more effective means of production and distribution than even the most effective scheme that an omniscient and well-intended ruler might propose. In the worst case scenario, when social policies are developed by interest groups rather than those genuinely concerned for the well-being of the society, the 'public' policies that result benefit only particular segments of society, while doing widespread harm to the whole.

This claim is the foundation of Smith's critique of three specific

---

more recently Vickers, 'Adam Smith and the status of the theory of money'; and Laidler, 'Adam Smith as monetary economist'.

14. For an account of the strength of these orders, see Maria Pia Paganelli, 'Adam Smith: why decentralized systems?', *The Adam Smith review* 2 (2006), p.203-208.

eighteenth-century proto-monetary policies. These approaches are not, strictly speaking, monetary policies as we would consider them today, since they generally differ in both motivation and implementation from modern forms. We think in terms of controlling the money supply to encourage or at least to fine-tune the economy through the actions of a central bank. But in Smith's time, attempts to control money supply in an effort to better the economy were in their infancy and central banks as we know them today had not yet been created. Nevertheless, efforts were made to control the money supply through certain proto-monetary policies – debasement, paper credit money, and tariffs – and Smith was critical of all of them.

The first proto-monetary policy considered by Smith is debasement. Debasement consists in decreasing the amount of metal in a coin while keeping its denomination constant. We hesitate to call this action 'policy' because it was generally meant explicitly to benefit the sovereign, and not to advance the general interests of society. Smith himself insists that debasement is not a public policy but a forcible abuse of power for the sake of personal benefit. It is indeed 'the avarice and injustice of princes and sovereign states' that promotes debasement to help debtors (the king) and ruin creditors (*WN* I.iv.10).

The second proto-monetary policy considered by Smith is the use of paper credit money. Smith recognises the necessity of paper credit money in the economy. The role of paper in domestic markets as a substitute for metallic money promotes the freeing of productive resources that would be otherwise unusable. Metals can be employed abroad while paper money is not accepted far from the place of issuing. Thus it is 'by rendering a greater part of that capital active and productive than would otherwise be so, that the most judicious operations of banking can increase the industry of the country' (*WN* II.ii.86). Yet paper is not a policy instrument because the 'judicious operations of banking' are not the result of rational planning, but the consequence of the uncoordinated operations of a multitude of private banks independent from and acting in competition with each other. Here again economic growth is the unintended consequence of a multitude of individual actions. Furthermore, when Smith has to face the possible use of credit as a policy instrument, he dismisses it as either a failure or an absurdity. In 1696, he pointed out, the Bank of England had to been obliged to suspend payments on its notes (*WN* II.ii.80), which exemplified the fact that when a central rational plan for banking is attempted the socio-economic order falls apart.[15] Smith even dismisses John Law's

---

15. Smith refers here to events of 6 May 1696, during the Recoinage, when a run on the Bank of England forced a partial suspension of cash payments. Two days earlier, clipped coins

paper experiments and his Mississippi Scheme, the most majestic of the rational schemes at the time. To improve the economy by increasing the money supply would be a disaster for industry, and Smith dismisses them as 'the most extravagant project both of banking and stock-jobbing that, perhaps, the world ever saw' (*WN* II.ii.78).[16] As Smith is reported to have explained in the lecture notes of his students: '[Mr Law] thought that national opulence consists in money, and that the value of gold and silver is arbitrary'. (*LJ*, p.270) Law's failure was inevitable because of 'the vanity of both these imaginations'.[17]

The third proto-monetary policy that Smith extensively analysed was mercantilism, to which he dedicated the whole of *WN* IV. Among the central mercantilist tenets was a commitment to increase the quantity of money in the economy in order to maximise the power of a country (in a zero-sum conception of economic rivalry).[18] The only form of money that mercantilists regarded as legitimate was precious metals. Paper is a mere shadow of metals, as it derives its value from representing gold and silver. To achieve their goal of increasing the quantity of money (that is, gold and silver), the mercantilists sought to limit imports (payments for which implied the exiting of gold and silver from the country) and to incentivise exports (which brought gold and silver into the country in the form of payments). The results of these policies, Smith argues, are catastrophic for at least two reasons. First he argues that the entire mercantile system rests on a fundamental misunderstanding of the nature and uses of money, namely the misperception that money is wealth: 'it would be too ridiculous to go about seriously to prove, that wealth does not consist in money, or in gold and silver' (*WN* IV.i.17). It follows that using resources to accumulate money not only prevents the allocation of those same resources to accumulating further wealth, but it is wasteful because 'Upon every account...the attention of government never was so unnecessarily employed, as when directed to watch over the preservation or increase of the quantity of money in any country' (*WN* IV.i.15). Second, mercantilism is based on special interests, not on general interest. Pursuing the betterment of one specific group at the

had ceased to be accepted by law but the Bank had insufficient stores of reminted money to answer demand. See Sir John Clapham, *The Bank of England: a history*, vol.1, p.32, 35-36.

16. For a detailed account of Smith and paper credit see Maria Pia Paganelli, 'Vanity and the Daedalian wings of paper money in Adam Smith', in *New voices on Adam Smith*, ed. Eric Schliesser and Leonidas Montes (London, 2006), p.271-89. For a critical account of Smith's analysis see Athol Fitzgibbons, *Adam Smith's system of liberty, wealth, and virtue: the moral and political foundations of the Wealth of nations* (Oxford, 1995).

17. Smith, 'Early draft', in *Lectures on jurisprudence*, p.42.

18. For a review of the central claims of mercantilism, see Jacob Viner, 'English theories of foreign trade before Adam Smith', *Journal of political economy* 38:4 (1930), p.249-301; and Mark Blaug, *Economic theory in retrospect*, 4th edn (Cambridge, 1985), p.10-18.

expense of the rest of society, Smith argues, necessarily leads to the impoverishment rather than the enrichment of society as a whole.[19] In illustrating the practical consequences of this aspect of mercantilist thought, Smith presents his fullest statement of the superior beauty and order of the system of natural liberty to a rationally constructed order.[20]

Mercantilism and money

Smith opens *WN* IV with a description of the mercantilist conception of money: 'That wealth consists in money, or in gold and silver, is a popular notion which naturally arises from a double function of money, as the instrument of commerce, and as the measure of value' (*WN* IV.i.1). Examination of this fallacy dominates the entirety of *WN* IV.i, which leads him into an eventual apology that he thought it 'necessary, though at the hazard of being tedious, to examine at full length this popular notion' (*WN* IV.i.34; see I.iv.18). In both places Smith calls attention to the fact that mercantilism rests on an unexamined opinion, an 'ambiguity of expression' in 'common language' that mercantilism's supporters have exploited to gain legislative support for their proposals (*WN* IV.i.34).[21] Smith's own strategy in arguing against mercantilism was to expose this sleight of hand, and thereby encourage his readers to pursue a more careful enquiry into the true nature of both money and wealth.[22]

19. See, among others, Jerry Evensky, 'The evolution of Adam Smith's views on political economy', *History of political economy* 21:1 (1989), p.123-45; Evensky, *Adam Smith's moral philosophy* (Cambridge, 2005).

20. In this sense, Smith's treatment of the mercantile misunderstanding has philosophical as well as economic significance, insofar as it is shaped by his understanding of epistemology. An important attempt to locate *The Wealth of nations* within Smith's wider philosophical commitments is offered in Samuel Fleischacker, *On Adam Smith's Wealth of nations: a philosophical companion* (Princeton, NJ, 2004), esp. p.21-31, which is particularly sensitive to Smith's commitment to the advantages of an epistemology grounded in 'common sense' rather than simple scepticism.

21. Smith's emphasis on the mercantilists' confusion of money and wealth has been noted by several commentators; see for example Laidler, 'Adam Smith as monetary economist', p.193; Viner, 'English theories of foreign trade before Adam Smith', p.264f; Donald Winch, *Riches and poverty: an intellectual history of political economy in Britain, 1750-1834* (Cambridge, 1996), p.110; Peter McNamara, *Political economy and statesmanship: Smith, Hamilton, and the foundation of the commercial republic* (DeKalb, IL., 1998), p.61-62; and Evensky, *Adam Smith's moral philosophy*, p.185. For Smith's sensitivity to the use and abuse of rhetoric in political and economic argument, see especially Andrew S. Skinner, 'Adam Smith: rhetoric and the communication of ideas', in *Methodological controversy in economics: historical essays in honour of T. W. Hutchison*, ed. A. W. Coats (London, 1983), p.71-88; Vivienne Brown, *Adam Smith's discourse: canonicity, commerce, conscience* (London, 1994); Charles Griswold, *Adam Smith and the virtues of Enlightenment* (Cambridge, 1999); and Fleischacker, *On Smith's Wealth of nations*, ch. 1.

22. In discussing *The Wealth of nations* IV, McNamara writes that 'Smith's inquiry is founded

Smith's attempt to bring his audience from a popular opinion concerning money to a true understanding of it depends on his ability to demonstrate that money is a matter of convention. In a passage Smith knew well, Aristotle had insisted that there is a fundamental distinction between money (*nomisma*, from *nomos*, or 'law' or 'custom') and wealth, which is tied to a natural capacity or need.[23] Smith's own discussion of money rests on the same distinction. The problem at the heart of the mercantile conception of money is that in it 'two values' are 'intimated somewhat ambiguously by the same word' – that is, money is taken to represent both the instrument of exchange and genuine wealth (*WN* II.ii.17). Consequently, what is needed is to move beyond the 'ambiguity of language' (*TMS* VII.ii.4.11)[24] – a call repeated in Smith's insistence in *WN* IV that 'we must in all cases attend to the nature of the thing, without paying any regard to the word' (*WN* IV.v.a.40).

In reconsidering the mercantile understanding of money, Smith thus seeks to move his audience beyond the false appearances of mere conventions, and instead encourages in them an appreciation of what is natural. The widespread success of the mercantile fallacy derived from the fact that its reliance on certain conventions appealed to the natural human propensity to prefer the plain and visible to the obscure and

---

upon an attempt to reach beyond the ordinary understanding of things by inventing a technical language for discussing the subject matter of political economy' (*Political economy and statesmanship*, p.63). The view developed below agrees with McNamara's claim that Smith sought to move his audience beyond the 'ordinary understanding' that the mercantilists exploited – a claim also made by Fleischacker, *On Smith's Wealth of nations*, p.16-17, who notes that the mercantilists 'appealed to a popular confusion', and Evensky, who argues that on Smith's account 'the mercantilists' sophistry was successful because they took advantage of an asymmetry of information' (*Adam Smith's moral philosophy*, p.190). But our argument below is that Smith's remedy for this practical problem lay principally neither in an 'invention' nor, on the other hand, in returning to 'thoughts couched in common language' (Fleischacker, *On Smith's Wealth of nations*, p.24-5), but rather in seeking to expand the vision of his readers.

23. See Aristotle, *Politics*, 1257b5-15; *Nicomachean ethics*, 1133a25-32; see Smith, *WN* I.iv.7.

24. Smith frequently notes confusions of words and calls attention to the limitations of popular understandings of terms (see, for example, *TMS* VI.iii.33-34; *TMS* VII.ii.1.10). In this sense his conception of speech parallels his treatment of money. Speech and commerce are both natural systems of exchange employing instruments of conventional value as a means – money in the case of commerce, and words in the case of speech – and in both cases the conventional instruments of each system are prone to misunderstanding. See especially Andreas Kalyvas and Ira Katznelson, 'The rhetoric of the market: Adam Smith on recognition, speech and exchange', *Review of politics* 63:3 (2001), p.568f; Charles Bazerman, 'Money talks: the rhetorical project of the *Wealth of nations*', in *Economics and language*, ed. Willie Henderson, Tony Dudley-Evans and Roger Backhouse (London, 1993), p.189, 194-95; and James Otteson, *Adam Smith's marketplace of life* (Cambridge, 2002), p.258-89. Especially helpful in elucidating this comparison is Otteson's analysis of how an 'unintended order' is discernible in the development of language (see p.270, 274).

abstract (see for example *LJ* vi.13). Money, like other visible objects, is trusted for its physical appearance. Smith admits that it is 'more natural' for 'the greater part of people' to make judgments on the basis of 'a plain palpable object', as opposed to an 'abstract notion, which, though it can be made sufficiently intelligible, is not altogether so natural and obvious' (*WN* I.v.5). Indeed for a butcher, brewer or baker, 'It is more natural and obvious' to estimate the value of a product 'by the quantity of money, the commodity for which he immediately exchanges them, than by that of bread and beer', and for this reason 'the exchangeable value of every commodity is more frequently estimated by the quantity of money, than by the quantity either of labour or of any other commodity which can be had in exchange for it' (*WN* I.v.6). This preference for the palpable is what explains the attractions of the mercantile fallacy, as it seems natural to ordinary people to trust tangible, seemingly 'lasting' gold to 'perishable' or 'consumable' commodities whose value appears unreliable (*WN* IV.i.19).[25]

Thus, Smith concludes, in ordinary economic transactions, 'we generally look no farther than money' (*LJ* vi.146). Yet sight, Smith knows, is a double-edged sword. The visible may have the advantage of being readily apprehended, but this can be a disadvantage if appearances are mistaken for the whole truth. As Smith seeks to show, if one hopes to understand a system in its entirety – and particularly the complex system of international political economy – one must take a broader view that encompasses more than that which is readily apparent.[26] Thus Smith does not mean to disabuse ordinary economic agents of their instinctive understanding of money; the common sense perspective, he notes, 'though not exact, is sufficient for carrying on the business of common life' (*WN* I.v.4). Rather, his intention is to expose how economic policymakers, and the mercantilists in particular, have exploited this instinctive but imprecise understanding, and it is in this spirit that he warns of

25. In this respect Smith's treatment of the appearance of money parallels his treatment elsewhere of the natural reverence that men have for moral appearances, in which he emphasises that money and wealth are desired less for their intrinsic utility than for the sake of how they make their possessor appear in the eyes of others (*TMS* I.iii.2.1; *WN* I.xi.c.31). Likewise Smith notes that in moral life we are frequently seduced by the 'dazzling' appearance of ornament and beauty, which often leads us to prefer 'the gaudy and glittering' to the solid and substantive (*WN* IV.vii.b.7; *TMS* I.iii.3.2), even though all that glitters is not necessarily good (*WN* IV.vii.a.17).

26. For an excellent discussion of Smith's subtle discrimination between the familiar but limited perspective of common life and the expanded vision of the philosopher, see Fleischacker, *On Smith's Wealth of nations*, p.30-31. On the problems of vision in Smith more generally and his debt to Bishop Berkeley's theory of vision see David M. Levy, 'Bishop Berkeley exorcises the infinite: fuzzy consequences of strict finitism', *Hume studies* 18:2 (1992), p.511-36; and Levy, 'The partial spectator in the *Wealth of nations*: a robust utilitarianism', *European journal of the history of economic thought* 2:2 (1995), p.299-326.

the dangers that come from erecting 'the sneaking arts of underling tradesmen' to the level of 'political maxims for the conduct of a great empire' (*WN* IV.iii.c.8).[27] Smith consistently emphasises that to judge on the basis of appearances is to judge in terms of partial and often incorrect knowledge. It is precisely this limited judgement, apt to promote intervention into complex systems, which he calls his audience of potential economic policymakers to transcend. By gradually bringing this audience to a more precise understanding of money, beyond that afforded by the popular understanding embodied in ordinary language, Smith encourages the development both of an appreciation of the significance of money beyond what its appearances reveal,[28] and, in turn, an awareness of the intricacy and complexity of the economic system as a whole. By so doing he hopes to foster an understanding which will render his readers less inclined to intervene in the economic system.

The science of the legislator

At the same time that Smith exposes the error in the understanding of money characteristic of mercantilism, he also means to provide a remedy for it. It is to this remedy that we now turn. Smith summarised the opposing approach to legislative intervention in his discussion of the man of system who, 'wise in his own conceit', thinks he can manage men as he can manipulate pieces on a chessboard (see *TMS* VI.ii.2.17). Lost in this reductive vision, Smith argues, is the moderation, scepticism and caution that are fundamental to the art of economic legislation. The moderate alternative to the approach of the man of system he calls the 'science of a statesman or legislator'.[29] The science of the legislator, applied to political economy, 'proposes to enrich both the people and the sovereign', and on these grounds alone it can be distinguished from mercantilism (*WN* IV.intro.1). Like the men of system, the merchants and manufacturers who support mercantilism are incapable of accounting for any interests beyond their own; all of their efforts are dedicated to advancing their own partial interests, and 'to know in what manner it enriched the country, was no part of their business' (*WN* IV.i.10). A great gap in fact separates these men from the general interest of the nation, as

27. On the misuses of mercantilism, see Evensky, 'The evolution of Adam Smith's views on political economy', and Evensky, *Adam Smith's moral philosophy*.
28. On the 'vulgar prejudices' on which mercantilism depends for its support, see for example, *WN* II.iii.25; IV.i.1; IV.vi.32; IV.ix.3.
29. For full explications of the 'science of the legislator' and its relationship to both natural jurisprudence and economic statesmanship, see Knud Haakonssen, *The Science of a legislator: the natural jurisprudence of David Hume and Adam Smith* (Cambridge, 1981), p.83-98; Winch, *Riches and poverty*, p.90-123; and McNamara, *Political economy and statesmanship*, p.77-94.

they in their 'sophistry' are 'always demanding a monopoly against their countrymen', in their effort to further interests 'directly opposite to that of the great body of the people' (*WN* IV.ii.38; IV.iii.c.10).[30] He explains that they are 'an order of men, whose interest is never exactly the same with that of the public, who have generally an interest to deceive and even oppress the publick, and who accordingly have, upon many occasions, both deceived and oppressed it' (*WN* I.xi.p.10). At their worst they even threaten political stability; hence his likening of them to 'an overgrown standing army' and his claim that 'they have become formidable to the government, and upon many occasions intimidate the legislature' (*WN* IV.ii.43; see IV.v.a.28). Insofar as they cannot consider interests beyond those of their own class, the mercantilists fall victim to the most vulgar sort of partiality that blinds them to the benefits of the system as a whole.

Smith seeks to counter such selfishness and partiality by encouraging his audience to cultivate an appreciation of this system in its entirety. Thus, where the mercantilists imposed on the simplicity of gentlemen in order to manipulate them (*WN* I.xi.p.10), Smith seeks to direct their generous and expansive imaginations to a vision of the beauty and order of the system as a whole, an appreciation of which he regards as the best defence against economic intervention. By so doing, he means to encourage their decent desire to promote rather than obstruct the improvement of the estates of their neighbours – that is to say, their intuitive anti-mercantilist appreciation of the fact that improvement is mutual (*WN* IV.ii.21).[31] Smith identifies an antecedent of this process in his description of how the principle of sympathy enables individuals to transcend the narrow egotism on which Hobbes and Mandeville founded their systems. Despite our natural preference for ourselves, he here explains, social order requires that we correct the 'otherwise natural inequality of our sentiments'. Thus, he explains,

> to the selfish and original passions of human nature, the loss or gain of a very small interest of our own, appears to be of vastly more importance, excites a much more passionate joy or sorrow, a much more ardent desire or aversion, than the greatest concern of another with whom we have no particular connexion. His interests, as long as they are surveyed from this station, can never be put into balance with our own, can never restrain us from doing

30. Smith is referring here to the situation in France under Colbert, although it is generally applicable as an example.
31. Smith's contrast between genuinely public-spirited political economy and the self-interested policies of the merchants and mercantilists is nicely developed in Jerry Z. Muller, *Adam Smith in his time and ours: designing the decent society* (Princeton, NJ, 1993), p.79-83; Winch, *Riches and poverty*, p.102-103; and Evensky, *Adam Smith's moral philosophy*, p.189-95, 201-204.

whatever may tend to promote our own, how ruinous soever to him. Before we can make any proper comparison of those opposite interests we must change our position. (*TMS* III.3.3)

Social order requires that we take a wider perspective beyond self-interest. It is precisely this perspective that he calls his would-be economic legislators to take in *WN* IV, in contrast to the narrow perspective adopted by mercantilism's advocates. Put this way, it is clear that Smith's appeal to the generosity of his audience is not addressed to their beneficence. Beneficence is not wholly absent from his anti-mercantilism,[32] yet in general his goal is not to encourage the sort of pity that leads to public activism, but rather the opposite: by revealing to his audience the intricacy and complexity, and thus the beauty of the system of international political economy as a whole, Smith hopes to encourage a reverence for this system and hence a temerity, humility and reticence to intervene in it – the direct opposite of the aggressive arrogance characteristic of the mercantilists.[33]

Smith explains this approach in *The Theory of moral sentiments*. The improvements that 'promote the public welfare [do not] always rise from pure sympathy with the happiness of those who are to reap the benefit of it'. Rather it is the case that these great systems, when taken as a whole, are themselves 'noble and magnificent objects', and that since 'We take pleasure in beholding the perfection of so beautiful and grand a system', we 'are uneasy till we move any obstruction that can in the least disturb or encumber the regularity of its motions'. This leads him to conclude that if one hopes to persuade men to support public policies which are genuinely public-spirited, one should not preach benevolence but rather one should 'describe the great system' that procures public advantages – 'the connexions and dependencies of its several parts, their mutual subordination to one another, and their general subserviency to the happiness of the society'. Most importantly, it is best

if you show how this system might be introduced into his own country, what it is that hinders it from taking place there at present, how those obstructions might be removed, and all the several wheels of the machine of government be made to move with more harmony and smoothness, without grating upon one another, or mutually retarding one another's motions. It is scarce possible that a man should listen to a discourse of this kind, and not

32. See *WN* IV.ii.35; IV.viii.4; IV.viii.17.
33. A point nicely developed in the account of the 'epistemic limits of statesmanship' given by Griswold, in which he explains that the science of the legislator, as developed by Smith, is itself 'a knowledge of ignorance, or of imperfection' (*Smith and the virtues of enlightenment*, p.304 and 309); see also Ryan Patrick Hanley, 'Enlightened nation building: the "science of the legislator" in Adam Smith and Rousseau', *American journal of political science* 52:2 (2008), p.219-34 (220-23, 230-31).

feel himself animated to some degree of public spirit. He will, at least for the moment, feel some desire to remove those obstructions, and to put into motion so beautiful and so orderly a machine. (*TMS* IV.1.11)

Smith's own anti-mercantilist argument in *WN* IV closely follows this advice.[34] By detailing the impediments and artifices of the mercantilists and their detrimental effects, he provides a blueprint for removing those obstructions that have impeded the realisation of the beauty and order of the system of natural liberty.

The Wealth of nations IV indeed traces a process in several stages, each of which successively expands the horizons of its audience and leads them from the natural, though partial, perspective of the mercantilists to the broader, more comprehensive perspective of the genuine legislator. He begins, as we have seen, by encouraging his audience to see the short-comings of the common sense understanding of money gleaned from its appearances. But after having revealed the failings of this ordinary perspective, he then moves on to the dangers of the nationalistic perspective, turning from 'private interest and the spirit of monopoly' to those risks that arise as the consequence of 'national prejudice and animosity' (*WN* IV.iii.a.1). Having ascended to this more encompassing view, Smith goes on to show the shortcomings of the ordinary perspec-tive when it is manifested at the national level, in which 'each nation has been made to look with an invidious eye upon the prosperity of all the nations with which it trades, and to consider their gain as its own loss. Commerce, which ought naturally to be, among nations, as among individuals, a bond of union and friendship, has become the most fertile source of discord and animosity' (*WN* IV.iii.c.9). As Smith hopes to show, a true understanding of the benefits of unhindered international trade can be achieved only when the system is regarded from the widest possible position: not from the perspective of that which is immediately visible, but from the point of view of 'the whole globe of the earth' (*WN* IV.iii.c.16).[35] Such cosmopolitanism is presented not as the product of global benevolence, but from Smith's attempt to put his imaginative audience in mind of the beauty and natural order of the system of international political economy. 'Were all nations to follow the liberal system of free exportation and free importation, the different states into which a great continent was divided would so far resemble the different

34. See Winch, *Riches and poverty*, p.95-6.
35. Evensky, *Adam Smith's moral philosophy*, esp. p.204-12, does an excellent job of demonstrat-ing Smith's commitment to transcending the narrow-mindedness characteristic of mer-cantilism, yet as we have sought to argue, Smith's goal seems less the recovery of the nationalistic perspective characteristic of civic humanism (as Evensky sometimes suggests; see p.205, 212) than the cultivation of a 'larger, international perspective' (as Evensky elsewhere emphasises; see p.207).

provinces of a great empire' (*WN* IV.v.b.39). For this reason, Smith presents the ordered beauty of the 'liberal system' as an alternative to the reductive jealousy, prejudice and 'national animosity' that characterises the mercantile system.

In this chapter, we have shown how Smith employs his theory of money to exemplify the superiority of market orders to rationally constructed orders. Smith's account of the history of money demonstrates that its evolution is the successful result of the undirected interactions of many individuals, rather than the fulfilment of one individual's rational project. He also shows how government intervention in the monetary order leads to results inferior to those produced by natural market forces. Smith's energetic intellectual commitment to the dismantling of mercantilism exemplifies his conviction that constructive orders would impoverish society, while the wealth of nations would increase only through the restitution of the system of natural liberty. In his treatment of money, indeed, Smith seeks to impress on his audience the beauty of the system of natural liberty so that they will both rescind the artificial obstacles to natural order created by men and also possess a degree of humility sufficient to prevent them from thinking that they can tamper with the system itself.

Pierre-Louis Rœderer, Adam Smith and the problem of inequality[1]

THOMAS HOPKINS

Smith's problematic French reception

Navigating the often treacherous waters of late eighteenth-century political and social theory poses particular challenges when trying to make sense of the reorientation of thinking about political economy that took place in France, as elsewhere, in the decades either side of the Revolution of 1789. The remarkable success of François Quesnay and his followers in dictating the terms of debate on the subject across much of Europe in the 1760s and early 1770s did not long survive the fall of Turgot's ministry in 1776.[2] Although distinguished representatives of what would latterly become known as the Physiocratic school remained active into the early nineteenth century, a more complex, and as yet still somewhat obscure, picture began to emerge in the 1780s and 1790s. Writing in 1803, the historian and political economist J.-C.-L. Simonde de Sismondi identified four systems of political economy that had gained widespread credence in the preceding decades.[3] Of the systems he named, three remain familiar enough, if somewhat weathered, features of the historiographical landscape: mercantilism, in the sense given the word by Adam Smith; Physiocracy; and the 'system of natural liberty' associated with Smith himself. The fourth school of thought to which he alluded, however, has all but disappeared from view in standard historical accounts. For Sismondi, its chief figure was the Swiss economist, Jean-Daniel Herrenschwand, a soldier who, under the patronage of the Duc de

1. I would like to thank Daniel Carey, Suzanne Marcuzzi, Michael Sonenscher and Keith Tribe for their comments on earlier drafts of this chapter, which draws on Thomas Hopkins, 'Say and Sismondi on the political economy of post-revolutionary Europe, *c*.1800-1842' (Doctoral dissertation, University of Cambridge, 2011). I would also like to take this opportunity to thank the Arts and Humanities Research Council for funding the research on which it is based.

2. T. J. Hochstrasser, 'Physiocracy and the politics of *laissez-faire*', in *The Cambridge history of eighteenth-century political thought*, ed. Mark Goldie and Robert Wokler (Cambridge, 2006), p.419-42, provides a useful overview.

3. J. C. L. Simonde [de Sismondi], *De la richesse commerciale: ou, Principes d'économie politique, appliqués à la législation du commerce*, 2 vols (Geneva, J. J. Paschoud, An XI [1803]), vol.1, p.7-11.

Choiseul, had risen high in the service of Louis XV. In 1786, Herrenschwand published a widely-read treatise entitled *De l'économie politique moderne*.[4] On Sismondi's account, Herrenschwand may be taken as standing for a range of positions that took as their starting point the idea that the exploitation of public credit, and of public control of the issue of money, could be used not only to meet the financial obligations of modern states, but to reshape their economies into forms more conducive to the common good than they had to date assumed. The signal importance of such ideas to the intellectual ferment that accompanied the French Revolution has begun to be detailed in recent scholarship.[5] It is now clear that the decision to issue government bonds backed by the sale of the *biens nationaux* in December 1789, and, in April 1790, to accord these *assignats* the status of a paper currency, was taken in an ideological climate torn between fear over the likely consequences of declaring the state bankrupt, and expectations that a sufficiently daring scheme of debt restructuring could provide the foundations for a more egalitarian social and political order.[6] This, as Michael Sonenscher has observed, amounted to an attempt to resurrect ancient republicanism upon the foundations of the modern commercial system, a project associated above all with the Girondin faction, including Jacques-Pierre Brissot, Etienne Clavière and Thomas Paine.[7]

Objections from within the republican camp came from two directions. The first, associated with the Jacobins, involved a more thorough-

4. [Jean-Daniel Herrenschwand], *De l'économie politique moderne: discours fondamental sur la population* (London, T. Hookham, 1786). A revised and expanded presentation of the work appeared under the title, *De l'économie politique et morale de l'espèce humaine*, 2 vols (London, Cooper and Graham, 1796). On Herrenschwand, see the recent study by Gabriel Poulalion, *L'Economiste Jean-Daniel Herrenschwand* (Aix-en-Provence, 2008). The extent of the confusion surrounding Herrenschwand's life and works is indicated by the failure of even the normally scrupulous editors of *The Cambridge history of eighteenth-century political thought* to distinguish the economist from his relative, the physician Jean-Frédéric Herrenschwand; see Goldie and Wokler (eds), *The Cambridge history of eighteenth-century political thought*, p.742.

5. Michael Sonenscher, *Before the deluge: public debt, inequality, and the intellectual origins of the French Revolution* (Princeton, NJ, 2007); Michael Sonenscher, *Sans-culottes: an eighteenth-century emblem in the French Revolution* (Princeton, NJ, 2008); see Istvan Hont, 'The rhapsody of public debt: David Hume and voluntary state bankruptcy', in *Jealousy of trade*, p.325-53.

6. On this episode, see the accounts given by Florin Aftalion, *The French Revolution: an economic interpretation* (Cambridge, 1990), p.61-85; and François Crouzet, *La Grande inflation: la monnaie en France de Louis XVI à Napoléon* (Paris, 1993), p.93-139.

7. An argument outlined in Michael Sonenscher, 'Property, community and citizenship', in *The Cambridge history of eighteenth-century political thought*, ed. Goldie and Wokler, p.465-94, and developed at greater length in Sonenscher, *Sans-culottes*. Gary Kates, *The Cercle social, the Girondins, and the French Revolution* (Princeton, NJ, 1985), remains the starting point for assessments of Girondin political thought, but is notably lacking in detailed treatment of their concern with political economy.

going rejection of the politics of modern commercial society. The second, however, which became linked to the complex of ideas subsequently known as *Idéologie*, took its stand upon the elaboration of a republican politics that would embrace the logic of modern commerce more fully, rejecting as anachronistic the political forms of the ancient world. Modern liberal republicanism, with its attempt to juggle political and civil equality with social inequality, was, in part, a product of this school of thought. It is perhaps natural to see affinities with Anglophone liberalism, and with the political economy of Adam Smith. The well-advertised allegiance of the economist Jean-Baptiste Say, very much a product of this intellectual environment, to Smith's position has long lent credence to the idea.[8] But if Smith did emerge as a touchstone for opponents of social 'levelling' under various guises, his reception in France was far from straightforward.

In the hands of early nineteenth-century admirers such as Say, Smithian political economy served two purposes. Firstly, Smith's 'system of natural liberty' provided the rationale for a rejection of ambitious schemes of political intervention in the economy, offering an authoritative check to interventionist projects such as those of the Girondins and their epigones. Secondly, as Cheryl Welch has emphasised, it offered an alternative grounding for liberal and republican politics to one couched in the more contentious language of natural rights.[9] It was for this reason that Say's political economy enjoyed such wide appeal, attracting the attention not only of liberal theorists such as Charles Dunoyer and Charles Comte, but also of Saint-Simon and, later, Proudhon.[10]

The intellectual climate of the late 1790s, when Smith's political economy first began to win widespread attention in France, was, however, somewhat different. Natural rights, typically grounded theoretically in

8. I have treated Say's role in these debates at greater length elsewhere; see Hopkins, 'Say and Sismondi on the political economy of post-revolutionary Europe'. There have been several attempts in recent years to situate Say more fully in his political context: see Forget, *The Social economics of Jean-Baptiste Say*; Richard Whatmore, *Republicanism and the French Revolution: an intellectual history of Jean-Baptiste Say's political economy* (Oxford, 2000); Sonenscher, *Before the deluge*, p.334-48.

9. Cheryl B. Welch, 'Social science from the French Revolution to positivism', in *The Cambridge history of nineteenth-century political thought*, ed. Gareth Stedman Jones and Gregory Claeys (Cambridge, 2011), p.171-99 (198).

10. On liberal 'industrialism' and Saint-Simon's debt to Say, see David Mercer Hart, 'Class, slavery and the industrialist theory of history in French liberal thought, 1814-1830: the contribution of Charles Comte and Charles Dunoyer' (Doctoral dissertation, University of Cambridge, 1994). On Proudhon's complex reading of Say, see Edward Castleton, 'Introduction: comment la propriété est devenue le vol, ou l'éducation de Pierre-Joseph Proudhon', in P.-J. Proudhon, *Qu'est-ce que la propriété?*, ed. Robert Damien and Edward Castleton (Paris, 2009), p.43-108 (82-96).

some form of sensationalist epistemology, provided the ideological underpinning of the republican regime of the Directory. Yet, at least for some of the more prominent French thinkers of the day, Smith could be read as committed to an account of human nature that sat uncomfortably with the idea of natural equality. This had important implications for the reception of his political economy in republican France. Digesting Smith for a republican audience required more than a rearrangement of the material presented in *The Wealth of nations*, it required a critique of Smith's anthropology, and of his model of the historical development of the European economy. The most extensive attempt to do this was made by Pierre-Louis Rœderer, former member of the *parlement* of Metz, and a close ally of the abbé Emmanuel-Joseph Sieyès.[11] In his critique of Smith, it is possible to get a fuller sense of the dense cluster of problems that came into play when the relationship between the modern European state system and the market economy was put into question. This chapter is concerned with Rœderer's attempts to provide a more robustly egalitarian foundation for political economy than it was supposed could be found in Smith. After a brief presentation of the intellectual background to the problem provided by the work of the Idéologues and the abbé Sieyès, I focus on Rœderer's reading of Smith as a critic of Rousseau, and his engagement with the work of Sophie de Grouchy, the translator of Smith's *Theory of moral sentiments*. From these disparate sources Rœderer attempted to weave a theory of 'social organisation' that could serve as a counterbalance to the politics of the 'levellers' without conceding ground on the subject of natural equality.

Ideology and social science

One way into Rœderer's thought is through the ideas commonly associated with the constellation of thinkers known to posterity as the Idéologues. The name was derived from the term 'Ideology' [*idéologie*], coined in 1796 by Antoine-Louis-Claude Destutt de Tracy in the course of a lecture series that, along with Pierre-George Cabanis, he gave before the Section on the Analysis of Sensations and Ideas, one of the six divisions of the Class of Moral and Political Sciences (CMPS) of the *Institut national*, established in Paris in 1795.[12] The two men had taken as

11. Rœderer's career is outlined by Kenneth Margerison, 'P.-L. Rœderer: political thought and practice during the French Revolution', *Transactions of the American philosophical society* 73:1 (1983), p.1-166.
12. Cheryl B. Welch, *Liberty and utility: the French Idéologues and the transformation of liberalism* (New York, 1984), p.34-35. Destutt de Tracy's first use of the term may be found in his *Mémoire sur la faculté de penser*, in *Mémoires de l'Institut national, classe des sciences morales et politiques*, 5 vols (Paris, Baudouin, Thermidor an VI-Fructidor an XII / 1798-1804), vol.1, p.283-450 (324).

their subject the physiological and rational aspects of analysis, with the object of providing some methodological grounding for the work of the CMPS as a whole. The neologism 'Ideology' was, it would seem, intended to provide an alternative to 'metaphysics' or 'psychology' in describing this foundational science of human understanding, on which could be built in turn the sciences of grammar, logic, instruction, education, morality and economy.[13] This was the basis of the system that Destutt de Tracy elaborated in the revised and expanded version of his lectures that he published in four volumes between 1801 and 1815 under the title, *Projet d'éléments d'idéologie*.[14]

The concept of 'Ideology' found an institutional focal point in the CMPS, amongst whose members were to be found the figures with which it became pre-eminently associated: Cabanis, Destutt de Tracy, Pierre Daunou, Dominique-Joseph Garat, Constantin-François Chassebœuf, known as Volney and, perhaps more loosely, Sieyès and Rœderer. It was here that the imperative need for a science of social organisation, identified variously by Sieyès, Talleyrand and Condorcet, was intended to be met.[15] The National Institute itself had been founded in 1795, under the terms of the constitution of the year III. Moral and Political Sciences formed the second of the three Classes into which it was initially divided, the first Class being that of the Physical and Mathematical sciences, the third, Belles-lettres and Fine Arts. In turn, the Classes were further divided into Sections, those of the second Class being six in number: Analysis of Sensations and Ideas, Ethics, Social Sciences and Legislation, Political Economy, History and Geography.[16] Several of the members of the second class would play important roles in the politics of the Directory and the early years of the Consulate – many of the key players in the Brumaire coup of 1799 would be drawn from its ranks. The political alliance between the Idéologues and the new First Consul quickly became strained, however, and the CMPS was an early victim of Napoleon's determination to eliminate politically troublesome elements within the state; it was abolished after the reorganisation of the Institute in 1803, not to be revived until 1832.[17] A second point of focus for Ideology was the journal, *La Décade philosophique, littéraire et politique*, established in 1794 as a republican review and forum for critical debate,

---

13. Destutt de Tracy, *Mémoire sur la faculté de penser*, p.287.
14. A.-L.-C. Destutt de Tracy, *Projet d'éléments d'idéologie à usage des écoles centrales de la République française*, 4 vols (Paris, Pierre Didot, 1800-1815).
15. Martin S. Staum, *Minerva's message: stabilizing the French Revolution* (Montreal and Kingston, 1996), p.19-32; and, more searchingly, Michael Sonenscher, 'Ideology, social science and general facts in late eighteenth-century French political thought', *History of European ideas* 35:1 (2009), p.24-37.
16. Staum, *Minerva's message*, p.3-4, 13-14.
17. Welch, *Liberty and utility*, p.37-40; Staum, *Minerva's message*, p.222-26.

which nurtured many of the rising intellectual stars of the day, including Say.[18]

Sonenscher has recently argued – and in spite of the wealth of scholarship on the subject – that whilst the centrality of Ideology to intellectual life under the Directory and the Consulate is reasonably clear, formidable difficulties remain in analysing what exactly it was intended to accomplish.[19] Destutt de Tracy's usage suggested that Ideology should constitute a sort of meta-science of the human understanding; but, this given, related questions remain of what kind of science this was supposed to be, and what the significance was of such a project in the last decades of the eighteenth century.

The first question can perhaps be answered with greater confidence than the second, although there remain elements of the story to be uncovered. The key point of reference for Cabanis and Destutt de Tracy was the work of the abbé Etienne Bonnot de Condillac, whose sensationalist epistemology, often associated with that of Locke, held out the appeal of potentially circumventing many of the arguments traded over the course of the second half of the eighteenth century between materialist and vitalist natural philosophies. Sonenscher has begun to demonstrate that this traditional picture may need to be considerably revised to accommodate the still hard-to-gauge role of Leibniz in late eighteenth-century French thought, but at a certain level it seems that Ideology will continue to hold a somewhat indeterminate middle ground between materialist and vitalist accounts of the mind-body relationship.[20] This points us in two directions. The first is towards an account of the individual in society, which tries to hold a balance between the idea of the individual as an ego possessed of interests interacting in unpredictable ways with similarly constituted beings, and the alternative, vitalist conception of an emergent order within society driven by the growing predomination of the spiritual over the physical in human life. Secondly, if we adopt Sonenscher's helpful suggestion that the concept of 'civilis-

18. The standard accounts remain Joanna Kitchin, *Un Journal 'philosophique': La Décade (1794-1807)* (Paris, 1965); and Marc Regaldo, *Un Milieu intellectuel: la Décade philosophique (1794-1807)*, 5 vols (Lille, 1976; Paris, 1976). See also *La Décade philosophique comme système, 1794-1807*, ed. Josiane Boulad-Ayoub, 9 vols (vols 8 and 9 co-edited by Martin Nadeau) (Rennes, 2003). The latter reproduces the journal's prospectus, published in 1794 and headed 'La Décade philosophique, littéraire et politique, par une société de républicains', vol.1, p.49-55; on the intellectual climate around the *Décade*, see Michael Sonenscher, '"The moment of social science": the *Décade philosophique* and late eighteenth-century French thought', *Modern intellectual history* 6:1 (2009), p.121-46.

19. Sonenscher, 'Ideology, social science and general facts in late eighteenth-century French political thought'; and for a similar argument see his review of *La Décade philosophique comme système*, ed. Boulad-Ayoub, in '"The moment of social science"'.

20. Sonenscher, 'Ideology, social science and general facts in late eighteenth-century French political thought', p.25-27. See also Sonenscher, *Sans-culottes*, p.119-26.

ation' may have played a large role in the development of Ideology, we can see that this materialist-vitalist division can be mapped onto alternative narratives of human moral progress: a utility-driven narrative versus an account resting on the notion of perfectibility. Rejecting the idea that priority should be assigned to either the physical or the spiritual side of human nature in accounting for the progress of civilisation, Ideology thus set itself the task of analysing the 'intellectual acquisitions' (the phrase is Sonenscher's[21]) made by mankind over the course of its history.[22]

In this respect, Sonenscher has argued, Cabanis and Destutt de Tracy's project could reasonably be affiliated with a variety of attempts to construct a meta-science of politics and society that would take heed of the criticisms Rousseau had levelled at the natural jurisprudence of Grotius, Hobbes and Pufendorf, whilst simultaneously rejecting his condemnation of modernity. It is this objective that links Ideology to the idea of social science, another concept that owes its origin to the revolutionary crisis. The first known use of the term *science sociale* occurs in the first edition of the abbé Sieyès's 1789 tract, *Qu'est-ce que le tiers état?*, after which it seems to have gained wider currency very rapidly, along with variants such as the *science de l'ordre social*, offered by Sieyès in subsequent editions of the pamphlet,[23] or the *science de l'organisation sociale*, that formed the subject of a series of lectures by Sieyès's political ally, Rœderer, in 1793.[24] In 1795, social science was paired with legislation as one of the Sections of the second Class of the Institute, a tribute as much to the centrality the concept had assumed in revolutionary intellectual debate as to the influence within the Institute of the man who had coined it.[25]

21. Sonenscher, 'Ideology, social science and general facts in late eighteenth-century French political thought', p.27.

22. A project similar in many respects to that of Condorcet. See the *Tableau historique des progrès de l'esprit humain: projets, esquisse, fragments et notes (1772-1794)*, ed. Jean-Pierre Schandeler and Pierre Crépel, with Eric Brian *et al.* (Paris, 2004), which now constitutes the essential edition to consult.

23. E.-J. Sieyès, 'What is the Third Estate?', trans. Michael Sonenscher, in *Political writings including the debate between Sieyès and Tom Paine in 1791*, ed. Michael Sonenscher (Indianapolis, IN, 2003), p.115, and the editor's introduction, esp. p.vii-xxii. Roberto Zapperi's edition of Sieyès, *Ecrits politiques* (Paris, 1985), p.139, does not note the change and follows the text of the later editions.

24. Pierre-Louis Rœderer, 'Cours d'organisation sociale; fait au Lycée en 1793 (l'an II de la République française)', not, however, published until over sixty years later, in *Œuvres du comte P.-L. Rœderer*, ed. A. M. Rœderer, 8 vols (Paris, 1853-1859), vol.8, p.129-305.

25. In addition to the texts by Sonenscher cited above, see, on the origins of social science, K. M. Baker, 'The early history of the term "social science"', *Annals of science* 20:3 (1964), p.211-26; and Robert Wokler, 'Ideology and the origins of social science', in *The Cambridge history of eighteenth-century political thought*, ed. Goldie and Wokler, p.688-710.

Sieyès's part in the political history of the Revolution is well known. In three pamphlets of the late 1780s, the *Essai sur les privilèges* of November 1788, *Qu'est-ce que le tiers état?* of January 1789, and the *Vue sur les moyens d'exécution dont les représentans de la France pourront disposer en 1789*, published in May 1789, but composed the previous year, he had established himself as a significant intellectual leader of the early years of the Revolution. This was a role in which he resurfaced in the months following the fall of Robespierre in 1794, playing a significant part in fashioning the constitution of the year III, which created the Directory. Along with Bonaparte, Sieyès was the figurehead for the Brumaire coup in 1799.[26]

The cornerstone of Sieyès's political thought was the concept of representation, which he invested with much of the weight carried in the late eighteenth century by that of the division of labour.[27] The rationale behind this was explained by Sieyès in the 'Préliminaire de la constitution, ou, reconnoissance et exposition raisonnée des droits de l'homme et du citoyen' that he presented to the constitutional committee of the National Assembly in July 1789. Sieyès argued that man had but one goal: his well-being. Subject to needs, he was possessed by nature of the means to meet these needs, in the form of his intellectual and physical faculties. Left to his own devices, the individual would develop these faculties, finding ways to bring his needs and his capacity to meet them into ever closer alignment.[28] In society, however, men could regard one another under two lights, either as means to the fulfilment of mutual needs, or as obstacles. The first perspective could provide the basis for social relations; the second implied only a state of war. The state of war was antithetical to the logic of reciprocal utility that was the only just basis for association. All men, Sieyès continued, were, as men, possessed in equal degree of the rights that derived from human nature: 'individual means are attached by nature to individual needs'. It was a matter of right that individuals be allowed to dispose of the means available to them freely.[29] Nature's favours, however, had not been evenly distributed

26. Jean-Denis Bredin, *Sieyès: la clé de la Révolution française* (Paris, 1988) is the standard biographical account. On Sieyès's political thought, see Murray Forsyth, *Reason and revolution: the political thought of the abbé Sieyès* (Leicester, 1987); Pasquale Pasquino, *Sieyès et l'invention de la constitution en France* (Paris, 1998); Sonenscher, 'Introduction', in Sieyès, *Political writings, including the debate between Sieyès and Tom Paine in 1791*, ed. Michael Sonenscher (Indianapolis, IN, 2003), p.vii-lxiv.

27. Forsyth, *Reason and revolution*, p.56-57; Pasquino, *Sieyès et l'invention de la constitution en France*, p.35-49; Sonenscher, 'Introduction', in Sieyès, *Political writings*, p.vii-xxii; Sonenscher, *Before the deluge*, p.263.

28. E.-J. Sieyès, 'Préliminaire de la constitution, ou, reconnoissance et exposition raisonnée des droits de l'homme et du citoyen', in *Ecrits politiques*, ed. Zapperi, p.192-93.

29. Sieyès, 'Préliminaire de la constitution', in *Ecrits politiques*, ed. Zapperi, p.193.

amongst men; it followed that there would be an inequality in their labour, in the product they derived from it and in what they might subsequently enjoy.

Nevertheless, this inequality did not destroy the primitive equality of rights, since these rights sprang from the same source.[30] The social union had as its stated aim the happiness of its members; but this was only to say that it favoured the development of individual means. Reciprocal respect for rights was the means by which society furthered this development by inviting individuals to employ one another as means to the common end; society did not strike at individual liberty, but extended it.[31] The maintenance of *natural or civil rights* thus described the goal of society. To this goal corresponded a means, namely, the constitution of the state, which described the organisation of the various branches of public power and their mutual relations.[32] As means and ends were correlative, *political rights* must likewise be equal, for an unequal distribution would result in privilege, or an exclusive and unjust claim upon the common good. The common good, however, must result from a common will, and this implied but a single common interest. This was why '[l']ordre social suppose nécessairement *unité* de but, et *concert* de moyens'.[33] The argument constituted a pointed critique of Rousseau's *Du contrat social* of 1762, and in particular Rousseau's claim that if, as he had contended, society was a state deeply at odds with human nature, then that nature could not itself provide the foundation for a society of free individuals. Rather, Rousseau had argued, the social contract must be a work of pure artifice, relying for its support not on any moral quality intrinsic to man in society, but on its members' ennobling love for the very object of their creation, the *patrie*.[34] On the contrary, Sieyès argued, people entered society for no other reason than the protection and furthering of their natural faculties; as society was a means to this end, there could be no possibility that the one would prove destructive of the other.

Construing society as a system of means and ends gave meaning to the concept of representation; it referred to the manner in which individuals can serve as means to one another. Sieyès's usage gave the term 'representation' an unusually broad compass; it implied that markets and

30. Sieyès, 'Préliminaire de la constitution', in *Ecrits politiques*, ed. Zapperi, p.193-94.
31. Sieyès, 'Préliminaire de la constitution', in *Ecrits politiques*, ed. Zapperi, p.194-95.
32. Sieyès, 'Préliminaire de la constitution', in *Ecrits politiques*, ed. Zapperi, p.198-99.
33. Sieyès, 'Préliminaire de la constitution', in *Ecrits politiques*, ed. Zapperi, p.199.
34. Jean-Jacques Rousseau, *Du contrat social*, I, ch.6, in *Œuvres complètes*, ed. Bernard Gagnebin and Marcel Raymond, 5 vols (Paris, 1959-1995), vol.3, p.360-62; *The Social contract and other later political writings*, ed. and trans. Victor Gourevitch (Cambridge, 1997), p.49-51; and see, helpfully, Michael Sonenscher, 'Property, community, and citizenship', in *The Cambridge history of eighteenth-century political thought*, p.477-79.

states alike could be considered as instantiations of the same principle.[35] But it also implied that these entities could not be collapsed one into the other. Applied to the functioning of government, a 'representative' system implied the creation of a political hierarchy based upon election, paralleling that created in the economic sphere by market competition. If these two hierarchies were consolidated into one, the result would be the emergence of privilege, and the perversion of the end of society. The key to keeping political and economic power separate lay in the elaboration of an alternative set of standards of value from that generated by the market.[36] Not wealth, Sieyès argued, but the patriotism of public service must be the foundation of the political order – whence Sieyès's interest in the system of graduated election that Rousseau had outlined in his *Considérations sur le gouvernement de Pologne*; whence the reorganisation of France into equal departments under the rubric of a nation 'one and indivisible'.[37]

Sieyès's 'science of the social order' established that the inequality of human faculties, and the social inequalities that derived from it, could co-exist with a robust account of the common interest underlying political union. This was the starting point for much of the political theorising conducted under the auspices of the CMPS. It suggested a way of tempering some of the more extravagant claims for equality that had been made in the course of the Revolution, and in particular, a way of rejecting much of what Rousseau had had to say about the foundations of the social contract, whilst paving the way for the reworking of his claim that if one were to secure the object of the general will, one must know how to bring individual interests into alignment with it.

This was the purpose of the *Cours d'organisation sociale*, delivered by Rœderer at the Paris Lycée in 1793, but not published until 1859.[38] Sonenscher has identified two targets in the lecture course. On the one hand there were the advocates of an egalitarian system of property distribution, such as Tom Paine, Jacques-Pierre Brissot and Etienne

---

35. Sonenscher, *Before the deluge*, p.263; Forsyth, *Reason and revolution*, p.56.
36. Sonenscher, 'Introduction', in Sieyès, *Political writings*, p.xxix-xxx.
37. Forsyth, *Reason and revolution*, p.151-66; Sonenscher, 'Introduction', in Sieyès, *Political writings*, p.xxx-xxxi.
38. P.-L. Rœderer, 'Cours d'organisation sociale', in *Œuvres*, vol.8, p.129-305. On Rœderer, see Sonenscher, *Before the deluge*, p.322-34; Gilbert Faccarello, 'Le legs de Turgot: aspects de l'économie politique sensualiste de Condorcet à Rœderer', in *La Pensée économique pendant la Révolution française*, ed. Gilbert Faccarello and Philippe Steiner (Grenoble, 1990), p.67-107; Ruth Scurr, 'Social equality in Pierre-Louis Rœderer's interpretation of the modern republic, 1793', *History of European ideas* 26:2 (2000), p.105-26; Scurr, 'Pierre-Louis Rœderer and the debate on forms of government in revolutionary France', *Political studies* 52:2 (2004), p.251-68; Michael James, 'Pierre-Louis Rœderer, Jean-Baptiste Say, and the concept of *industrie*', *History of political economy* 9:4 (1977), p.455-75.

Clavière. On the other were the advocates of a system of common ownership: Diderot (mistaken for the author of the *Code de la nature* of Etienne-Gabriel Morelly) and Gabriel Bonnot de Mably. Rœderer rejected the claims of both these sets of 'levellers', and set out to vindicate the juxtaposition of what Sonenscher terms 'real inequality, but formal legal and political equality' that Sieyès had described in the 'Préliminaire de la constitution'.[39] Bringing means and ends together in this way required some kind of answer to Rousseau's bleak warnings about the troubling interplay between the human desire for distinction and the indeterminacy of needs. But, if Sieyès's grounding of social science on a doctrine of natural equality were to be maintained, it might also require an answer to Rousseau's most formidable late-eighteenth-century critic, Adam Smith.

Smith as a critic of Rousseau

In his moral philosophy and political economy, Smith had provided a careful reworking of aspects of the modern natural law tradition. Under this guise, the claim that economics and politics followed differing logics could be understood to entail taking a determinate position on the nature of human sociability. Smith presented society as founded upon commerce, or the reciprocal fulfilment of mutual needs in the light of self-interest, and the bonds thus created as compatible with, but not causally dependent upon, political union.[40] 'Moral sentiments' he derived from the action of 'sympathy', the faculty that allowed us to place ourselves in the position of others, and to 'judge of the propriety or impropriety of the Affections of other Men, by their concord or dissonance with our own'.[41] This made moral perfectibility a consequence of the expansion in scope of our imaginative sensibilities, the principal stimulus to which was, in the widest sense of the word, our commerce with others. The advance of the division of labour in society thus underwrote progress both in morals and in wealth, and it was this

39. Rœderer, 'Cours d'organisation sociale', in *Œuvres*, vol.8, p.134; Sonenscher, *Before the deluge*, p.322-23.

40. Istvan Hont, 'The language of sociability and commerce: Samuel Pufendorf and the theoretical foundations of the "four stages theory"', in *The Languages of political theory in early-modern Europe*, ed. Anthony Pagden (Cambridge, 1987), p.253-76, reprinted in Hont, *Jealousy of trade*, p.159-84, with further remarks at p.37-51. On the 'modern', post-Grotian tradition of natural law, Richard Tuck, 'The "Modern" theory of natural law', in *The Languages of political theory in early-modern Europe*, ed. Anthony Pagden (Cambridge 1987), p.99-119; and on Smith's relation to it, see Knud Haakonssen, *The Science of a legislator*, and Haakonssen, *Natural law and moral philosophy: from Grotius to the Scottish Enlightenment* (Cambridge, 1996).

41. Adam Smith, *The Theory of moral sentiments* [1759], ed. D. D. Raphael and A. L. Macfie (1976; Indianapolis, IN, 1982), p.16.

linkage that supplied much of the normative appeal that Smith ascribed to the notion of 'commercial society'.

One way of reading this argument was as a powerful riposte to Rousseau's *Discours sur l'origine et les fondemens de l'inégalité parmi les hommes*, published four years before the first edition of Smith's *Theory of moral sentiments* in 1755, and which Smith had himself reviewed for an Edinburgh journal.[42] Rousseau had famously distinguished between *amour de soi-même*, or the natural self-love of sentient beings that inclines them to their own self-preservation, 'which, guided in man by reason and modified by pity, produces humanity and virtue', and *amour-propre*, or vanity, 'a relative sentiment, factitious and born in society'.[43] *Amour-propre* was a product of our capacity to compare, to rank and to accord ourselves pre-eminence in our own estimation. It was, as Frederick Neuhouser has recently put it, a 'drive for recognition'. Even if, as Neuhouser emphasises, this drive was at the root of what it meant to be recognisably human and recognisably rational, the very subjectivity it entailed was the progenitor of the complex of passions that conspired to make social life a state of inequality and unfreedom.[44] Rousseau placed the blame for society's ills upon humankind's inability to tame its desires, and more particularly to rein in the imagination that spurred them. The tendency of man in society consistently to conflate the demands of self-preservation with those of *amour-propre* entailed an extreme fluidity in the relationship between needs and desires. From this sprang the spiralling range of physical and emotional needs to which men in society were subject. This was at the root of the division of labour and of the distinction of ranks, and the motor for the slow entrammelling of the individual in relations of inequality and mutual dependence.[45]

Smith met this argument on its own terrain. He did not set out to break the causal connection that Rousseau had drawn between the imagination and inequality. He did, however, seek to demonstrate how the imaginative stimulus to the sense of self that society provided would

42. Adam Smith, 'A letter to the authors of the *Edinburgh review*' [1756], in *Essays on philosophical subjects*, ed. W. P. D. Wightman and J. C. Bryce (1980; Indianapolis, IN, 1982), p.242-56; Smith's reply to Rousseau is an under-explored subject; Dennis C. Rasmussen, *The Problems and promise of commercial society: Adam Smith's response to Rousseau* (University Park, PA, 2008), has highlighted some points of contact. In what follows I am indebted to the discussion in Sonenscher, *Before the deluge*, p.328-29.

43. Rousseau, *Discours sur l'origine et fondemens de l'inégalité*, in *Œuvres complètes*, vol.3, p.219; *The Discourses and other early political writings*, ed. and trans. Victor Gourevitch (Cambridge, 1997), p.218.

44. Frederick Neuhouser, *Rousseau's theodicy of self-love: evil, rationality, and the drive for recognition* (Oxford, 2008), p.1, 187-91.

45. Rousseau, *Discours sur l'origine et fondemens de l'inégalité*, in *Œuvres complètes*, vol.3, p.171-75; *Discourses*, ed. Gourevitch, p.167-71.

itself furnish a check upon the self's more destructive tendencies in the form of what Smith termed the 'impartial spectator', or the capacity to judge according to standards laid down by the continued operations of sympathy.[46] Rousseau had supposed that the natural sentiment of pity, the foundation of virtue, would become attenuated in society. Putting sympathy in its place implied, perhaps, leaving virtue at a certain remove from natural sentiment, but as a reflective construct it would gain in force with the strengthening of social bonds. None of this implied that it would prove any easier for individuals to measure their desires by what was strictly necessary for their survival. Smith, like Rousseau, took it as given that the attractions of wealth appealed rather to our self-interest than to physiological necessity. Indeed, he claimed that it was 'chiefly from this regard to the sentiments of mankind, that we pursue riches and avoid poverty'.[47] Mankind, Smith argued, was inclined to sympathise more entirely with joy than sorrow.[48] In consequence, we tended to make a show of our good fortune; it suited our vanity to meet with greater sympathy than we would in the case of misfortune.[49] He concluded, 'Upon this disposition of mankind, to go along with all the passions of the rich and powerful, is founded the distinction of ranks, and the order of society'.[50]

Nevertheless, though the desire for distinction might govern the passions, there was sufficient reality in the physiological basis of our subsistence needs (which might be indeterminate but were not illimitable) to ensure that however vast the fortunes of the rich might grow, the basic needs of the poor would still be met. This was the central argument of Book III of *The Wealth of nations*, which examined how it was that Europe had come to follow an 'unnatural and retrograde order' in which the economy was driven by trade rather than agriculture. The fourth chapter of Book III picked up the argument at the point where the medieval revival of urban commerce began to penetrate the countryside, still in the hands of the great feudal landlords. The landlords received enormous wealth from the cultivation of the land in produce, but as there was nothing for which to exchange it – and they soon reached the limits of their own consumption – they were obliged to consume the surplus 'in rustick hospitality', namely in the maintenance of large, dependent retinues.[51] Wealth in such circumstances translated

46. Smith, *Theory of moral sentiments*, p.109-13; D. D. Raphael, *The Impartial spectator: Adam Smith's moral philosophy* (Oxford, 2007), p.32-42; see Sonenscher, *Before the deluge*, p.328.
47. Smith, *Theory of moral sentiments*, p.50.
48. Smith, *Theory of moral sentiments*, p.43-50.
49. Smith, *Theory of moral sentiments*, p.50-51.
50. Smith, *Theory of moral sentiments*, p.52.
51. Smith, *Wealth of nations*, vol.1, p.413 (III.iv.5).

immediately into command over manpower, an acceptable enough result, for, as Smith had noted elsewhere, 'The pride of man makes him love to domineer'.[52] The introduction of commerce in luxuries changed all this: 'For a pair of diamond buckles perhaps, or for something as frivolous and useless, they exchanged the maintenance, or what is the same thing, the price of the maintenance of a thousand men for a year, and with it the whole weight and authority which it could give them.'[53] Presented with the opening of new avenues for the gratification of 'the most childish vanity' – their 'sole motive' in this transaction – the great proprietors relinquished the direct authority they had exercised over their retainers, and instead undertook to maintain, indirectly and indifferently, a crowd of manufacturers and traders whose only dependence was on the extent of the market for their produce.[54] The implication of this 'great revolution' was that commerce likewise carried a self-correcting mechanism against the excesses of the unbridled ego, even as it satisfied the fancies of the rich. An expanding market furthered the division of labour, increasing the productive output of society. The reciprocal basis of commerce would serve to ensure that this product was distributed amongst all classes of society, in such a way that although inequality would remain, all would partake in the greater prosperity. Economic growth, its benefits percolating down the social scale, would take the sting from the inequality of distribution; the moral legitimacy of commercial society could rest, if on nothing else, on the fact that 'the accommodation of an European prince does not always so much exceed that of an industrious and frugal peasant, as the accommodation of the latter exceeds that of many an African king, the absolute master of the lives and liberties of ten thousand naked savages'.[55]

Taken together, the *Theory of moral sentiments* and *The Wealth of nations* could be read as an extended explanation of why the passions unleashed by inequality did not constitute an overweening impediment to the establishment of a stable social order based on commerce. This was an argument that would appear to have been somewhat easier to follow in the late eighteenth century than it would later become; if there was an 'Adam Smith problem' for his contemporaries, it did not lie in the purported incommensurability of the positions adopted in his two most celebrated works.[56] Rather, as Rœderer made clear, the problem with

52. Smith, *Wealth of nations*, vol.1, p.388 (III.ii.10).
53. Smith, *Wealth of nations*, vol.1, p.418-9 (III.iv.10).
54. Smith, *Wealth of nations*, vol.1, p.422 (III.iv.17); for the context of the argument, Istvan Hont, 'Adam Smith and the political economy of the "unnatural and retrograde order"', in Hont, *Jealousy of trade*, p.354-88.
55. Smith, *Wealth of nations*, vol.1, p.24 (I.i.11); see Hont, *Jealousy of trade*, p.90-91.
56. On the history of the nineteenth-century 'Adam Smith problem', see August Onken, 'The

Smith was that, in taking sympathy as his starting point, 'il reconnaît un *principe naturel* de l'inégalité des conditions parmi les hommes'.[57] Rœderer recognised the significance of Smith's concept of sympathy; it could supply what he found wanting in the concept of self-interest, particularly in the formulation offered by Helvétius.[58] Helvétius had taken as his starting point the natural sensibility with which mankind was endowed. This, he had argued, made physical pleasure or pain the foundation of all the passions. Gratification or affliction could be immediate, or the object of foresight. Government and the division of property and of labour arose from attempts to act on this foresight.[59] Once instituted, they led progressively to the distinction of ranks:

> Lorsque les sociétés en seront à ce point de perfection, alors toute égalité entre les hommes sera rompue: on distinguera des supérieurs & des inférieurs: alors ces mots de *bien* de *mal*, créés pour exprimer les sensations de plaisir ou de douleur physiques que nous recevons des objets extérieurs, s'étendront généralement à tout ce qui peut nous procurer l'une ou l'autre de ces sensations, les accroître ou les diminuer; telles sont les richesses & l'indigence: alors les richesses & les honneurs, par les avantages qui y seront attachés, deviendront l'objet général du désir des hommes. De-là naîtront, selon la forme différente des gouvernements, des passions criminelles ou vertueuses; telles sont l'envie, l'avarice, l'orgueil, l'ambition, l'amour de la patrie, la passion de la gloire, la magnanimité, et même l'amour, qui, ne nous étant donné par la nature que comme un besoin, deviendra, en se confondant avec la vanité, une passion factice, qui ne sera, comme les autres, qu'un développement de la sensibilité physique.[60]

Adam Smith problem', in *Adam Smith: critical responses*, ed. Hiroshi Mizuta, 6 vols (London, 2000), vol.5, p.84-105, trans. from the *Zeitschrift für Socialwissenschaft* 1 (1898), p.25-33, 101-108, 276-87; and for commentary, Keith Tribe, ' "Das Adam Smith problem" and the origins of modern Smith scholarship', *History of European ideas* 34:4 (2008), p.514-25.

57. Rœderer, 'Cours d'organisation sociale', in *Œuvres*, vol.8, p.200; cited in Sonenscher, *Before the deluge*, p.329.

58. Rœderer, 'Cours d'organisation sociale', in *Œuvres*, vol.8, p.186-87.

59. [C. A. Helvétius], *De l'esprit* (Paris, Durand, 1758), p.322-24 ; see Rœderer, 'Cours d'organisation sociale', in *Œuvres*, vol.8, p.186.

60. Helvétius, *De l'esprit*, p.324. The contemporary English translation reads, 'When societies are arrived at this point of perfection, all equality between men will be destroyed: they will be distinguished into superiors and inferiors; then the words good and evil, formed to express the natural sensations of pleasure and pain we receive from external objects, will generally extend to every thing that can procure, increase, or diminish either of these sensations; such are riches and indigence: and then riches and honours, by the advantages annexed to them, will become the general object of the desires of mankind. Hence will arise, according to the different forms of government, criminal or virtuous passions, such as envy, avarice, pride, and ambition, patriotism, a love of glory, magnanimity, and even love, which being given by nature only as a want, will be confounded with vanity, and become an artificial passion, that will, like the others, arise from the unfolding of the natural sensibility.' *De l'esprit: or, essays on the mind, and its several faculties* (London, printed for the translator, 1759), p.162.

Sympathy could enrich this account, giving it added force by offering greater insight into the workings of the imagination. The superficial opposition between the two principles could be resolved if one recognised their common origin in sensibility.[61] Nevertheless, Rœderer claimed, Smith's position presented a difficulty that was not evident in Helvétius's work, insofar as he placed 'un principe d'inégalité sociale dans notre organisation physique'.[62] This carried inequality into the very foundation of the natural rights on which society was grounded. If sympathy were to form part of the toolkit of the science of social organisation, it would have to be separated from Smith's emphasis on its role in establishing the distinction of ranks.

Sophie de Grouchy and the 'Lettres sur la sympathie'

Rœderer found the means to do so in the arguments presented in the 'Lettres sur la sympathie' by Sophie de Grouchy, the former Marquise de Condorcet, and appended to her translation of Smith's *Theory of moral sentiments*. Though not published until 1798, the 'Lettres' had been circulating in manuscript within the Condorcet circle since 1790.[63] Rœderer complained that he had lacked sufficient time to study the manuscript in detail; but it nevertheless formed the starting point for his reflections. De Grouchy presented her 'Lettres' as a critical commentary on Smith's text, and in particular on its opening chapters, but a commentary in which she had followed as much the thread of her own ideas as those of her subject of study, Smith.[64] Her views involved grounding sympathy firmly in a sensationalist psychology that owed rather more to Helvétius and to Condillac than to Smith. One fault of Smith's account of sympathy, de Grouchy wrote, was that he contented himself with remarking its existence, and then proceeded to examine its principal effects, but without pausing to pursue the phenomenon back to its first cause.[65] The key to understanding sympathy, de Grouchy argued, lay in recognising the composite nature of our experience of pleasure and pain. Physical gratification or injury produces both a localised sensation of pleasure or pain in the organ immediately afflicted, and a more

---

61. Rœderer, 'Cours d'organisation sociale', in *Œuvres*, vol.8, p.194.
62. Rœderer, 'Cours d'organisation sociale', in *Œuvres*, vol.8, p.194.
63. Sophie de Grouchy, marquise de Condorcet, 'Lettres sur la sympathie', in Adam Smith, *Théorie des sentimens moraux, ou essai analytique sur les principes des jugemens que portent naturellement les hommes, d'abord sur les actions des autres, et ensuite par leurs propres actions: suivi d'une dissertation sur l'origine des langues; par Adam Smith; traduit de l'anglais, sur la septième et dernière édition, par S. Grouchy Ve. Condorcet. Elle y a joint huit lettres sur la sympathie*, 2 vols (Paris, F. Buisson, An VI / 1798), vol.2, p.353-507.
64. De Grouchy, 'Lettres sur la sympathie', in *Théorie des sentimens moraux*, vol.2, p.356.
65. De Grouchy, 'Lettres sur la sympathie', in *Théorie des sentimens moraux*, vol.2, p.357.

generalised impression of pleasure or discomfort in the body as a whole, which can survive the passing of the localised sensation that caused it. Through the workings of memory and imagination, this impression can be recreated independently of further physical stimulus: it is, in the case of affliction, 'un effet de douleur qui suit également et sa présence physique et sa présence morale'.[66] In these mental recreations of such impressions, however abstracted from the sensations that originally gave rise to them, we find the proximate origin of the sympathy that we feel for the physical pleasure or ailments of others; thus sentiment is abstracted from our own experiences. However, it would be but a passing sentiment, were it not for our capacity for reflection. Reflection comes to our aid in forcing 'notre compassion à être active en lui offrant de nouveau les objets qui n'avaient fait sur elle qu'une impression momentanée'.[67] Reflection prompts us to connect sensations with their causes, and to give greater extension to the range of pleasures and pains with which we can be brought to sympathise. It is reflection that establishes sympathy as a permanent sentiment with us, that refines our sensibilities to the sufferings of others, and awakens within us the desire to work for the good of humanity.[68]

This phenomenon raised the question how it was that such humanitarian sentiments could find their particular object in certain individuals. What was it that interested us in the fate of some more than others? De Grouchy's answer was that our sympathy with individuals derived, in the first instance, from the relations of dependence in which we found ourselves. The child was born into a world in which her dependence on the care of others would only be replaced in time with a new dependence, of greater or lesser extent depending on circumstance, on her ability to interest others in her livelihood. Our sympathy for those upon whom we depend, or with whom, through the division of labour, we engage in relations of mutual dependence, was that much more acute than for those we had but little contact with.[69] To be sure, in an advanced state of civilisation, we might embrace within this circle those with whom we had a somewhat more tenuous relationship – people we might look to for aid, for example, or who shared with us certain tastes or opinions. In any case, the foundation remained the enlarged conceptions formed of pleasure or pain that governed the imagination.[70]

This account gives a physiological cast to the theory of sympathy that

66. De Grouchy, 'Lettres sur la sympathie', in *Théorie des sentimens moraux*, vol.2, p.360.
67. De Grouchy, 'Lettres sur la sympathie', in *Théorie des sentimens moraux*, vol.2, p.370.
68. De Grouchy, 'Lettres sur la sympathie', in *Théorie des sentimens moraux*, vol.2, p.371.
69. De Grouchy, 'Lettres sur la sympathie', in *Théorie des sentimens moraux*, vol.2, p.375-77.
70. De Grouchy, 'Lettres sur la sympathie', in *Théorie des sentimens moraux*, vol.2, p.377-78.

Smith had largely eschewed. But de Grouchy made clear that she was not engaged in mere window-dressing. Smith's moral philosophy had, as we have seen, pointed to an explicit endorsement of the distinction in ranks in society. In correlating sympathy with propriety, he had set out to demonstrate how sympathy could serve as the basis for a scale of values, in which not only virtue or merit, but power, wealth and authority would be rewarded with esteem.[71] To de Grouchy, this was hard to square with a commitment to humanity's natural equality, which she took to be the necessary starting point for republican government.[72] Tracking sympathy back to its origins in sensory experience pointed the way towards making the imagination safe for republicanism. For her, Smith's fault had been to make sympathy too much a product of the imagination, neglecting its physical stimuli.[73] As a result he was apt to neglect the ways in which the imagination was structured by our experience of the world. A being deprived of stimuli would not develop any degree of sensibility and would thus be incapable of any measure of sympathy. This view assigned considerable importance to the education of infants, whose exposure to varying forms of pleasure and pain would in effect determine their capacity for sympathy in later life.[74]

Just as significant as initial exposure to stimuli, however, was the development of the capacity for reflection. In this context individuals were most marked by the inequality of conditions. A peasant labourer had little time for reflection upon his experiences; his life was passed in endless toil to meet the most basic of necessities. His sensibilities thus remained coarse and unrefined, his sympathies constricted. Only a life with its own measure of relative ease could guarantee the development of his faculties in such a manner as to make him capable of the kind of extended sympathies one might meet with amongst the leisured classes.[75] In an equitably constituted society this would be the fruit of the division of labour, and from the reciprocity of exchange would follow the reciprocity of sympathy amongst a population in which none lived in conditions of misery.[76] If sympathy was governed not by the unchecked stirrings of imagination, but by our reasoning upon sensory experience, then the issue was not the illimitable human tendency towards vanity, but the distribution of pleasures and pains in society and the ways in which they would shape our responses. It was, in short, as Helvétius had

---

71. Smith, *Theory of moral sentiments*, p.52.
72. De Grouchy, 'Lettres sur la sympathie', in *Théorie des sentimens moraux*, vol.2, p.407-408.
73. De Grouchy, 'Lettres sur la sympathie', in *Théorie des sentimens moraux*, vol.2, p.409.
74. De Grouchy, 'Lettres sur la sympathie', in *Théorie des sentimens moraux*, vol.2, p.365-67.
75. De Grouchy, 'Lettres sur la sympathie', in *Théorie des sentimens moraux*, vol.2, p.372-73.
76. De Grouchy, 'Lettres sur la sympathie', in *Théorie des sentimens moraux*, vol.2, p.474-75.

suggested, a question of institutions. If morality – a product of the extension of sympathy – was wanting, this happened because of the impact of vicious institutions.[77]

Rœderer was quick to grasp the central point. Smith, he argued, had held to the notion that sympathy derived 'uniquement de l'imagination'.[78] This was as much as to say that, as with Rousseau's *amour-propre*, it was a product of our mental and physical dependence on others. However, such an account was not sufficient to produce a robust conception of individual rights. But placing the origin of sympathy in natural sensibility was sufficient to demonstrate its origin in a phenomenon of our physiology that could only be 'individual, personal', and also served to correlate sympathy with self-interest. This analysis did not, he made clear, imply that the two were identical; they were 'modes' of sensibility that could give rise to differing kinds of passions.[79] Such observations, as Sonenscher suggests, allowed Rœderer to tie the discussion to a distinction derived from contemporary advances in physiology. 'Les sens internes', he wrote, 'sont des sentinelles intérieures de l'économie animale, placées sur le siège de nos besoins, ou plutôt sont les organes de nos besoins; au lieu que les sens externes sont les organes des sensations qui appartiennent à nos besoins et de celles qui n'y appartiennent pas.'[80] This distinction, Sonenscher maintains, created the possibility of producing the alternate hierarchies of value that provided the foundation of Sieyès's politics.[81] Moral passions, the product of the external senses, could be 'graduated' because they were less deep-seated than physical passions. Hence, as de Grouchy had suggested, it would be possible to shape the passions of individuals through legislation, by paying careful attention to the distribution of rewards and punishments. In this manner, 'consideration' could be elevated above power and wealth in the ambitions of the citizenry.[82]

But taking sensibility as the starting point also suggested what it would take to reconstruct Smith's political economy in such a way as to avoid the preponderant role he assigned to luxury, whilst providing sufficient motive for progressive accumulation. Rœderer argued that the earth, consistent with the principle of natural equality, was held in trust by the owners of property. The right each had to realise the means to his own well-being implied a right to the fruits of the earth that no property

77. De Grouchy, 'Lettres sur la sympathie', in *Théorie des sentimens moraux*, vol.2, p.485.
78. Rœderer, 'Cours d'organisation sociale', in *Œuvres*, vol.8, p.187.
79. Rœderer, 'Cours d'organisation sociale', in *Œuvres*, vol.8, p.194.
80. Rœderer, 'Cours d'organisation sociale', in *Œuvres*, vol.8, p.225; cited in Sonenscher, *Before the deluge*, p.331.
81. Sonenscher, *Before the deluge*, p.332-34.
82. Rœderer, 'Cours d'organisation sociale', in *Œuvres*, vol.8, p.205-206.

regime could annul.[83] Property must, therefore, have as its object not the restriction but the extension of the productive faculties of man.[84] In order to explain how property achieved that end, Rœderer reverted to the sequence described by Turgot in his *Réflexions sur la formation et distribution des richesses* of 1766.[85] Turgot had explained how cultivation of the land required three kinds of wealth: the land itself, capital advanced to prepare it for use and capital advanced to the labourers who were to work it.[86] Combined with labour, these produced a net product that could then be distributed amongst the rest of society.[87] Once all available land had an owner, those without a share were obliged to exchange their labour for its produce, either by cultivating it themselves in exchange for a share of the product, or by providing services to property owners.[88] However, the necessity of capital, either as a fixed investment, or as an advance on the costs of production, opened a third way to wealth other than through labour or ownership of lands.[89] To Rœderer, this suggested a way of revising Smith's account of the origins of Europe's 'unnatural and retrograde order'.[90] On Rœderer's reading, the Germanic invasions that had destroyed the western Roman Empire had brought into the conquerors' possession lands already in cultivation, already supplied with the necessary capital to put labour to work. The surpluses that accrued to the conquerors, Rœderer explained, could have no other outlet than in supporting their serfs in either the 'rude arts inseparable from agriculture' or in the production of household goods. In this way, their surplus was distributed not amongst an idle retinue, but to productive labourers who could gradually amass capital of their own, that they could, in turn, advance to set in motion further manufactures or commerce.[91] Society was thus composed of two classes: capitalists and labourers, each divided across the agricultural, manufacturing, and

---

83. Rœderer, 'Cours d'organisation sociale', in *Œuvres*, vol.8, p.134; Sonenscher, *Before the deluge*, p.324.
84. Rœderer, 'Cours d'organisation sociale', in *Œuvres*, vol.8, p.152-53.
85. A. R. J. Turgot, 'Réflexions sur la formation et distribution des richesses' [1766], in *Formation et distribution des richesses*, ed. Joël-Thomas Ravix and Paul-Marie Romani (Paris, 1997), p.155-226.
86. Turgot, 'Réflexions sur la formation et distribution des richesses', in *Formation et distribution des richesses*, p.158-60.
87. Turgot, 'Réflexions sur la formation et distribution des richesses', in *Formation et distribution des richesses*, p.160-62.
88. Turgot, 'Réflexions sur la formation et distribution des richesses', in *Formation et distribution des richesses*, p.165-67.
89. Turgot, 'Réflexions sur la formation et distribution des richesses', in *Formation et distribution des richesses*, p.174.
90. Contra Sonenscher, I would suggest that Smith is more likely a target than Rousseau at this point of Rœderer's argument; see Sonenscher, *Before the deluge*, p.325.
91. Rœderer, 'Cours d'organisation sociale', in *Œuvres*, vol.8, p.141.

commercial sectors.[92] In the continual exchange between the two, the fruits of the earth would be diffused throughout society. The foundation of the system was labour. In guaranteeing the rights of persons and property, one guaranteed nothing other than the right to the enjoyment of the fruits of labour and capital. Needs set labour in motion, but it was the expectation of reward that prompted the renewal of efforts when needs had been met. The result of this continual spurring was to ensure that the means to meet future needs were constantly generated anew.[93] This suggested a rather closer alignment of means and ends than was evident in Smith's luxury-based system, and consequently a rather more robust defence of private property as a social institution consistent with the equality of both natural and political rights.

Rœderer on rights, labour and morality

In 1795, the CMPS had established a prize competition, which asked what institutions were best suited to undertake the establishment of morality amongst a people. Finding the initial results unsatisfactory, the judges decided to issue a clarification of their intentions; Rœderer was an obvious candidate for the task. The result, Rœderer's 'Précis des observations sur la question proposée par l'Institut national', published in the *Décade philosophique* in 1797, whilst brief, is worth considering in some detail, for it points to the nub of his argument against Smith.

Rœderer began by noting that in confining the question's remit to the *institutions* conducive to morality rather than the broader question of *means* in general, the class had sought to circumscribe an otherwise unmanageable subject. Furthermore, he added, the emphasis on morality should have made it plain that entries ought to concern themselves with one set of social institutions only – those properly described as moral institutions rather than civil, political or religious.[94] Moral institutions, Rœderer continued, could be categorised as of three kinds: those that enlightened the mind, such as public education; those that elevated the soul, such as monuments and national festivities and solemnities; and those which governed men through custom, such as the institutions of domestic life.[95] It was the latter that posed the most difficult problem for the modern legislator. Ancient legislation, such as that of Lycurgus,

92. Scurr, 'Social equality in Pierre-Louis Rœderer's interpretation of the modern republic, 1793', p.112.
93. Rœderer, 'Cours d'organisation sociale', in *Œuvres*, vol.8, p.145-46.
94. Pierre-Louis Rœderer, 'Précis des observations sur la question proposée par l'Institut national pour le sujet du premier prix de la Classe des Sciences Morales et Politiques', *La Décade philosophique, politique et littéraire*, An VI, 1er trimestre (Paris, Au Bureau de la Décade, 1797), p.534.
95. Rœderer, 'Précis des observations sur la question proposée par l'Institut national', p.535.

Moses or Confucius, had placed great emphasis on the regulation of domestic life to an extent that was inconsistent with the respect for natural rights that Rœderer took to follow from the public as well as the private interest.[96] The key to resolving this problem, Rœderer argued, lay in what he termed the 'omnipotence' of human labour, considered not merely as a means to the meeting of material needs, but also, by the discipline it instils in the individual, as a regulator of domestic habits:

C'est cette institution pleine et entière du travail, qui développant tous les talens, multipliant toutes les richesses, grossissant le patrimoine commun, peut seule ennoblir et resserrer les relations d'homme à homme. C'est elle seule qui peut rendre sensible et faire goûter avec douceur, l'égalité de droits dans les inégalités de fait, en donnant au riche de la modestie et de la frugalité, au pauvre de la dignité et des jouissances; en mettant tous les talens en regard et en les obligeant, par le sentiment de leur mutuelle dépendance, à une estime et à des égards réciproques. C'est elle qui forme la plus puissante garantie de la propriété, parce qu'elle apprend à tous que le bien ne s'acquiert qu'avec de la peine, et parce que le travail offre à tous du bien à acquérir. C'est elle qui forme la plus puissante garantie de la liberté, parce qu'elle double pour le riche le besoin qu'il a du pauvre, et qu'elle affranchit celui-ci de tout ce qu'il y avait dégradant dans sa dépendance. C'est elle qui attache le père aux enfans, les enfans aux pères, et les époux les uns aux autres. C'est elle enfin qui, assurant un bonheur propre et durable, plaçant chez le pauvre l'espérance près du besoin, ranimant dans le riche le désir près de la satiété, entretenant en tous le ressort nécessaire à la faculté de jouir, préserve l'âme de ces passions inquiètes, tracassières, malfesantes que l'ennui fait naître, dirai-je pour le soulagement ou pour le châtiment des âmes inoccupées?[97]

96. Rœderer, 'Précis des observations sur la question proposée par l'Institut national', p.535-36.

97. Rœderer, 'Précis des observations sur la question proposée par l'Institut national', p.536-37. 'It is, plainly and simply, this institution of labour that, in developing every talent, multiplying all wealth, expanding the common inheritance, can alone ennoble and strengthen the relations between men. It alone may make sensible and palatable the notion of the equality of rights amidst inequality in fact, by giving to the rich modesty and frugality, and the poor dignity and joy; by valuing all contributions and making everyone, recognizing their mutual dependence, acknowledge and respect one another. This institution is the most powerful guarantee of property, because it teaches everyone that benefit is acquired only through pain, and because labour offers to all the opportunity to acquire. It is this institution that is the most powerful guarantee of liberty, because it doubles the need the rich have of the poor, and it liberates the poor from the degradation of dependence. It is this institution that bonds the father to his children, the children to their fathers, and the spouses to each other. It is this institution, finally, that, ensuring a durable and proper happiness, placing hope beside need for the poor, reawakening desire among the rich and setting it alongside satiation, providing for all the resources necessary for enjoyment, preserves the mind from these evil, uncertain passions that boredom creates to soothe or to stimulate unoccupied minds.' I have revised the translation in Forget, *Social economics of Jean-Baptiste Say*, p.194.

This dense presentation of the argument of the *Cours d'organisation sociale* made plain the manner in which the guarantee of natural rights was supposed to generate the range of moral habits that would serve to keep inequality in check. Hope *and* need, the moral passions *and* the physical, were what kept society in motion and served to reconcile 'equality in rights' with 'inequality in fact'.

Rœderer did not openly discuss the evident political subtext that lay behind the question, the dilemma faced by the republican political elites: after making a republic, how did one set about making good republicans of the citizens? Terror was no longer the order of the day. But it could not be said that the republic of the Directory stood on a particularly sure footing. The politics of 'levelling' had not gone away, as demonstrated by Gracchus Babeuf's Conspiracy of the Equals. Nor would it. The opposition of idleness and industry, and the privileging of property rights would become the subject of much debate in the following decades.[98] But Rœderer's attempt to make French republicanism sit comfortably with the new political economy would prove a rather fragile intellectual endeavour, lasting little more than a generation. Nevertheless, it remains one of the most ambitious attempts of the revolutionary period to square the theoretical circle of combining political equality and material inequality.

---

98. For discussion, see Giovanna Procacci, *Gouverner la misère: la question sociale en France (1789-1848)* (Paris, 1993).

Summaries

Introduction: money and political economy in the era of Enlightenment
Daniel Carey

The emergence of political economy as a philosophical preoccupation constitutes a defining feature of the Enlightenment but there was no 'position' on this subject that attracted consensus. This introduction charts different sources in the period for thinking about issues of money, trade, banking, the role of the state, including political arithmetic, the impact of the Financial Revolution, the Great Recoinage in the 1690s and republican political philosophy. The argument shows that attention to political economy problematises efforts to periodise Enlightenment, and that determining what was progressive and what was 'backward looking' proves more difficult to assess on closer inspection.

Sir Robert Filmer, usury and the ideology of order
Johann P. Sommerville

Sir Robert Filmer's patriarchalist theory of political society is often linked to a traditionalist ideology of order, which based claims on the Bible and on analogies between different parts of the natural world. John Locke, by contrast, is said to have argued from reason, rejected traditional ideas and adopted political and economic principles which were well suited to an increasingly commercial society, for instance defending usury. This chapter questions these contentions, showing that Filmer and Locke held much the same views on usury, that Filmer was no conservative adherent to the ideology of order and that Filmer was arguably more of an innovator than Locke on questions of political theory.

John Locke's philosophy of money
Daniel Carey

This chapter discusses Locke's philosophy of money formulated in the midst of the crisis of English coin caused by the radical depletion of silver during the Nine Years' War (1688-1697). Rampant clipping had reduced the average weight of coins by fifty per cent but Locke resisted the solution of devaluing the currency and instead defended the sanctity of the existing monetary standard. To explain Locke's commitment I consider his political position and his philosophy of language. Locke emerges as a defender of intersubjective agreements even where discretion exists for changing the meaning of terms like money; specifically he insists on the independent measure or rule for regulating exchange, in this case silver by weight (not its stamp or denomination).

The Great Recoinage of 1696: Charles Davenant and monetary theory
Charles Larkin

The English re-coinage of 1696 was one of the great monetary events in history. By 1695 almost 50% of the specie content was missing from coinage in circulation, causing a monetary crisis. In May 1696 England's debased coinage was demonetised and new full-weight coins were issued, setting in motion events instrumental in the creation of the British Gold Standard. Charles Davenant, an author of economic tracts, politician and civil servant, was an important voice during formulation of the re-coinage policy. This chapter looks beyond the debate between John Locke, Isaac Newton and William Lowndes into the deeper theoretical and political concepts behind the final decision to re-coin the English currency.

'Mysterious politicks': land, credit and Commonwealth political economy, 1656-1722
Justin Champion

This chapter engages with ongoing debate about the economic sophistication of the post-Harringtonian republican tradition after 1660. The discussion focuses on the collaboration and responses of two key figures in the reception and fashioning of this later tradition – John Toland (1670-1722), editor of Harrington's works and proposer of new banking systems, and Viscount Robert Molesworth (1656-1725), landowner and politician – particularly their involvement with and perspective on the greatest moment of financial speculation, the South Sea Bubble. The essay suggests that these later republican thinkers had a much more sophisticated and complex understanding of the relationship between land, money, credit and public virtue than is commonly recognised.

Berkeley and the idea of a national bank
Patrick Kelly

Though George Berkeley's *The Querist* (1735-1737) advocated a national bank as the key to transforming the Irish economy, the excision of his extensive critique of banking from the second (and generally used) edition of 1750 has marginalised his ideas on the subject. Berkeley's analysis of banking ventures in Europe and America provided the blueprint for an effective public bank, able to mobilise national resources for the benefit of the whole population, and dependent on parliament for its establishment and supervision. What is not altogether clear is why Berkeley opted for a land-bank model for Ireland, since the examples he cited suggest other forms of bank were less vulnerable to fraud or abuse.

Adam Smith on money, mercantilism and the system of natural liberty
Ryan Patrick Hanley and *Maria Pia Paganelli*

Adam Smith's theory of money played a key role in his development of one of the conclusions for which he is most famous today: the superiority of the system of natural liberty to mercantilism. This chapter examines the part played by money in this argument, and specifically Smith's theory of money's origins and evolution, and its relevance to his theory of natural liberty. The chapter goes on to show how his position contributes to his critique of mercantilism and other proto-monetary policies as illustrative of his wider objection to interventionism, in conjunction with his understanding of the 'science of the legislator' in promoting the realisation of the system of natural liberty.

Pierre-Louis Rœderer, Adam Smith and the problem of inequality
Thomas Hopkins

The work of Adam Smith was subjected to intense scrutiny in Revolutionary France, even before the publication of Garnier's celebrated translation of *The Wealth of nations* in 1802, and of the avowedly 'Smithian' works of Say and Sismondi in 1803. This article is concerned with Pierre-Louis Rœderer's reading of Smith as a trenchant critic of Rousseau and the problems this raised for any attempt to retool Smith's moral philosophy and political economy as the basis of a republican social science. For Rœderer, Smith's moral philosophy and political economy alike appeared dangerously indifferent to the principle of natural equality, and therefore needed radical reconstruction.

List of contributors

Daniel Carey is a Professor in the School of Humanities, National University of Ireland, Galway. His publications include the monograph *Locke, Shaftesbury and Hutcheson: contesting diversity in the Enlightenment and beyond* (2006), and the edited volumes *The Empire of credit: the financial revolution in the British Atlantic world, 1688-1815*, with Christopher J. Finlay (2011), and *The Postcolonial Enlightenment: eighteenth-century colonialism and postcolonial theory*, with Lynn Festa (2009). He is a former editor of the journal *Eighteenth-century Ireland*.

Justin Champion studied history at Cambridge and has taught at Royal Holloway, University of London since 1990, holding a Chair in the History of Early Modern Ideas. He has published on the history of freethinking and irreligion, in particular exploring the ideas and life of John Toland and his circle. He is currently completing a volume of Hobbes's writings on religion for the Clarendon Works of Thomas Hobbes. Committed to Public History, he is a frequent broadcaster on the BBC on early modern topics. He was recently made an Honorary Fellow of the Historical Association.

Ryan Patrick Hanley is Associate Professor of Political Science at Marquette University. He is author of *Adam Smith and the character of virtue* (Cambridge, 2009), editor of the Penguin Classics edition of Smith's *Theory of moral sentiments*, and editor of the forthcoming *Adam Smith: a Princeton guide*. He is a past president of the International Adam Smith Society.

Thomas Hopkins is a temporary Lecturer in History at Queen Mary, University of London. He was a post-doctoral researcher at the University of Helsinki from 2009 to 2013. He holds a PhD in History from the University of Cambridge and is currently working on a monograph on political economy in post-Napoleonic Europe, with particular reference to the thought of Jean-Baptiste Say and J.-C.-L. Simonde de Sismondi.

Patrick Kelly is a former lecturer in History at Trinity College, Dublin. He has edited *Locke on money* (2 vols, Oxford, 1991), and published articles on Locke and Irish intellectual and social history of the seventeenth and eighteenth centuries. He is currently completing an edition of William Molyneux's *Case of Ireland [...] stated* (1698).

Charles Larkin is an Adjunct Lecturer and Research Associate at the School of Business, Trinity College Dublin, and Lecturer in Economics and Finance at Cardiff Metropolitan University. He has a PhD from Trinity College Dublin. He specialises in financial history and public policy economics. He is also a special advisor to Senator Sean Barrett in Seanad Eireann.

Maria Pia Paganelli teaches economics at Trinity University in San Antonio, Texas. She works on Adam Smith, David Hume, eighteenth-century monetary theories and the links between the Scottish Enlightenment and behavioural economics. She is the book review editor for the *Journal of the history of economic thought* and co-edited the *Oxford handbook of Adam Smith* (2013).

Johann P. Sommerville is Professor of History at the University of Wisconsin, Madison. His writings include *Royalists and patriots: politics and ideology in England 1603-1640* (2nd edn, 1999), *Thomas Hobbes: political ideas in historical context* (1992), and editions of the political works of King James VI and I and Sir Robert Filmer in the series Cambridge Texts in the History of Political Thought, published by Cambridge University Press.

Bibliography

Manuscript sources

Bodleian Library, Oxford
  MS Locke f.10.
  MS Locke b.3.
  MS Rawlinson D 677

British Library
  Add MSS 4295
  Add MSS 4465

Huntington Library
  HM 43212

The National Archives (UK)
  PRO 30/24/47/4

University of Kansas
  Spencer Mss G23

Primary sources

An abstract of their majesties commission under the great seal, dated the 15th day of June 1694: for taking subscriptions for the bank, pursuant to the late act of parliament (London, s. n., 1694).

Andrewes, Lancelot, *De usuris, theologica determinatio* in *Opuscula quaedam posthuma* (Oxford, 1852), p.117-50.

–, *De usuris, theologica determinatio* (1585), in *Opuscula quaedam posthuma* (London, Felix Kyngston for R[ichard] B[adger] & Andræa Hebb, 1629), p.111-38.

Aquinas, St Thomas, *In decem libros ethicorum Aristotelis ad Nicomachum expositio*, ed. Angeli M. Pirotta and Martini-S. Gillet (Turin, 1934).

–, *Summa theologiae* (Alba, 1962).

Aristotle, *Nicomachean ethics*, in *The Complete works of Aristotle: the revised Oxford translation*, 2 vols, ed. Jonathan Barnes (Princeton, NJ, 1984).

–, *Politics*, in *The Complete works of Aristotle: the revised Oxford translation*, 2 vols, ed. Jonathan Barnes (Princeton, NJ, 1984).

Asgill, John, *Several assertions proved, in order to create another species of money than gold and silver* (London, s. n., 1696).

Bacon, Francis, *The Oxford authors: Francis Bacon*, ed. Brian Vickers (Oxford, 1996).

Barbon, Nicholas, *A Discourse concerning coining the new money lighter* (London, Richard Chiswell, 1696).

–, *A Discourse of trade* (London, Tho. Milbourn for the author, 1691).

Berkeley, George, *Alciphron: or, the minute philosopher*, 2 vols (Dublin, G. Risk, G. Ewing, and W. Smith, 1732).

–, *A Discourse addressed to magistrates and men in authority. Occasioned by the enormous licence, and irreligion of the times* (Dublin, George Faulkner, 1738).

–, *An Essay towards preventing the ruine of Great Britain* (London, J. Roberts, 1721).

–, 'The Irish patriot or Queries upon queries' (1738), rptd in Joseph Johnston, *Bishop Berkeley's Querist in historical perspective* (Dundalk, 1970), p.210-13.

-, 'A manuscript of Bishop Berkeley', ed. J. M. Hone, in *The Times literary supplement* (13 March 1930), p.21; corrected version ed. R. J. Best in *The Times literary supplement* (3 April 1930), p.295.

-, [with Anne Berkeley?], *Maxims concerning patriotism: by a lady* (Dublin, s. n.,1750).

-, 'The plan or sketch of a national bank. To A. B. *Esq.*', in Berkeley, *Queries relating to a national bank, extracted from the Querist. Also the letter containing a plan or sketch of such bank. Republished with notes* (Dublin, George Faulkner, 1737), p.34-40.

-, *Queries relating to a national bank, extracted from the Querist. Also the letter containing a plan or sketch of such bank. Republished with notes* (Dublin, George Faulkner, 1737).

-, *The Querist, containing several queries, proposed to the consideration of the public* (Dublin, R. Reilly for G. Risk, G. Ewing, and W. Smith, 1735-1737).

-, *A Treatise concerning the principles of human knowledge*, ed. Jonathan Dancy (Oxford, 1998).

-, *The Works of George Berkeley Bishop of Cloyne*, ed. A. A. Luce and T. E. Jessop, 9 vols (London, 1948-1957).

Bindon, David, *An Essay on the gold and silver-coin currant in Ireland* (Dublin, E. Dobson, 1729).

-, *Some reasons shewing the necessity the people of Ireland are under, for continuing to refuse Mr Wood's coinage* (Dublin, 1724).

Blaxton, John, *The English usurer; or usury condemned by the most learned and famous divines of the church of England* (Oxford, John Norton for Francis Bowman, 1634).

Bodin, Jean, *Les Six livres de la république* (Paris, Jacques du Puys, 1576).

-, *The Six bookes of a commonweale*, trans. Richard Knolles (1606),

facsimile ed. Kenneth Douglas McRae (Cambridge, MA, 1962).

Boulter, Hugh, *Letters written by his excellency Hugh Boulter, D. D., lord primate of all Ireland*, 2 vols (Dublin, George Faulkner and James Williams, 1770).

Briscoe, John, *A Discourse of the late funds of the Million-Act, Lottery-Act, and Bank of England* (London, J. D. for Andrew Bell, 1696).

C., D., *An Essay towards the deciding of the so much, and so long controverted case of usury [...] By D. C.* (London, John Rothwell, 1661).

Cantillon, Richard, *Essai sur la nature du commerce en général* (London, Fletcher Gyles, 1755).

Capel, Richard, *Tentations: their nature, danger, cure: the fourth part. [...] by Richard Capel, sometimes fellow of Magdalen Colledge in Oxford. To all which is added an appendix touching usury* (London, T. R. and E. M. for John Bartlet, 1655).

The Case of Sir Theodore Janssen, one of the late directors of the South-Sea company (London, s. n., 1721).

Cato's letters, ed. Ronald Hamowy, 2 vols (Indianapolis, IN, 1995).

Child, Sir Josiah, *A Discourse about trade* ([London], A. Sowle, 1690).

Cicero, *On Duties*, ed. M. T. Griffin and E. M. Atkins (Cambridge, 1991).

-, *Philippics 1-6*, ed. and trans. D. R. Shackleton Bailey, revd John T. Ramsey and Gesine Manuwald (Cambridge, MA, 2009).

Cobbett, William, *Parliamentary history of England*, 36 vols (London, R. Bagshaw, 1806-1820).

Condorcet, Marie Jean Antoine Nicolas de Caritat, marquis de, *Tableau historique des progrès de l'esprit humain: projets, esquisse, fragments et notes (1772-1794)*, ed. Jean-Pierre Schandeler and Pierre Crépel with Eric Brian *et al.* (Paris, 2004).

Culpeper, Sir Thomas, *Tract against usury* (London, William Jaggard for Walter Burre, 1621).

Davanzati, Bernardo, *A Discourse upon coins*, trans. John Toland (London, J. D. for Awnsham and John Churchill, 1696).
Davenant, Charles, *The Political and commercial works of that celebrated writer Charles D'Avenant, LL.D.*, ed. Sir Charles Whitworth, 5 vols (London, R. Horsfield *et al.*, 1771).
–, *Two manuscripts by Charles Davenant*, ed. Abbott Payson Usher (Baltimore, MD, 1942).
La Décade philosophique comme système, 1794-1807, ed. Josiane Boulad-Ayoub, 9 vols (vols 8 and 9 co-edited by Martin Nadeau) (Rennes, 2003).
De Grouchy, Sophie (marquise de Condorcet), 'Lettres sur la sympathie', in Adam Smith, *Théorie des sentimens moraux, ou Essai analytique sur les principes des jugemens que portent naturellement les hommes, d'abord sur les actions des autres, et ensuite par leurs propres actions: suivi d'une dissertation sur l'origine des langues; par Adam Smith; traduit de l'anglais, sur la septième et dernière édition, par S. Grouchy Ve. Condorcet. Elle y a joint huit lettres sur la sympathie*, 2 vols (Paris, F. Buisson, An VI / 1798), vol.2, p.353-507.
Destutt de Tracy, A.-L.-C., *Mémoire sur la faculté de penser*, in *Mémoires de l'Institut national, classe des sciences morales et politiques*, 5 vols (Paris, Baudouin, Thermidor an VI-Fructidor an XII / 1798-1804), vol.1, p.283-450.
–, *Projet d'éléments d'idéologie à usage des écoles centrales de la République française*, 4 vols (Paris, Pierre Didot, 1800-1815).
Downam, George, *Lectures on the XV. Psalme* (London, Adam Islip for Cuthbert Burbie, 1604).

Fenton, Roger, *A Treatise of usurie, divided into three bookes* (London, Felix Kyngston for William Aspley, 1611).
Filmer, Sir Robert, *Patriarcha and other writings*, ed. Johann P. Sommerville (Cambridge, 1991).
–, *A Discourse whether it may be lawful to take use for money* (London, Will. Crook, 1678).
–, *Quaestio quodlibetica, or a discourse, whether it may bee lawfull to take use for money* (London, Humphrey Moseley, 1653).
–, *Observations concerning the originall of government*, in Filmer, *Patriarcha and other writings*, ed. Johann P. Sommerville (Cambridge, 1991).
A Further essay for the amendment of the gold and silver coins: with the opinion of Mr. Gerrard de Malynes, who was an eminent merchant in the reign of Queen Elizabeth, concerning the standard of England (London, T. Hodgkin, 1695).

Gibbon, Charles, *A Work worth the reading: wherein is contayned, fiue profitable and pithy questions* (London, Thomas Orwin, 1591).
Gordon, Thomas, *The Conspirators; or, the case of Catiline*, 9th edn (London, J. Roberts, 1721).

Hakluyt, Richard, 'A discourse of western planting', in *The Original writings & correspondence of the two Richard Hakluyts*, ed. E. G. R. Taylor, 2 vols (London, 1935).
The Harleian miscellany, ed. William Oldys and Thomas Park, 10 vols (London, 1808-1813).
Harrington, James, *The Common-wealth of Oceana* (London, J. Streater for Livewell Chapman, 1656).
–, *The Political works of James Harrington*, ed. J. G. A. Pocock (Cambridge, 1977).
–, *The Prerogative of popular government* (London, [G. Dawson] for Tho. Brewster, 1658).

–, *The Oceana of James Harrington and his other works*, ed. John Toland (London, John Darby, 1700).

Helvétius, C. A., *De l'esprit* (Paris, Durand, 1758).

–, *De l'esprit: or, essays on the mind, and its several faculties* (London, printed for the translator, 1759).

[Herrenschwand, Jean-Daniel], *De l'économie politique moderne: discours fondamental sur la population* (London, T. Hookham, 1786).

–, *De l'économie politique et morale de l'espèce humaine*, 2 vols (London, Cooper and Graham, 1796).

[Hill, Abraham], *A Letter about raising the value of coin* (London, Randal Taylor, 1690).

Historical Manuscripts Commission: report on manuscripts in various collections, vol.8 (London, 1913).

Hodges, James, *The Present state of England, as to coin and publick charges* (London, Andr. Bell, 1697).

Hooker, Richard, *Of the laws of ecclesiastical polity: preface. Book I. Book VIII*, ed. Arthur Stephen McGrade (Cambridge, 1989).

Huddleston, John, *Usury explain'd; or, conscience quieted in the case of putting out mony at interest* (London, D. Edwards, 1695/6).

Hume, David, *Essays, moral, political and literary*, ed. Eugene F. Miller (Indianapolis, IN, 1985).

–, *Political discourses* (Edinburgh, R. Fleming for A. Kincaid and A. Donaldson, 1752).

J., R., *A Letter of advice to a friend about the currency of clipt-money* (London, A. and J. Churchill, 1696).

Janssen, Sir Theodore, *A Discourse concerning banks* (London, James Knapton, 1697).

–, *Sir Theodore Janssen, Kt Bart. his particular and inventory* (London, Jacob Tonson, Bernard Lintot and William Taylor, 1721).

The Journals of the House of Commons of the kingdom of Ireland, 19 vols (Dublin, George Grierson *et al*, [vols 16 and 17], 1795-1800).

Journals of the House of Lords [Ireland], 8 vols (Dublin, William Sleater, 1779-1800).

Law, John, *Money and trade considered, with a proposal for supplying the nation with money* (Edinburgh, Heirs and Successors of Andrew Anderson, 1705).

Layton, Henry, *Observations concerning money and coin* (London, Peter Buck, 1697).

Le Blanc, François, *Traite historique des monnoies de France: depuis le commencement de la Monarchie jusques a present* (Paris, Jean Jombert, 1690).

A Letter to a Member of Parliament (London, s. n., 1721).

Locke, John, 'Answer to My Lord Keepers queries', in *Locke on money*, ed. Patrick Hyde Kelly, 2 vols (Oxford, 1991), vol.2, p.381-97.

–, *The Correspondence of John Locke*, ed. E. S. de Beer, 8 vols (Oxford, 1976-1989).

–, *An Essay concerning human understanding*, ed. Peter H. Nidditch (Oxford, 1975).

–, 'Of ethick in general', in *Writings on religion*, ed. Victor Nuovo (Oxford, 2002), p.9-14.

–, *Further considerations concerning raising the value of money* (1695), in *Locke on money*, ed. Patrick Hyde Kelly, 2 vols (Oxford, 1991).

–, 'Guineas', in *Locke on money*, ed. Patrick Hyde Kelly, 2 vols (Oxford, 1991), vol.2, p.363-64.

–, *A Letter concerning toleration*, trans. William Popple (London, Awnsham Churchill, 1689).

–, *Mr Locke's reply to the Right Reverend the Lord Bishop of Worcester's answer to his second letter* (London, H[annah]. C[lark]. for A. and J. Churchill, 1699).

–, 'A paper given to Sir William

Trumbull which was written at his request September 1695', in *Locke on money*, ed. Patrick Hyde Kelly, 2 vols (Oxford, 1991), vol.2, p.365-73.

–, *Some considerations of the consequences of the lowering of interest, and raising the value of money* (1692), in *Locke on money*, ed. Patrick Hyde Kelly, 2 vols (Oxford, 1991).

–, *Two treatises of government*, ed. Peter Laslett (Cambridge, 1988).

Lowndes, William, *A Report containing an essay for the amendment of the silver coins* (London, Charles Bill and the executrix of Thomas Newcomb, 1695).

M., H. [Sir Humphry Mackworth], *England's glory, or, the great improvement of trade in general, by a royal bank, or office of credit* (London, T[homas]. W[arren]. for Tho. Bever, 1694).

Machiavelli, Niccolò, *Discourses on Livy*, trans. Harvey C. Mansfield and Nathan Tarcov (Chicago, IL, 1996).

Madden, Samuel, *Reflections and resolutions proper for the gentlemen of Ireland* (Dublin, R. Reilly for George Ewing, 1738).

Malynes, Gerard, *Consuetudo, vel lex mercatoria, or The Ancient law-merchant* (London, Adam Islip, 1622).

Mandeville, Bernard, *The Fable of the bees: or, private vices publick benefits* (London, J. Roberts, 1714).

–, *The Grumbling hive: or, Knaves turn'd honest* (London, Sam. Ballard, 1705).

Manley, Thomas, *Usury at six per cent. examined* (London, Thomas Ratcliffe and Thomas Daniel for Ambrose Isted, 1669).

Marsilius of Padua, *Defensor pacis*, trans. Alan Gewirth (Toronto, 1980).

Misselden, Edward, *Free trade. Or, the meanes to make trade florish* (London, Iohn Leggatt for Simon Waterson, 1622).

Molesworth, Robert, *An Account of Denmark, with Francogallia and Some considerations for the promoting of agriculture and employing the poor*, ed. Justin Champion (Indianapolis, IN, 2011).

–, *Some considerations for the promoting of agriculture, and employing the poor* (Dublin, George Grierson, 1723).

–, 'The translator's preface', in François Hotman, *Franco-Gallia: or, an account of the ancient free state of France*, 2nd edn (London, Edward Valentine, 1721), p.i-xxxvi.

Mun, Thomas, *England's treasure by forraign trade* (London, J. G. for Thomas Clark, 1664).

Perkins, William, *A Discourse of conscience* (Cambridge, John Legate, 1596).

–, *Epieikeia: a treatise of Christian equitie and moderation* (Cambridge, Iohn Legat, 1604).

Petty, William, *Political arithmetick* (London, Robert Clavel and Hen. Mortlock, 1690).

–, *Quantulumcunque concerning money* [1682] (London, A. and J. Churchill, 1695).

–, 'Verbum sapienti' [1664], in *The Economic writings of Sir William Petty*, ed. Charles Henry Hull, 2 vols (Cambridge, 1899), vol.1, p.99-120.

Plutarch, *Parallel lives*, trans. Bernadette Perrin, 11 vols (London, 1914-26)

Prior, Thomas, *Observations on coin in general. With some proposals for regulating the value of coin in Ireland* (Dublin, A. Rhames for R. Gunne, 1729).

A Proposal for the relief of Ireland, by a coinage of monies, of gold and silver; and establishing a national bank (Dublin, s. n., 1734).

Pufendorf, Samuel, *De jure naturae et gentium libri octo*, ed. and trans. C. H. Oldfather and W. A. Oldfather, 2 vols (Oxford, 1934).

–, *Le Droit de la nature et des gens*, ed. and trans. Jean Barbeyrac, 2 vols (Amsterdam, Henri Schelte, 1706).

A Review of the universal remedy for all diseases incident to coin: with application to our present circumstance. In a letter to Mr. Locke (London, A. and J. Churchill, 1696).

Robbins, Caroline (ed.), *Two English republican tracts* (Cambridge, 1969).

Rœderer, Pierre-Louis, 'Cours d'organisation sociale; fait au Lycée en 1793 (l'an II de la République française)', in *Œuvres du comte P.-L. Rœderer*, ed. A. M. Rœderer, 8 vols (Paris, 1853-1859), vol.8, p.129-305.

–, 'Précis des observations sur la question proposée par l'Institut national pour le sujet du premier prix de la Classe des Sciences Morales et Politiques', *La Décade philosophique, politique et littéraire*, l'an VI, 1er trimestre (Paris, Au Bureau de la Décade, 1797), p.534-37.

Rousseau, Jean-Jaques, *Discours sur l'origine et fondemens de l'inégalité parmi les hommes*, in *Œuvres complètes*, ed. Bernard Gagnebin and Marcel Raymond, 5 vols (Paris, 1959-1995).

–, *The Discourses and other early political writings*, ed. and trans. Victor Gourevitch (Cambridge, 1997).

–, *Du contrat social*, in *Œuvres complètes*, ed. Bernard Gagnebin and Marcel Raymond, 5 vols (Paris, 1959-1995).

–, *The Social contract and other later political writings*, ed. and trans. Victor Gourevitch (Cambridge, 1997).

Salmasius, Claudius (Claude de Saumaise), *De modo usurarum* (Leiden, Bonaventura and Abraham Elzevier, 1639).

–, *De usuris liber* (Leiden, Bonaventura and Abraham Elzevier, 1638).

–, *Dissertatio de foenore trapezitico, in tres libros divisa* (Leiden, Joannes Maire, 1640).

'The secret history of the South-Sea scheme', in *A Collection of several pieces of Mr John Toland*, ed. Pierre Desmaizeaux, 2 vols (London, J. Peele, 1726), vol.1, p.404-47.

Sieyès, E.-J., 'What is the Third Estate?', trans. Michael Sonenscher, in *Political writings including the debate between Sieyès and Tom Paine in 1791*, ed. Michael Sonenscher (Indianapolis, IN, 2003), p.92-162.

–, *Ecrits politiques*, ed. Roberto Zapperi (Paris, 1985).

Simonde [de Sismondi], J. C. L., *De la richesse commerciale: ou, Principes d'économie politique, appliqués à la législation du commerce*, 2 vols (Geneva, J. J. Paschoud, An XI [1803]).

Smith, Adam, 'Early draft of part of *The Wealth of nations*', in *Lectures on jurisprudence*, ed. R. L. Meek, D. D. Raphael and P. G. Stein (1978; Indianapolis, IN, 1982).

–, *An Inquiry into the nature and causes of the wealth of nations* [1776], gen. eds R. H Campbell and A. S. Skinner, textual ed. W. B. Todd, 2 vols (1976; Indianapolis, IN, 1981).

–, *Lectures on jurisprudence*, ed. R. L. Meek, D. D. Raphael and P. G. Stein (Oxford, 1978; Indianapolis, IN, 1982).

–, 'A letter to the authors of the *Edinburgh review*' [1756], in *Essays on philosophical subjects*, ed. W. P. D. Wightman and J. C. Bryce (1980; Indianapolis, IN, 1982), p.242-56.

–, *The Theory of moral sentiments* [1759], ed. D. D. Raphael and A. L. Macfie (1976; Indianapolis, IN, 1982).

Some observations by way of answer, to a pamphlet, called England's glory; or, the royal bank (London, John Whitlock, 1694).

Soto, Domingo de, *De iustitia et iure* (Salamanca, Andreas a Portonariis, 1553).

Steele, Sir Richard, *The Crisis of property* (London, W. Chetwood *et al.*, 1720).

Stewart, Dugald, *Lectures on political economy*, in *The Collected works of Dugald Stewart*, ed. Sir William Hamilton, 11 vols (Edinburgh, 1854-1858).

Stillingfleet, Edward, *The Bishop of Worcester's answer to Mr. Locke's second letter* (London, J[ohn]. H[eptinstall]. for Henry Mortlock, 1698).

Suárez, Francisco, *Tractatus de legibus ac Deo legislatore* [1612] (Naples, 1872).

Swift, Jonathan, *The Examiner* 13 (2 November 1710).

Toland, John, *The Art of governing by partys* (London, Bernard Lintott, 1701).

–, *A Collection of several pieces of Mr. John Toland, now first publish'd from his original manuscripts*, ed. Pierre Desmaizeaux, 2 vols (London, J. Peele, 1726).

–, 'To the Lord Mayor, Aldermen, Sherifs, and Common Council of London', in *The Oceana of James Harrington and his other works*, ed. John Toland (London, [John Darby], 1700), p.i-vi.

–, 'Preface', in *The Oceana of James Harrington and his other works*, ed.

John Toland (London, [John Darby], 1700), p.vii-x.

–, 'The scheme, or practical model, of a national bank', in *A Collection of several pieces of Mr John Toland, now first publish'd from his original manuscripts*, ed. Pierre Desmaizeaux, 2 vols (London, J. Peele, 1726), vol.1, p.448-74.

Turgot, A. R. J., 'Réflexions sur la formation et distribution des richesses' [1766], in *Formation et distribution des richesses*, ed. Joël-Thomas Ravix and Paul-Marie Romani (Paris, 1997), p.155-226.

Tusser, Thomas, *A Hundreth good pointes of husbandrie* (London, Richard Tottel, 1557).

The Usury debate in the seventeenth century: three arguments (New York, 1972).

Vaughan, Rice, *A Discourse of coin and coinage* (London, Th. Dawks for Th. Basset, 1675).

William of Ockham, *Dialogus*, in *Monarchia S. Romani imperii*, ed. Melchior Goldast, 3 vols (Hanover, Thomas Willierius, 1611-14, vol. 2, 392-957; facsimile reissue Graz, 1960).

Wilson, Thomas, *A Discourse upon usury*, ed. R. H. Tawney (London, 1925).

[Wren, Matthew], *Considerations on Mr. Harrington's common-wealth of Oceana* (London, Samuel Gellibrand, 1657).

Secondary sources

Aftalion, Florin, *The French Revolution: an economic interpretation* (Cambridge, 1990).

Annas, Julia, 'Cicero on Stoic moral philosophy and private property', in *Philosophia togata*, ed. Miriam

Griffin and Jonathan Barnes (Oxford, 1989), p.151-73.

Appleby, Joyce Oldham, *Economic thought and ideology in seventeenth-century England* (Princeton, NJ, 1978).

–, 'Locke, liberalism, and the natural law of money', *Past & present* 71 (May 1976), p.43-69.

Ashton, Robert, 'Usury and high finance in the age of Shakespeare and Jonson', *University of Nottingham Renaissance and modern studies* 4 (1960), p.14-43.

Aspromourgos, Tony, *On the origins of classical economics: distribution and value from William Petty to Adam Smith* (London, 1996).

Ayers, Michael, *Locke: epistemology and ontology*, 2 vols (London, 1991).

Baker, K. M., 'The early history of the term "social science"', *Annals of science* 20:3 (1964), p.211-26.

Balen, Malcolm, *A Very English deceit: the secret history of the South Sea Bubble and the first great financial scandal* (London, 2002).

Bazerman, Charles, 'Money talks: the rhetorical project of the *Wealth of nations*', in *Economics and language*, ed. Willie Henderson, Tony Dudley-Evans and Roger Backhouse (London, 1993), p.173-99.

Becker, Carl L., *The Heavenly city of the eighteenth-century philosophers* (1932; New Haven, CT, 1974).

Bernanke, Ben S., and Cara C. Lown, 'The credit crunch', *Brookings papers on economic activity* 1991:2 (1991), p.205-47.

Blaug, Mark, *Economic theory in retrospect*, 4th edn (Cambridge, 1985).

Böhm-Bawerk, Eugen von, *Capital and interest*, vol.1: *History and critique of interest theories* (South Holland, IL, 1959).

Braddick, Michael J., 'The early modern English state and the question of differentiation, from 1550 to 1700', *Comparative studies in society and history* 38:1 (1996), p.92-111.

–, *State formation in early modern England c.1550-1700* (Cambridge, 2000).

Bredin, Jean-Denis, *Sieyès: la clé de la Révolution française* (Paris, 1988).

Brown, Vivienne, *Adam Smith's discourse: canonicity, commerce, conscience* (London, 1994).

Brewer, John, *The Sinews of power: war, money and the English state, 1688-1783* (London, 1989).

Burns, J. H. (ed.), with the assistance of Mark Goldie, *The Cambridge history of political thought 1450-1700* (Cambridge, 1991).

Caffentzis, Constantine George, *Clipped coins, abused words, & civil government: John Locke's philosophy of money* (New York, 1989).

–, *Exciting the industry of mankind: George Berkeley's philosophy of money* (Dordrecht, 2000).

–, 'The failure of Berkeley's bank: money and libertinism in eighteenth-century Ireland', in *The Empire of credit: the financial revolution in the British Atlantic world, 1688-1815*, ed. Daniel Carey and Christopher J. Finlay (Dublin, 2011), p.229-48.

–, 'Hume, money, and civilization; or, why was Hume a metallist?', *Hume studies* 27:2 (2001), p.301-35.

Cannan, Edwin (ed.), *The Paper pound of 1797-1821*, 2nd edn (London, 1925).

Carey, Daniel, 'John Locke, money, and credit', in *The Empire of credit: the financial revolution in the British Atlantic world, 1688-1815*, ed. Daniel Carey and Christopher J. Finlay (Dublin, 2011), p.25-51.

–, *Locke, Shaftesbury, and Hutcheson: contesting diversity in the Enlightenment and beyond* (Cambridge, 2006).

–, 'Locke's species: money and philosophy in the 1690s', *Annals of science* 70:3 (2013), p.357-80.

–, and Christopher J. Finlay (eds), *The Empire of credit: the financial revolution in the British Atlantic world, 1688-1815* (Dublin, 2011).

Carswell, John, *The South Sea Bubble*, revd edn (Stroud, 1993).

Carter, J. M., 'Cicero: politics and philosophy', in *Cicero and Virgil: studies in honour of Harold Hunt*, ed. John R. C. Martyn (Amsterdam, 1972), p.15-36.

Cassirer, Ernst, *The Philosophy of the Enlightenment* (1951; Princeton, NJ, 1979).

Castleton, Edward, 'Introduction: comment la propriété est devenue le vol, ou l'éducation de Pierre-Joseph Proudhon', in P.-J. Proudhon, *Qu'est-ce que la propriété?*, ed. Robert Damien and Edward Castleton (Paris, 2009), p.43-108.

Champion, Justin, 'Introduction', in Robert Molesworth, *An Account of Denmark, with Francogallia and Some Considerations for the promoting of agriculture and employing the poor*, ed. Justin Champion (Indianapolis, IN, 2011), p.ix-xl.

–, *Republican learning: John Toland and the crisis of Christian culture, 1696-1722* (Manchester, 2003).

Chartier, Roger, *The Cultural origins of the French Revolution*, trans. Lydia G. Cochrane (Durham, NC, 1991).

Checkland, S. G., *Scottish banking: a history* (Glasgow, 1975).

Clapham, Sir John, *The Bank of England: a history*, 2 vols (Cambridge, 1944).

Clark, J. C. D., *English society 1688-1832: ideology, social structure and political practice during the Ancien Régime* (Cambridge, 1985).

Clément, Pierre, *Histoire de Colbert et de son administration*, 2 vols (Paris, 1874).

–, *Les Questions monétaires avant 1789, et spécialement sous le ministère de Colbert* (Paris, 1870).

Coleman, D. C., 'Mercantilism revisited', *Historical journal* 23:4 (1980), p.773-91.

Coleman, William Oliver, *Rationalism and anti-rationalism in the origins of economics: the philosophical roots of 18th century economic thought* (Aldershot, 1995).

Continisio, Chiara, 'La "politica" aristotelica: un modello per la convivenza ordinata nella trattatistica politica italiana dell'Antico Regime', *Cheiron* 11:22 (1994), p.149-65.

Cooper, Thompson, 'John Dormer (1636-1700)', in the *Dictionary of national biography*, 22 vols, ed. Sir Leslie Stephen and Sir Sidney Lee (London, 1885-1901).

–, revised by Ruth Jordan, 'Huddleston [*alias* Dormer, Shirley], John (1636–1700)', in *Oxford dictionary of national biography* (Oxford, 2004).

Cossa, Luigi, *An Introduction to the study of political economy*, trans. Louis Dyer (London, 1893).

Creedy, John, 'On the King-Davenant "law" of demand', *Scottish journal of political economy* 33:3 (1986), p.193-212.

Cromartie, Alan, 'Harringtonian virtue: Harrington, Machiavelli, and the method of the *Moment*', *Historical journal* 41:4 (1998), p.987-1009.

Crouzet, François, *La Grande inflation: la monnaie en France de Louis XVI à Napoléon* (Paris, 1993).

–, 'The Huguenots and the English Financial Revolution', in *Favorites of fortune: technology, growth, and economic development since the Industrial Revolution*, ed. Patrice Higonnet, David S. Landes and Henry Rosovsky (Cambridge, MA, 1991), p.221-66.

Cullen, Louis, 'Landlords, bankers and merchants: the early Irish banking world, 1700-1820', in *Economists and the Irish economy from the eighteenth century to the present day*, ed. Antoin E. Murphy (Dublin, 1984), p.25-44.

Daly, James, *Sir Robert Filmer and English political thought* (Toronto, 1979).

Davies, Godfrey, and Marjorie Scofield, 'Letters of Charles Davenant', *Huntington library quarterly* 4:3 (1941), p.309-42.

Dawson, Hannah, 'Locke on private language', *British journal for the history of philosophy* 11:4 (2003), p.609-38.

–, *Locke, language, and early-modern philosophy* (Cambridge, 2007).

Dempsey, Bernard W., 'The historical emergence of quantity theory', *Quarterly journal of economics* 50:1 (1935), p.174-84.

Deringer, William Peter, 'Calculated values: the politics and epistemology of economic numbers in Britain, 1688-1738' (Doctoral dissertation, Princeton University, 2012).

Desmedt, Ludovic, 'Money in the "body politick": the analysis of trade and circulation in the writings of seventeenth-century political arithmeticians', *History of political economy* 37:1 (2005), p.79-101.

–, 'Les fondements monétaires de la "révolution financière" anglaise: le tournant de 1696', in *La Monnaie dévoilée par ses crises*, ed. Bruno Theret, 2 vols (Paris, 2007), vol.1, p.311-38.

Dickson, P. G. M., *The Financial Revolution in England: a study in the development of public credit, 1688-1756* (London, 1967).

Ehrenpreis, Irvin, *Swift: the man, his works and the age*, 3 vols (Cambridge, MA, 1962-1983).

Eltis, Walter, 'John Locke, the quantity theory of money and the establishment of a sound currency', in Mark Blaug *et al.*, *The Quantity theory of money: from Locke to Keynes and Friedman* (Cheltenham, 1995), p.4-26.

Endres, A. M., 'The functions of numerical data in the writings of Graunt, Petty, and Davenant', *History of political economy* 17:2 (1985), p.245-64.

–, 'The King-Davenant "law" in classical economics', *History of political economy* 19:4 (1987), p.621-38.

Ernst, Wolfgang, 'The glossators' monetary law', in *The Creation of the ius commune: from Casus to Regula*, ed. John W. Cairns and Paul J. du Plessis (Edinburgh, 2010), p.219-46.

Evensky, Jerry, *Adam Smith's moral philosophy* (Cambridge, 2005).

–, 'The evolution of Adam Smith's views on political economy', *History of political economy* 21:1 (1989), p.123-45.

Faccarello, Gilbert, 'Le legs de Turgot: aspects de l'économie politique sensualiste de Condorcet à Rœderer', in *La Pensée économique pendant la Révolution française*, ed. Gilbert Faccarello and Philippe Steiner (Grenoble, 1990), p.67-107.

Feavearyear, Sir Albert, *The Pound sterling: a history of English money*, 2nd edn revd E. Victor Morgan (Oxford, 1963).

Ferguson, Niall, *The Cash nexus: money and power in the modern world, 1700-2000* (London, 2001).

Fest, Joachim, *Der zerstorte Traum: vom Ende des utopischen Zeitalters* (Berlin, 1991).

Fetter, Frank Whitson, *Development of British monetary orthodoxy 1797-1875* (Cambridge, MA, 1965).

Finkelstein, Andrea, *Harmony and the balance: an intellectual history of seventeenth-century English economic thought* (Ann Arbor, MI, 2000).

Finlay, Christopher J., 'Commerce and the law of nations in Hume's theory of money' in *The Empire of credit: the financial revolution in the*

British Atlantic world, 1688-1815, ed. Daniel Carey and Christopher J. Finlay (Dublin, 2011), p.53-72.

Fitzgibbons, Athol, *Adam Smith's system of liberty, wealth, and virtue: the moral and political foundations of the Wealth of nations* (Oxford, 1995).

Fleischacker, Samuel, *On Adam Smith's Wealth of nations: a philosophical companion* (Princeton, NJ, 2004).

Forget, Evelyn L., *The Social economics of Jean-Baptiste Say: markets and virtue* (London, 1999).

Forsyth, Murray, *Reason and revolution: the political thought of the abbé Sieyès* (Leicester, 1987).

Foucault, Michel, *The Order of things: an archeology of the human sciences* (1970; New York, 1994).

Fox, D., 'The *Case of Mixt Monies*: confirming nominalism in the common law of monetary obligations', *Cambridge law journal* 70:1 (2011), p.144-74.

Gaskill, Malcolm, *Crime and mentalities in early modern England* (Cambridge, 2000).

Gauci, Perry, 'Malynes, Gerard (*fl*.1585-1641)', *in Oxford dictionary of national biography* (Oxford, 2004).

George, Charles H., 'English Calvinist opinion on usury, 1600-1640', *Journal of the history of ideas* 18:4 (1957), p.455-74.

Giacomin, Alberto, 'Paper money: a reassessment of Adam Smith's view', in *Money and markets: a doctrinal approach*, ed. Alberto Giacomin and Maria Christina Marcuzzo (London, 2007), p.181-99.

Goldie, Mark, and Robert Wokler (eds), *The Cambridge history of eighteenth-century political thought* (Cambridge, 2006).

Goldsmith, M. M., *Private vices, public benefits: Bernard Mandeville's social and political thought* (Cambridge, 1985).

Gordon, Daniel, *Citizens without sovereignty: equality and sociability in French thought, 1670-1789* (Princeton, NJ, 1994).

Greaves, Richard L., 'Asgill, John (*bap.* 1659, *d.* 1738)', in *Oxford dictionary of national biography* (Oxford, 2004).

Greenleaf, W. H., *Order, empiricism and politics: two traditions of English political thought 1500-1700* (London, 1964).

Griffith, William P., 'Mackworth, Sir Humphry (1657-1727)', *in Oxford dictionary of national biography* (Oxford, 2004).

Griswold, Charles, *Adam Smith and the virtues of Enlightenment* (Cambridge, 1999).

Guyer, Paul, 'Locke's philosophy of language', in *The Cambridge companion to Locke*, ed. Vere Chappell (Cambridge, 1994), p.115-45.

Haakonssen, Knud, *The Science of a legislator: the natural jurisprudence of David Hume and Adam Smith* (Cambridge, 1981).

–, *Natural law and moral philosophy: from Grotius to the Scottish Enlightenment* (Cambridge, 1996).

Hamilton, Earl J., *American treasure and the price revolution in Spain, 1501-1650* (Cambridge, MA, 1934).

Hamowy, Ronald, '*Cato's* letters, John Locke, and the Republican paradigm', *History of political thought* 11:2 (1990), p.273-94.

Hanley, Ryan Patrick, 'Enlightened nation building: the "science of the legislator" in Adam Smith and Rousseau', *American journal of political science* 52:2 (2008), p.219-34.

Hart, David Mercer, 'Class, slavery and the industrialist theory of history in French liberal thought, 1814-1830: the contribution of Charles Comte and Charles Dunoyer' (Doctoral dissertation, University of Cambridge, 1994).

Hawkes, David, *The Culture of usury in Renaissance England* (New York, 2010).

Hayton, D. W., 'Mackworth, Sir Humphrey', in *The History of Parliament: the House of Commons 1690-1715*, ed. Eveline Cruickshanks, Stuart Handley and D. W. Hayton, 5 vols (Cambridge, 2002), vol.4, p.724-35.

Heckscher, Eli F., *Mercantilism* [1935], trans. Mendel Shapiro, revd edn, ed. E. F. Söderlund, 2 vols (London, 1955).

–, 'Revisions in economic history: V. Mercantilism', *Economic history review* 7:1 (1936), p.44-54.

Hochstrasser, T. J., 'Physiocracy and the politics of *laissez-faire*', in *The Cambridge history of eighteenth-century political thought*, ed. Mark Goldie and Robert Wokler (Cambridge, 2006), p.419-42.

Hollander, Jacob H., 'The development of the theory of money from Adam Smith to David Ricardo', *Quarterly journal of economics* 25:3 (1911), p.429-70.

Hont, Istvan, *Jealousy of trade: international competition and the nation-state in historical perspective* (Cambridge, MA, 2005).

–, 'The language of sociability and commerce: Samuel Pufendorf and the theoretical foundations of the "four stages theory"', in *The Languages of political theory in early-modern Europe*, ed. Anthony Pagden (Cambridge, 1987), p.253-76.

Hopkins, Thomas, 'Say and Sismondi on the political economy of post-revolutionary Europe, *c.*1800-1842' (Doctoral dissertation, University of Cambridge, 2011).

Hoppit, Julian, 'Attitudes to credit in Britain, 1680-1790', *Historical journal* 33:2 (1990), p.305-22.

–, 'Davenant, Charles (1656-1714)', in *Oxford dictionary of national biography* (Oxford, 2004).

–, 'The myths of the South Sea Bubble', *Transactions of the Royal Historical Society* 12 (2002), p.141-65.

Horsefield, J. Keith, *British monetary experiments 1650-1710* (Cambridge, MA, 1960).

–, 'The duties of a banker II: the effects of inconvertibility', in *Papers in English monetary history*, ed. T. S. Ashton and R. S. Sayers (Oxford, 1953), p.16-36.

Horwitz, Henry, 'The East India trade, the politicians, and the constitution: 1689-1702', *Journal of British studies* 17:2 (1978), p.1-18.

–, *Parliament, policy and politics in the reign of William III* (Manchester, 1977).

–, (ed.), *London politics 1713-1717: minutes of a Whig club 1714-1717* (London, 1981).

Hutchison, Terence, *Before Adam Smith: the emergence of political economy, 1662-1776* (Oxford, 1988).

Israel, Jonathan I., *Radical Enlightenment: philosophy and the making of modernity, 1650-1750* (Oxford, 2001).

Jacob, Margaret, *The Newtonians and the English Revolution, 1689-1720* (Hassocks, 1976).

James, Michael, 'Pierre-Louis Rœderer, Jean-Baptiste Say, and the concept of *industrie*', *History of political economy* 9:4 (1977), p.455-75.

Jevons, W. Stanley, *The Theory of political economy* (London, 1871).

Johnston, Joseph, *Bishop Berkeley's Querist in historical perspective* (Dundalk, 1970).

Jolley, Nicholas, *Locke: his philosophical thought* (Oxford, 1999).

Jones, D. W., *War and economy in the Age of William III and Marlborough* (Oxford, 1988).

Jones, Norman, *God and the moneylenders: usury and law in early modern England* (Oxford, 1989).

Jurdjevic, Mark, 'Virtue, commerce and the enduring Florentine republican moment: reintegrating Italy into the Atlantic republican debate', *Journal of the history of ideas* 62:4 (2001), p.721-43.

Kalyvas, Andreas, and Ira Katznelson, 'The rhetoric of the market: Adam Smith on recognition, speech and exchange', *Review of politics* 63:3 (2001), p.549-79.

Kates, Gary, *The Cercle social, the Girondins, and the French Revolution* (Princeton, NJ, 1985).

Kaye, Joel, *Economy and nature in the fourteenth century: money, market exchange, and the emergence of scientific thought* (Cambridge, 1998).

Kelly, Patrick Hyde, 'Anne Donnellan: Irish proto-bluestocking', *Hermathena* 154 (1993), p.39-68.

–, 'General introduction: Locke on money', in *Locke on money*, ed. Patrick Hyde Kelly, 2 vols (Oxford, 1991), vol.1, p.1-109.

–, 'Industry and virtue versus luxury and corruption: Berkeley, Walpole, and the South Sea Bubble crisis', *Eighteenth-century Ireland / Iris an dá chultúr* 7 (1992), p.57-74.

–, '"Monkey business": Locke's "College" correspondence and the adoption of the plan for the Great Recoinage of 1696', *Locke studies* 9 (2009), p.139-65.

–, 'The politics of political economy in mid-eighteenth century Ireland', in *Political ideas in eighteenth-century Ireland*, ed. S. J. Connolly (Dublin, 2000), p.105-29.

Kerridge, Eric, *Usury, interest, and the Reformation* (Aldershot, 2002).

Keynes, Sir Geoffrey, *A Bibliography of George Berkeley Bishop of Cloyne: his works and critics in the eighteenth century* (Oxford, 1976).

Keynes, John Maynard, *The General theory of employment, interest, and money* (New York, 1936).

Kindleberger, Charles Poor, *International economics*, 3rd edn (Homewood, IL, 1963).

Kirshner, Julius, and Kimberly Lo Prete, 'Peter John Olivi's treatises on contracts of sale, usury and restitution: Minorite economics or minor works?', *Quaderni fiorentini per la storia del pensiero giuridico moderno* 13 (1984), p.233-86.

Kitchin, Joanna, *Un Journal 'philosophique': La Décade (1794-1807)* (Paris, 1965).

Kleer, Richard A., ' "Fictitious cash": English public finance and paper money, 1689-1697', in *Money, power, and print: interdisciplinary studies on the Financial Revolution in the British Isles*, ed. Charles Ivar McGrath and Chris Fauske (Newark, DE, 2008), p.70-103.

–, ' "The folly of particulars": the political economy of the South Sea Bubble', *Financial history review* 19 (2012), p.175-97.

–, ' "The ruine of Diana": Lowndes, Locke, and the bankers', *History of political economy* 36:3 (2004), p.533-56.

Kwarteng, Kwasi, 'The political thought of the recoinage crisis of 1695-1697' (Doctoral dissertation, University of Cambridge, 2000).

Laidler, David, 'Adam Smith as a monetary economist', *Canadian journal of economics/Révue canadienne d'économique* 14:2 (1981), p.185-200.

Langford, Paul, *Public life and the propertied Englishman, 1689-1798* (Oxford, 1991).

Laslett, Peter, 'Introduction', in Sir Robert Filmer, *Patriarcha and other political works* (Oxford, 1949), p.1-46.

Levy, David M., 'Bishop Berkeley exorcises the infinite: fuzzy consequences of strict finitism', *Hume studies* 18:2 (1992), p.511-36.

–, 'The partial spectator in the *Wealth of Nations*: a robust utilitarianism', *European journal of the history of economic thought* 2:2 (1995), p.299-326.

Li, Ming-Hsun, *The Great Recoinage of 1696 to 1699* (London, 1963).

Lovejoy, Arthur O., *The Great chain of being* (1936; Cambridge, MA, 1982).

Luce, Arthur Aston, *The Life of George Berkeley, Bishop of Cloyne* [1949], intro. by David Berman (London, 1992).

McCormick, Ted, *William Petty and the ambitions of political arithmetic* (Oxford, 2009).

McCulloch, J. R., 'Note on the re-coinage of 1696-1699', in *A Select collection of scarce and valuable tracts on money*, ed. J. R. McCulloch (London, 1856), p.261-65.

MacDonald, Michael, 'An Early seventeenth-century defence of usury', *Historical research* 60 (1987), p.353-60.

McNamara, Peter, *Political economy and statesmanship: Smith, Hamilton, and the foundation of the commercial republic* (DeKalb, IL, 1998).

Macpherson, C. B., 'Harrington as realist: a rejoinder', *Past & present* 24 (1963), p.82-85.

–, *The Political theory of possessive individualism: Hobbes to Locke* (Oxford, 1962).

Magnusson, Lars, *Mercantilism: the shaping of an economic language* (London, 1994).

Margerison, Kenneth, 'P.-L. Rœderer: political thought and practice during the French Revolution', *Transactions of the American philosophical society* 73:1 (1983), p.1-166.

Mayhew, Nicholas, 'Silver in England 1600-1800: coinage outputs and bullion exports from the records of the London Tower Mint and the London Company of Goldsmiths', in *Money in the pre-industrial world: bullion, debasements and coin substitutes*, ed. John H. Munro (London, 2012), p.97-109.

–, *Sterling: the rise and fall of a currency* (London, 1999).

Mehta, Pratap Bhanu, 'Liberalism, nation, and empire: the case of J. S. Mill', in *Empire and modern political thought*, ed. Sankar Muthu (Cambridge, 2012), p.232-60.

Mehta, Uday Singh, *Liberalism and empire: a study in nineteenth-century British liberal thought* (Chicago, IL, 1999).

Monod, Paul Kléber, *The Power of kings: monarchy and religion in Europe, 1589-1715* (New Haven, CT, 1999).

Montes, Leonidas, *Adam Smith in context: a critical reassessment of some central components of his thought* (New York, 2004).

Moore, Seán D., *Swift, the book, and the Irish financial revolution: satire and sovereignty in colonial Ireland* (Baltimore, MD, 2010).

Muldrew, Craig, *The Economy of obligation: the culture of credit and social relations in early modern England* (Houndmills, 1998).

Muller, Jerry Z., *Adam Smith in his time and ours: designing the decent society* (Princeton, NJ, 1993).

Murphy, Anne L., *The Origins of English financial markets: investment and speculation before the South Sea Bubble* (Cambridge, 2009).

Murphy, Antoin E., *The Genesis of macroeconomics: new ideas from Sir William Petty to Henry Thornton* (Oxford, 2009).

–, 'John Law and the Scottish Enlightenment', in *A History of Scottish economic thought*, ed. Alexander Dow and Sheila Dow (London, 2006), p.9-26.

–, *John Law: economic theorist and policy-maker* (Oxford, 1997).

–, *Richard Cantillon: entrepreneur and economist* (Oxford, 1986).

Neal, Larry, '*I am not master of events': the speculations of John Law and Lord Londonderry in the Mississippi and South Sea Bubbles* (New Haven, CT, 2012).

Neal, Larry, and Stephen Quinn, 'Markets and institutions in the rise of London as a financial center in the seventeenth century', in *Finance, intermediaries, and economic development*, ed. Stanley L. Engerman, Philip T. Hoffman, Jean-Laurent Rosenthal and Kenneth L. Sokoloff (Cambridge, 2003), p.11-33.

Nelson, Benjamin, *The Idea of usury: from tribal brotherhood to universal otherhood*, 2nd edn (Chicago, IL, 1969).

Nelson, Eric, *The Greek tradition in republican thought* (Cambridge, 2004).

Neuhouser, Frederick, *Rousseau's theodicy of self-love: evil, rationality, and the drive for recognition* (Oxford, 2008).

New, John F. H., 'Harrington, a realist?', *Past & present* 24 (1963), p.75-81.

–, 'The meaning of Harrington's agrarian', *Past & present* 25 (1963), p.94-95.

Nicholson, Linda J., *Gender and history: the limits of social theory in the age of the family* (New York, 1986).

Nisbet, Robert A., *History of the idea of progress* (New York, 1980).

Nogués-Marco, Pilar, 'Competing bimetallic ratios: Amsterdam, London, and bullion arbitrage in mid-eighteenth century', *Journal of economic history* 73:2 (2013), p.445-76.

Noonan, John T., Jr., *The Scholastic analysis of usury* (Cambridge, MA, 1957).

North, Douglass C., and Barry R. Weingast, 'Constitutions and commitment: the evolution of institutions governing public choice in seventeenth-century England', *Journal of economic history* 49:4 (1989), p.803-32.

Norton, Mary Beth, *Founding fathers and mothers: gendered power and the forming of American society* (New York, 1997).

O'Brien, Patrick K., 'Fiscal exceptionalism: Great Britain and its European rivals from Civil War to triumph at Trafalgar and Waterloo', in *The Political economy of British historical experience, 1688-1914*, ed. Donald Winch and Patrick K. O'Brien (Oxford, 2002), p.245-65.

–, 'The political economy of British taxation, 1660-1815', *Economic history review* (2nd ser.), 41:1 (1988), p.1-32.

Ogborn, Miles, 'The capacities of the state: Charles Davenant and the management of the Excise, 1683-1698', *Journal of historical geography* 24:3 (1998), p.289-312.

O'Kane, Finola, *Landscape design in eighteenth-century Ireland: mixing foreign trees with the natives* (Cork, 2004).

Onken, August, 'The Adam Smith problem' in *Adam Smith: critical responses*, ed. Hiroshi Mizuta, 6 vols (London, 2000), vol.5, p.84-105, trans. from the *Zeitschrift für Socialwissenschaft* 1 (1898), p.25-33, 101-108, 276-87.

Orphanides, Athanasios, 'Taylor rules', in *The New Palgrave dictionary of economics*, 2nd edn, ed. Steven N. Durlauf and Lawrence E. Blume, 8 vols (Houndmills, 2008), vol.8, p.200-204.

Ormazabal, Kepa, 'Lowndes and Locke on the value of money', *History of political economy* 44:1 (2012), p.157-80.

Otteson, James, *Adam Smith's marketplace of life* (Cambridge, 2002).

Paganelli, Maria Pia, 'Adam Smith: why decentralized systems?', *The*

Adam Smith review 2 (2006), p.203-208.

–, 'Vanity and the Daedalian wings of paper money in Adam Smith', in *New voices on Adam Smith*, ed. Eric Schliesser and Leonidas Montes (London, 2006), p.271-89.

Pasquino, Pasquale, *Sieyès et l'invention de la constitution en France* (Paris, 1998).

Pateman, Carole, *The Sexual contract* (Stanford, CA, 1988).

Paul, Helen J., *The South Sea Bubble: an economic history of its origins and consequences* (New York, 2011).

Phillipson, Nicholas, *Adam Smith: an enlightened life* (London, 2011).

Pincus Steve, 'Neither Machiavellian moment nor possessive individualism: commercial society and the defenders of the English commonwealth', *American historical review* 103:3 (1998), p.705-36.

–, 'Rethinking mercantilism: political economy, the British Empire, and the Atlantic World in the seventeenth and eighteenth centuries', *William and Mary quarterly* 69:1 (2012), p.3-34.

–, *1688: the first modern revolution* (New Haven, CT, 2009).

–, and Alice Wolfram, 'A proactive state?: the land bank, investment and party politics in the 1690s', in *Regulating the British economy, 1660-1850*, ed. Perry Gauci (Farnham, 2011), p.41-62.

Pittock, M. G. H., 'John Law's theory of money and its roots in Scottish culture', *Proceedings of the antiquarian society of Scotland* 133 (2003), p.391-403.

Pitts, Jennifer, *A Turn to empire: the rise of imperial liberalism in Britain and France* (Princeton, NJ, 2005).

Pocock, J. G. A., 'Early modern capitalism: the Augustan perception', in *Feudalism, capitalism and beyond*, ed. Eugene Kamenka and R. S. Neale (London, 1975), p.62-83.

–, 'Historical introduction', in *The Political works of James Harrington*, ed. J. G. A. Pocock (Cambridge, 1977), p.1-152.

–, *The Machiavellian moment: Florentine political thought and the Atlantic republican tradition* (Princeton, NJ, 1975).

–, *Virtue, commerce, and history: essays on political thought and history, chiefly in the eighteenth century* (Cambridge, 1985).

–, (ed.), *The Varieties of British political thought, 1500-1800* (Cambridge, 1993).

Porter, Roy, *The Creation of the modern world: the British Enlightenment* (New York, 2000).

Poulalion, Gabriel, *L'Economiste Jean-Daniel Herrenschwand* (Aix-en-Provence, 2008).

Procacci, Giovanna, *Gouverner la misère: la question sociale en France (1789-1848)* (Paris, 1993).

Purcell, Nicholas, 'The Roman *villa* and the landscape of production', in *Urban society in Roman Italy*, ed. T. J. Cornell and Kathryn Lomas (London, 1995), p.151-79.

Quinn, Stephen, 'Gold, silver, and the Glorious Revolution: arbitrage between bills of exchange and bullion', *Economic history review* 44:3 (1996): 473-90.

Rand, Benjamin, *Berkeley and Percival: the correspondence of George Berkeley, afterwards Bishop of Cloyne, and Sir John Percival, afterwards first Earl of Egmont* (Cambridge, 1914).

Raphael, D. D., *The Impartial spectator: Adam Smith's moral philosophy* (Oxford, 2007).

Rasmussen, Dennis C., *The Problems and promise of commercial society: Adam Smith's response to Rousseau* (University Park, PA, 2008).

Rawson, Elizabeth, 'The Ciceronian aristocracy and its properties', in *Studies in Roman property*, ed. M. I.

Finley (Cambridge, 1976), p.85-102.

Redish, Angela, *Bimetallism: an economic and historical analysis* (Cambridge, 2000).

Regaldo, Marc, *Un Milieu intellectuel: la Décade philosophique (1794-1807)*, 5 vols (Lille, 1976; Paris, 1976).

Richards, R. D. 'The Exchequer bill in the history of English governmental finance', *Economic history* 3:11 (1936), p.193-211.

–, 'The first fifty years of the Bank of England', in *History of the principal public banks*, ed. J. G. van Dillen (The Hague, 1934), p.219-30.

–, 'The lottery in the history of English government finance', *Economic history* 3:9 (1934), p.57-76.

Ridley, Ronald T., '*Leges agrariae*: myths ancient and modern', *Classical philology* 95:4 (2000), p.459-67.

Rose, Craig, *England in the 1690s: revolution, religion and war* (Oxford, 1999).

Rosenmeier, Jesper, 'John Cotton on usury', *William and Mary quarterly* 47:4 (1990), p.548-65.

Roseveare, Henry, *The Financial Revolution 1660-1760* (London, 1991).

Rössner, Philipp Robinson, *Deflation – devaluation – rebellion: Geld im Zeitalter der Reformation* (Stuttgart, 2012).

Rubini, Dennis, 'Politics and the battle for the banks, 1688-1697', *English historical review* 85 (1970), p.693-714.

Ryder, Michael, 'The Bank of Ireland, 1721: land, credit and dependency', *Historical journal* 25:3 (1982), p.557-82.

Ste Croix, G. E. M. de, *The Class struggle in the ancient Greek world from the archaic age to the Arab conquests* (London, 1981).

Sargent, Thomas J., and François R.

Velde, *The Big problem of small change* (Princeton, NJ, 2002).

Saville, Richard, *Bank of Scotland: a history 1695-1995* (Edinburgh, 1996).

Schliesser, Eric, 'Wonder in the face of scientific revolutions: Adam Smith on Newton's "proof" of Copernicanism', *British journal for the history of philosophy* 13:4 (2005), p.697-732.

Schumpeter, Joseph A., *History of economic analysis*, ed. Elizabeth Boody Schumpeter (New York, 1954).

Scott, Jonathan, *England's troubles: seventeenth-century English political instability in European context* (Cambridge, 2000).

–, ' "Good night Amsterdam": Sir George Downing and Anglo-Dutch statebuilding', *English historical review* 118 (2003), p.334-56.

Scurr, Ruth, 'Pierre-Louis Rœderer and the debate on forms of government in revolutionary France', *Political studies* 52:2 (2004), p.251-68.

–, 'Social equality in Pierre-Louis Rœderer's interpretation of the modern republic, 1793', *History of European ideas* 26:2 (2000), p.105-26.

Sedgwick, Romney, *The House of Commons 1715-1754*, 2 vols (London, 1970).

Shapiro, James, *Shakespeare and the Jews* (New York, 1996).

Shaw, William, *The History of the currency 1252 to 1894* (London, 1895).

– (ed.), *Select tracts and documents illustrative of English monetary history 1626-1730* (1896; London, 1935).

Singer, Brian C. J., *Society, theory and the French Revolution* (New York, 1986).

Skinner, Andrew S., 'Adam Smith: rhetoric and the communication of ideas', in *Methodological controversy in economics: historical essays in honour of T. W. Hutchison*, ed. A. W. Coats (London, 1983), p.71-88.

Skinner, Quentin, *The Foundations of modern political thought*, vol.2: *The Age of Reformation* (Cambridge, 1978).

Slack, Paul, 'Measuring the national wealth in seventeenth-century England', *Economic history review* 57:4 (2004), p.607-35.

Sommerville, Johann, 'Conscience, law, and things indifferent: arguments on toleration from the Vestiarian controversy to Hobbes and Locke', in *Contexts of conscience in early modern Europe, 1500-1700*, ed. Harald E. Braun and Edward Vallance (Houndmills, 2004), p.166-79.

–, *Royalists and patriots: politics and ideology in England 1603-1640*, 2nd edn (Harlow, 1999).

Sonenscher, Michael, *Before the deluge: public debt, inequality, and the intellectual origins of the French Revolution* (Princeton, NJ, 2007).

–, 'Ideology, social science and general facts in late eighteenth-century French political thought', *History of European ideas* 35:1 (2009), p.24-37.

–, 'Introduction', in *Political writings including the debate between Sieyès and Tom Paine in 1791*, ed. Michael Sonenscher (Indianapolis, IN, 2003), p.vii-lxiv.

–, '"The moment of social science": the *Décade philosophique* and late eighteenth-century French thought', *Modern intellectual history* 6:1 (2009), p.121-46.

–, 'Property, community and citizenship', in *The Cambridge history of eighteenth-century political thought*, ed. Mark Goldie and Robert Wokler (Cambridge, 2006), p.495-94.

–, *Sans-culottes: an eighteenth-century*

emblem in the French Revolution (Princeton, NJ, 2008).

Spooner, Frank C., *The International economy and monetary movements in France, 1493-1725*, 2nd edn (Cambridge, MA, 1972).

Staum, Martin S., *Minerva's message: stabilizing the French Revolution* (Montreal and Kingston, 1996).

Stern, Philip J., and Carl Wennerlind (eds), *Mercantilism reimagined: political economy in early modern Britain and its empire* (Oxford, 2013).

Stigler, Stephen M., 'Jevons on the King-Davenant law of demand: a simple resolution of a historical puzzle', *History of political economy* 26:2 (1994), p.185-91.

Stone, Lawrence, *The Family, sex and marriage in England 1500-1800* (New York, 1977).

Sullivan, Robert E., *John Toland and the deist controversy: a study in adaptations* (Cambridge, MA, 1982).

Thirsk, Joan, and J. P. Cooper (eds), *Seventeenth-century economic documents* (Oxford, 1972).

Tribe, Keith, ' "Das Adam Smith problem" and the origins of modern Smith scholarship', *History of European ideas* 34:4 (2008), p.514-25.

–, *Land, labour and economic discourse* (London, 1978).

Tuck, Richard, 'The "Modern" theory of natural law', in *The Languages of political theory in early-modern Europe*, ed. Anthony Pagden (Cambridge, 1987), p.99-119.

Van Dillen, J. G., 'The Bank of Amsterdam', in *History of the principal public banks*, ed. J. G. van Dillen (The Hague, 1934), p.79-123.

Veale, Elspeth, 'Sir Theodore Janssen, Huguenot and merchant of London *c.*1658-1748', *Proceedings of the Huguenot society of Great*

Britain and Ireland 26:2 (1995), p.264-88.

Venturi, Franco, *The End of the Old Regime in Europe, 1776-1789*, trans. R. Burr Litchfield, 2 vols (Princeton, NJ, 1991). Translation of *Settecento riformatore*, vol.4, *La Caduta dell'Antico Regime (1776-1789)*, vol.1, *I Grandi stati dell'Occidente* [1984], and vol.2, *Il Patriottismo repubblicano e gli imperi dell'Est* [1984]).

–, *The End of the Old Regime in Europe, 1768-1776: the first crisis*, trans. R. Burr Litchfield (Princeton, NJ, 1989). Translation of *Settecento riformatore*, vol.3. *La Prima crisi dell'Antico Regime (1768-1776)* [1979].

Vickers, Douglas, 'Adam Smith and the status of the theory of money', in *Essays on Adam Smith*, ed. Andrew S. Skinner and Thomas Wilson (Oxford, 1975), p.482-503.

–, *Studies in the theory of money 1690-1776* (1959; New York, 1968).

Viner, Jacob, 'English theories of foreign trade before Adam Smith', *Journal of political economy* 38:4 (1930), p.249-301.

–, 'Mercantilist thought', in Viner, *Essays on the intellectual history of economics*, ed. Douglas A. Irwin (Princeton, NJ, 1991), p.262-76.

Waddell, D. A. G., 'The career and writings of Charles Davenant (1656–1714)', (Doctoral dissertation, University of Oxford, 1954).

–, 'Charles Davenant (1656-1714) – a biographical sketch', *Economic history review* 11:2 (1958), p.279-88.

Walcot, P., 'Cicero on private property: theory and practice', *Greece and Rome*, 2nd series, 22:2 (1975), p.120-28.

Walcott, Robert, 'The East India interest in the general election of 1700-1701', *English historical review* 71 (1956), p.223-39.

Walsh, Patrick, 'Irish money on the London market: Ireland, the Anglo-Irish and the South Sea Bubble of 1720', *Eighteenth-century life*, forthcoming 2014.

Weber, Max, *The Protestant ethic and the spirit of capitalism*, trans. Talcott Parsons (London, 1930).

Welch, Cheryl B., *Liberty and utility: the French Idéologues and the transformation of liberalism* (New York, 1984).

–, 'Social science from the French Revolution to positivism', in *The Cambridge history of nineteenth-century political thought*, ed. Gareth Stedman Jones and Gregory Claeys (Cambridge, 2011), p.171-99.

Wennerlind, Carl, 'An artificial virtue and the oil of commerce: a synthetic view of Hume's theory of money', in *David Hume's political economy*, ed. Carl Wennerlind and Margaret Schabas (London, 2008), p.105-26.

–, *Casualties of credit: the English Financial Revolution, 1620-1720* (Cambridge, MA, 2011).

–, 'The link between David Hume's *Treatise of human nature* and his fiduciary theory of money', *History of political economy* 33:1 (2001), p.139-60.

Whatmore, Richard, *Republicanism and the French Revolution: an intellectual history of Jean-Baptiste Say's political economy* (Oxford, 2000).

Whewell, William, 'Mathematical exposition of some doctrines of political economy, second memoir' [1850], in *Mathematical exposition of some doctrines of political economy* (New York, 1971).

Wicksteed, Philip H., 'On certain passages in Jevons' theory of political economy', *Quarterly journal of economics* 3:3 (1889), p.293-314.

Winch, Donald, *Riches and poverty: an intellectual history of political economy in Britain, 1750-1834* (Cambridge, 1996).

Wokler, Robert, 'Ideology and the origins of social science', in *The Cambridge history of eighteenth-century political thought*, ed. Mark Goldie and Robert Wokler (Cambridge, 2006), p.688-710.

Wood, Neal, *Cicero's social and political thought* (Berkeley, CA, 1988).

Worden, Blair, 'James Harrington and "The Commonwealth of Oceana", 1656', in *Republicanism, liberty, and commercial society, 1649-1776*, ed. David Wootton (Stanford, CA, 1994), p.82-110.

–, 'Harrington's "Oceana": origins and aftermath, 1651-1660', in *Republicanism, liberty, and commercial society, 1649-1776*, ed. David Wootton (Stanford, CA, 1994), p.111-38.

–, 'Marchamont Nedham and the beginnings of English republicanism, 1649-1656', in *Republicanism, liberty, and commercial society, 1649-1776*, ed. David Wootton (Stanford, CA, 1994), p.45-81.

–, 'Republicanism and the Restoration, 1660-1683', in *Republicanism, liberty, and commercial society, 1649-1776*, ed. David Wootton (Stanford, CA, 1994), p.139-93.

Wrightson, Keith, *Earthly necessities: economic lives in early modern Britain* (New Haven, CT, 2000).

Yule, G. Udney, 'Crop production and price: a note on Gregory King's law', *Journal of the Royal Statistical Society* 78 (1915), p.296-98.

Index